INVENTION, ARRANGEMENT, AND STYLE:
Rhetorical Criticism of Jude and 2 Peter

SOCIETY
OF BIBLICAL
LITERATURE

DISSERTATION SERIES
J. J. M. Roberts, Old Testament Editor
Charles Talbert, New Testament Editor

Number 104

INVENTION, ARRANGEMENT, AND STYLE:
Rhetorical Criticism of Jude and 2 Peter

by
Duane Frederick Watson

Duane Frederick Watson

INVENTION, ARRANGEMENT, AND STYLE:
Rhetorical Criticism of Jude and 2 Peter

Scholars Press
Atlanta, Georgia

INVENTION, ARRANGEMENT, AND STYLE:
Rhetorical Criticism of Jude and 2 Peter

Duane Frederick Watson

BS
2815.2
. W37
1988

Ph.D., 1986
Duke University

Advisor:
Franklin W. Young

© 1988
Society of Biblical Literature

Library of Congress Cataloging-in-Publication Data

Watson, Duane Frederick.
  Invention, arrangement, and style.

  (Dissertation series / Society of Biblical
Literature ; no. 104)
  Bibliography: p.
  1. Bible. N.T. Jude—Language, style.
2. Bible. N.T. Peter, 2nd—Language, style.
I. title. II. Series: Dissertation series (Society
of Biblical Literature) ; no. 104.
BS2815.2.W37   1988   227'.93066   87-13010
ISBN 1-55540-155-4 (alk. paper)
ISBN 1-55540-156-2 (pbk. : alk. paper)

Printed in the United States of America

For Dr. JoAnn Ford Watson

λύχνος μου φαίνων ἐν αὐχμηρῷ τόπῳ.

Contents

List of Figures

Abbreviations

Ar. *Poet.*	Aristotle, *Poetica*
Ar. *Rhet.*	Aristotle, *Rhetorica*
Ar. *Top.*	Aristotle, *Topica*
Aug. *De Doct. Chr.*	Augustine, *De Doctrina Christiana*
Cic. *Brut.*	Cicero, *Brutus*
Cic. *De Or.*	Cicero, *De Oratore*
Cic. *Inv.*	Cicero, *De Inventione*
Cic. *Opt. Gen.*	Cicero, *De Optimo Genera*
Cic. *Or.*	Cicero, *Orator*
Cic. *Part. Or.*	Cicero, *De Partitione Oratoriae*
Cic. *Top.*	Cicero, *Oratorum Topica*
Demetr. *Eloc.*	Demetrius, *Elocutione*
Her.	*Rhetorica ad Herennium*
Long. *Subl.*	Longinus, *De Sublime*
Pl. *Phdr.*	Plato, *Phaedrus*
Quint.	Quintilian, *Institutio Oratoria*
Rhet. ad Alex.	*Rhetorica ad Alexandrum*

Acknowledgments

I would like to thank Drs. Franklin Young, George Kennedy, D. Moody Smith, Dan Via, and Roland Murphy for their tutelage and their work on my doctoral committee. Particular appreciation is extended to Drs. Young and Kennedy for their painstaking reading of an earlier draft of this work and numerous suggestions for improvement, and for their encouragement throughout the project. May I be as helpful an advisor to my students as they have been to me.

Quotations of Scripture, the Dead Sea Scrolls, Pseudepigrapha, the Apocrypha, and classical sources are acknowledged to be from the Revised Standard Version, Vermes, Hennecke-Schneemelcher, Charlesworth, and Loeb translations respectively, unless otherwise noted.

1
Introduction

This initial chapter is divided into two parts. First, the developments in rhetorical criticism of the Old and New Testaments will be presented, with an emphasis upon New Testament studies.[1] Secondly, the methodology of rhetorical criticism of the New Testament will be outlined not only to state the method used in the rhetorical analyses to follow, but also to provide a terminological and conceptual basis for them as well.

THE DEVELOPMENT OF RHETORICAL CRITICISM
IN BIBLICAL STUDIES

The use of rhetorical criticism in biblical studies and an initial methodology were first proposed by James Muilenburg in his presidential address delivered at the annual meeting of the Society of Biblical Literature in 1968.[2] Muilenburg, while praising form criticism for moving beyond historical criticism and making many lasting contributions, pointed out limitations of the form critical method which needed correction and supplementation. First, while emphasizing the role of convention and custom in literary composition and expecting each genre or *Gattung* to exhibit similar structural forms, terminology, style, and *Sitz-im-Leben,* form criticism stresses the typical and representative so that the individual, personal, unique, and unrepeatable features of a given pericope are ignored.[3] Second, form criticism has an over-aversion to biographical or psychological interpretations and resistance to placing a pericope in an historical context.[4]

---

[1] For a brief overview of the rhetoric of the Old and New Testaments, see George A. Kennedy, *Classical Rhetoric and its Christian and Secular Tradition from Ancient to Modern Times* (Chapel Hill: University of North Carolina Press, 1980) 120–32.

[2] This address is reproduced as "Form Criticism and Beyond," *JBL* 88 (1969) 1–18. Prior to this address, Muilenburg himself had written pioneering works using stylistic and rhetorical devices. Two such examples are "A Study in Hebrew Rhetoric: Repetition and Style," *VTSup* 1 (1953) 97–111 and "The Book of Isaiah: Chs. 40–66," in *The Interpreter's Bible,* gen. ed. George Arthur Buttrick, 12 vols. (New York: Abingdon, 1952–57) 5:381–773.

[3] Ibid., 4–5.

[4] Ibid., 5–6.

Muilenburg argued that form critical analysis needed to be supplemented with a careful inspection of the unique features or a literary unit, features lying "beyond the spectrum of genre" in the realm of "artistry." The words and motifs in a literary composition need careful examination to discover how the thought of the author has been woven into linguistic patterns. This enables the exegete "to think the thoughts of the biblical writer after him."[5]

> What I am interested in, above all, is in understanding the nature of Hebrew literary composition, in exhibiting the structural patterns that are employed for the fashioning of a literary unit, whether in poetry or in prose, and in discerning the many and various devices by which the predictions are formulated and ordered into a unified whole. Such an enterprise I should describe as rhetoric and the methodology as rhetorical criticism.[6]

Muilenburg continued by offering a simple methodology for rhetorical criticism in which the limits or scope of the literary unit is first defined, observing the major motif usually given at the beginning, points of climax, and *inclusio*.[7] Second, the structure of the unit is determined and the configuration of its parts discovered. The rhetorical devices marking the sequence and movement of the unit and the shifts in the development of the author's thought are carefully noted. These include parallelism, sequence of units within cola, meter, strophes, particles, rhetorical questions, and repetitions.[8]

Muilenburg's challenge and methodology were enthusiastically received, and were immediately echoed by David Greenwood in his article, "Rhetorical Criticism and Formgeschichte: Some Methodological Considerations."[9] Having directed his remarks mainly to Old Testament studies, Muilenburg's proposals had their greatest initial impact on Old Testament studies. A fairly steady flow of rhetorical-critical works on the Old Testament has followed. The chief early work is *Rhetorical Critisism: Essays in Honor of James Muilenburg,* edited by Jared J. Jackson and Martin Kessler,[10] which contains rhetorical analyses of several Old Testament pericopes. Three other works of a larger scale are Yehoshua Gitay's *Prophecy and Persuasion: A Study of Isaiah 40–48,*[11] Jack R. Lundbom's *Jeremiah: A Study in Ancient Hebrew Rhetoric,*[12] and *Art and Meaning: Rhetoric in Biblical Literature,* edited by D. J. A. Clines et al.[13] Several important articles are Jack R. Lundbom, "Poetic Structure and Prophetic

---

[5] Ibid., 7.
[6] Ibid., 8.
[7] Ibid., 9–10.
[8] Ibid., 10–18.
[9] *JBL* 89 (1970) 418–26.
[10] (Pittsburg: Pickwick Press, 1974).
[11] ForTLing 14 (Bonn: Linguistica Biblica, 1981).
[12] SBLDS 18 (Missoula, MT: Scholars Press, 1975).
[13] JSOTSup 19 (Sheffield: JSOT, 1982).

Rhetoric in Hosea";[14] Yehoshua Gitay, "A Study of Amos's Art of Speech: A Rhetorical Analysis of Amos 3:1–15";[15] Anthony Ceresko, "A Rhetorical Analysis of David's 'Boast' (1 Samuel 17:34–37): Some Reflections on Method";[16] and Alan Hauser, "Jonah: In Pursuit of the Dove."[17]

Rhetorical criticism of the New Testament has its own prominent forerunners: Amos Wilder and Robert Funk. In fact, Amos Wilder has been hailed as "the father of rhetorical analysis."[18] In his work, *Early Christian Rhetoric: The Language of the Gospel*,[19] Wilder makes the case that literary forms and genres reveal the patterns of consciousness, the social-historical setting, and the exigence of the author, an observation which lead to an appreciation of the rhetorical quality of such forms. Robert Funk, building on the work of Wilder, in his book *Language, Hermeneutic, and Word of God*,[20] examines parables and letters and concludes that parables act like metaphors and letters like oral communication, like structured speech. He writes that the letter form " 'is almost as flexible as oral speech itself,' and the style of Paul betrays on every page the marks of oral expression . . ."[21] The analyst is thus directed to identify the form, style, and sequence of a work in order to understand the author's thought which he wishes to communicate,[22] that is, to perform a rudimentary rhetorical analysis.

Shortly after these works came out and the same year as Muilenburg's clarion call, E. A. Judge wrote an article entitled "Paul's Boasting in Relation to Contemporary Professional Practice"[23] in which he raised the issue of the extent, if any, of Paul's training in and use of Greco-Roman rhetoric, and called for a systematic analysis of the rhetoric of the New Testament. He thus made explicit one of the many issues raised by Wilder and Funk, namely that literary form and sequence may not only reveal an author's situation and thought, but may have been constructed with a conscious or unconscious use of a known rhetorical system.

---

[14] *VT* 29 (1979) 300–308.

[15] *CBQ* 42 (1980) 293–309.

[16] *CBQ* 47 (1985) 58–74.

[17] *JBL* 104 (1985) 21–37. Before leaving this section, it bears mention that a fifteenth century scholar, Judah Messer Leon, used the Old Testament to teach classical rhetoric, and used classical rhetoric to perform exegesis. See his *The Book of the Honeycomb's Flow*, trans. and ed. Isaac Rabinowitz (Ithaca, New York and London: Cornell University Press, 1983).

[18] Vernon K. Robbins and John H. Patton, "Rhetoric and Biblical Criticism," *The Quarterly Journal of Speech* 66 (1980) 328.

[19] (Cambridge: Harvard University Press, 1971). Originally published as *The Language of the Gospel: Early Christian Rhetoric* (New York: Harper and Row, 1964).

[20] (New York: Harper and Row, 1966).

[21] Ibid., 248, quoting Wilder, 39.

[22] Ibid, 254.

[23] *AusBR* 16 (1968) 37–50.

It quickly became apparent that rhetorical criticism of the Old and New Testaments was going to develop along both similar and different lines. Contributing to similarity is the fact that both can utilize the "new rhetoric" represented by Chaim Perelman,[24] W. J. Brandt,[25] Kenneth Burke,[26] and others. Contributing to difference in development is the fact that the rhetoric of the Old Testament was formed in the context of the Ancient Near East, whereas the rhetoric of the New Testament derives mainly from the conceptualization of rhetoric by the Greeks and its borrowed and modified Roman form. On the one hand, the rhetoric of the Ancient Near East is reconstructed by examination of the literature of the period and used to analyze the Old Testament. Often Greco-Roman conceptions, especially those of style, also can be used because of the highly conceptualized nature of Greco-Roman rhetoric. On the other hand, Greco-Roman rhetoric is clearly systematized and stated in extant ancient handbooks from the New Testament era and can directly inform an analysis of the New Testament.

As rhetorical criticism of the New Testament has developed in the last two decades, one branch has focused on the ancient rhetorical handbooks as well as other related works of Greece and Rome to determine their contribution to New Testament studies. With the re-evaluation of these works, New Testament scholars have broadened their perspective of the nature and scope of classical rhetoric and have placed the New Testament documents in the larger Greco-Roman literary heritage to which it is increasingly obvious they are obligated.

These recent developments have precedent, for there has always been limited classical rhetorical criticism of the New Testament. This has almost always pertained to stylistic matters, especially figures of speech and thought, and matters of genre and form. For example, Saint Augustine analyzed the rhetorical style of the biblical writers, especially Paul, in Book IV of his work *On Christian Doctrine*,[27] and the Venerable Bede in his *De schematibus et tropis* analyzed figures and tropes in both Testaments.[28]

Near the turn of this century in Germany, numerous important works regarding the rhetoric of the New Testament were published. Johannes Weiss

[24] Chaim Perelman and L. Olbrechts-Tyteca, *The New Rhetoric: A Treatise on Argumentation,* trans. John Wilkinson and Purcell Weaver (Notre Dame: University of Notre Dame Press, 1969).

[25] *The Rhetoric of Argumentation* (New York: Bobbs-Merrill, 1970).

[26] *The Rhetoric of Religion* (Berkeley: University of California Press, 1970). For a very important work on the rhetoric of the New Testament using a variety of literary and rhetorical-critical methods, see Vernon K. Robbins, *Jesus the Teacher: A Socio-Rhetorical Interpretation of Mark* (Philadelphia: Fortress, 1984).

[27] Trans. D. W. Robertson, Jr., The Library of Liberal Arts (Indianapolis, IL.: Bobbs Merrill, 1958).

[28] "Bede's *De schematibus et tropis*—A Translation," trans. Gussie Hecht Tannenhaus, *Quarterly Journal of Speech* 48 (1962) 237–53, also in *Readings in Medieval Rhetoric,* ed. Joseph M. Miller et al. (Bloomington and London: Indiana University Press, 1973) 96–122.

wrote two works on Pauline rhetoric, "Beiträge zur Paulinischen Rhetoric" (1897)[29] and *Die Aufgaben der neutestamentlichen Wissenschaft in dem Gegenwart* (1908)[30] in which the sentence structure, style, and rhetorical devices of Paul are analyzed. Eduard Norden published *Die antike Kunstprosa vom VI Jahrhunderts vor Christus in die Zeit der Renaissance* (1898)[31] which surveys rhetorical prose from the sixth century B.C. to the Renaissance and includes a discussion of New Testament rhetoric. He followed this with *Agnostos Theos* (1913)[32] which contains special studies on several rhetorical aspects of the New Testament. These works were accompanied by Eduard König's classic *Stilistik, Rhetoric, und Poetik in Bezug auf die biblische Literatur* (1900)[33] which is an encyclopedia of linguistic and rhetorical phenomena in the Bible providing parallels from classical literature. Under the influence of his mentor, Johannes Weiss, Rudolf Bultmann wrote a doctoral dissertation entitled *Der Stil der paulinischen Predigt und die kynisch-stoische Diatribe* (1910)[34] which relies heavily upon an analysis of rhetorical devices in Paul's letters in an attempt to show that Paul used the Cynic-Stoic diatribe form. Meanwhile in England, E. W. Bullinger had published his massive *Figures of Speech Used in the Bible* (1898)[35] which identifies numerous figures of speech and thought and illustrates them with examples from both Testaments.

Since this outpouring at the turn of the century, the rhetoric of the New Testament has received only limited treatment. Of course, New Testament grammars have traditionally dealt on a minimal basis with rhetoric. For example, the standard Blass-Debrunner-Funk grammar of the New Testament has a discussion of the continuous and periodic style, and a section on figures of speech and thought.[36] Nigel Turner's *A Grammar of New Testament Greek: Style*[37] evaluates the style of every New Testament book from a grammatical and syntactical standpoint, and C. F. D. Moule's *An Idiom Book of New Testament Greek* contains a section entitled "Miscellaneous Notes on Style."[38]

---

[29] In *Theologische Studien. Herrn Wirkl. Oberkonsistorialrath Professor D. Bernhard Weiss zu seinem 70* (Göttingen: Vandenhoeck and Ruprecht, 1897) 165-247.

[30] (Göttingen: Vandenhoeck and Ruprecht, 1908).

[31] Two vols. (Leipzig and Berlin: B. G. Teubner, 1898) 4th ed., 1923.

[32] (Leipzig and Berlin: B. G. Teubner, 1913).

[33] (Leipzig: Theodor Weicher, 1900).

[34] FRLANT 13 (Göttingen: Vandenhoeck and Ruprecht, 1910).

[35] (London: Eyre and Spottiswoode, 1898; repr. ed. Grand Rapids: Baker Book House, 1968).

[36] F. Blass and A. Debrunner, *A Greek Grammar of the New Testament,* trans. and rev. Robert W. Funk (Chicago and London: University of Chicago Press, 1961) 239-48, §458-72; 256-63, §485-96.

[37] In *A Grammar of New Testament Greek,* gen. eds. James Hope Moulton and Nigel Turner, 4 vols. (Edinburgh: T. & T. Clark, 1906-76) 4 (1976).

[38] Second ed. (Cambridge: Cambridge University Press, 1959) 193-201.

Other than reference grammars, works using ancient rhetoric are few and often use ancient rhetorical concepts divorced from their classical roots. There is E. von Dobschütz's article, "Zwei- und dreigliedrige Formeln,"[39] which among other things discusses parallelism in both the Old and New Testaments. There are two studies on chiasmus: Nils Lund's *Chiasmus in the New Testament*[40] and the response of Joachim Jeremias, "Chiasmus in den Paulusbriefen."[41] E. K. Lee, in an article entitled "Words Denoting 'Pattern' in the New Testament,"[42] in part examines the role of δεῖγμα and ὑπόδειγμα in the New Testament. Norbert Schneider has published a study of Pauline antithesis entitled *Die rhetorische Eigenart der paulinischen Antithesis.*[43] Finally, there is also a series of articles on the *topos* of the New Testament led by David Bradley's "The Topos as a Form in the Pauline Paraenesis,"[44] followed by Terence Mullin's critique, "Topos as a New Testament Form,"[45] neither of which brings classical sources to bear. This discussion is enhanced significantly by John Brunt's article, "More on the *Topos* as a New Testament Form,"[46] which utilizes the treatments of *topos* from the rhetorical handbooks.

In 1975, Hans Dieter Betz produced what to my knowledge is the first rhetorical analysis of a portion of the New Testament using Greco-Roman rhetoric. In his article, "The Literary Composition and Function of Paul's Letter to the Galatians,"[47] Betz subjects Galatians to a brief analysis concentrating on invention and arrangement and argues that it is an "apologetic letter" akin to forensic rhetoric used for defense in a court of law. This article was followed by his commentary on Galatians[48] in which he consistently utilizes matters of invention and arrangement in the analysis and interpretation.

He was followed by F. Forrester Church's article, "Rhetorical Structure and Design in Paul's Letter to Philemon,"[49] which subjects the letter of Philemon to a fine cursory rhetorical analysis utilizing the ancient handbooks and a knowledge of the letter form, concentrating on invention and arrangement. In another important study, "Greek Rhetoric and Pauline Argumentation," Wilhelm Wuellner focuses on 1 Corinthians in an attempt to show "that digressions in Paul's letters are illustrative of his rhetorical sophistication and that they serve to support his argumentation."[50] The hymn of Philippians 2:6–11 is shown

---

[39] *JBL* 50 (1931) 117–47.
[40] (Chapel Hill: University of North Carolina Press, 1942).
[41] *ZNW* 49 (1958) 145–56.
[42] *NTS* 8 (1961/62) 166–73.
[43] HermUnT 11 (Tübingen: Mohr-Siebeck, 1970).
[44] *JBL* 72 (1953) 238–46.
[45] *JBL* 99 (1980) 541–47.
[46] *JBL* 104 (1985) 495–500.
[47] *NTS* 21 (1975) 353–79.
[48] Hermeneia (Philadelphia: Fortress Press, 1979).
[49] *HTR* 71 (1978) 17–33.
[50] In *Early Christian Literature and the Classical Intellectual Tradition. In Honorem*

to conform to classical rhetorical conventions of periodic structure in Charles Robbin's article, "Rhetorical Structure of Philippians 2:6-11."[51] In his investigation, "Hellenistic Rhetoric in the Christological Proof of Luke-Acts,"[52] William Kurz uses Hellenistic rhetoric to argue that Luke's Christological proof in Luke-Acts is an adaptation of the enthymeme of Aristotle, and conforms so well that is can be posited that Luke formally studied rhetoric.

In a series of related articles, Karl Donfried, Wilhelm Wuellner, and Robert Jewett use classical rhetoric to analyze Romans as a situational letter. Donfried[53] criticizes Bultmann's doctoral dissertation in which Bultmann attempted to demonstrate the relationship between the Cynic-Stoic diatribe and the Pauline letters. Donfried argues that Paul's use of rhetorical devices does not necessarily mean that he was using the diatribe form, but rather indicates Paul was a child of his culture. Wuellner[54] brings both the new and classical rhetoric to bear on the issue of the nature of Romans. He argues that Paul's letters should be approached primarily as argumentative and rhetorical rather than through genre or historical-situational studies. After extensively analyzing the *exordium* (1:1-15) and *peroratio* (15:14-16:23) of Romans and their connections within the argumentation of the epistle, he concludes that Romans is epideictic rhetoric. Jewett,[55] refining the work of Wuellner, also classifies Romans as epideictic, but, based on the work of Theodore Burgess,[56] classifies it more specifically as an ambassador's speech with elements of three other subtypes: the parenetic letter, the hortatory letter, and the philosophical diatribe.

Thorough rhetorical analyses of New Testament books using classical rhetoric have yet to be performed. Betz's work on Galatians is still the most complete, but it does not exhaust all the features of Greco-Roman rhetoric that are present in Galatians, especially where style is concerned. Forrester's article only treats the rhetoric of Philemon in a cursory fashion. Other studies only deal with a specific pericope or particular issue(s).

What these studies have shown is the actual and potential contributions classical rhetoric can make to structuring and interpreting the New Testament. One purpose of this study is therefore to provide a complete rhetorical analysis of Jude and 2 Peter according to the Greco-Roman system of rhetoric. It is the

---

Robert M. Grant, eds. William R. Schoedel and Robert L. Wilken, Theologie Historique 54 (Paris: Éditions Beauchesne, 1979) 177.

[51] *CBQ* 42 (1980) 73-82.

[52] *CBQ* 42 (1980) 171-95.

[53] "False Propositions in the Study of Romans," *CBQ* 36 (1974) 332-55, or *The Romans Debate,* ed. Karl P. Donfried (Minneapolis: Augsburg, 1977) 120-48.

[54] "Paul's Rhetoric of Argumentation in Romans: An Alternative to the Donfried-Karris Debate Over Romans," *CBQ* 38 (1976) 330-51, or *Romans Debate,* 152-74.

[55] "Romans as an Ambassadorial Letter," *Int* 36 (1982) 5-20.

[56] "Epideictic Literature," *University of Chicago Studies in Classical Philology* 3 (1902) 89-261.

intent of this study to identify specifically and evaluate in every detail the rhetoric of these works according to the conventions of their own age.

Jude and 2 Peter were chosen for another purpose as well. The role rhetorical criticism can legitimately play in dealing with literary questions regarding the interrelationships of New Testament books is virtually unexplored. It is my contention that rhetorical criticism can substantially contribute to solving the question of the literary unity of 2 Peter and the question of the literary dependence between Jude and 2 Peter. Therefore, this study will identify and formulate the contribution that conventions of Greco-Roman rhetoric can provide for answering these literary questions of the integrity of 2 Peter and the nature of the dependence between Jude 4-18 and 2 Pet 2:1-3:3.

THE METHODOLOGY OF RHETORICAL CRITICISM
OF THE NEW TESTAMENT

The rhetorical analysis of Jude and 2 Peter will be conducted according to the methodology proposed by George A. Kennedy in his book *New Testament Interpretation Through Rhetorical Criticism.*[57] This methodology consists of five interrelated steps which are outlined in the following pages and elaborated where it will conveniently serve as a terminological and conceptual basis for the analyses to follow.[58]

Determine the Rhetorical Unit

First, a determination of the rhetorical unit is made. The unit must have a decided introduction, body, and conclusion, and may either comprise an entire work or be a part of a larger one. If part of a larger work, signs of *inclusio* must be sought and the rhetoric of the overall work may need to be examined to illumine the analysis of the designated unit.

Analyze the Rhetorical Situation

Secondly, the rhetorical situation of the rhetorical unit is analyzed. The concept of the rhetorical situation was first proposed by Lloyd Bitzer.[59] He asserts that any given discourse originates because a situation elicits it, and this situation conditions the discourse much like a question controls an answer or a problem the solution.[60] He defines the rhetorical situation as ". . . a complex of persons, events, objects, and relations presenting an actual or potential exigence

---

[57] (Chapel Hill: University of North Carolina Press, 1984) esp. 33-38.
[58] See Edward P. J. Corbett, *Classical Rhetoric for the Modern Student,* 2d ed. (New York: Oxford University Press, 1971) for an examination of the role classical rhetoric does and can play in modern works. Pages 31-40 offer a helpful brief outline of classical rhetorical theory.
[59] "The Rhetorical Situation," *Philosophy and Rhetoric,* 1 (1968) 1-14.
[60] Ibid., 5-6.

which can be completely or partially removed if discourse, introduced into the situation, can so constrain human decision or action as to bring about the significant modification of the exigence."[61]

According to this definition, there are three constituents of the rhetorical situation: the exigence, the audience, and the constraints brought to the situation by the rhetor. The exigence is ". . . an imperfection marked by urgency; it is a defect, an obstacle, something waiting to be done, a thing which is other than it should be."[62] The exigence colors the rhetoric and is often clearly detected in the introduction (*exordium*) or beginning of the body (*probatio*) of a rhetorical work. These three constituents must be examined in detail in the rhetorical analysis, and that is where they are more conveniently discussed in this study.

Determine the Species of Rhetoric,
the Question, and the Stasis

In the third step of the proposed methodology, the species of rhetoric, the basic question, and the stasis of the argument are carefully determined. Regarding the first, there are three main species of rhetoric:[63] judicial,[64] deliberative,[65] and epideictic.[66] Judicial rhetoric is concerned with accusation and defense,

---

[61] Ibid., 6.

[62] Ibid.

[63] Ar. *Rhet.* 1.3.1358b.3; 1359a.9; Cic. *Inv.* 1.5.7; *Top.* 24.91; Her. 1.2.2; Quint. 2.21.23; 3.3.14–15; 3.4.12–15; cf. Cic. *De Or.* 1.31.141. For further details see the discussions in Ar. *Rhet.* 1.3.15; *Rhet. ad Alex.* 1.1421b.7ff.; Cic. *Inv.* 2.4.12–59.178; *De Or.* 2.81.333–85.349; Quint. 3.4. *Rhet. ad Alex.* adds the investigational (1.1421b.7–8; 5.1427b.12–30; 37). Heinrich Lausberg, *Handbuch der literarischen Rhetorik. Eine Grundlegung der Literaturwissenschaft,* 2d ed., 2 vols. (Munich: Max Heuber, 1973) 1:51–61, §53–65; Josef Martin, *Antike Rhetorik: Technik und Methode.* HbAltW 2.3 (Munich: C. H. Beck, 1974) 9–10, 15–210; George Kennedy, *The Art of Rhetoric in the Roman World: 300 B.C.–A.D. 300* (Princeton: Princeton University Press, 1972) 7–23.

[64] Δικανικόν (Ar. *Rhet.* 1.3.1358b.3; *Rhet. ad Alex.* 1.1421b.7–8); δίκαι (Ar. *Rhet.* 1.3.1359a.9); *iudicialis* (Cic. *Inv.* 1.5.7; *Top.* 24.91; Her. 1.2.2; Quint. 3.3.14; 3.4.15; cf. Cic. *De Or.* 1.31.141). For full discussions, see Ar. *Rhet.* 1.10–15; *Rhet. ad Alex.* 4, 36; Cic. *Inv.* 2.4.14–51.154; *Part. Or.* 4.14–5.15; 28–37; *Top.* 24.92–26.96; Quint. 3.9; Lausberg, 1:86–123, §140–223; Martin, 15–166; Kennedy, *Roman World,* 7–18.

[65] Συμβουλευτικόν (Ar. *Rhet.* 1.3.1358b.3), συμβουλή (Ar. *Rhet.* 1.3.1359a.9), *deliberativus* (Cic. *Inv.* 1.5.7; *Top.* 24.91; Her. 1.2.2; Quint. 2.21.23; 3.3.14; 3.4.15; cf. Cic. *Or.* 1.31.141). For full discussions, see Ar. *Rhet.* 1.4–8; *Rhet. ad Alex.* 1–2, 29–34; Cic. *De Or.* 2.81.333–83.340; *Inv.* 2.51.155–58.176; *Part. Or.* 4.13; 24–37; Her. 3.2–5; Quint. 3.8; Lausberg, 1:123–29, §224–38; Martin, 167–76; Kennedy, *Roman World,* 18–21.

[66] Ἐπιδεικτικόν (Ar. *Rhet.* 1.3.1358b.3; 1359a.9; *Rhet. ad Alex.* 1.1421b.7–8; Cic. *Or.* 11.37; Quint. 3.4.12), *demonstrativus* (Cic. *Inv.* 1.5.7; Her. 1.2.2; Quint. 3.4.14), *laudativus* (Quint. 2.21.23; 3.3.14; 3.4.12), *laudatio* (Cic. *De Or.* 2.84.341; *Top.* 24.91; cf. Cic. *De Or.* 1.31.141), ἐγκωμιαστικόν (Quint. 3.4.12), *panegyricus* (Quint. 3.4.13). For full discussions, see Ar. *Rhet.* 1.9; *Rhet. ad Alex.* 3, 35; Cic. *Inv.* 2.59.178; *De Or.* 2.11.45–46; 2.84–85; *Or.* 11.37; *Part. Or.* 4.12; 21–23; Her. 3.6–8; Quint. 3.4.3; 3.7; Lausberg, 1:129–38, §239–54;

particularly in the legal setting,[67] and its end is the just and the unjust.[68] Its time reference is the past since it pertains to actions in the past for which accusation and defense are made.[69] Deliberative rhetoric is advice giving, persuasion and dissuasion,[70] and its end is the possible or impossible, advantageous or harmful, necessary or unnecesary, expedient or inexpedient.[71] Its time reference is mainly future since advice is generally given on future things,[72] although the present is sometimes appropriate.[73] Epideictic rhetoric praises and blames[74] and its end is the honorable or the dishonorable with a view to increasing or decreasing assent to some value.[75] Its characteristic time reference is present since persons and things are praised or blamed for what they are doing,[76] but the past is often recalled and the future anticipated.[77] Epideictic is often used purely for pleasure.[78] All three species of rhetoric rely on the others, each often temporarily using the other.[79]

Concerning questions,[80] every case in which there is an accusation and defense consists of one or more controversial questions. A question or cause is any subject on which two or more opinions can be offered. If one question is

---

Martin, 177–210; Kennedy, *Roman World,* 21–23; Walter H. Beale, "Rhetorical Performative Discourse: A New Theory of Epideictic," *Philosophy and Rhetoric* 11 (1978) 221–46; Richard J. Chase, "The Classical Conception of Epideictic," *Quarterly Journal of Speech* 47 (1961) 293–300; Christine Oravec, " 'Observation' in Aristotle's Theory of Epideictic," *Philosophy and Rhetoric* 9 (1976) 162–74.

[67] Ar. *Rhet.* 1.3.1358b.3; *Rhet. ad Alex.* 4.1426b.22ff; Cic. *Inv.* 1.5.7; Quint. 3.4.6–7, 9.

[68] Ar. *Rhet.* 1.3.1358b.5; Cic. *Inv.* 2.4.12; 2.51.155–56; *Top.* 24.91; cf. Quint. 3.4.15.

[69] Ar. *Rhet.* 1.3.1358b.4; 2.18.1392a.5; Cic. *Part. Or.* 20.69; cf. Cic. *Part. Or.* 3.10.

[70] Ar. *Rhet.* 1.3.1358b.3; *Rhet. ad Alex.* 1.1421b.17–23; Cic. *Inv.* 1.5.7; *Part. Or.* 24.83ff.; Her. 1.2.2; Quint. 3.4.6, 9; 3.8.1–6, 67–70; cf. Cic. *De Or.* 1.31.141.

[71] Ar. *Rhet.* 1.3.1358b.5; *Rhet. ad Alex.* 1.1421b.21ff.; Cic. *Inv.* 2.4.12; 2.51.155–58.176; *Part. Or.* 24.83–87; *Top.* 24.91; Her. 3.2.3–5.9; Quint. 3.8.1–6, 22–35; cf. Cic. *De Or.* 2.82.333–36; Quint. 3.4.16.

[72] Ar. *Rhet.* 1.3.1358b.4; 1.4.1359a.1–2; 2.18.1392a.5; Quint. 3.4.7; 3.8.6; cf. Cic. *Part. Or.* 3.10; 20.69.

[73] Ar. *Rhet.* 1.6.1362a.1; 1.8.1366a.7.

[74] Ar. *Rhet.* 1.3.1358b.3; Cic. *Inv.* 1.5.7; 2.4.12; *Part. Or.* 21.70; Her. 1.2.2; Quint. 3.4.6–9, 12–14; cf. *Rhet. ad Alex.* 3.1425b.35; Cic. *Inv.* 2.59.177; *De Or.* 1.31.141.

[75] Ar. *Rhet.* 1.3.1358b.5; *Rhet. ad Alex.* 3.1425b.36–39; Cic. *Inv.* 2.4.12; 2.51.155–56; *Top.* 24.91; Her. 3.6.10; cf. Quint. 3.4.16.

[76] Ar. *Rhet.* 1.3.1358b.4; cf. Cic. *Part. Or.* 3.10; 20.69.

[77] Ar. *Rhet.* 1.3.1358b.4; Quint. 3.4.7; cf. Cic. *Part. Or.* 21.71.

[78] Cic. *Part. Or.* 3.10–4.12.

[79] *Rhet. ad Alex.* 5.1427b.31ff.; Quint. 3.4.16. Quintilian notes that Isocrates claimed that praise and blame are found in every type of oratory (3.4.11). Cornificius says epideictic often constitutes extensive parts of judicial and deliberative causes (Her. 3.8.15).

[80] Lausberg, 1:61–64, §66–78; Martin, 15ff.

involved, the case is simple, and if there is more than one question, it is complex. The questions of the complex case may all be of the same kind, or they may be different.[81] A third and different question is the comparative in which the desirability of one thing or person over another is determined by comparison.[82] All questions are concerned either with what is or what is not written, the former being legal questions (νομικόν) and the latter being rational questions (λογικόν).[83]

All questions are either definite and special, or indefinite and general.[84] "Definite questions involve facts, persons, time and the like."[85] "Indefinite questions are those which may be maintained or impugned without reference to persons, time or place and the like."[86] Indefinite questions involve matters of knowledge and action. Knowledge consists of the three subdivisions: whether a thing exists, what it is, and what its nature or quality is. Action involves how to obtain or avoid something and how to use something.[87] The indefinite question is broader than and logically prior to the indefinite question, for in every definite question the indefinite is implied.[88] Most judicial and epideictic questions are definite, and most deliberative questions are indefinite.[89]

Stasis theory[90] is a system for determining the basic definite question at

[81] Cic. *Inv.* 1.12.17; Quint. 3.10.1-2; cf. Quint. 7.2.8.

[82] Quint. 3.10.3. Cic. *Inv.* 1.12.17 considers comparison as one of two varieties of the complex question, the other being several questions.

[83] Cic. *Inv.* 1.12.17; Quint. 3.5.4-5.

[84] Cic. *Inv.* 1.6.8; *Part. Or.* 1.4; 18.61ff.; *Top.* 21.79-22.86; Quint. 3.5.5ff.

[85] Quint. 3.5.7. for a similar understanding, see Cic. *Inv.* 1.6.8 (stating Hermagorus' understanding); *De Or.* 1.31.138; 2.19.78; 3.28.109; *Part. Or.* 1.4; *Top.* 21-22. The definite question was called an hypothesis by the Greeks and a cause by the Romans according to Cic. *Part. Or.* 18.61; *Top.* 21.79; and Quint. 3.5.7.

[86] Quint. 3.5.5. For a similar understanding, see Cic. *Inv.* 1.6.8 (stating Hermagorus' understanding); *De Or.* 1.31.138; 2.10.42; 2.19.78; 3.28.109; *Or.* 14.46; *Part. Or.* 1.4; *Top.* 21-22. The indefinite question was called a thesis by the Greeks and a proposition by the Romans according to Cic. *Part. Or.* 18.61; *Top.* 21.79; and Quint. 3.5.5. It is called a thesis by Cic. *Or.* 14.46.

[87] Cic. *Part. Or.* 18.61-19.67; *Top.* 21.79-22.86; Quint. 3.5.5-6; cf. Cic. *De Or.* 3.29.111-30.118.

[88] Cic. *Part. Or.* 18.61; *Top.* 21.80; Quint. 3.5.8-16; cf. Cic. *De Or.* 3.30.119-20; *Or.* 14.45-46; *Top.* 22.86. Cicero states that the indefinite question does not concern the rhetor (*Inv.* 1.6.8). Quintilian takes him to task for this because of the interrelationship of the definite and indefinite question (3.5.4-15).

[89] Cic. *De Or.* 2.10.42-43; 3.28.109.

[90] Στάσις (Cic. *Top.* 25.93; Quint. 3.6.3), *status* (Cic. *Top.* 25.93; Quint. 3.6.1), *constitutio* (Cic. *Inv.* 1.8.10; Quint. 3.6.2). Stasis theory is generally discussed as part of inventional theory.

Stasis theory originated with Hermagorus in the second century B.C. and had profound and lasting effects on Greek and Roman rhetoric. Unfortunately, as Quintilian points out, there were as many varieties of stasis theory as there were teachers of rhetoric (3.6.22), and his own discussion evaluates theories espousing anywhere from one to eight stases (3.6.23-62). Quintilian himself developed two basic theories in his own lifetime (3.6.63ff.).

issue in a case when it may be obscure or when numerous questions may be present. It is particularly important in legal situations to determine the question basic for defense or offense. The stasis or basis is not the first conflict or causes or opinions,[91] but is the kind of question that arises from the first conflict of causes.[92] To use Quintilian's example, a first conflict of causes would be "You did it" and "I did not do it," and the question which arises is "Did he do it?" The stases underlying this question is one of fact as we will see shortly.[93]

Rational questions give rise to and rest upon one of three stases: fact (or conjecture), definition, and quality.[94] All questions in a case involve whether a thing is, what it is, and of what kind it is.[95] With the stasis of fact, the question is whether something was ever done, or was done by the person accused.[96] The stasis of definition involves admitting the facts while denying they are to be defined as they have been.[97] With the stasis of quality, the act is admitted, but that any wrong was committed is denied; a claim is made that it was the best course of action to take under the circumstances;[98] or

---

For the discussion to follow, I will be dependent upon Quintilian's mature theory (3.6.63–82), for it dates from the New Testament era and represents the mainstream of the theory as espoused by Hermagorus and Cicero (George A. Kennedy, *Quintilian,* Twayne World Author Series [New York: Twayne Publishers, 1969] 61).

For other discussions of stasis, see Cic. *Inv.* 1.8–14; 2.4.14–54.177; *De Or.* 2.24.104–26.113; *Or.* 14; 34.121–22; *Part. Or.* 9.33–12.4; 18.61ff.; 29.101ff.; *Top.* 21–25; Her. 1.11–16; Lausberg, 1:64–85; §79–138; Martin, 28–52; Hermogenes, "Hermogenes' *On Stases:* A Translation with an Introduction and Notes," trans. and ed. Ray Nadeau, *Speech Monographs* 31 (1964) 361–424.

[91] As asserts Cic. *Inv.* 1.8.10; 1.14.19.

[92] Quint. 3.6.5; cf. 3.6.17.

[93] Quint. 3.6.5.

[94] Cic. *De Or.* 2.25.104–9; 2.30.132; *Part. Or.* 9.33; 29.101; 37.131; Quint. 3.6.66–67, 86. Cic. *Inv.* 1.8.10 gives four stases: fact, definition, quality, and translative or legal. Her. 1.11.18 and 1.14–15 has two rational stases: the conjectural or fact, and the judicial or quality. Cornificius includes the stasis of definition under legal stases (Her. 1.12.21; 2.12.17). Ar. *Rhet.* 3.17.1417b.1 argues that there are four disputed points: the fact, the claim no harm is done (definition), the claim that it is not so important (definition), and that the act was just (quality).

[95] Cic. *De Or.* 1.31.139; 2.26.113; *Or.* 14.45; Quint. 3.6.44, 80. Cf. Cic. *Or.* 34.121 and *Part. Or.* 18.64–19.66 which discuss these three questions under the indefinite questions.

[96] Cic. *Inv.* 1.8.11; Quint. 3.6.83. For full discussion, see Cic. *Inv.* 2.4.14–16.5; *De Or.* 2.25.105; *Part. Or.* 10.34–11.40; *Top.* 23.87; Her. 1.11.18; 2.2.3–8.12; Quint. 7.2; cf. Cic. *De Or.* 2.30.132.

[97] Cic. *Inv.* 1.8.11; Quint. 3.6.83. For full discussion, see Cic. *Inv.* 2.17–20; *De Or.* 2.25.106–9; *Part. Or.* 12.41; *Top.* 23.87–88; Quint. 7.3; cf. Cic. *De Or.* 2.30.132; Her. 1.12.21; 2.12.17.

[98] Cic. *Inv.* 1.9.12; Quint. 3.6.83. For full discussion, see Cic. *Inv.* 1.9.12–11.15; 2.21–39; *De Or.* 2.25.106; *Part. Or.* 12.42; *Top.* 23.89–90; Her. 1.14–15; 2.13–29; Quint. 7.4; cf. Cic. *De Or.* 2.30.132.

there is inquiry into the nature of a thing.[99]

Legal questions can be divided into four subspecies related to questions of law. These are questions of word and intent of the law, contradictory laws, syllogism (attempting to include a case under a law that does not specifically provide for it), and ambiguous law.[100] These four subspecies of legal questions are not stases per se, but they can have the same three stases as rational questions (i.e., fact, definition, and quality).[101] For example, according to Quintilian, when one is dealing with the word and intention of the law or contradictory laws, the stases involved are those of fact or quality respectively. With the legal question of syllogism or ambiguous laws, the stases are those of quality and fact respectively.[102]

It is important to note that since a case may involve more than one question, it may also contain subsidiary stases. However, only one stasis will predominate.[103] The main stasis is the point upon which the whole matter turns and upon which the audience focuses attention.[104] These three basic stases are utilized by the three main species of rhetoric: deliberative, epideictic, and judicial.[105] However, they and their discussions are most applicable to judicial rhetoric where opposing views are necessarily involved. Whereas judicial rhetoric may utilize any of the stases quite effectively, epideictic and deliberative usually find the stasis of quality most effective.[106]

Analyze Invention, Arrangement, and Style

The art of rhetoric was generally considered to consist of five parts: invention, arrangement, style, memory, and delivery;[107] only the first three of which concern rhetorical criticism of written works. The fourth step in a rhetorical criticism is the careful analysis of invention, arrangement, and style in every line of the rhetorical unit, with special attention to how the rhetor handles the

[99] Quint. 7.4.1ff.

[100] Quint. 3.6.66, 68. For full discussion, see Cic. *De Or.* 1.31.139–140; 2.26.110–12; *Part. Or.* 31.107–8; 38–39; Her. 1.11.19–13.23; 2.9–12; Quint. 7.5–9. Cic. *De Or.* 1.31.139–40; 2.26.110–12; *Part. Or.* 31.107–9; and *Top.* 25.96 exclude syllogism. Her. 1.12.20–21 and 2.12.17–18 add transference in which the defendant wants postponement, change of plaintiff, or judge; and definition in which the name by which an act should be called is in question. Cic. *Inv.* 1.12.7–13.18 and 2.40.116–51.154 contain these four and add a definitional-legal stasis. Cf. Ar. *Rhet.* 1.15.1375a.3–1375b.12.

[101] Quint. 3.6.82, 86–89; cf. Cic. *Or.* 34.121.

[102] Quint. 3.6.88. Cicero makes the point that legal questions are not a separate category, but fall under the category of quality or nature (*De Or.* 2.26.113).

[103] Cic. *Inv.* 1.12.17; Quint. 3.6.7–9, 21, 81, 91ff.

[104] Quint. 3.6.9, 12, 21.

[105] Cic. *Inv.* 2.4.12; Quint. 3.6.81; cf. Cic. *De Or.* 2.51.155.

[106] For detailed discussions on how stasis works with each type of rhetoric, see Cic. *Inv.* 2.4–59 and Quint. 3.7–9; 7.2–10.

[107] Cic. *Inv.* 1.7.9; *De Or.* 1.31.142; *Or.* 13.43; *Opt. Gen.* 2.4–5; Her. 1.2.3; Quint. 3.3.1; cf. Cic. *De Or.* 2.19.79.

exigence. This analysis should be provided with a detailed outline structured according to the elements of arrangement and showing particular concern for matters of invention.

Invention

"Invention[108] is the devising of matter, true or plausible, that would make the case convincing."[109] Invention begins with the determination of the species of rhetoric, the question, and the stasis as already discussed, but is mainly concerned with the development of proofs to best support the case. The two types of proofs used in invention are the inartificial and the artificial.[110] Inartificial proofs (ἄτεχνοι)[111] are those not manufactured by the rhetor[112] and include witnesses, evidence extracted by torture, informal agreements, contracts, laws, decisions of previous courts, rumors, documents, and oaths.[113] Inartificial proofs mainly belong to judicial rhetoric.[114] Artificial proofs (ἔντεχνοι)[115] are those constructed from propositions and supporting material gathered from the facts of the case,[116] and include ethos, pathos, and logos.[117]

Ethos (ἦθος)[118] is moral character and conduct, the course of life.[119] It ". . . is

[108] *Inventio*— Cic. *Inv.* 1.7.9; Her. 1.2.3; Quint. 3.3.1; Lausberg, 1:146–240, §260–442; Martin, 15–210; George A. Kennedy, *The Art of Persuasion in Greece* (Princeton: Princeton University Press, 1963) 87–103 (pertaining to Aristotle); Kennedy, *New Testament Interpretation*, 14–23.

[109] Her. 1.2.3. Cf. Cic. *Inv.* 1.7.9 for a similar definition.

[110] Lausberg, 1:191–235, §350–426; Martin, 97–135.

[111] Lausberg, 1.191–93, §351–54; Martin, 97–101.

[112] Ar. *Rhet.* 1.2.1355b.2; Cic. *De Or.* 2.27.116; 2.39.163; *Part. Or.* 2.5–6; 13.48; Quint. 5.1.1; cf. Cic. *Or.* 34.122. *Rhet. ad Alex.* 7.1428a.16ff. considers this type of proof as supplementary (ἐπίθετοι).

[113] Ar. *Rhet.* 1.2.1355b.2; 1.15.1375a.1–2; 1375b.13–1377b.30; *Rhet. ad Alex.* 7.1428a.22–23; 14.1431b.10–17.1432a.45; Cic. *De Or.* 2.27.116; *Part. Or.* 2.6; 14.48–51; Quint. 5.1–7. Cf. Her. 2.13.19 which gives a similar list of proofs for legal stasis. *Rhet. ad Alex.* 7.1428a.22–23 and 14.1431b.10 add the opinion of the rhetor. Cic. *Part. Or.* 2.6 classifies such evidence as either divine or human. Under divine he lists "oracles, auspices, prophecies, the answers of priests, augurs, and diviners." Cf. Quint. 5.11.43–44 and below, p. 17 n. 143. Cic. *Part. Or.* 14.48–51 gives a methodology for handling inartificial proofs.

[114] Ar. *Rhet.* 1.15.1375a.1.

[115] Lausberg, 1:193–235, §355–426; Martin, 101–35.

[116] Ar. *Rhet.* 1.2.1355b.2; Cic. *De Or.* 2.27.116; 2.39.163; *Part. Or.* 2.5–7; Quint. 5.1.1; 5.8.1; cf. Cic. *Or.* 34.122. *Rhet. ad Alex.* 7.1428a.16ff. considers these proofs drawn from the words and actions of persons.

[117] Ar. *Rhet.* 1.2.1356a.3–6; Cic. *De Or.* 2.27.115; Quint. 5.12.9–12 (pathos only). *Rhet. ad Alex.* 7.1428a.16ff gives the list: probabilities, examples, tokens, enthymemes, maxims, signs, and refutations.

[118] Lausberg, 1:141–42, §257; Martin, 158–61; Kennedy, *Art of Persuasion in Greece*, 91–93.

[119] Ar. *Rhet.* 1.2.1356a.3–4; 1.8.1366a.6; Cic. *De Or.* 2.43.182–84; Quint. 6.2.8–19.

related to men's nature and character, their habits and all the intercourse of life . . ."[120] As a means of artificial proof, the rhetor seeks to show his own and his client's ethos in the best light and his opponent's in the worst![121] Ethos is an ethical proof based on the demonstration through the speech of the rhetor's goodness, goodwill, and moral uprighteousness, all of which enhances the persuasiveness and perceived truth of the message![122] Ethos was often considered the most effective means of proof![123]

Pathos (πάθος, *adfectus*)[124] is emotion and, as a means of proof, is arousal of the emotion of the audience for or against both the matter at hand and those representing it![125] The rhetor seeks to elicit positive pathos for his own case and negative pathos for his opponent's case![126] Proofs using pathos include the rhetor

[120] Cic. *Or.* 37.128.

[121] For strategy for using ethos, see Ar. *Rhet.* 2.1.1377b.1–1378a.7; Cic. *De Or.* 2.43.182–84.

[122] Ar. *Rhet.* 1.8.1366a.6. Aristotle conceived of ethos as an actual moral uprighteousness inherent in the speech (*Rhet.* 1.2.1356a.3; 1.8.1366a.6). Cicero revised Aristotle's understanding of ethos, pathos, and logos. These became three duties of the rhetor: to charm, to move, and to teach respectively (*De Or.* 2.43.182–84). Ethos thus shifted more to a perceived rather than an actual goodness, to a pleasant and gracious manner. This shift is evident in the quotation: "For by means of particular types of thought and diction, and the employment besides of a delivery that is unruffled and eloquent of good nature, the speakers are made to appear upright, well-bred and virtuous men" (*De Or.* 2.43.184).

Quintilian derives his conception of ethos and pathos from Cicero. He further conceives of ethos and pathos as differing degrees of emotion (6.2.8, 9, 12, 17; Cic. *Or.* 37.128). Ethos designates calm and gentle emotions inducing goodwill (6.2.9, 12; Cic. *Or.* 37.128), and pathos as describing more violent emotion meant to command and disturb (6.2.9, 12, 20–24; Cic. *Or.* 37.128). However, Aristotle's conception of ethos as inherent in the speech reappears to a degree (6.2.13, 17, 18). Quintilian says ethos in an orator ". . . is commended to our approval by goodness more than aught else and is not merely calm and mild; but in most cases ingratiating and courteous and such as to excite pleasure and affection in our hearers" (6.2.13).

According to Quintilian, ethos in all its forms requires a man of good character and courtesy (6.2.18). Ethos of this kind in the person of the rhetor is particularly necessary when dealing with intimates or offering admonition (6.2.14), which is the case with biblical writers. See Kennedy, *Quintilian,* 74–75, and *Art of Persuasion in Greece,* 91–96.

[123] Ar. *Rhet.* 1.2.1356a.4; Quint. 4.1.7; 5.12.9; Aug. *De Doct. Chr.* 37.59–60. Cf. *Rhet. ad Alex.* 14.1431b.10ff., which states that the rhetor's opinion is a form of supplementary proof, and Quint. 3.8.12–13, which states that ethos is the most effective means of proof in deliberative rhetoric.

[124] Lausberg, 1:140–41, §257; Martin, 158–66; Kennedy, *Art of Persuasion in Greece,* 93–96.

[125] Ar. *Rhet.* 1.2.1356a.3, 5; Cic. *De Or.* 2.42.178; 2.44.185–87; *Or.* 37.128; Quint. 6.2.20–24; cf. 5.8.1–3.

[126] For strategy using pathos, see Ar. *Rhet.* 2.1.1378a.8–17.1391b.6; Cic. *De Or.* 2.44.185–87; 2.51–52; Quint. 6.2.25ff.

perceived as a good man (rather than being a good man as with ethos), assevera-
tion or positive and earnest affirmation, and giving an element of character and
supporting it with a plausible reason.[127]

There are two modes of reasoning from logos: example and argument, or
induction and deduction respectively.[128] "Induction is a form of argument which
leads the person with whom one is arguing to give assent to certain undisputed
facts; through this assent it wins his approval of a doubtful proposition because
it resembles the facts to which he has assented."[129] Deduction is ". . . a form of
argument which draws a probable conclusion from the fact under consideration
itself . . ."[130]

Examples[131] used in proof include examples from history,[132] fables,[133] com-
parisons,[134] fictions of poets,[135] and judgments.[136] Historical parallels were
considered very useful, particularly because they can be related in detail as the
case demands.[137] They are especially useful in deliberative oratory because, since
the future resembles the past, they aid deliberation on what is likely to happen.[138]
Fables, like those of Aesop, were considered useful because they are easier to
provide than historical examples,[139] and are especially useful in convincing the
rude and uneducated.[140] The fictions of the poets can be used but have less force

---

[127] Quint. 5.12.9–13. Quintilian makes the observation that stylistic ornamant is persuasive (8.3.1–6). This type of persuasion is most akin to pathos, being derived from pleasure
in listening.

[128] Ar. *Rhet.* 1.2.1356b.8; Cic. *Inv.* 1.31–41.

[129] Cic. *Inv.* 1.31.51.

[130] Cic. *Inv.* 1.34.57.

[131] Παράδειγμα (Ar. *Rhet.* 1.2.1357a.13; 2.20.1393a.1; *Rhet. ad Alex.* 7.1428a.16ff.; Quint.
5.11.1–2), *exemplum* (Cic. *Inv.* 1.30.49; Quint. 5.11.6). For a full discussion, see Ar. *Rhet.*
2.20; *Rhet. ad Alex.* 8; Cic. *Inv.* 1.30.49; Quint. 5.11; Lausberg, 1:227–35, §410–26; Martin,
119–24. Cicero (*Inv.* 1.30.49) considers similitude, parallel, and *exemplum* as separate
categories of argument using comparison. Quintilian makes the point that while many
Roman writers (like Cicero) distinguish examples from comparison (παραβολή, similitude),
he considers both together under example because example involves comparison and
comparison is of the nature of example (5.11.1–2). In this he agrees with Aristotle who
considers comparison a type of example (*Rhet.* 2.20.1393a.2). Quintilian notes that
similitudes are akin to examples, ". . . more especially when drawn from things nearly
equal without any admixture of metaphor . . ." (5.11.22).

[132] Ar. *Rhet.* 2.20.1393a.2–1393b.4; *Rhet. ad Alex.* 8; Cic. *Inv.* 1.30.49; Quint. 5.11.1, 8,
15–16.

[133] Ar. *Rhet.* 2.20.1393a.2; 1393b.5–1394a.8; Quint. 5.11.19–21.

[134] Ar. *Rhet.* 2.20.1393a.2; 1393b.4.

[135] Quint. 5.11.17–18.

[136] Cic. *Inv.* 1.30.48; Quint. 5.11.36–44.

[137] Quint. 5.11.8, 15–16.

[138] Ar. *Rhet.* 2.20.1394a.8; Quint. 5.11.8; cf. 3.8.66.

[139] Ar. *Rhet.* 2.20.1394a.9.

[140] Quint. 5.11.19–21.

than other forms of examples![141] Judgments or κρίσεις are ". . . whatever may be regarded as expressing the opinion of nations, peoples, philosophers, distinguished citizens, or illustrious poets,"[142] and include common sayings, popular beliefs, and supernatural oracles![143]

Proof from example involves induction[144] and is ". . . the adducing of some past action real or assumed which may serve to persuade the audience of the truth of the point which we are trying to make."[145] It always involves comparison of likes, unlikes, and contraries,[146] usually like to like within a genus![147] The parallel between the example and the point proven can be complete or partial,[148] and the proof may argue from the greater to the lesser or the lesser to the greater![149] Arguments from unlikes are most suitable to exhortation[150] as is true in New Testament usage.

The argument, the other form of artificial proof from logos, is defined as ". . . a process of reasoning which provides proof and enables one thing to be inferred from another and confirms facts which are uncertain by reference to facts which are certain."[151] What are regarded as certainties for use in arguments are: things perceived by the senses (e.g., signs), things about which there is general agreement, things established by law or passed into current usage, and what is admitted by either party, what has been proven, or whatever is not disputed by the opposition![152]

There are three types of argument: the syllogism, the epicheireme, and the enthymeme![153] The syllogism[154] has three parts:[155] the major premise which

---

[141] Quint. 5.11.17–18.

[142] Quint. 5.11.36. Cf. Cic. *Inv.* 1.30.48 for a similar definition.

[143] Quint. 5.11.37, 42–44. Quintilian argues against an opposing position stating that authoritative sources are inartificial proofs because the rhetor receives them ready-made. He asserts to the contrary that they are external to the case until the rhetor uses art and applies them to the case, and are thus artificial proofs (5.11.43–44). Cf. Cic. *Part. Or.* 2.6 which classifies authoritative sources like "oracles, auspices, prophecies, the answers of priests, augurs, and diviners" as inartificial proofs.

[144] Ar. *Rhet.* 1.2.1356b.8; 1357a.13; 2.20.1393a.1; Quint. 5.11.2–6; cf. Cic. *Inv.* 1.31.51–32.53.

[145] Quint. 5.11.6. For similar deffinitions, see *Rhet. ad Alex.* 8.1429a.20ff.; Cic. *Inv.* 1.30.49.

[146] *Rhet. ad Alex.* 8.1429a.20ff.; Cic. *Inv.* 1.30.49; Quint. 5.11.1–7.

[147] Ar. *Rhet.* 1.2.1357b.19.

[148] Quint. 5.11.5–7.

[149] Quint. 5.11.9ff.

[150] Quint. 5.11.10.

[151] Quint. 5.10.11.

[152] Quint. 5.10.12–15.

[153] For detailed discussion of the syllogistic or deductive form of argument, see Cic. *Inv.* 1.34–41; Lausberg, 1:197–227, §366–409; Martin, 101–19; Kennedy, *New Testament Interpretation,* 16–17, and *Art of Persuasion in Greece,* 96–101.

[154] Συλλογισμός (Ar. *Rhet.* 1.2.1357a.13), *syllogismus* (Quint. 5.14.14).

[155] Cf. the lengthy discussion in Cic. *Inv.* 1.34–41 where Cicero examines the various

presents the principle underlying the syllogism, the minor premise which supports the point of the major premise needed to proof, and the conclusion.[156] The major and minor premises themselves may or may not need supporting proof![157] Since the syllogism is a structure of formal logic, it is rarely found in pure form in a rhetorical context.[158]

An epicheireme[159] consists of three parts: the major premise or the subject or inquiry, the minor premise or the proof of the major premise, and the conclusion or the agreeable element of the major and minor premises.[160] The premises may be admitted facts or need proof.[161] In these regards, the epicheireme is like a syllogism. However, the epicheireme varies from the syllogism in that it deals with statements that are often no more than credible, whereas a syllogism always infers truth from truth.[162]

An enthymeme[163] is usually regarded as an "incomplete syllogism,"[164] "a proposition with a reason."[165] Whereas the syllogism ". . . always has its premises and conclusion and effects its proof by the employment of all its parts, the enthymeme is content to let its proof be understood without explicit statement."[166] It may be drawn from a denial of consequents and consist of a proposition and a proof, or be drawn from incompatibles (a stronger form), or consist in a reason subjoined to a dissimilar or contrary proposition (the most effective form).[167] Like the epicheireme, an enthymeme may be necessary or only probable.[168]

The premises of arguments are often signs,[169] or what normally precede or

---

views on the subject of how many parts deductive arguments in syllogistic form should have and decides on five parts. Cf. Her. 2.18.28–29.46 for a five part scheme for arguments in general.

[156] Cf. Cic. *Inv.* 1.37.67.

[157] Cf. Cic. *Inv.* 1.34.57ff.

[158] Quint. 5.14.27ff.

[159] Ἐπιχείρημα (Quint. 5.10.1), *epichirema* (Quint. 5.10.4; 5.14.5, 14).

[160] Quint. 5.14.5–6; cf. 5.10.5.

[161] Quint. 5.14.5–9, 13; cf. 5.10.8ff.

[162] Quint. 5.14.14.

[163] Ἐνθύμημα (Ar. *Rhet.* 1.2.1357a.13; *Rhet. ad Alex.* 7.1428a.20; 10.1430a.23; Quint. 5.10.1), *enthymema* (Quint. 5.10.1; 5.14.1). For a detailed discussion, see Ar. *Rhet.* 1.2.1357a.13–14; 2.22–26; 3.17.1418a.6–1418b.17; *Rhet. ad Alex.* 10; Quint. 5.10.1–3; 5.14.1–4, 24–26.

[164] Quint. 5.14.2. For a similar understanding, see Ar. *Rhet.* 2.22.1395b.1–3; cf. 1.2.1357a.13.

[165] Quint. 5.10.2.

[166] Quint. 5.14.24. See Ar. *Rhet.* 1.2.1357a.13 for a similar definition. Cf. Quint. 5.10.2–3.

[167] Quint. 5.10.2; 5.14.1–4, 25; cf. Cic. *Inv.* 1.40.73–74.

[168] Ar. *Rhet.* 1.2.1357a.14.

[169] Σημεῖον (*Rhet. ad Alex.* 7.1428a.21; 12.1430b.30; Quint. 5.9.9), *signum* (Cic. *Inv.*

accompany or follow a thing.[170] They are either necessary[171] or unnecessary.[172] Necessary signs are those which involve a set conclusion and are irrefutable, offering no dispute as to facts. Thus they are normally used as the premises and conclusions of syllogisms.[173] Unnecessary signs are those offering only a probability[174] and are used with other signs and extraneous material to strengthen their value in proof.[175]

Each of the three species of rhetoric is characterized by a particular type of argumentation. Epideictic usually employs amplification to stir emotion rather than arguments to effect proof.[176] Deliberative chiefly relies upon ethos[177] and examples and comparison of examples,[178] whereas judicial is characterized by the use of enthymeme.[179]

Both inductive and deductive proofs are formulated using topics,[180] ". . . the secret places where arguments reside, and from which they must be drawn forth."[181] There are two basic types of topics, the common and the specific. Common topics supply arguments applicable to all species of rhetoric and all

---

1.29.47; Quint. 5.9.1), *indicium* (Quint. 5.9.9; 5.10.11), *vestigium* (Quint. 5.9.9). For a full discussion, see *Rhet. ad Alex.* 12; Quint. 5.9.1-16; Lausberg, 1:195-97, §358-65; Martin, 106-7.

[170] *Rhet. ad Alex.* 12.1430b.30ff. Cic. *Inv.* 1.30.48 gives a similar definition.

[171] Σημεῖον ἄλυτον (Quint. 5.9.3), *signum necessarium* (Quint. 5.9.3), *signum insolubile* (Quint. 5.9.3), *signum indubitatum* (Quint. 5.9.2), *signum immutabile* (Quint. 5.10.74), τεκμήρια (Ar. *Rhet.* 1.2.1357b.16; Pl. *Phdr.* 266E 51; Quint. 5.9.3).

[172] Σημεῖον εἰκός (Quint. 5.9.8), *signum non necessarium* (Quint. 5.9.8), *signum dubium* (Quint. 5.9.2).

[173] Ar. *Rhet.* 1.2.1357b.16-17; *Rhet. ad Alex.* 12; Quint. 5.9.3-7; cf. *Rhet. ad Alex.* 9.

[174] *Rhet. ad Alex.* 12; Quint. 5.9.8-16.

[175] Quint. 5.9.8-11.

[176] Ar. *Rhet.* 1.9.1368a.38-40; 2.18.1392a.5; 3.17.1417b.3; *Rhet. ad Alex.* 3.1426b.19ff.; 6.1428a.1ff; Cic. *Part. Or.* 21.71; cf. Her. 3.8.15.

[177] Quint. 3.8.12-13.

[178] Ar. *Rhet.* 1.9.1368a.40; 2.20.1394a.8; 3.17.1418a.5; *Rhet. ad Alex.* 32.1438b.29ff.; Quint. 3.8.34, 66; cf. 5.11.8.

[179] Ar. *Rhet.* 1.9.1368a.40; 3.17.1418a.5; *Rhet. ad Alex.* 6.1428a.5ff.

[180] Τόποι (Ar. *Rhet.* 1.2.1358a.21), *loci* (Cic. *Top.* 2.8; Quint. 5.10.20). For further discussion, see Ar. *Rhet.* 1.2.1358a.21-22; 1.3.1359a.8-9; 1.4.14; 2.18-19; 2.22.1396a.8; 2.23-24; *Top.; Rhet. ad Alex.* 1.1421b.21-1423a.11; 3.1425b.36-1426a.19; Cic. *Inv.* 1.24-28; 1.53-56; 2.14.47-18.56; 2.20.61; 2.22.68; 2.23.71; 2.26.77-78; 2.28.85-86; 2.30.91, 94; 2.33.101-3; 2.36.108-9; 2.38-39; 2.48.143; 2.49.147; 2.50.152-59.178; *De Or.* 2.30.130-31; 2.39-40; 2.84.341-85.350; *Or.* 14.46-47; *Part. Or.* 2.5-7; 21.70-23.82; *Top.; Her.* 2.6.10; 2.14-17; 2.30.47-31.50; 3.2.3-5.9; 3.8; Quint. 2.4.22-23; 5.8.4-5; 5.10.20-118; 5.13.57; Lausberg, 1:201-20, §373-99; Martin, 107-19, 155-57, 162-65; Kennedy, *New Testament Interpretation*, 20-21; *Classical Rhetoric*, 82-85; *Art of Persuasion in Greece*, 100-103; John C. Brunt, "More on the *Topos* as a New Testament Form," *JBL* 104 (1985) 495-500.

[181] Quint. 5.10.20. Cf. Cic. *Or.* 14.46; *Part. Or.* 2.5; *Top.* 2.8 for similar definitions.

classes of things,[182] whereas specific topics are applicable to particular species of rhetoric or particular classes of things.[183] Common topics include the possible-impossible, past fact, future fact, and degree (more-less, greater-lesser).[184] Specific topics for judicial rhetoric include the just-unjust and equity-inequity;[185] for deliberative include happiness-unhappiness, expediency-harm, honor dishonor, necessary-unnecessary, and the good and degrees thereof;[186] and for epideictic include the noble-disgraceful and virtue-vice.[187]

Arrangement

"Arrangement[188] is the ordering and distribution of the matter, making clear the place to which each thing is assigned."[189] Arrangement has its fullest structure in judicial rhetoric and was considered to have four to six parts.[190] These are the *exordium*,[191] the *narratio*,[192] the *partitio*,[193] the *probatio*,[194] the

---

[182] Ar. *Rhet.* 1.2.1358a.21–22; Cic. *Inv.* 2.14.47–15.48.

[183] Ar. *Rhet.* 1.2.1358a.21–22; Cic. *De Or.* 1.31.141; cf. Quint. 5.13.57.

[184] Ar. *Rhet.* 1.2.1358a.21; 1.3.1359a.8–9; 2.18–19; 2.23–24; *Top.* 2.1–7.3; Cic. *Inv.* 1.24–28; 2.14.47–15.50; *De Or.* 2.39–40; *Part. Or.* 2.5–7; *Top.* 1.1–23.90; Her. 2.6–10; Quint. 5.8.4–5; 5.10.20–99.

[185] Ar. *Rhet.* 1.10.1368b.1ff.; 2.22.1396a.8; Cic. *Inv.* 2.16–18; 2.20.61; 2.23.71; 2.26.77–78; 2.28.85–86; 2.30.91, 94; 2.33.101–3; 2.36.108–9; 2.38–39; 2.48.143; 2.49.147; 2.50.152–53; *Top.* 23.90; Her. 2.6.9; 2.9–10; 2.14–17.

[186] Ar. *Rhet.* 1.4–8; 2.22.1396a.8; *Rhet. ad Alex.* 1.1421b.21–1423a.11; 6.1427b.39–40; Cic. *Inv.* 2.52–58; *Top.* 23.89; *Part. Or.* 24–27; Her. 3.2.3–5.9; Quint. 3.8.10–28.

[187] Ar. *Rhet.* 1.9; 2.22.1396a.8; *Rhet. ad Alex.* 3; 35.1440b.14–1441b.29; Cic. *Inv.* 2.59.177; *De Or.* 2.84–85; *Part. Or.* 21–23; *Top.* 23.89; Her. 3.6–8; cf. Cic. *De Or.* 2.11.46.

[188] *Dispositio* — Her. 1.2.3; Quint. 3.3.1; 7.1.2; Lausberg, 1:241–47, §443–52; Martin, 211–43; Kennedy, *New Testament Interpretation,* 23–25.

[189] Her. 1.2.3. Cf. Cic. *Inv.* 1.7.9 and Quint. 7.1.1–2 for similar definitions.

[190] For the debate, see Quint. 3.9.1–5. The four part scheme includes the *exordium, narratio, probatio,* and *peroratio,* the *partitio* and *refutatio* being considered as part of the *narratio* and *probatio* respectively (Ar. *Rhet.* 3.13; Cic. *De Or.* 2.80.326ff.; *Part. Or.* 1.4; 8.27; *Top.* 26.97–98). The five part scheme adds the *refutatio* (Quint. 3.9.1–6). Cf. Cic. *Or.* 15.50. The six part scheme is obvious (Cic. *Inv.* 1.14.19; Her. 1.3.4).

[191] Προοίμιον (Ar. *Rhet.* 3.13.1414b.3; Pl. *Phdr.* 266D 51; *Rhet. ad Alex.* 28.1436a.32; Quint. 4.1.1), *prooemium* (Her. 1.4.6; Quint. 3.9.1); *principium* (Cic. *De Or.* 2.78.315; Her. 3.9.16; Quint. 4.1.1), *initium* (Cic. *Part. Or.* 8.27); *exordium* (Cic. *Inv.* 1.14.19; Her. 1.3.4; Quint. 4.1.1).

[192] Πρόθεσις (Ar. *Rhet.* 3.13.1414a.2), *narratio* (Cic. *Inv.* 1.14.19; 1.19.27; *De Or.* 2.80.326; *Part. Or.* 8.27; 9.31; Her. 1.3.4; 3.9.1, 16).

[193] *Partitio* (Cic. *Inv.* 1.14.19; 1.22.31; Quint. 3.9.1–2; 4.5.1), *divisio* (Her. 1.3.4; 3.9.16), *propositio* (Quint. 3.9.2).

[194] βεβαίωσις (*Rhet. ad Alex.* 32.1438b.29), πίστις (Ar. *Rhet.* 3.13.1414b.4), διήγησις (Pl. *Phdr.* 266E 51), *confirmatio* (Cic. *Inv.* 1.14.19; 1.24.34; *De Or.* 2.81.331; *Or.* 34.122; *Part. Or.* 1.4; 8.27; Her. 1.3.4; 3.9.16); *probatio* (Quint. 3.9.1).

refutatio,[195] and the *peroratio*.[196]

The *exordium* is the beginning component of a rhetorical unit which aims to make the audience attentive, well-disposed, and receptive to the speech that follows.[197] The *narratio* is ". . . the persuasive exposition of that which either has been done, or is supposed to have been done . . . a speech instructing the audience as to the nature of the case in dispute."[198] The *partitio* is ". . . the enumeration in order of our own propositions, those of our adversary, or both."[199] The *probatio* ". . . is the part of the oration which by marshalling arguments lends credit, authority, and support to our case."[200] In the *refutatio*, ". . . arguments are used to impair, disprove, or weaken the confirmation or proof in our opponent's speech."[201] The *peroratio*[202] is the conclusion of the rhetoric. It has the two main functions and divisions of recapitulating the main points of the *probatio*[203] and arousing emotions for our case and against that of the opposition through amplification.[204]

---

[195] *Confutatio* (Her. 1.3.4; 3.9.16); *reprehensio* (Cic. *Inv.* 1.14.19; *De Or.* 2.81.331), *refutatio* (Quint. 3.9.1).

[196] Ἐπίλογος (Ar. *Rhet.* 3.13.1414b.3; 3.19.1419b.1), *epilogus* (Her. 2.30.47; Quint. 6.1.7), *conclusio* (Cic. *Inv.* 1.14.19; 1.52.98; Her. 1.3.4; 2.30.47; 3.9.16), *peroratio* (Cic. *Or.* 34.122; *Part. Or.* 1.4; 8.27; 15.52; Quint. 3.9.1).

[197] Ar. *Rhet.* 3.14.1415a.7; *Rhet. ad Alex.* 29.1436a.33ff.; Cic. *Inv.* 1.15.20; *Or.* 14.122; *Part. Or.* 8.28; *Top.* 26.97; Her. 1.3.4; 1.4.6; Quint. 4.1.5, 37, 41, 50–51; cf. Cic. *De Or.* 1.31.143; 2.19.80; *Or.* 15.50; Quint. 4.1.61–62; 4.2.24; 10.1.48. For detailed discussions, see Ar. *Rhet.* 3.14–15; *Rhet. ad Alex.* 29; Cic. *Inv.* 1.15–18; *De Or.* 2.77.315–80.325; *Part. Or.* 8.28–30; Her. 1.3.4–7.11; Quint. 4.1; Lausberg, 1:150-63, §263–88; Martin, 60–75.

[198] Quint. 4.2.31. For similar understandings, see Cic. *Inv.* 1.19.27; *Or.* 34.122; *Part. Or.* 9.31; cf. Cic. *De Or.* 1.31.143; 2.19.80; Quint. 4.2.86. For detailed discussions, see Ar. *Rhet.* 3.16; *Rhet. ad Alex.* 30–31; Cic. *Inv.* 1.19–21; *Part. Or.* 9.31–32; Her. 1.8–9; Quint. 4.2–3; Lausberg, 1:163–90, §289–347; Martin, 75–89.

[199] Quint. 4.5.1. For similar understandings, see Cic. *Inv.* 1.22.31; Her. 1.3.4; cf. Cic. *De Or.* 1.31.143. For detailed discussions, see Cic. *Inv.* 1.22–23; Her. 1.10.17; Quint. 3.9.1–5; 4.4–5; Martin, 91–95.

[200] Cic. *Inv.* 1.24.34. For similar understandings, see Cic. *Or.* 34.122; Her. 1.3.4; cf. Cic. *De Or.* 1.31.143; 2.19.80. For detailed discussions, see Ar. *Rhet.* 3.17; *Rhet. ad Alex.* 32–33; Cic. *Inv.* 1.24.34–41.77; *Part. Or.* 9.33–14.51; Her. 3.9–10; Quint. 5.1–12; Lausberg, 1:191–235, §350–426; Martin, 95–137.

[201] Cic. *Inv.* 1.42.78. For similar understandings, see Ar. *Rhet.* 2.25.1402a.1–2; 3.13.1414b.4; Her. 1.3.4; Quint. 3.9.5; 5.13.1; cf. Cic. *De Or.* 1.31.143; 2.81.331. For detailed discussions, see Ar. *Rhet.* 2.25; *Rhet. ad Alex.* 34.1439b.37–1440a.25; Cic. *Inv.* 1.42.78–51.96; *De Or.* 2.53.215–16; *Part. Or.* 12.44; Quint. 5.13; Martin, 124–33.

[202] Ar. *Rhet.* 3.19.1419b.1–6; Cic. *Inv.* 1.52–56; *Or.* 34.122; *Part. Or.* 15–17; *Top.* 26.98; Her. 2.30-31; Quint 6.1; Lausberg, 1:236–40, §431–42; Martin, 147–66.

[203] *Repetitio* (*Rhet. ad Alex.* 20.1433b.29; Quint. 6.1.1), *enumeratio* (Cic. *Inv.* 1.52.98; *Part. Or.* 15.52; Her. 2.30.47; Quint. 6.1.1). For detailed discussions, see Ar. *Rhet.* 3.19.1419b.1; 1419b.4–1420a.6; *Rhet. ad Alex.* 20–21; 36.1444b.21-35; Cic. *Inv.* 1.52; *De Or.* 2.19.80; *Part. Or.* 17.59–60; Her. 2.30.47; Quint. 6.1.1–8; cf. Cic. *De Or.* 1.31.143.

[204] *Adfectus* (Quint 6.1.1, 9). For detailed discussions, see Ar. *Rhet.* 3.19.1419b.1–3;

Style

Style[205] is defined as ". . . the fitting of the proper language to the invented matter,"[206] and "the adaptation of suitable words and sentences to the matter devised."[207] In the ancient handbooks, style is usually discussed under two headings: *lexis* (or diction) and synthesis (or composition).[208] *Lexis* is making a correct choice of words, and usually concerns such matters as proper designations, metaphorical usage, and new coinages.[209] Synthesis concerns the manner in which words are fashioned into phrases, clauses, and sentences; the most important aspects of which are symmetry and rhythm,[210] and tropes and figures.

A trope[211] is ". . . the transference of expressions from their natural and principle significance to another, with a view to the embellishment of style . . . the transference of words and phrases from the place which is strictly theirs to another to which they do not properly belong."[212] Tropes include

---

Rhet. ad Alex. 34; 36.1443b.15–22; Cic. *Inv.* 1.53–56; *Or.* 34.122; *Part. Or.* 15.52–17.58; *Top.* 26.98; Her. 2.30.47–31.50; Quint. 6.1.9–55.

[205] Λέξις (Ar. *Rhet.* 3.1.1403b.2), φράσις (Quint. 8.1.1), *oratio* (Cic. *De Or.* 1.31.142; *Part. Or.* 5.16; Quint 1.5.1), *elocutio* (Cic. *Inv.* 1.7.9; Her. 4.1.1; Quint 3.3.1). For extensive discussions of style, see Ar. *Rhet.* 3.1–12; *Rhet. ad Alex.* 22.1434a.35–28.1436a.13; Long. *Subl.* (all); Demetr. *Eloc.* (all); Cic. *De Or.* 3.5.19–55.212 (with the exclusion of the digressions of 3.20.74–24.90 and 3.28–36); *Or.* 19.61–31.112; 35.123–25; 39.134–71.237; *Part. Or.* 5.16–7.24; *Opt. Gen.* (all); Her. 4; Quint. 1.5; 8–9. Lausberg, 1:248–525, §458–1082; Martin, 247–345; Kennedy, *New Testament Interpretation,* 25–30; J. W. H. Atkins, *Literary Criticism in Antiquity,* 2 vols. (Cambridge: Cambridge University Press, 1934; repr. ed., Peter Smith, 1961); G. M. A. Grube, *The Greek and Roman Critics* (Toronto: University of Toronto Press, 1965); A. D. Leeman, *Orationis Ratio: The Stylistic Theories and Practice of the Roman Orators Historians and Philosophers,* 2 vols. (Amsterdam: Adolf M. Hakkert, 1963); D. A. Russell, *Criticism in Antiquity* (Berkeley/Los Angeles: University of California Press, 1981) 129–47.

[206] Cic. *Inv.* 1.7.9.

[207] Her. 1.2.3.

[208] *Rhet. ad Alex.* 23.1434b.33–37; Cic. *De Or.* 3.37.149; *Or.* 24.80; *Part. Or.* 5.16–17; Quint. 1.5.1–2.

[209] Ar. *Rhet.* 3.2–4; *Rhet. ad Alex.* 23; Demetr. *Eloc.* 1.5; Cic. *De Or.* 3.37.149–43.170; *Or.* 24.80; *Part. Or.* 5.16–17; Quint 1.5; 8, pr. 23ff.; 8.3.24.39; Lausberg, 1:279–82, §542–51.

[210] Ar. *Rhet.* 3.8–9; *Rhet. ad Alex.* 23–28; Demetr. *Eloc.* (all); Cic. *De Or.* 3.43.171–51.199; *Or.* 44.149–71.237; *Part. Or.* 6.18–22; Quint. 9.4. Lausberg, 1:455–507, §911–1054; Martin, 315–28; Leeman, 1:149–55 (on Cic. Or.), 1:307–10 (on Quint.).

[211] Τρόπος (Cic. *Brut.* 17.69), *tropus* (Quint. 8.6.1), *tropos* (Quint. 9.1.4). For further information, see Quint. 8.6; 9.1.1–9; Lausberg, 1:282–307, §552–98; Martin, 261–70; Leeman, 1:302–4 (on Quint.).

[212] Quint. 9.1.4. Quint 8.6.1 gives a similar definition. Cf. Cic. *Or.* 27, 92–93; *Brut.* 17.69.

metaphor, metonomy, antonomasia, metalepsis, synecdoche, catachresis, allegory, hyperbole, onomatopoeia, periphrasis, and epithet.[213]

A figure[214] occurs ". . . when we give our language a conformation other than the obvious and ordinary."[215] It involves a "rational change in meaning or language from the ordinary and simple form,"[216] and is "poetically or rhetorically altered from the simple and obvious method of expression."[217] It is ". . . a form of expression to which a new aspect is given by art."[218] A figure does not necessarily involve alteration of order or the strict sense of words as does a trope.[219]

There are two classes of figures: figures of speech[220] and figures of thought.[221] Figures of speech pertain to words, dictions, expression, language or style, and figures of thought to feeling and conception.[222] The figure of speech disappears if words are altered, but the figure of thought remains whatever words are used.[223] "It is a figure of diction if the adornment is comprised in the fine polish of the language itself. A figure of thought derives from a certain distinction from the idea, not from the words."[224]

---

[213] Quint. 9.1.3, 5–6. Her 4.31.42ff. adds hyperbaton and deletes metalepsis and epithet from this list. Cf. Cic. Or. 27.93-94 which lists allegory, catachresis, metaphor, and metonomy as "transferred words."

[214] For general discussion, see Quint. 9.1.1-36; Lausberg, 1:308-9, §600-603; Martin, 270-75; Leeman, 1:33-42; Bullinger (all).

[215] Quint. 9.1.4.

[216] Quint. 9.1.11.

[217] Quint. 9.1.13.

[218] Quint. 9.1.14.

[219] Quint. 9.1.7.

[220] *Conformatio verborum* (Cic. De Or. 3.52.200; Quint. 9.2.1), *figurae quaeque in verbis sunt* (Quint. 2.13.11; *schemata, id est figurae, quae* λέξεως *vocantur* (Quint. 1.8.16); *figurae orationis* (Quint. 9.4.117), *figurae verborum* (Quint. 8.6.67; 9.1.3; 9.3.1), *verborum exornatio* (Her. 4.13.18). For further information, see Demetr. *Eloc.* 2.59-67; Cic. De Or. 3.54.206-8; Or. 24.80; 39.134-35; Her. 4.13-34; Quint. 9.3.1-99; Lausberg, 1:310-74, §607-754; Martin, 295-315; Leeman, 1:33-39 (on Her.).

[221] *Conformatio senteniarum* (Cic. De Or. 3.52.201; Quint. 9.2.1), *conformatio sententia* (Cic. Or. 39.136), *figurae quaeque in sensibus sunt* (Quint. 2.13.11), *schemata, id est figurae quae* διανοίας *vocantur* (Quint. 1.8.16), *figurae mentis quae* σχήματα διανοίας *dicuntur* (Quint. 6.3.70), *figurae sententia* (Quint. 9.1.3), *figurae quae ad mentem pertinent* (Quint. 9.1.19), *sententiarum exornatio* (Her. 4.13.18). For further information, see Cic. De Or. 3.53.202-54.206; Or. 24.81; 39.136-40.139; Her. 4.35-55; Quint. 9.2; Lausberg, 1:375-455, §755-910; Martin, 275-95; Leeman, 1:39-42 (on Her.).

[222] Quint. 9.1.17.

[223] Cic. De Or. 3.52.200; Or. 24.81.

[224] Her. 4.13.18.

In ancient rhetoric, there are three basic styles:[225] the Grand,[226] the Middle,[227] and the Plain.[228] All three styles are generally used in a single work as purpose, occasion, audience, case, or portion of a case require;[229] the most predominant style classifying the work.[230] The Grand Style[231] is a "smooth and ornate arrangement of impressive words"[232] and is characterized by a "power of thought and majesty of diction."[233] It is forceful,[234] yet stately and opulent.[235] It is the most ornamented style, using the most ornate words available[236] and all figures of speech and thought,[237] particularly

[225] Cic. *De Or.* 3.52.199–200; 3.45.177; *Or.* 5.20–6.21; 21.69–29.101; *Opt. Gen.* 1.2; Her. 4.8–11; Quint. 12.10.58–72; Aug. *De Doct. Chr.* 4.19.38; 4.24.54–26.56; Lausberg, 1:519–25, §1078–82; Martin, 331–45; Leeman, 1.29–32 (on Her.); 1:145–59 (on Cic. *Or.*); Kennedy, *Art of Persuasion in Greece*, 279–82.

There are exceptions to this threefold scheme. Demetrius' discussion shows there was considerable debate in his time whether or not there were two or four basic styles: the elevated (μεγαλοπρεπής), the elegant (γλαφυρός), the plain (ἰσχνός), and the forceful (δεινός) (*Eloc.* 2.36). Cicero postulates only two styles: the "simple, concise" or plain and the "elevated and abundant" or grand (*Brut.* 55.201), or the mild and the emotional (*De Or.* 2.53.212–15; cf. 2.49.200). Quintilan makes it clear that the threefold division is arbitrary and there are numerous gradations of each of the three styles (12.10.66–68).

[226] *Grandiloquus* (Cic. *Or.* 5.20), *gravis* (Cic. *De Or.* 3.45.177; Her. 4.8.11; 4.11.16), ἁδρός (Quint. 12.10.58).

[227] *Medius et quasi temperatus* (Cic. *Or.* 6.21; cf. *De Or.* 3.45.177), *mediocris* (Her. 4.8.11; 4.11.16), ἀνθηρός (Quint. 12.10.58).

[228] *Plena* (Cic. *De Or.* 3.52.199), *subtilis* (Cic. *Or.* 21.69; *De Or.* 3.45.177; Quint. 12.10.58), *extenuata* (Her. 4.8.11), *atenuatus* (Her. 4.11.16), ἰσχνός (Demetr. *Eloc.* 2.36; Quint. 12.10.58).

[229] Cic. *De Or.* 3.52.199; *Or.* 21.70–22.74; 35.123; Her. 4.11.16; Quint. 12.10.69–72; Aug. *De Doct. Chr.* 4.19.38; 22–23; cf. Demetr. *Eloc.* 2.36. For discussion of how styles interrelate in a work, see Demetr. *Eloc.* 2.36; Cic. *Or.* 28.99–31.112; Her. 4.11.16; Aug. *De Doct. Chr.* 4.22–23. These discussions are contradictory and highly idiosyncratic.

The orators have various schemes based on the assumption that the three styles are suited to different purposes. The grand style is for moving (Quint. 12.10.59) or persuading (Cic. *Or.* 21.69; Aug. *De Doct. Chr.* 4.19.38), the middle for charming (Quint. 12.10.59; Cic. *Or.* 21.69) or praising and condemning (Aug. *De Doct. Chr.* 4.19.38) and the plain for instruction (Quint. 12.10.59; Aug. *De Doct. Chr.* 4.19.38) and proof (Cic. *Or.* 21.69; Quint. 12.10.59). Another scheme is that the plain is suited to trivial matters, the middle to those of moderate significance, and the grand to weighty affairs (Cic. *Or.* 29.101).

[230] Aug. *De Doct. Chr.* 4.22.51.

[231] Cic. *Or.* 5.20; 28.97–99; Her. 4.8.11–12; Quint. 12.10.61–62. Her. 4.8.12 provides an example of the grand style.

[232] Her. 4.8.11.

[233] Cic. *Or.* 5.20.

[234] Quint. 12.10.58, 61; Aug. *De Doct. Chr.* 4.20.42.

[235] Cic. *Opt. Gen.* 1.2.

[236] Her. 4.8.11.

[237] Her. 4.8.11; Aug. *De Doct. Chr.* 4.20.42.

hyperbole.[238] Amplification is found throughout.[239]

The middle style[240] does not have the intellectual appeal of the plain style or the force of the grand.[241] It does not use impressive words, but not colloquial words either.[242] It is a relaxed style, but not ordinary prose.[243] It uses all the figures of speech and many of thought.[244] Metaphor is to be used most frequently.[245]

The plain style[246] is characterized as ". . . plain, to the point, explaining everything and making every point clear rather than impressive, using a refined, concise style stripped of ornament."[247] It is restrained, concise, avoiding long clauses which tend to elevation of style.[248] It uses current idiom, colloquial language,[249] avoids compound words and ambiguity, and uses natural word order.[250] The plain style has no force or vigor,[251] utilizes only moderate amplification,[252] and avoids accumulation.[253] However, it does try to be vivid through the use of *enargeia*.[254]

The plain style uses few figures[255] and such use is subdued. Figures should be spread throughout the speech. Figures of speech are more suited than figures of thought, and when figures of thought are used they should not be glaring. Maxims are a dominant feature. Metaphors should be used most of all because

---

[238] Quint. 12.10.62.

[239] Quint. 12.10.62. Cf. Cic. *Or.* 5.20 and Her. 4.8.11 which state that the grand style uses the thoughts of amplification and appeals to pity.

[240] Cic. *Or.* 6.21; 26.91–27.96; Her. 4.9.13; Quint. 12.10.60. Her. 4.9.13 provides an example of the middle style.

[241] Cic. *Or.* 6.21.

[242] Her. 4.8.11.

[243] Her. 4.9.13.

[244] Cic. *Or.* 27.95. *Or.* 6.21 says "simple" figures of speech and thought, but how one is to distinguish these is not explained. Those figures discussed by Cicero as characteristic of the middle style are said to be "transferred." These are tropes as later defined, and Cicero lists metaphor, metonymy, catachresis, and allegory as figures appropriate to the middle style (*Or.* 27.92–94).

[245] Quint. 12.10.60.

[246] Demetr. *Eloc.* 4.190–222; Cic. *Or.* 6.20; 23.75–26.90; Her. 4.10.14; Quint. 12.10.59. Her. 4.10.14 gives an example of the plain style.

[247] Cic. *Or.* 6.20.

[248] Demetr. *Eloc.* 4.204.

[249] Her. 4.8.11; 4.10.14; Cic. *Or.* 23.76; Demetr. *Eloc.* 4.192.

[250] Demetr. *Eloc.* 4.191, 196, 199.

[251] Cic. *De Or.* 3.52.199.

[252] Demetr. *Eloc.* 4.202.

[253] Cic. *Or.* 25.85.

[254] Demetr. *Eloc.* 4.209–20.

[255] Cic. *Or.* 25.83. Cic. *Or.* 6.20; 23.79 state, in contradiction, that no figures or ornament are to characterize the plain style. However, among orators and Cicero himself elsewhere in *Or.*, this is an extreme position.

they are usually colloquial, but they should be used modestly and be of a mild nature. Parisosis, homoeoteleuton, paronomasia, and all figures of repetition are unsuited to the plain style because they are obvious art.[256]

Amplification

Closely tied to invention, arrangement, and style is amplification.[257] "Amplification . . . is a sort of weighter affirmation, designed to win credence in the source of speaking by arousing emotion."[258] It is ". . . a sort of forcible method of arguing, argument being aimed at effecting proof, amplification at exercising influence."[259]

There are several methods of amplification and attentuation.[260] One, the use of strong words,[261] can be effected by the use of powerful, yet ordinary words, synonyms, exaggerated words, or words used metaphorically.[262] The use of strong words in amplification can be strengthened by making a comparison between a stronger word and the one for which it substitutes or by using epithets.[263]

A second method, augmentation,[264] is effected in four ways: 1) the use of a series increasing in intensity to the highest degree and pointing out that what is discussed goes beyond the highest category; 2) by beginning with the superlative and superimposing a still higher degree; 3) by making it clear that there is no greater degree than what is said; 4) by a continuous series in which each word is stronger than the last.[265]

A third method is comparison (*comparatio*) which also uses gradation. Comparison seeks to raise from the lesser to the greater in an effort to raise the greater. Also, a parallel can be used to make something that is desirable to exaggerate seem greater.[266] Reasoning (*ratiocinatio*) is a fourth method of amplification and occurs when something is magnified and by a rational process

---

[256] Cic. *Or.* 24.79–25.86.

[257] Αὔξησις, *amplificatio.* For detailed discussions, consult Ar. *Rhet.* 1.9.1368a.38–40; Cic. *De Or.* 3.26.104–27.107; *Part. Or.* 15.52–17.58; Long. *Subl.* 11.1–12.2; Quint. 8.4; Lausberg, 1:220–27, §400–403, Martin, 153–58, 208–10. Cf. Cic. *Inv.* 1.53–54 and Her. 2.30.47–49 after him, for amplification using commonplaces in the *peroratio.*

[258] Cic. *Part. Or.* 15.52.

[259] Cic. *Part. Or.* 8.27.

[260] The methods of attenuation are virtually the same as those of amplification outlined below (Quint. 8.4.28) except, of course, with negative emphasis.

[261] Cic. *Part. Or.* 15.53; Quint. 8.4.1–3.

[262] Cic. *Part. Or.* 15.53.

[263] Quint. 8.4.2–3.

[264] Cic. *Part. Or.* 15.54; Quint. 8.4.3–9.

[265] Quint. 8.4.3–9.

[266] Quint. 8.4.9–14. Quintilian warns not to confuse parallel in amplification with parallel in proof. Amplification using parallel compares whole with whole, part with part, whereas proof using parallels only compares whole with whole (8.4.12–14).

is used to effect a corresponding magnification of something else. Reasoning may use physical characteristics, subsequent events, antecedent circumstances, horrible circumstances, allusion to something else, reference to something said for another purpose, or description.[267]

Fifth, amplification can be effected through accumulation, the amassing of words and sentences identical in meaning.[268] Climax is reached by the amassing, not by a continuous series of steps,[269] and can be made stronger by making each successive word or phrase stronger.[270] Sixth, amplification can use the topics or commonplaces,[271] such as a vigorous attack on vices or offenses supported by proof, depreciation of the charges, or giving the pro and con on topics of ". . . virtue, duty, equity and good, moral worth and utility, honour and disgrace, reward and punishment."[272]

A seventh method of amplification is the use of facts with the topics of proof.[273] This includes accumulation of definitions, recapitulation of consequences, juxtaposition of contraries, discrepant and contradictory statements, causes and consequences, analogies and instances, and personification of imaginary persons and objects.[274] Eighth, matters of great importance can be discussed, such as heavenly and divine objects, things with obscure causes,

---

[267] Quint. 8.4.15-26. This type of amplification is akin to the figure of thought called emphasis, but emphasis derives its effects from the words, whereas reasoning derives its effects from inference from facts and is more impressive (Quint. 8.4.26).

[268] Quint. 8.4.26-27. Cf. "Longinus'" definition: ". . . amplification consists in accumulating all the aspects and topics inherent in the subject and thus strengthening the argument by dwelling upon it" (*Subl.* 12.2). Cf. Her. 4.40.52-53.

[269] Quint. 8.4.26-27. Cf. Cic. *Part. Or.* 16.55- "accumulations of definitions" as a type of amplification.

[270] Quint. 8.4.27. Cf. Cic. *Part. Or.* 15.54- "gradual rise from lower to higher terms" is a type of amplification. Cf. "Longinus'" definition of amplification in general as "one great phrase after another is wheeled on to the stage with increasing force" (*Subl.* 11.1).

Quintilian points out that amplification by accumulation is akin to the figure called συναθροισμός by the Greeks in which "a number of different things . . . are accumulated," but it differs in that in amplification by accumulation "all the accumulated details have but one reference" (8.4.27). συναθροισμός is equivalent to the figure of thought called *frequentio* by Cornificius which ". . . occurs when the points scattered throughout the whole cause are collected in one place so as to make the speech more impressive or sharp or accusatory" (Her. 4.40.52). Cf. the Greek figure of speech called διαλλαγή or *consummatio*, "a mixture of words, some identical and others different in meaning" (Quint. 9.3.49; cf. 9.3.48 for a similar definition), or "a number of different arguments are used to establish one point (Quint. 9.2.103). This is a mixture of accumulation and synonymy (Lausberg, 1:340, §674). (Quintilain denies it is a figure because it is a "straight forward method of speaking" [9.2.103]).

[271] Long. *Subl.* 11.2; Cic. *De Or.* 3.27.104-7.

[272] Cic. *De Or.* 3.27.106-7.

[273] Cic. *Or.* 37.126; *Part. Or.* 16.55.

[274] Cic. *Part. Or.* 16.55.

wonders of earth and sky, things advantageous or detrimental to humankind, love of god, affection for relatives, and moral considerations like virtue.[275] Finally, several miscellaneous methods are praise and censure,[276] exaggeration,[277] personification,[278] and with individual sentences, asyndeton, repetition, iteration, doubling of words, and a rise from lower to higher terms.[279]

Amplification should be appropriate to the case. For example, if for pleasure, it should arouse emotion, and if for exhortation, it should enumerate things good and evil.[280] It should also fit the rhetor's role as prosecutor or defendant, arousing anger or compassion for example.[281] Amplification should be spread throughout the speech,[282] especially after proof or refutation,[283] and amplify in the midst of arguments, especially in the *peroratio*.[284] It must always be proportionate to the needs of the subject.[285]

Evaluate Rhetorical Effectiveness

The fifth and final step in the methodology of rhetorical analysis is an evaluation of the overall effectiveness of the rhetorical unit in adhering to conventional rhetorical principles of invention, arrangement, and style. More importantly is the estimation of the rhetoric's effectiveness in meeting the rhetorical exigence that it attempts to change and in convincing and motivating the audience to change it as desired.

This concludes the discussion of the history and methodology of New Testament rhetorical criticism. The following two chapters offer a detailed rhetorical analysis of both Jude and 2 Peter using the above methodology. These analyses will be conveniently cross-referenced to the elaboration of rhetorical conventions in the second section of this chapter.

---

[275] Cic. *Part. Or.* 16.55–56.

[276] Cic. *De Or.* 3.27.105.

[277] Long. *Subl.* 11.2. Cf. Cic. *Part. Or.* 15.53 which espouses the use of exaggerated words for amplification, and Quint. 8.4.29 which notes that hyperbole was once considered a form of amplification.

[278] Cic. *De Or.* 3.53.205; *Part. Or.* 16.55.

[279] Cic. *Part. Or.* 15.53–54.

[280] Cic. *Part. Or.* 8.27; 17.58; *Or.* 36.126.

[281] Cic. *Part. Or.* 17.58.

[282] Cic. *Or.* 36.126.

[283] Cic. *Or.* 36.127; *Part. Or.* 15.52.

[284] Cic. *Or.* 36.127.

[285] Ar. *Rhet.* 3.2.1404b.4.

2
The Epistle of Jude:
A Rhetorical Analysis

THE RHETORICAL UNIT

Being an epistle, Jude is a clearly defined unit. Unlike the longer epistles of 2 Corinthians, Philippians, and 2 Peter, Jude is considered to be a unified, non-composite work. There is no debate about its unity or indication of redaction. Thus Jude can be justifiably treated as an original rhetorical unit.

THE RHETORICAL SITUATION

The situation which prompted the writing of the Epistle of Jude is decidedly rhetorical in nature and conforms to Bitzer's definition of the rhetorical situation.[1] As noted above, a rhetorical situation has three constituents: the exigence, the audience to be constrained in decision and action, and the constraints which influence the rhetoric and which the rhetor beings to bear upon the audience.[2] These constituents are now defined and examined in relation to the rhetorical situation of Jude.

A rhetorical exigence is one which can be modified or eliminated by discourse and which specifies the audience to be addressed and the change to be effected.[3] The exigence of the situation prompting the author of Jude to write is rhetorical, being subject to modification by discourse and specifying the audience to be addressed and the change to be made.

The exigence is the sudden and troubling infiltration (v 4) of the church or churches by a doctrinally and ethically divergent group which has successfully attempted to gather a following (vv 19, 22-23) for its own gain (vv 11, 16). The language of v 4, "admission has been secretly gained," indicates that the group may be itinerant prophets or teachers, a common affliction in early Christianity.[4] As the discussion to follow will show, their nature as false teachers seeking financial gain is indicated in vv 11-13. They deny the authority of the Law of

---

[1] Bitzer, 6.
[2] Bitzer, 6.
[3] Bitzer, 7.
[4] Matt 7:15; 2 Cor 10-11; 1 John 4:1; 2 John 10; *Did.* 11-12; Ign. *Eph.* 9:1.

Moses (vv 8–10) and Christ himself (vv 4, 8), possibly on the basis of a claim to prophetic revelation (v 8; cf. v 19). As a corrolary of this rejection they are immoral, especially in a sexual sense (vv 6–8, 10, 16).[5]

The author of Jude clearly perceives the exigence to be acute. He considers the sect to be evil on a number of counts, the division they create in the church(es) to be heinous (v 19), and those who follow the sect to be heading for eternal destruction along with its members (vv 22–23). He regards the exigence as urgent and demanding of immediate attention because such teaching and behavior is a precursor of the eschaton (vv 14–15, 18), and those esposing them will be destroyed at the eschaton (vv 14–15, 23). The exigence is particularly urgent because the eschaton is near (vv 14–16, 17–19, 21, 23). Our author is so convinced that the exigence is urgent that he forsakes the subject which had first motivated him to write so that he can exhort the church regarding it (v 3). The audience also perceives the exigence, for some have followed the sectarians (vv 19, 22–23), but to what degree the audience perceives it, what interest they have in it, what quality they ascribe to it, and what they see as the consequences of it are impossible to determine with the data given.[6]

The exigence is expected to continue. It is a precursor of the end of the world and will remain until then (vv 14–15, 18). However, the effects of the exigence can be minimized by the modification of the overall situation. The author desires that the audience be convinced that the sectarians are the ungodly of prophecy (vv 14–19) and are headed for destruction (vv 5–16), cling to traditional doctrine (vv 3, 20), bolster their spiritual lives (vv 20–21), and actively convince those already persuaded by the infiltrators to abandon them and their ways (vv 22–23). In this way he hopes to put an end to the influence of the sectarians and save the congregation from sharing their destruction.

---

[5] For further information on the opponents and exigence of the situation behind Jude, see Richard J. Bauckham, *Jude, 2 Peter*, WBC 50 (Waco, TX: Word, 1983) 11–13; J. Cantinat, *Les Epîtres de Saint Jacques et de Saint Jude*, SB (Paris: Gabalda, 1973) 227–82, 287–88; I. H. Eybers, "Aspects of the Background of the Letter of Jude," *Neot* 9 (1975) 113–23; Eric Fuchs and Pierre Reymond, *La Deuxième Épître de Saint Pierre; L'Épitre de Saint Jude*, CNT 2/13b (Paris: Delachaux & Neistlé, 1980) 142–43; J. N. D. Kelly, *A Commentary on the Epistles of Peter and Jude*, BNTC (London: A.& C. Black, 1969) 228–31; Gerhard Krodel, "The Letter of Jude," in *Hebrews, James, 1 and 2 Peter, Jude, Revelation*, PC (Philadelphia: Fortress Press, 1977) 92–93; D. J. Rowston, "The Setting of the Letter of Jude" (Ph.D. dissertation, Southern Baptist Theological Seminary, 1971) 6–34; K. H. Schelkle, *Die Petrusbriefe, der Judasbriefe*, HTKNT 13/2, 2d ed. (Frieburg/Basel/Vienna: Herder, 1964) 137–38; W. Schrage, *Die "katholischen" Briefe: Die Briefe des Jakobus, Petrus, Johannes und Judas*, NTD 10, 12th ed. (Göttingen: Vandenhoeck & Ruprecht, 1961) 223–25; E. M. Sidebottom, *James, Jude and 2 Peter*, NCB (London: Thomas Nelson, 1967) 75–76; the Frederik Wisse, "The Epistle of Jude in the History of Heresiology," in *Essays on the Nag Hanmnmadi Texts in Honor of Alexander Böhlig*, ed. Martin Krause, NHS 3 (Leiden: E. J. Brill, 1972) 133–43.

[6] For an analysis of the audience's perception of the exigence based on the nature of the *exordium*, see below, pp. 34–35.

The second constituent of the rhetorical situation, the rhetorical audience, consists of "those persons who are capable of being influenced by discourse and of being mediators of change."[7] The audience to which Jude addresses his letter is such an audience. It is an unspecified Christian community or group of communities which have been infiltrated by an ungodly group (v 4) which is responsible for its division (vv 19, 22–23) and corruption (vv 12, 23–24).[8] This audience is subject to the exigence and capable of modifying is as requested. Full confidence that the community can and will favorably respond as advised is the underlying tone of the epistle (especially noted in vv 3, 20–23).

The third constituent, rhetorical constraints, have the power to direct the decision and action needed to modify the exigence. These include beliefs, attitudes, documents, facts, traditions, images, interests, motives, and, once the rhetor adds discourse, the rhetor's ethos, proofs, and style. These constitute two main types of constraint: those created by the rhetor and his discourse, and those inherent in the situation.[9]

The constraints operative within the epistle of Jude are rhetorical in nature, having the power to constrain the decision and action of the audience so as to achieve the modification of the exigence. They are numerous, and many have their point of origin in the authority of Jude himself and in the church which he represents, that is, in ethos. Acting as a major constraint is the ethos of Jude the brother of James, the bishop of Jerusalem, and of Jesus Christ (v 1), and his personal authority and reputation as a leader in the church to demand change and expect it to be effected according to church doctrine.[10]

Owing to his position, Jude's teachings and exhortations themselves act as authoritative constraints. His teaching that the sect will be severely punished by God (vv 10–13, 14–16) and his depiction of this punishment in traditional horrifying images (vv 5–7, 13, 15, 23) serve as effective constraints against joining the

---

[7] Bitzer, 8.

[8] For further information on the nature of Jude's audience, see Bauckham, 16; Cantinat, 287–88; Eybers, 113–23; Fuchs and Reymond, 144; Kelly, 227–28; J. Michl, *Die Katholischen Briefe*, RNT 8/2, 2d ed. (Regensburg: Friedrich Pustet, 1968) 71–73; Schelkle, 137; Sidebottom, 73–75.

[9] Bitzer, 8.

[10] There is more than considerable debate concerning the authorship of Jude, whether Jude the brother of Jesus and James or a pseudonymous author using Jude's name penned the epistle. For our purposes in rhetorical analysis the issue is somewhat mute. We need only be alert to the options and realize that, whether authentic or pseudonymous, the ethos of Jude, the brother of Jesus and James, is at play. The only exception would be if the recipients knew the epistle to be pseudonymous whereby the ethos of Jude would cease to be a factor. The preservation of the epistle and its use by 2 Peter (to be discussed in ch. 4) argues against this exception. Throughout the remainder of the study the author of Jude will be referred to simply as Jude.

For recent discussions of this issue, see Bauckham, 14–16, 21–23; Cantinat, 283–87; Fuchs and Reymond, 144–48; Kelly, 231–34; Michel, 70–71; Rowston, 67–88; Schelkle, 140–43; Schrage, 225–26; Sidebottom, 78–79.

sect and risking punishment. Also effective are his promise of heavenly reward for those who obey his exhortations (vv 21–23, 25), as well as those exhortations themselves (vv 4, 20–25).

Not only Jude's explicit teaching and exhortations, but, owing to his position, his characterizations serve as constraints. His characterization of the congregation as "called beloved in God the Father and kept for Jesus Christ" (v 1) provides a constraint, for the audience is reminded of their identity, of the behavior befitting it, and of their privilege of allowing God to keep them from corruption. Jude's extremely negative characterization of the sectarians serves as a constraint providing a foil for desired behavior. Those desiring to win both Jude's and divine approval would be restrained not to act in this way and receive a like condemnation.

For additional constraints, Jude can also appeal to a substantial body of literature and oral tradition which was previously delivered to his audience and is held authoritative by them (vv 3, 5, 17–19). This body includes the Old Testament and Jewish tradition based on it (vv 5–7, 11), the *Testament of Moses* (v 9), *1 Enoch* (vv 14–15), and apostolic tradition (vv 17–18). This material is most constraining because it contains prophecies believed to pertain to the coming of the sectarians and their condemnation (vv 4, 14–15, 17–18).

THE SPECIES OF RHETORIC, THE QUESTION, AND THE STASIS

The Epistle of Jude is to be classified as deliberative rhetoric, for it exhibits the major characteristics of this species.[11] First, the epistle is clearly intended to advise and dissuade the audience with reference to a particular action.[12] This is the intention specified in the exhortation of v 3 to contend for a particular doctrine and practice: ". . . I found it necessary to write appealing to you to contend for the faith which was once for all delivered to the saints." Second, the time referent is mainly future[13] with the stress upon the future punishment of the sectarians (vv 10–13, 15) and the future reward of the faithful (vv 21, 24). However, as characteristic of deliberative rhetoric, the time referent is occasionally present,[14] since the identification of the sectarians relies on their present activity (vv 8, 10, 11–13, 16, 19), and the matters exhorted in vv 20–23 are to be implemented presently. Third, the epistle involves what is advantageous and harmful, expedient and inexpedient.[15] Finally, the main basis of

---

[11] For a discussion of deliberative rhetoric, see ch. 1.

[12] Ar. *Rhet.* 1.3.1358b.3; *Rhet. ad Alex.* 1.1421b.17–23; Cic. *Inv.* 1.5.7; *Part. Or.* 24.83ff.; Her. 1.2.2; Quint. 3.4.6, 9; 3.8.1–6, 67–70; cf. Cic. *De Or.* 1.31.141.

[13] Ar. *Rhet.* 1.3.1358b.4; 1.4.1359a.1–2; 2.18.1392a.5; Quint. 3.4.7; 3.8.6; cf. Cic. *Part. Or.* 3.10; 20.69.

[14] Ar. *Rhet.* 1.6.1362a.1; 1.8.1366a.7.

[15] Ar. *Rhet.* 1.3.1358b.5; *Rhet. ad Alex.* 1.1421b.21ff.; Cic. *Inv.* 2.4.12; 2.51.155–58.176; *Part. Or.* 24.83–87; *Top.* 24.91; Her. 3.2.3–5.9; Quint. 3.8.1–6, 22–35; cf. Cic. *De Or.* 2.82.333–36; Quint. 3.4.16.

proof is example and comparison of example![16]

However, this classification is too neat, for the bulk of Jude (vv 4-19) is clearly of a demonstrative nature and is essentially a barbed denunciation of the sectarians based on their character and deeds. Verse 4 distinctly states that what follows is a condemnation (τὸ κρίμα),[17] and, as stated above, much material has a present time reference. Demonstrative nature and present time reference are characteristic of epideictic rhetoric![18] Therefore, Jude is to be classified as deliberative rhetoric which relies heavily upon epideictic in it efforts to advise and dissuade. Deliberative and epideictic rhetoric are complementary in that what deliberative advises and dissuades, epideictic praises and blames![19] Epideictic lends itself well to supporting any attempt at advising and dissuading.[20]

There are two related questions[21] behind Jude's rhetoric and thus it is a complex rather than simple case.[22] One question is: "Are the sectarians within the church the ungodly whose presence and judgment in the last days has been foretold?" The other question is: "Are the sectarians ungodly in word and deed and subject to judgment?" Both questions are rational questions rather than legal questions because they do not involve written law,[23] and both are definite rather than indefinite questions because they involve facts and persons.[24]

A reconstruction of the conflicting causes giving rise to the questions underlying the stasis would look like the following:

Cause 1:   Jude would identify the sectarians as the ungodly whose presence and judgment in the last days has been foretold.

Cause 2:   The sectarians (and followers) would deny being so identified.

Question 1: Are the sectarians the ungodly whose presence and judgment in the last days has been foretold?

Cause 1:   Jude would assert that the sectarians are ungodly in word and deed and are subject to judgment.

---

[16] Ar. *Rhet.* 1.9.1368a.40; 2.20.1394a.8; 3.17.1418a.5; *Rhet. ad Alex.* 32.1438b.29ff.; Quint. 3.8.34, 66; cf. 5.11.8.

[17] There is considerable debate on the referent of τοῦτο τὸ κρίμα, whether to the sentence of condemnation of vv 5-19 or to the parousia judgment to which these condemnations refer. See Bauckham, 35-37 for a detailed discussion. The question can be elucidated by rhetoric. It is likely that κρίμα designates the species of rhetoric to follow as epideictic using vituperation. Thus, the sentence of condemnation itself, not the parousia judgment to which it refers, is probably central.

[18] For more on epideictic, see ch. 1.

[19] Quint. 3.7.28.

[20] Her. 3.8.15; cf. Quint. 3.4.11.

[21] For more on question, see ch. 1.

[22] Cic. *Inv.* 1.12.17; Quint. 3.10.1-2; 7.2.8.

[23] Cic. *Inv.* 1.12.17; Quint. 3.5.4-5.

[24] Cic. *Inv.* 1.6.8; *De Or.* 1.31.138; 2.19.78; 3.28.109; *Part. Or.* 1.4; *Top.* 21.79-22.86; Quint. 3.5.7.

Cause 2:   The sectarians (and followers) would deny this accusation.
Question 2: Are the sectarians ungodly in word and deed and subject to judgment?

The stasis,[25] as is typical of deliberative of epideictic rhetoric, is mainly one of quality.[26] It concerns the nature of a thing, in this case whether or not the words and deeds of the sectarians are ungodly and subject to judgment. This is the main stasis upon which the rhetoric focuses.[27] However, Jude has two questions of differing nature and thus two stases. The subsidiary stasis is one of fact, for it concerns whether a thing is; in this case it concerns whether the sectarians are those whose presence and judgment in the last days has been foretold.

INVENTION, ARRANGEMENT, AND STYLE

The following is a detailed consideration of Jude's use of invention, arrangement, and style to enable his audience to recognize the exigence, to define it and ascribe to it the qualities he proposes, and to modify it as he desires. The reader is referred to the conclusion of this chapter for a rhetorical outline of Jude which visually summarizes the results of this analysis pertaining to invention and arrangement and which will be useful for reference when reading this section. For matters of style and topics, see appendixes 1 and 3.

The Exordium (v 3)

Dismissing the epistolary prescript momentarily, we will examine the first element of arrangement: the *exordium*.[28] The epistle, as deliberative rhetoric, need not have an *exordium* per se,[29] especially if the audience requested the deliberation[30] or is prepared for what is to be said,[31] but its beginning must have some resemblance to an *exordium*.[32] In deliberative rhetoric, this beginning may amount to no more than a mere heading[33] which sets forth the rhetor's concern and intention, the subjects to be dealt with, and a call for a hearing.[34] From the rhetor's perspective, if the audience does not properly perceive the exigence in negative terms or it attaches too little importance to the problem, then an *exordium* may be provided to prepare the audience for deliberation.[35]

[25] For more on stasis, see ch. 1.
[26] Quint. 3.8.4; 7.4.1-3; cf. 3.7.28.
[27] According to Quintilian, one stasis predominates (3.6.9, 12, 21).
[28] For more on the *exordium*, see ch. 1.
[29] Ar. *Rhet.* 3.14.1415b.12; Cic. *Part. Or.* 4.13.
[30] Quint. 3.8.6.
[31] Ar. *Rhet.* 3.14.1415b.8; Quint. 4.1.72.
[32] Quint. 3.8.6, 10.
[33] Ar. *Rhet.* 3.14.1415b.8; Quint. 3.8.10; cf. Cic. *Part. Or.* 4.13.
[34] Cic. *Part. Or.* 27.97.
[35] Ar. *Rhet.* 3.14.1415b.12; cf. Quint. 4.1.72.

Jude, although deliberative and brief, does possess a concise *exordium* in v 3: "Beloved, being very eager to write to you of our common salvation, I found it necessary to write appealing to you to contend for the faith which was once for all delivered to the saints." Unfortunately it is impossible to determine from the *exordium* if Jude's audience did or did not perceive the exigence. On the one hand, the *exordium* may be short owing to the intended length of the epistle, its deliberative nature, or because the audience requested deliberation and fully perceives the exigence. On the other hand, the *exordium* may be provided because deliberation has not been requested, or the audience does not perceive the exigence negatively or to be as important as Jude considers it.

There are five kinds of causes which may underlie the *exordium*.[36] These are the honorable,[37] the mean,[38] the doubtful or ambiguous,[39] the difficult or extraordinary,[40] and the obscure.[41] A cause is honorable "when we either defend what seems to deserve defense by all men, or attack what all men seem in duty bound to attack."[42] The cause is doubtful or ambiguous when the point for decision is doubtful[43] or "when it is partly honourable and partly discreditable."[44] The cause is mean or petty "when the matter . . . is considered unimportant,"[45] and obscure when matters are difficult to grasp.[46] The cause is discreditable "when something honourable is under attack or when something discreditable is being defended."[47] Jude's *exordium* is prompted by an honorable cause. The cause is honorable to his audience because it defends the faith they share in common with Jude, a faith delivered to them by the apostles, a faith they are not yet persuaded by sectarians to give up.

There are two types of approach to take in the *exordium*: the *principium* or *prooimion,* and the *insinuatio* or *ephodos*.[48] The *principium* directly and immediately prepares the audience to hear what follows. It makes a direct appeal to

[36] Cic. *Inv.* 1.15.20–16.21; Her. 1.3.5; Quint. 4.1.40-41.

[37] Ἔνδοξον (Quint. 4.1.40), *honestum* (Cic. *Inv.* 1.15.20; Her. 1.3.5; Quint. 4.1.40).

[38] Ἄδοξον (Quint. 4.1.40), *humile* (Cic. *Inv.* 1.15.20; Her. 1.3.5; Quint. 4.1.40).

[39] Ἀμφίδοξον (Quint. 4.1.40), *anceps* (Cic. *Inv.* 1.15.20; Quint. 4.1.40), *dubium* (Her. 1.3.5; Quint. 4.1.40).

[40] Παράδοξον (Quint. 4.1.40), *admirabile* (Cic. *Inv.* 1.15.20; Quint. 4.1.40). The cause is extraordinary from the jurors' perspective because they find it difficult to believe anyone would defend such a cause.

[41] Δυσπαρακολούθητον (Quint. 4.1.40), *obscurum* (Cic. *Inv.* 1.15.20; Quint. 4.1.40). Her. 1.3.5 excludes the obscure and instead has the discreditable or scandalous (*turpe*). Quint. 4.1.40 mentions that some rhetors add the discreditable and notes it is often put under the mean or extraordinary.

[42] Her. 1.3.5.

[43] Cic. *Inv.* 1.15.20.

[44] Her. 1.3.5.

[45] Her. 1.3.5.

[46] Cic. *Inv.* 1.15.20.

[47] Her. 1.3.5.

[48] Cic. *Inv.* 1.15–17; Her. 1.4–7; Quint. 4.1.42–51; cf. *Rhet. ad Alex.* 29.1437b.33ff.

audience goodwill and attention[49] and is particularly suited to the honorable cause.[50] The *insinuatio* is a subtle and gradual attempt to ingratiate the audience to the cause.[51] It is often used when the cause is discreditable and alienates the audience or when the audience has been won over to the opposition and is hostile to the cause.[52]

Jude takes the *principium*. His cause is honorable and his audience is assumed not to have been persuaded by the opponents. Although some fellow Christians have been persuaded (vv 19, 21-23), the epistle is not directed to them. Now with the honorable cause no *exordium* is needed[53] because it wins approval by its very nature.[54] However, if one is used, it must take the *principium*[55] and must show why the cause is honorable, briefly announce what will be discussed,[56] and/or use the topics designed to produce goodwill so as to increase an advantage already enjoyed.[57] This Jude does, making known that his cause is honorable because he is contending for the faith which was once for all delivered to the saints, and announcing that he will be presenting an appeal.

The bulk of discussion of the *exordium* in the ancient world pertained to its three main functions of making the audience attentive, receptive, and well-disposed.[58] The *exordium* of Jude performs these three functions well. According to rhetorical theory, there are a variety of ways to gain audience attention. The rhetor can show that what follows is an important, new, unusual, incredible, agreeable, scandalous, or alarming matter. He can point out that the matter pertains to the welfare of all, the audience itself, illustrious men, the interests of the state, or the worship of the gods; and is likely to set a precedent. There are also the more obvious methods of bidding the audience's attention, creating the impression that one will stick closely to the point, taking only points most applicable to the case, and presenting the case clearly.[59] Expressions of hope, wishing, fear, and detestation, as well as admonitions, entreaties, and falsehood can supplement these methods.[60] Overall, the ethos of the rhetor has a large role in his ability to gain attention.[61]

---

[49] Cic. *Inv.* 1.15.20; Her. 1.4.6; Quint. 4.1.42.

[50] Her. 1.4.6.

[51] Cic. *Inv.* 1.15.20; Her. 1.7.11; Quint. 4.1.42.

[52] Cic. *Inv.* 1.15.20; 1.17.23; Her. 1.4.6; 1.6.9; Quint. 4.1.42, 48.

[53] Cic. *Inv.* 1.15.21; Her. 1.4.6; cf. *Rhet. ad Alex.* 29.1437b.33ff.

[54] Cic. *Inv.* 1.15.20; Quint. 4.1.41; cf. Her. 1.3.5.

[55] Cic. *Inv.* 1.15.21; Her. 1.4.6.

[56] Her. 1.4.6.

[57] Cic. *Inv.* 1.15.21-16.23; Her. 1.4.7-5.8.

[58] See ch. 1.

[59] Ar. *Rhet.* 3.14.1415a-1415b.7; *Rhet. ad Alex.* 29.1436b.5-15; Cic. *Inv.* 1.16.23; *Part. Or.* 8.29-30; Her. 1.4.7; Quint. 4.1.33-34; 10.1.48.

[60] Quint. 4.1.33; cf. 6.1.14. Quint. 4.1.20-21 discusses the role of fear in obtaining goodwill.

[61] Ar. *Rhet.* 3.14.1415a.7.

Jude makes his audience attentive by stressing the importance of what he is to discuss, by making it clear that it pertains to the audience and the worship of God, by stating his main purpose in writing, and by his ethos. He accentuates the importance of what follows by creating a tone of anxiety and urgency which begins here and pervades the epistle. This urgent tone is engendered by his acknowledgement that it was his original intention to write to them concerning their common salvation, but, in light of the situation, he must suddenly alter his plans and appeal to them to contend for the faith. Attention is also gained by amplification, for the contrast between the original and subsequent intent to write constitutes amplification based upon juxtaposition of contraries and amplification using matters of great importance.[62] The very need to appeal to a faith that was "once for all delivered" should awaken their interest. This entire scheme gives an air of importance and credibility to the whole epistle and is most conducive to begin deliberation on doctrinal and ethical matters.

Receptivity is gained by providing a brief summary of the case in plain language[63] and follows naturally from gaining audience attention.[64] Having used skillful means of gaining attention, Jude can also be expected to have gained receptivity.

To gain the goodwill of the audience and make it well-disposed, the rhetor can concentrate upon the facts of the case and upon the persons connected with the case, the latter including the person of the rhetor, the audience, and the opposition.[65] Jude does not deal with either the opponents or the audience specifically, and deals only slightly more with the facts of the case. Jude's concentration falls upon himself as rhetor, that is, in establishing his ethos. This one-sided emphasis is expected in deliberative rhetoric in which it is conventional for the rhetor to begin with a reference to self or opponents,[66] and in the honorable cause which wins approval by its very nature.

Concerning goodwill connected with the person of the rhetor, the pleader believed to be a good man was considered the strongest influence in the case.[67] He must give the impression of being a reliable witness, of having undertaken the case because of a sense of duty to a friend or relative, patriotism, a serious moral consideration, or because of being forced to take action by some weighty and honorable reason. The undertaking of the case must be free from suspicion of meanness, personal spite, or ambition. The rhetor must not appear to have designs on the judges' integrity, must avoid the impression of being abusive or proud, and must refer to his own acts and services without arrogance. The rhetor

---

[62] Cic. *Part. Or.* 16.55–56.

[63] Ar. *Rhet.* 3.14.1415a.6; Cic. *Inv.* 1.16.23; Quint. 4.1.34; 10.1.48.

[64] Cic. *Inv.* 1.16.23; Her. 1.4.7; Quint. 4.1.34.

[65] Ar. *Rhet.* 3.14.1415a.7; Cic. *Inv.* 1.16.22; *De Or.* 2.79.321–22; *Part. Or.* 8.28; Her. 1.4.8–5.8; Quint. 4.1.6–15.

[66] Quint. 3.8.8 after Ar. *Rhet.* 3.14.1415a.7.

[67] Ar. *Rhet.* 1.2.1356a.3–4; 3.14.1415a.7; Quint. 4.1.7; Aug. *De Doct. Chr.* 4.27.

must present himself as struggling against difficulties and misfortunes, and that he is unwilling to place his hope in anyone else but his audience. He must give the impression that his words are presided over by the gods, and weaken the effect of charges or suspicions of less honorable dealings which have been cast upon him.[68]

If the rhetor being perceived as a good man is the strongest influence in obtaining goodwill, then the person of Jude as brother of Jesus and James would foster goodwill. He certainly would be perceived as a reliable witness. Addressing his audience as "beloved" ('Αγαπητοί) and expressing his eagerness to write demonstrates that he undertook the case out of a sense of duty to friends. His assumption that he and the audience share a common salvation emphasizes his relation to the audience—the corporate nature of his own and their salvation.

Jude makes it clear that his original intention to write the audience about their common salvation has been usurped by an immediate and pressing necessity (ἀνάγκη) to have them contend for the faith. This tactic gains goodwill by intimating that his writing is motivated by a serious moral consideration and necessity. The anxiety latent in this statement prevents him from losing goodwill by seeming arrogant.

Jude's ethos is strengthened by the assertion that he is urging his audience to contend for a faith that was "once for all delivered." Those who delivered the gospel to Jude's audience were partly the apostles referred to in vv 17-18.[69] By expressing concern for the message the apostles delivered, Jude is associated with them and comes to share the positive ethos and goodwill they enjoy.

Concerning goodwill connected with the audience, Cicero writes:

> Good-will will be sought from the persons of the auditors if an account is given of acts which they have performed with couragge, wisdom, and mercy, but so as not to show excessive flattery: and if it is shown in what honourable esteem they are held and how eagerly their judgment and opinion are awaited.[70]

Quintilian adds: "We shall win the good-will of the judge not merely by praising him . . . but by linking his praises to the furtherance of our own case."[71] Also, a reason can be given why the audience is expected to agree with the rhetor.[72]

In regard to goodwill obtained from the auditors, Jude's designation of

---

[68] Cic. *Inv.* 1.16.22; *Part. Or.* 8.28; Her. 1.4.8–5.8; Quint. 4.1.7–10, 33; 10.1.48; cf. Cic. *De Or.* 2.79.321.

[69] παραδιδόναι, as well as παραλαμβάνειν, are technical terms in early Christianity derived from the Hebrew, technical terms for the passing on of tradition. Jude's use of παραδιδόναι corresponds to Paul's use of this term and παραλαμβάνειν to refer to his initial instruction of the churches he founded. See 1 Cor 11:2, 23; 15:3; Gal 1:9; Phil 4:9; Col 2:6; 1 Thess 2:13; 2 Thess 2:15; 3:16; cf. Rom 6:17. Friedrich Büchsel, "δίδωμι." *TDNT* 2.171; Gerhard Delling, "λαμβάνω," *TDNT* 4:11–14.

[70] Cic. *Inv.* 1.16.22. There is similar instruction in Her. 1.5.8.

[71] Quint. 4.1.16.

[72] Cic. *Part. Or.* 8.28; cf. *De Or.* 2.79.321-22.

them as "beloved" and his assertion that both he and they share a common salvation show in what honorable esteem he holds them, without using excessive flattery. He makes it very clear that he is eager (σπουδή) to write and there is the implication that he is just as eager to receive their response to his accounting of the matter. The reference to a common salvation also gives grounds for why the audience should agree with him.

Cicero also suggests that "Good-will may come from the circumstances themselves if we praise and exalt our own case, and depreciate our opponent's with contemptuous allusions."[73] Jude takes this tack, his phrasing making a clear allusion to an immediate and pressing danger to the faith that must receive attention.

These three aims of the *exordium*, to elicit attention, receptivity, and goodwill, while characteristic of the *exordium*, should characterize the entire rhetorical piece.[74] This is particularly true of the desire to elicit goodwill through ethos, for, as stated above, the ethos of the rhetor was considered the strongest influence in the case. As the analysis will show, Jude's rhetoric achieves these three aims throughout.

The *exordium* also functions to indicate briefly the points which the rhetor proposes to address, that is, it introduces the points which serve the purposes of the *probatio*.[75] In the *exordium*, Jude states that his main reason for writing was to have his audience ". . . contend for the faith that was once for all (ἅπαξ) delivered to the saints." As the *probatio* begins in v 5, Jude reminds his audience that they were "once for all" (ἅπαξ) fully informed. These two verses carry the implicit argument that since faith has been "once for all delivered," there should be no need for Jude to write to dissuade his audience from teachings of a contradictory nature and that these conflicting teachings are superfluous.

The *exordium* should also attempt to elicit the pathos desired from the audience.[76] Quintilian advises that it is sometimes necessary to frighten the audience in the *exordium* in order to gain desired objectives.[77] Obtaining goodwill and attention may require expressions of wishing, detestation, entreaty, or anxiety to stir up hope and fear.[78] Jude is taking this tack, for the use of the emotive phrase πᾶσαν σπουδήν ("very eager") creates a sense of urgency. The use of the metaphorical term ἐπαγωνίζεσθαι ("to contend")[79] enhances Jude's attempt

---

[73] Cic. *Inv.* 1.16.22. There is similar instruction in Her. 1.5.8; cf. Cic. *De Or.* 2.79.322.
[74] Cic. *De Or.* 2.79.323; Her. 1.7.11; Quint. 4.1.5; cf. Ar. *Rhet.* 3.14.1415b.9.
[75] Cic. *De Or.* 2.80.325; Quint. 4.1.23–27. Cf. Cic. *De Or.* 2.79.320 which states that the *exordium* provides a statement of the whole case, an approach to and preparation for the case, or mere ornament.
[76] Cic. *De Or.* 2.77.311; *Part. Or.* 8.27.
[77] Quint. 4.1.20–22.
[78] Quint. 4.1.33; cf. 4.1.20–22.
[79] A metaphor is a trope and ". . . occurs when a word applying to one thing is transferred to another, because the similarity seems to justify this transference" (Her. 4.34.45). Cf. Ar. *Poet.* 21.1457b.7 and Quint. 8.6.5 for similar definitions. A metaphor "is a shorter

to stir his audience by conveying his appeal in the terms of an athletic contest.[80]

The same pathos which the rhetor seeks to elicit in the *exordium* should be elicited with greater intensity in the *peroratio*.[81] Having set forth the case, in the *peroratio* the rhetor seeks to elicit the same emotions strongly enough that the audience will act on the exigence as he has advised. In the section of the *peroratio* devoted to emotional appeal (vv 20–23), Jude employs highly emotional exhortation to convey the urgency of the situation and the manner in which to contend for the faith. That Jude is purposely connecting the *exordium* and *peroratio* is indicated by the repetition of topics (ἁγίοις πίστει, v 3 and ἁγιωτάτῃ . . . πίστει, v 20; σωτηρίας, v 3 and σωτῆρι, v 25; cf. ἔλεος, v 21) and the relationship of admonition-implementation (contend, v 3; practical steps for contending, vv 20–23).

The *exordium* should be appropriate to and drawn from the case. The *exordium* is faulty if it is suited to a number of different cases (vulgar), can equally well be used by the opposition (common), can be used by the opponent to his advantage (interchangeable), is irrelevant to the case (detached), or is drawn from another speech (transferred). The *exordium* is also faulty on another level if it is tedious with an overabundance of words and ideas, contrary to convention, fails to perform its three functions, or produces a result different than the case requires.[82] None of these faults characterize Jude's *exordium*.

The Epistolary Prescript or "Quasi-Exordium" (vv 1–2)

Now that the rhetorical qualities of the *exordium* have been outlined, we may return to consider the rhetorical function of the epistolary prescript

---

form of simile" with the difference that ". . . in the latter we compare some object to the thing which we wish to describe, whereas in the former this object is actually substituted for the thing" (Quint. 8.6.8). Cf. the interpolated definition in Cic. *De Or.* 3.39.157. For further discussion, see Ar. *Rhet.* 3.2.1404b.6–1405b.13; 3.10.1410b.5–11.1413b.16; Ar. *Poet.* 21.1457b.7–16; Long. *Subl.* 32; Demetr. *Eloc.* 2.78–90; Cic. *De Or.* 3.38.155–43.170; Or. 27.92–93; Her. 4.34–45; Quint. 8.6.4–18; Lausberg, 1:285–91, §558–64; Martin, 266–68; Leeman, 1:126–32; Bullinger, 735–43; G. B. Caird, *The Language and Imagery of the Bible* (Philadelphia: Westiminster Press, 1980) 131–71.

[80] Ἐπαγωνίζεσθαι is one of many verbs widely found in Hellenistic Judaism (and especially in Stoic moral philosophy), used metaphorically of athletic contests to portray life as a moral contest. Using the verb ἀγών and its compounds, this metaphorical usage is found in the primitive church in Paul (Rom 15:30; 1 Cor 9:24–27; Phil 1:27–30, 4:3; Col 1:29–2:1; 4:12–13; 1 Tim 4:10; 6:12; 2 Tim 4:7) and elsewhere (*1 Clem.* 2:4; 7:1; 35:4; *2 Clem.* 7; 20:2; *Barn.* 4:11). See V. C. Pfitnzer, *Paul and the Agon Motif,* NovTSup 16 (Leiden: E. J. Brill, 1967) ch. 3; E. Stauffer, "ἀγνώ, ἀγωνίζομαι," TDNT 1:134–40. This athletic metaphor grew pale with use and often suggested only exertion or striving (Pfitzner, 72). Whether or not the metaphor is vibrant here is difficult to tell, but either way the idea of striving is rhetorically effective.

[81] Quint. 4.1.28; 6.1.9–55; cf. Cic. *De Or.* 2.77.310–11; *Part. Or.* 1.4.

[82] Cic. *Inv.* 1.18.26; *De Or.* 2.78.315, 318–19; Her. 1.7.11; Quint. 4.1.71.

(vv 1-2). The epistolary prescript, although necessitated by the epistolary form of the discourse and not technically a recognized element in rhetorical arrangement, does function like the *exordium*. This is particularly true of making the audience attentive, receptive, and well-disposed; establishing desired ethos; and introducing topics to be developed in the *probatio*.

In the parties formula (v 1) Jude's self-designation helps establish his ethos. The phrase "servant of Jesus Christ" ('Ιησοῦ χριστοῦ δοῦλος) used in the New Testament as a self-designation most likely denotes specific office as a Christian leader,[83] being derived from the honorific title "servant of God" used of Jewish leaders.[84] This self designation reminds Jude's audience of his authority to address them. In stating that he is the brother of James he also increases ethos, for his audience recognizes him as brother of the bishop of Jerusalem and Jesus Christ himself.[85]

Concerning goodwill derived from the person of the rhetor, since "servant of Christ (God)" is also a redemptive title applied to Christians in general,[86] the designation also gives Jude a common footing with the audience. Since the rhetor perceived as a good man is the strongest influence in the case,[87] then the person of Jude used in writing to a congregation on good terms obtains much goodwill.

With regard to obtaining goodwill from the persons of the audience, in the parties formula (v 1) there is the threefold designation of the addresses as "called, beloved[88] in God the Father, and kept for Jesus Christ." Like Jude, early Christian epistles often contain an extended theological characterization of the addresses, often using the binitarian formula.[89] This acts to show in what honorable esteem the audience is held, and such an aspect is directed by convention to foster goodwill[90] and positive pathos. Also according to convention, this praise is linked to the furtherance of the case,[91] for, as shown below, Jude's

---

[83] The self-designation δοῦλος 'Ιησοῦ χριστοῦ is found in the salutations of Rom 1:1; Phil 1:1 (pl. of Paul and Timothy); Titus 1:1; Jas 1:1; and 2 Pet 1:1, as well as in the body of a letter in Gal 1:10. The self-designation is always by Christian leaders. A few Christian leaders are given the title by others (Col 4:12—Paul to Epaphras; 2 Tim 2:24—Paul to Timothy). Karl Rengstorf, "δοῦλος," *TDNT* 2:276-77.

[84] E.g., Moses (Josh 14:7; Neh 9:14; Jos. *Ant.* 5.39), Joshua (Josh 24:29; Judg 2:8), Abraham (Ps 105:42), David (Ps 89:3). Rengstorf, *TDNT* 2:267-68.

[85] On the person of Jude, see above, p. 31, n. 10.

[86] Rengstorf, *TDNT* 2:275-76; 1 Cor 7:22-23; Eph 6:6; 1 Pet 2:16; Rev 7:3.

[87] See above, p. 37, n. 67.

[88] For ἠγαπημένοις, some manuscripts (KLP) have ἠγιασμένοις, "sanctified," probably modeled on 1 Cor 1:2. The reading ἠγαπημένοις is much better attested (p⁷²אAB). Bruce Metzger, *A Textual Commentary on the Greek New Testament* (United Bible Societies, 1971) 725.

[89] Rom 1:7; 1 Cor 1:2; 1 Thess 1:1; 1 Pet 1:2; *1 Clem.* inscr.; all the letters of Ignatius.

[90] Cic. *Inv.* 1.16.22; Her. 1.5.8.

[91] Quint. 4.1.16.

purpose in his deliberative rhetoric is to persuade his audience to keep themselves in God's love.

The salutation (v 2) is the threefold blessing, "may mercy, peace, and love be multiplied to you."[92] The theological passive πληθυνθείη indicates Jude is exhorting God to bless his audience generously. The blessing elicits goodwill and positive pathos from the audience by showing in what esteem they are held,[93] and consequently bolsters Jude's ethos as well.

Jude uses triple expressions in the prescript in his self-designation, designation of his audience, and in his blessing. The triple expression is a favorite stylistic device found throughout Jude (vv 1, 2, 5-7, 8, 11, 19, 20-21 [double], 22-23, 25)[94] and constitutes amplification by accumulation. It is the listing of different words or ideas to leave an impact of greater number and quantity upon the audience.[95] Here the list of self-designations increases ethos and the list of designations and blessings effectively increases audience goodwill and positive pathos.

In vv 1-2, as is proper in an *exordium*, Jude introduces topics which will play a greater role in the rhetoric of the letter.[96] A primary topic is "keeping and being kept." In v 1 he designates his audience as "those being kept (τετηρημένοις) by God for Christ." Later in v 21 he commands the audience to keep themselves in God's love (τηρήσατε), and in v 24 he defines Christ as the one able to keep (φυλάξαι) his audience from falling into sin. On the other hand, in v 6 he accuses the angels of not keeping (μὴ τηρήσαντας) their own position, and in v 8 by implication he accuses the sectarians of the same thing. As a consequence, angels are kept (τετήρηκεν) in nether gloom (v 6), a fate awaiting the sectarians (v 13).

Mercy, peace, and love are also topics. In v 2, Jude wishes mercy (ἔλεος) to be multiplied to his audience. In v 21 he admonishes his audience to wait for the mercy (ἔλεος) unto eternal life, and in vv 22-23 he exhorts them to have mercy (ἐλεᾶτε) on others. Also in v 2, Jude wishes peace (εἰρήνη) to be multiplied to his audience. In v 12 Jude is concerned with the disruptive activity of the ungodly during love feasts, in v 16 with the grumbling and malcontention of the ungodly, and in v 19 with their divisiveness. In vv 1-2, Jude designates his audience as those beloved of God (ἠγαπημένοις, v 1) and wishes that love (ἀγάπη, v 2) be multiplied to them. He later twice designates his audience as ἀγαπητοί (vv 17, 20). In v 12 he is concerned with the negative influence of the ungodly upon the love feasts (ἀγάπαις) and in v 21 he admonishes them to keep themselves in the love

---

[92] Cf. blessings in other early Christian salutations—1 Tim 1:2; 2 Tim 1:2; 2 John 3; *Mart. Pol.* inscr.; 3 Cor 3:40 (epistle ending).

[93] Cic. *Inv.* 1.16.22; Her. 1.5.8.

[94] J. B. Mayor, *The Epistles of St. Jude and the Second Epistle of St. Peter* (London: Macmillan and Co., 1907; repr. ed. Grand Rapids: Baker, 1979) lvi, lix; Turner, 139; Bauckham, 6.

[95] Quint. 8.4.26-27. For more detail, see ch. 1.

[96] Cic. *De Or.* 2.80.325; Quint. 4.1.23-26; cf. *De Or.* 2.79.320.

(ἀγάπη) of God. As will be shown more fully later, Jude has followed standard rhetorical procedure in introducing a topic in the *exordium* (here quasi-*exordium*), developing it in the *probatio* (vv 5-16, except the topic of mercy), and reiterating it in the *peroratio* (vv 17-25).[97]

The Narratio *(v 4)*

Verse 4 comprises the *narratio* of Jude, the second element which instructs the audience as to the nature of the case.[98] The preposition γάρ which begins v 4 typically marks the transition from *exordium* to *narratio*.[99] As γάρ indicates, the *narratio* provides the concerns for which the *exordium* has striven to obtain the audience's attention, receptivity, and goodwill. It describes the exigence and the points upon which the rhetor would like the audience to render judgment.[100] Some cases, like Jude, are so brief that they require only a concise *narratio*, occasionally only a single sentence. This is especially true when the facts and effects of the case are familiar to the audience.[101] In situations where the audience is fully aware of the facts of the case, no *narratio* is needed at all.[102] Deliberative oratory, of which Jude is classified, being future oriented does not use a *narratio* unless the narration of past events helps make a decision about future events.[103] The decision Jude desires his audience to make about the exigence is aided by the narration of past events, for the fact that the sectarians have infiltrated the church and were once designated for condemnation should help motivate the audience to contend for the faith.

As was the case with the *exordium*, Jude's use of the *narratio* does not indicate how his audience perceived the exigence. On the one hand, it may be brief owing to the intended length of the letter, the simplicity of the case, and/or the familiarity of his audience with the exigence. On the other hand, a brief *narratio* may indicate the audience is not fully aware of the facts, does not perceive them negatively as Jude does, and/or the narration of the facts will facilitate decision-making about the future.

There are three types of *narratio*.[104] In one, διηγήσεις ἐπὶ κριτῶν λεγόμεναι, the facts of the case are related so as to turn every detail to the rhetor's advantage![105]

---

[97] For the relation of *exordium* and *probatio*, see Cic. *De Or.* 2.80.325; Quint. 4.1.23-26. For the relation of *probatio* and *peroratio*, see Ar. *Rhet.* 3.19.1419b.1, 4-6; *Rhet. ad Alex.* 20-21; 36.1444b.21-35; Cic. *Inv.* 1.52; *De Or.* 2.19.80; *Part. Or.* 15.52; 17.59-60; Her. 2.30.47; Quint. 6.1.1-8; cf. Cic. *De Or.* 1.31.143.

[98] For further discussion of the *narratio*, see ch. 1.

[99] Cf. Quint. 4.1.76-79 which recommends that the transition from *exordium* to *narratio* be obvious.

[100] Quint. 4.2.1, 31.

[101] Quint. 4.2.4-8.

[102] Cic. *Inv.* 1.21.30; *De Or.* 2.81.330; Quint. 3.8.10; 4.2.20-23.

[103] Ar. *Rhet.* 3.16.1417b.11; Cic. *Part. Or.* 4.13.

[104] Quint. 4.2.2-4 advises against subtle divisions of the *narratio* into classes.

[105] Cic. *Inv.* 1.19.27; Her. 1.8.12; Quint. 4.2.11.

Another, παραδιήγησις, is an incidental *narratio* which goes beyond the strict limits of the case for the purpose of making a comparison, amusing the audience, amplifying, winning belief, incriminating an adversary, effecting a transition, or setting the stage for what follows![106] The third type, διηγήσεις καθ' ἑαυτάς, is used for practice and amusement![107]

Jude's *narratio* is clearly of the first variety, for it is directly related to the case at hand and every detail is designed to work to his advantage. In one sentence he points to prophecy as proof and destroys the ethos of his opponents with a characterization of their nature and activity that is nothing but incriminating. In deliberative rhetoric a decision has to be rendered, and this variety of *narratio* is well suited to this purpose. It was advised that the *narratio* begin with reference to some person who is to be praised if on the rhetor's side, or abused if on the side of the opponent![108] Jude's *narratio* is constituted completely of abuse of the opponent.

Jude's *narratio* also has the virtues of brevity, clarity, and plausibility that should characterize the *narratio*[109] and all the rhetoric as well![110] To achieve brevity in the *narratio*, the rhetor is advised to start at the point of the case which concerns the audience and not to narrate the facts further than the point of decision. Irrelevance and digressions are to be avoided, everything that neither helps nor harms the case being omitted and summaries used which include few details. The case is to be clearly stated so that things not mentioned can be inferred from what has been mentioned, each idea being expressed once in simple terms![111]

Jude achieves brevity in his *narratio* in just this fashion. He starts at the point which concerns his audience: the secret admission of ungodly individuals. He does not narrate past the point of decision: the nature and fate of the sectarians. He includes only material relevant and helpful in explicating the case, summarizes with few details, and expresses each idea only once. For example, he describes his opponents as "ungodly." The ἀσεβ- root in the Greek world signified irreverence for the gods and neglect of cultus. In Hellenistic Judaism it signified sinful behavior originating in irreverence towards God, and is often found in contexts in which the ungodly are judged![112] Its use appropriately encapsulates

---

[106] Cic. *Inv.* 1.19.27; Her. 1.8.12; Quint. 4.2.11. Quint. 9.2.107 states that some consider it a figure of thought.

[107] Cic. *Inv.* 1.19.27; Her. 1.8.12–13.

[108] Quint. 4.2.129–31.

[109] *Rhet. ad Alex.* 30.1438a.20ff.; Cic. *Inv.* 1.20.28–21.30; *Or.* 34.122; Her. 1.9.14–16; Quint. 4.2.31–60. Ar. *Rhet.* 3.16.1416b.4 scorns brevity in favor of a proper mean, Cic. *Part. Or.* 9.31–32 adds charm, Cic. *De Or.* 2.80.326–29 excludes plausibility, and Cic. *Top.* 26.97 adds the virtues of plain, restrained, and dignified.

[110] Cic. *De Or.* 2.19.83.

[111] *Rhet. ad Alex.* 30.1438a.38ff.; Cic. *Inv*, 1.20.28; *De Or.* 2.80.326–28; *Part. Or.* 6.19; 9.32; Her. 1.9.14; Quint. 4.2.40–51, 103–4.

[112] Werner Foerster, "σέβομαι," *TDNT* 7:185–91; *1 Enoch* 10.20; *T. Zeb.* 10.3; Rom 1:18; 1 Pet 4:18; 2 Pet 2:6; 3:7; *1 Clem.* 14:5; 57:7; *2 Clem.* 10:1; 18:1; *Barn.* 10:5; 11:7; 15:5.

much that Jude will subsequently explicate: the sectarians' rebellion against divine authority has issued in unethical behavior subject to judgment. The brevity of Jude's *narratio* qualifies it for the designation σύντομος, a statement of fact which is free from superfluous matters without omitting something that requires statement![113]

To achieve clarity in the *narratio* the rhetor was advised to set forth the case in words that are appropriate and significant, not ignoble, far-fetched, or unusual; to give precise account of fact, persons, times, places, and causes; to relate events in chronological order; to present nothing in confused or intricate style; to avoid digression; and to observe the rules for obtaining brevity![114] Jude follows these conventions. He uses words and phrases appropriate and significant to the exigence: "secretly gained," "designated for this condemnation," "ungodly," "pervert the grace of God into immorality," "licentiousness," and "deny." Details like the persons, time, place, and cause of the case are all given to some degree. The persons are those who secretly gained admission, who fit the description given, and exhibit the behavior described. The time is clearly understood as the immediate past and the present. The place is the church assembly. The cause is the sinners' ungodly doctrine and behavior. The *narratio* does not possess a confused or intricate style and observes the rules for obtaining brevity.

To attain plausibility, the *narratio* must correspond to and not contradict nature and real life, the habits of ordinary people, the beliefs of the audience, law, custom, or religion. It must assign reasons and motives for the facts, and demonstrate the ability to do the deed, the time opportune, and the scene of the action suitable to the events narrated. The character of the people involved must be kept in accordance with the facts desired to be believed. Inconsistency and contradiction must be avoided. Hints of the proofs and reasons for things that seem improbable should be given![115]

Jude's *narratio* corresponds to real life, for it is not hard to believe that a perverse group could infiltrate the assembly. It also corresponds to the beliefs and religion of his audience, for he alludes to prophecy as having designated the facts of the case (prophecy he later assumes his audience knows). The scene of the activity, the assembly, is suited to the events narrated. The character of the opponents is in keeping with the facts Jude desires to be believed, for it is implied that their admission into the assembly involved stealth and deception, and they are designated as ungodly persons who pervert grace and deny the lordship of Christ. The proofs are hinted at, for the phrase "long ago were designated" implies that examples of the historical type and supernatural oracle will be used to prove the nature of the opponents.

[113] Quint. 4.2.42.

[114] *Rhet. ad Alex.* 30.1438a.20ff.; Cic. *Inv.* 1.20.29; *Part. Or.* 6.19; 9.31–32; Her. 1.9.15; Quint. 4.2.36–39; cf. 4.2.103–4.

[115] *Rhet. ad Alex.* 30.1438b.1ff.; Cic. *Inv.* 1.21.29; *Part. Or.* 9.31.32; Her. 1.9.16; Quint. 4.2.52–60.

These three qualities of brevity, clarity, and plausibility should especially characterize the *narratio*. If the audience fails to comprehend the case, the remainder of the rhetoric will evade it. However, if the rhetoric is to remain effective, then these qualities must also be found throughout the speech![116] As we will discover, Jude's rhetoric is characterized by these three qualities throughout.

The credibility of the *narratio* greatly depends on the credibility or ethos of the rhetor which derives from both his life and his rhetorical style. Honesty, integrity, and truth in the rhetor add plausibility and authority to the rhetoric![117] The more dignified the style, the greater authority the rhetor and the rhetoric will possess. However, the *narratio* should not suggest artful design, seem fictitious, or betray anxiety, but should seem to derive naturally from the case![118] The ethos of Jude, or a pseudonymous author so portraying himself, would certainly bring credibility to the *narratio*. His straightforward *narratio* in dignified style would also increase his ethos and that of his rhetoric. In contrast, the extremely negative characterization of the sectarians' nature and deeds would severely lessen their ethos.

As is desirable, the *narratio* evokes in briefer form, and to a lesser degree, the emotional response or pathos that Jude desires to elicit from his audience in the *peroratio*:[119] extreme urgency and disgust. He elicits this pathos, not by the use of explicit emotional appeal, as is one option, but by vivid and emotive words[120] such as "pervert" (μετάτιθημι), "licentiousness" (ἀσέλγεια), and "certain men have infiltrated" (παρεισέδυσαν . . . τινες ἄνθρωποι), a phrase which connotes secrecy and bad intent![121] This is also amplification based on powerful yet ordinary words![122] Also as desirable, Jude's *narratio* introduces in a highly condensed form the worst features of his opponents![123] It was advised that in more important cases, the rhetor could excite horror by narrating abominable wrongs, by giving an outline of the wrongs to be more fully dealt with later![124] Jude's *narratio* outlines the terrible deeds of his opponents which should excite horror in the faithful of his audience.

---

[116] Cic. *Part. Or.* 9.31; *Top.* 26.97; Quint. 4.2.35.

[117] Cic. *Part. Or.* 9.31–32; Quint. 4.2.125–27.

[118] Quint. 4.2.125–27; cf. Cic. *Part. Or.* 9.31–32.

[119] Quint. 4.2.111–15.

[120] Quint. 4.2.113.

[121] The verb παρεισδύ(ν)ειν is a NT hapax, but the noun παρείσδυσις is used of Satan's activity in *Barn.* 2:10 and 4:9. Παρείσακτος and παρεισέρχεσθαι are used in Gal 2:10 and in 2 Pet 2:1 of heretical teaching. Παρεισπορεύεσθαι is used with λεληθότως in 2 Macc 8:1. Wilhelm Michaelis, "παρεισάγω," *TDNT* 5:824–26.

"Certain persons" is often used with a nuance of disparagement to describe a definite group who are opponents of the rhetor and/or the audience (Rom 3:8; 1 Cor 4:18; 15:34; 2 Cor 3:1; 10:12; Gal 1:7; 1 Tim 1:3, 19; 2 Pet 3:9; Ign. *Eph.* 7:1; 9:1).

[122] Cic. *Part. Or.* 15.53; Quint. 8.4.1–3.

[123] Quint. 4.2.129–31.

[124] Quint. 4.2.120.

Before leaving the discussion of pathos, it is noteworthy that Jude describes his opponents in three ways: they are ungodly, pervert the grace of God into licentiousness, and deny the Master and Lord Jesus Christ. This constitutes amplification by accumulation.[125] By putting together phrases of a similar thrust, Jude leaves his audience with a magnified impression of the ungodliness of the sectarians.

At the close of the *narratio* is usually found the *partitio,* the element of arrangement which contains the proposition(s) to be developed in the *probatio.*[126] A *partitio* is not needed in Jude because the case he addresses is simple, hinging on two interrelated propositions,[127] and the *narratio* ends where the main question begins.[128] In this case the *narratio* contains the points to be developed in the *probatio,*[129] and the *narratio* functions as the propositions.[130] As demonstrated below, the *probatio* develops the propositions that the sectarians in the church are ungodly, and are the ungodly whose judgment was previously predicted.

This interplay of *narratio* and *probatio* is partially indicated by the topics they share. The topic of judgment (κρίμα) occurs twice in the *probatio* (κρίσις — vv 6, 15). The topic of ungodliness, referred to twice in the *narratio* using paronomasia[131] (ἀσεβεῖς and ἀσέλγεια), is developed in the *probatio* using derivations of the root ἀσεβ- in both prophecies which serve as the artificial proofs of the propositions of the *narratio* (vv 14–15, 18).[132] The topic of denying authority (τὸν μόνον δεσπότην καὶ κύριον ἡμῶν Ἰησοῦν χριστὸν ἀρνούμενοι) occurs again in the *probatio* in vv 8–11 (κυριότητα δὲ ἀθετοῦσιν, v 8). The epithet[133] τὸν μόνον δεσπότη καὶ κυρίος in the *narratio* emphasizes the nature of Christ's authority and enhances the topic[134] containing the implicit argument that if Christ is the only lord, his authority should not be rejected.

Verses 3–4 correspond to the body-opening of the Greek letter which is

---

[125] Quint. 8.4.26–27. For further information, see ch. 1.

[126] For further details, see ch. 1.

[127] Cic. *Inv.* 1.23.33 and Quint. 4.5.8 state that no *partitio* is needed when only one proposition is involved.

[128] Quint. 4.4.1–2.

[129] Quint. 4.2.54, 79, 86.

[130] Quint. 4.4.9 describes this technique.

[131] Paronomasia has a variety of related manifestations. One, described as "words lack so close a resemblance, and yet are not dissimilar" (Her. 4.22.30), is used here. For further information, see Her. 4.21.29–23.32; Quint. 9.3.66ff.; Lausberg, 1:322–25, §637–39; Martin, 304–5; Bullinger, 307–20.

[132] Ἀσεβεῖς (v 4); ἀσεβεῖς (twice), ἀσέβεια, ἀσεβέω (v 15); ἀσεβέω (v 18).

[133] An epithet is a trope and occurs ". . . when an adjective or noun is used, which adds to the sense of thing spoken of by simply holding forth some attribute, character, or quality descriptive of it" (Bullinger, 440). For further information, see Ar. *Rhet.* 3.2.1405b.14; Quint. 8.6.40–43; Lausberg, 1:341–44, §676–85; Martin, 264; Bullinger, 440–41.

[134] Quint. 8.6.40 describes the epithet's role in enhancing meaning.

"... the point at which the principal occasion for the letter is usually indicated."[135] The body-opening often begins with a vocative such as is found here in ἀγαπητοί.[136] More important, it was customary as the letter opened to establish the common ground between both parties. This common ground is provided either by allusion to information shared by both parties or by the disclosure of new information.[137] Jude's reference to a letter in which he intended to write about "our common salvation" (v 3) is an allusion to shared information and establishes common ground between himself and the audience.

Jude gives the purpose of his letter in the form of a petition common to both official and private requests in literature of this era. This petition has three basic elements: background, petition verb, and desired action. Optional embellishments, including the address,[138] can be added. Jude 3-4 exhibits these elements.[139] Verse 4 provides the background of the petition as γάρ indicates. Verse 3 contains the appeal in the verb παρακαλῶν ("appealing"), the most personal and intense of the four verbs usually used for petitions in personal letters.[140] Verse 3 contains the desired action in ἐπαγωνίζεσθαι, "to carry on the fight." Verse 3 also contains the optional element of an address in 'Αγαπητοί, ὑμῖν, "Beloved, you."

Jude 5-23 provides further background for Jude's petition in vv 3-4. Jude 5-19 explains the situation of v 4 that requires the appeal of v 3, namely, that the presence now and the future punishment of the sectarians has been prophesied. Jude 20-23 further elaborates the desired action described merely as "contend" in v 3. The topical connections between v 3 and vv 20-23 and between v 4 and vv 5-19 substantiate this relationship and are given above.

It can be concluded that the body-opening of the Greek letter, especially when using the petition form, performs the functions of the *exordium* and *narratio*. Like the *exordium*, it establishes a bond of commonality between rhetor and audience and introduces the main purpose or theme of the letter upon which the audience is to act. Like the *narratio* it provides the background facts which prompt the rhetor to address the audience, and the main points to be proven in the remainder of the letter. Thus, by using the letter form according to convention, Jude automatically incorportes desirable elements of rhetorical arrangement.

The Probatio (vv 5-16)

The next element of rhetorical arrangement is the *probatio*,[141] and in the case of Jude it comprises vv 5-16. The *probatio* is the section of a rhetorical

---

[135] John Lee White, *The Body of the Greek Letter*, SBLDS 2 (Missoula, MT: Scholars Press, 1972) 18.

[136] White, 15-17. This holds true for the body-middle and body-closing as well.

[137] White, 18-19, 24-25, 31, 39.

[138] T. Y. Mullins, "Petition as a Literary Form," *NovT* 5 (1962) 46-54.

[139] Bauckham, 28-29.

[140] Mullins, 48-49.

[141] For more on the *probatio*, see ch. 1.

work in which the rhetor attempts to persuade the audience of the legitimacy of his case through a presentation of propositions and corresponding proofs; it is the ". . . verification of the facts as put forward in the statement."[142] These facts or propositions may be contained in the *partitio* in which they are specifically listed,[143] be found at the beginning of every proof,[144] and/or be implicit or explicit in the *narratio*,[145] as in Jude. The propositions given in Jude's *narratio* are that the sectarians are ungodly and are the very ungodly who were to appear as foretold. Jude's *probatio* develops these propositions: the first in vv 5-10, and vv 11-13, and the second in vv 14-16 (and in the *peroratio* in vv 17-19).

As predominately deliberative rhetoric, Jude attempts to dissuade his audience from heeding the sectarians' doctrine or following their practice and thereby coming under like judgment. His attempt to dissuade depends heavily upon epideictic rhetoric aimed at invective which destroys the ethos of the sectarians. The *probatio* proves, in terms of radical Christian rhetoric,[146] that the sectarians are sinners under judgment whose appearance was previously predicted. These proofs are properly embellished with stylistic devices which enhance the negative portrayal of both the sin and the judgment.

The proofs Jude uses to support his propositions are artificial, inductive.[147] The main basis of proof in deliberative rhetoric is usually example and comparison of examples,[148] and we find this true of Jude's deliberation. He employs examples of the narrow historical type which adduce a past action that is real or assumed real which may serve to persuade the audience,[149] as well as judgments,[150] especially of the type of supernatural oracles.[151] This use of example was anticipated in the *narratio* with the phrase "those who long ago were designated" (οἱ πάλαι προγεγραμμένοι).

The tradition, the examples, and the testimony used in vv 5-19 are known to his audience, as indicated by the fact that Jude merely needs to remind them of it (vv 5, 17). Also, since his references and allusions to the Old Testament and apocryphal materials are not always self-explanatory, he assumes his audience's familiarity with them. Probably, this material comes in large part from their

---

[142] Quint. 4.2.79.

[143] Quint. 4.5.1-25. For more on the *probatio*, see ch. 1.

[144] Quint. 4.4.1.

[145] Quint. 3.9.7; 4.2.54, 79, 86; cf. 4.4.9.

[146] Radical Christian rhetoric is defined by Kennedy as "a doctrine . . . purely proclaimed and not couched in enthymemes" (*New Testament Interpretation*, 7), that is, it is not rationally proven.

[147] See ch. 1 for a discussion of this type of proof.

[148] Ar. *Rhet.* 1.9.1368a.40; 2.20.1394a.7-8; 3.17.1418a.5; *Rhet. ad Alex.* 32.1438b.29ff.; Quint. 3.8.34, 66; cf. 5.11.8.

[149] Ar. *Rhet.* 2.20.1393a.2-1393b.4; *Rhet. ad Alex.* 8.1429a.20; 8.1430a.5ff.; Cic. *Inv.* 1.30.49; Quint. 5.11.1, 8, 15-16.

[150] Cic. *Inv.* 1.30.48; Quint. 5.11.36-44.

[151] Quint. 5.11.43-44. See ch. 1 for further discussion.

previous instruction (vv 3, 5) (some by apostles —v 17), and would be persuasive in deliberation.

In v 5 Jude uses a transitional form known as a "disclosure" formula: ". . . a formulaic phrase conveying either the addressor's desire or command that the addressees 'know' something."[152] The type of disclosure formula used here is the full disclosure formula employing the idea of "wishing" the addresses know something[153] This formula signifies a major transition from the body-opening to the body middle[154] and is marked by the use of verbs of saying and informing[155] as found in Jude in the phrase εἰδότας ὑμᾶς πάντα. The body-middle both develops the subject introduced in the body-opening and introduces new material[156] Therefore, the body-middle of the letter here corresponds to the *probatio* in rhetoric.

Jude employs a traditional Jewish and Christian practice of reminding the audience to recall their traditions to prevent falling away[157] Jude states that what follows is tradition about which his audience was once fully informed and merely needs to be reminded (cf. v 3)[158] By reminding his audience (cf. v 17) and stating in an aside that reminding is all that is necessary since they were already fully informed, Jude assumes their knowledge and lessens the possibility of offending them by seeming to speak from a superior position. He agains enhances his ethos and invites positive pathos.

The First Proof (vv 5-10)

The first major development of the proposition is vv 5-10. This section comprises an artificial and inductive proof based on example[159] of the type employing comparison of like example[160] The common topic of past and future

---

[152] White, 2.

[153] White, 3–5.

[154] White, 32, 38, 41. It also marks the transition from letter-opening to body-opening (White, 2–5, 18–19, 41).

[155] White, 32–36, 38, 41.

[156] White, 38–39.

[157] Jude 5, 17; Num 15:39–41; Mal 4:4; *Jub.* 6:22; *2 Apoc. Bar.* 84:2, 7–9; Rom 15:15; 1 Cor 11:2; 2 Thess 2:5; 2 Tim 2:8, 14; 2 Pet 1:12; 3:1–2; Rev 3:3.

[158] Of the variant readings for Jude 5, I am choosing the reading εἰδότας ὑμᾶς ἅπαξ πάντα, ὅτι [ὁ] κύριος over the reading εἰδότας ὑμᾶς πάντα, ὅτι [ὁ] κύριος ἅπαξ. The latter reading probably arose from a desire to move ἅπαξ within the ὅτι clause to modify σώσας so as to complement the following τὸ δεύτερον with a word like πρῶτον. The chosen reading corresponds well with the phrase ἅπαξ παραδοθείσῃ, "once for all delivered," in v 3. For further information, see Metzger, 726; Wikgren, "Some Problems in Jude 5," in *Studies in the History and Text of the New Testament in honor of Kenneth Willis Clark,* ed. B. L. Daniels and M. Suggs, SD 29 (Salt Lake City: University of Utah Press, 1967) 147–52; Carroll D. Osburn, "The Text of Jude 5," *Bib* 62 (1981) 107–15.

[159] For a discussion of example, see ch. 1.

[160] *Rhet. ad Alex.* 8.1429a.20ff.; Cic. *Inv.* 1.30.49; Quint. 5.11.1–7.

fact supplies the argument.[161] Jude first presents three examples of ungodly people, their sins, and their judgment (vv 5-7). Then the sectarians are compared to the examples in order to establish that they are also sinners and subject to judgment (vv 8-10).

Jude's argument employs examples of an historical type.[162] It was thought advisable to use historical examples in deliberative rhetoric when speaking about what is likely to happen.[163] These examples should be like or nearly equal that to which they are compared.[164] In deliberative rhetoric, speaking about future judgment, Jude properly uses historical examples nearly equal to what is compared, providing partial rather than complete parallel.[165] The examples are probably not elaborated because they are familiar to Jude's audience and only their main point, that of sin, is suited to the case.[166]

These examples of vv 5-7 derive from a traditional Jewish Christian schema for illustrating that sin incurs judgment.[167] They also reflect the early church's practice of comparing false teachers to examples of the sinful in the Old Testament.[168] Being a familiar and accepted method of argumentation using familiar illustrations, this comparison should be effective in proof. An audience is more easily persuaded by the familiar, and this is especially true in deliberative rhetoric where the rhetor seeks to muster evidence to persuade the audience to hold to something they have always believed but are in danger of abandoning.

In v 5 Jude sets out the example of the Israelites in the wilderness who, after receiving the spies' report, disbelieved God could give them Canaan, refused to enter, and then, with the exception of Joshua and Caleb, were destroyed for their disbelief.[169] In both Jewish and Christian literature, this was a common example used to illustrate the themes of sin and judgment,[170] particularly that disbelief issues in disobedience.[171] Part of the message here is that Christians, like the Israelites, although once saved, can later perish in judgment for their unbelief

[161] Ar. *Rhet.* 1.3.1359a.8; 2.18.1391b.3; 2.19.1392b.16–1393a.25.

[162] Ar. *Rhet.* 2.20.1393a.2–1393b.4; *Rhet. ad Alex.* 8.1429a.20; 1430a.5ff.; Cic. *Inv.* 1.30.49; Quint. 5.11.1, 8, 15–16. Jude's examples were historical to his audience in the first century A.D., but today their relation to history is, of course, debated.

[163] Ar. *Rhet.* 2.20.1394a.8; Quint. 5.11.8; cf. 3.8.66.

[164] Quint. 5.11.8.

[165] Quint. 5.11.5–7.

[166] Quint. 5.11.15–16.

[167] Sir. 16:7–10; CD 2:17–3:12; 3 Macc 2:4–7; *T. Napht.* 3:4–5; *m. Sahn.* 10:3; 2 Pet 2:4–8; K. Berger, "Hartherzigkeit und Gottes Gesetz, die Vorgeschichte des anti-jüdischen Vorwurfs in Mc 10⁵," *ZNW* 61 (1970) 27–36; J. Schlosser, "Les jours de Noé et de Lot: A propos de Luc, XVII, 26–30," *RB* 80 (1973) 26–34; Bauckham, 46–47.

[168] 2 Tim 3:8–9; Rev 2:14, 20; 2 Peter 2 after Jude.

[169] Num 14; 26:64–65. Disbelief is also mentioned in other accounts of the incident: Deut 1:32; 9:23; Ps 106:24; *Bib. Ant.* 15.6; Heb 3:19; 4:2.

[170] CD 3:7–9; Sir 16:10; Ps 95:8–11; Heb 3:7–4:13.

[171] Deut 9:23; Ps 106:25; Heb 3:19; 4:6, 11.

and disobedience. This is a counterpart of the topic of keeping the faith and not being kept for punishment found in vv 1, 6, 13, 21, and 24.

This first example, the wilderness disobedience, is out of chronological order. The change may have been intentional, either to group together the other two examples which deal with immorality, or to place it first in order to emphasize that God's people have been judged before for disobedience, or most likely, to effect a climax, as will be discussed below. It is preferable rhetorically, to present things in their natural order unless there is a compelling reason to do otherwise![172]

In v 6 Jude presents a second example of sin and punishment with which to compare the sectarians: the evil angels, the Watchers, of Gen 6:1-4. Gen 6:1-4 in the literature of the period often associated the sexual union of the Watchers with human females with the corruption of humanity, an event necessitating the Flood![173] Jude is dependent upon *1 Enoch* 6-19, especially ch. 10 where the reference to the Watchers being punished by being bound under the earth until the Day of Judgment is found![174] Verse 6 works out the topic of judgment found in the *narratio* as the use of synonyms indicates: κρίμα (v 4) — κρίσις (v 6). Verse 6 is reiterated and amplified in v 13. There the sectarians are explicitly compared to the evil angels (i.e., wandering stars) and are said to share the same judgment: nether gloom.

Jude embellishes this example using refining,[175] *regressio*,[176] word play using *reflexio*,[177] and transplacement![178] The statement the angels "did not keep their own position" but "left their proper dwelling" both repeats the idea in different form (refining) and draws a distinction regarding the place of the Watchers' habitation (*regressio*). This statement placed in contrast with "have been

---

[172] Quint. 9.4.23.

[173] *1 Enoch* 6-19, 21, 86-88; 106:13-15, 17; *Jub.* 4:15, 22; 5:1; CD 2:17-19; 1QapGen. 2:1; *Tg. Ps.-J.* Gen 6:1-4; *T. Reub.* 5:6-7; *T. Napht.* 3:5; *2 Apoc. Bar.* 56:10-14; 1 Pet 3:19-20; 2 Pet 2:4; phps. 1 Cor 11:10; 1 Tim 2:9.

[174] For detailed demonstration of this dependence, see Bauckham, 51-53.

[175] Refining or *expolitio* is a figure of thought which ". . . consists in dwelling on the same topic and yet seeming to say something ever new" (Her. 4.42.54). It may be accomplished in one of two ways: by repeating the idea in different form or by altering the idea (Her. 4.42.54). For further discussion, see Her. 4.42.54-44.58; Lausberg, 1:413-19, §830-42; Bullinger, 399-400.

[176] *Regressio* or ἐπάνοδος is a figure of speech, a ". . . form of repetition which simultaneously reiterates things that have already been said, and draws distinctions between them" (Quint. 9.3.35). For further discussion, see Quint. 9.3.35-36; Lausberg, 1:393-95, §798-99. Cf. Bullinger, 299-300, 913.

[177] *Reflexio* or ἀντανάκλασις is a figure of thought ". . . where the same word is used in two different meanings" (Quint. 9.3.68). For further discussion, see Her. 4.14.21; Lausberg, 1:335-36, §663-64; Martin, 316; Bullinger, 286.

[178] Transplacement is a figure of speech. It is both the frequent reintroduction of the same word and a word used in various functions (Her. 4.14.20-21; Quint. 9.3.41-42). For further discussion, see Lausberg, 1:333, §658-59; Martin, 306; Bullinger, 286-93.

kept . . . in the nether gloom" forms a word play, for the reiterated forms of τηρέω (μὴ τηρήσαντας and τετήρηκεν—transplacement) are not used in the same sense (*reflexio*). Since the Watchers have not "kept" their position, the Lord now "keeps" them chained. These figures allow Jude to dwell on the topic of rebellion (v 4) so that the comparison drawn to the sectarians in v 8 can be more pointed. As previously stated, keeping is a topic in Jude (vv 1, 6, 13, 21, 24) and is used in a play on words not only here in v 6 but also in a larger contrast in Jude as a whole. In Jude the Christians are kept for blessing (vv 1, 24) because they kept themselves in God's love (v 21) in contrast to the evil angels and sectarians who did not keep their positions (v 6) and are kept for nether gloom (vv 6, 13).[179]

In v 7 Jude presents what was probably considered the classic cases of sin and divine judgment in Jewish and Christian literature: Sodom and Gomorrah.[180] It is noteworthy that Jude specifically identifies this story as a δεῖγμα, an example.[181] "Serve as an example by undergoing a punishment of eternal fire" probably alludes not only to the example of Sodom and Gomorrah in tradition but also to them as an observable example as well. It was believed that the hot springs and sulfurous nature of the region south of the Dead Sea was the smoldering ruins of Sodom and Gomorrah.[182]

The example of Sodom and Gomorrah is antithetical to the previous examples of the Watchers. Whereas in the previous example angels lust after humans, in this example humans lust after angels. In both cases God's order is broken and the message is that breaking God's established order leads to punishment of eternal fire.[183] In describing the sin as "acted immorally" and "indulged in unnatural lust," Jude uses the figure *regressio* in which what precedes is reiterated and distinctions are drawn.[184] This reiteration amplifies the sin through repetition[185] and provides for a more pointed comparison to the sectarians in v 8. This example is again alluded to in the *peroratio* in v 23 as part of Jude's attempt to instill the proper pathos of urgency and fear in his audience by urging them to "snatch from the fire" those who follow the sectarians.

This section, vv 5–7, illustrates Jude's love of climax. The punishment increases in specificity and grows in horror. In vv 5–7 the intensification is from

---

[179] There is a similar play on words in John 17:6, 11–12; Rev 3:10.

[180] Gen 19:4–11; Deut 29:23; Isa 1:9; 13:19; Jer 23:14; 49:18; 50:40; Lam 4:6; Hos 11:8; Amos 4:11; Zeph 2:9; Sir 16:8; 3 Macc 2:5; *Jub.* 16:5–6, 9; 20:5; 22:22; 36:10; *T. Asher* 7:1; Philo *Quaest. Gen.* 4.51; Jos. *BJ* 5.566; Matt 10:15; 11:24; Mark 6:11; Luke 10:12; 17:19.

[181] Lee, 167.

[182] Cf. Josephus: ". . . vestiges of the divine fire and faint traces of five cities are still visible" (*BJ* 4.483); Philo: ". . . to the present day the memorials to the awful disaster are strewn in Syria, ruins and cinders and brimstone and smoke, and the dusky flame still arises as though fire were smouldering within" (*Mos.* 2.56; cf. *Abr.* 141).

[183] These two examples are also brought together in *T. Napht.* 3.4–5.

[184] For a discussion of *regressio,* see above, p. 52, n. 176.

[185] Cic. *Part. Or.* 15.54.

destruction in this life by natural death, to capture in eternal chains until judgment, to punishment by eternal fire. A climactic movement is also found in vv 11-13 as discussed below. This is the use of amplification by augmentation[186] of the type in which each member of a series is stronger than the previous member![187]

Throughout Jude, οὗτοι marks the transition from an example or type to the comparison with the sectarians, and from prediction to identification of the sectarians with the subject of the prediction![188] In v 8 transition is so marked and is also indicated by change in verb tense. The verbs in vv 5-7 are present tense (except πρόκεινται in v 7 which indicates the example is still present) and those of vv 8-10 are in the past tense (except in the quotation of v 9).

In vv 8-10 Jude makes his comparison explicit. He has set forth three examples of sin and judgment which serve to illustrate sin and which act as proofs that sin is judged (vv 5-7). He now reiterates the sins in summary fashion and identifies the sins of the sectarians as those of the paradigms he set forth, concluding that the sectarians are sinners and subject to judgment. Like the Watchers and the inhabitants of Sodom and Gomorrah, the sectarians defile the flesh; like the Israelites, Watchers, and Sodomites, they reject authority; and like the Sodomites, they revile angels![189]

Jude makes his explicit comparison in v 8 with verbal finesse. "Yet in like manner" (ὁμοίως μέντοι καί) adds a twist of persuasive pathos, implying that in light of such examples of sin and judgment as those in vv 5-7, it is hard to conceive of anyone sinning in similar fashion. "Defiling the flesh" is an expression used of the Watchers[190] and Sodomites![191] In the phrase "rejecting authority" (κυριότητα), the abstract form of the noun κύριος develops the topic of lordship and rejecting authority begun with reference to Christ and God as rejected κύριοι in vv 4 and 5. "Reviling the glorious ones," that is, angels, recalls the sin of the inhabitants of Sodom and Gomorrah.

The construction μέν . . . δέ . . . δέ structures v 8 to correspond to the second proposition of the *narratio* (v 4). The sectarians' perversion of the grace of God into licentiousness corresponds to "defile the flesh," and their denial of the Master and Lord, Jesus Christ, corresponds to "reject authority and revile the glorious ones."[192] The three conjunctions μέν . . . δέ . . . δέ constitute

---

[186] Cic. *Part. Or.* 15.54; Quint. 8.4.3-9.

[187] Quint. 8.4.8-9.

[188] Ὁμοίως μέντοι καὶ οὗτοι, v 8; οὗτοι δέ, v 10; οὗτοί εἰσιν, vv 12, 19; οὗτοί εἰσιν, v 16. These form the transitions from vv 5-7 to vv 8-10; v 11 to vv 12-13; vv 14-15 to v 16; and vv 17-18 to v 19 respectively.

[189] Although in a different fashion. Rather than desiring the angels for sexual purposes, Jude probably means that they reviled angels who gave the law to Moses, uphold the order of creation, and condemn their licentious behavior. Bauckham, 58-59, 62-63.

[190] *1 Enoch* 7:1; 9:8; 10:11; 12:4; 15:3-4; cf. 69:5.

[191] *Jub.* 16:5.

[192] Verse 10 does the same in reverse order.

polysyndeton[193] which emphasizes the sins of the sectarians[194] and makes them seem more important and numerous.[195] These conjunctions and the triple expression of which they are a part produce amplification by accumulation[196] using the figure διαλλαγή,[197] the amassing of different characteristics. This amplification is aided also by homoeoteleuton,[198] for the three cola end in the verbs μιαίνουσιν, ἀθετοῦσιν, and βλασφημοῦσιν.

Apparently, the sectarians base their doctrine and practice upon the authority of their own visionary experience, for Jude claims that these are related to dreaming. Ἐνυπνιαζόμενοι ("dreamings") is a reference to the dreams of prophetic revelation, and, although able to refer to authentic revelation,[199] in the Old Testament usually refers to the dreams of false prophets.[200] With the word and its connotations Jude implicitly argues that the sectarians' authority is false, thus effectively decreasing their ethos and that of their doctrine and practice.

Verses 9-10 serve as amplification of v 8, as amplification after proof[201] using the common topic of degree.[202] This is antithesis[203] using amplification,[204] and amplification by reasoning in which reasoning from given facts effects a magnification of something else.[205] As noted above, in v 8 Jude uses ὁμοίως μέντοι

---

[193] Polysyndeton is a figure of speech characterized by an excessive number of connecting particles (Quint. 9.3.50). For further discussion, see Quint. 9.3.50-54; Lausberg, 1:345, §686-87; Martin, 308; Bullinger, 208-37.

[194] Demetr. *Eloc.* 2.63; Quint. 9.3.54.

[195] Demetr. *Eloc.* 2.54, 63.

[196] Quint. 8.4.26-27. For further discussion, see ch. 1.

[197] Quint. 9.2.103; 9.3.49. For further discussion, see ch. 1.

[198] Homoeoteleuton is a figure of speech which occurs when ". . . clauses conclude alike, the same syllables being placed at the end of each" (Quint. 9.3.77). For further discussion, see Her. 4.20.28; Demetr. *Eloc.* 1.26; Lausberg, 1:361-63, §725-28; Martin, 311-12; Bullinger, 177.

[199] LXX Dan 2:1; Joel 2:28=Acts 2:17; cf. *1 Enoch* 85:1.

[200] LXX Deut 13:2, 4, 6; Isa 56:10; Jer 23:25; 36:8. Cf. ἐνύπνια ψευδῆ (false dreams) in Jer 23:32 and Zech 10:2. Cf. *1 Enoch* 99:8 where the sinners of the last days "shall become wicked on account of the folly of their hearts; their eyes will be blindfolded on account of the fear of their hearts, the vision of their dreams." Horst Balz, "ὕπνος," *TDNT* 8:550-55.

[201] Cic. *Or.* 36.127; *Part. Or.* 15.52.

[202] Ar. *Rhet.* 1.2.1358a.21; 1.3.1359a.9; 2.18.1391b.4; 2.19.1393a.26-27; Cic. *De Or.* 2.40.172; *Part. Or.* 2.7; Quint. 5.10.86-93.

[203] Antithesis is a figure of speech in which ". . . either terminology or meaning, or both at once, are opposite in the opposed clauses" (*Rhet. ad Alex.* 26.1435b.25ff.). Cf. Ar. *Rhet.* 3.9.1409b.7; Demetr. *Eloc.* 1.22; Cic. *Or.* 50.166; Her. 4.15.21 for similar definitions. For further discussion, see Ar. *Rhet.* 3.9.1409b.7-1410b.10; *Rhet. ad Alex.* 26; Cic. *Or.* 49.166-50.167; Her. 4.15.21; 4.45.58; Quint. 9.3.81-86.

[204] Cic. *Part. Or.* 16.55.

[205] Quint. 8.4.15-26.

χαὶ to imply how unbelievable it is to sin in light of punishment, and in vv 9–10 he further attempts to increase the pathos of startled disbelief by observing that even the archangel Michael acted only in accord with a higher moral authority when contending with the evil angel Satan. By contrast, the sectarians revile good angels associated with the Mosaic law and thus usurp the role of the Lord.

Verse 9 is an example of the figure of thought called exemplification, "the citing of something done or said in the past, along with the definite naming of the doer or author" used to embellish, clarify, and vivify.[206] For his amplifying example, Jude uses a recognized and authoritative source, *T. Mos.*, which itself includes a quotation from an authoritative source, Zech. 3:2 — ἐπιτίμησαι σοι χύριος,"May the Lord rebuke you."[207] This gives his amplification the additional support of the ethos of *T. Mos.* and the Old Testament. The example is adorned with paronomasia of the type in which words lack a close resemblance, but are not dissimilar:[208] διαβόλῳ διακρινόμενος διελέγετο.

Like v 8, v 10 is an outworking of the two points of the *narratio*, but here developed in reverse order. First Jude shows that the sectarians reject authority (vv 4b, 10a), and then that they are licentious (vv 4a, 10b). In v 10, Jude draws his comparison with v 9 while amplifying the application of v 8. Whereas the archangel Michael will not revile Satan (v 9), the sectarians "revile what they do not understand," that is, they revile the angelic guardians of the law (v 8), a sin similar to the sin of the Sodomites (v 7). This development of the topic of reviling angels is aided by the thrice used βλασφημεῖν (vv 8–10), an example of transplacement which here supports amplification of the topic by repetition.[209] The similitude,[210] "those things that they know by instinct as irrational animals do," vivifies and amplifies[211] the sectarians' behavior through comparison.[212] It also refers back to "defiling the flesh" in v 8, for φυσικῶς ("instinct") corresponds to

---

[206] Her. 4.49.62. See also Bullinger, 467.

[207] For a detailed discussion of the background and source of Jude 9, see Bauckham, 47–48, 65–76.

[208] Her. 4.22.30.

[209] Cic. *Part. Or.* 15.54.

[210] A similitude is a figure of thought, ". . . a manner of speech that carries over an element of likeness from one thing to a different thing" (Her. 4.45.59). Cf. Cic. *Inv.* 1.30.49 for a similar definition. For further discussion, see Her. 4.45.59–47.60; Quint. 8.3.72–81; Lausberg, 1:419–22, §843–47; Martin, 253–54; Bullinger, 751–53; Marsh McCall, *Ancient Rhetorical Theories of Simile and Comparison*, Loeb Classical Monographs (Cambridge: Harvard University Press, 1969); Caird, 144–71.

[211] The purpose of a similitude is to embellish, help prove, clarify, or vivify (Her. 4.45.59; Quint. 8.3.72ff.; cf. 5.11.22).

[212] The similitude has four forms: contrast, negation, detailed parallel, and abridged comparison (Her. 4.45.59–47.60). Quintilian adds a fifth called reciprocal representation in which the correspondence between the resemblances is exact and both subjects of comparison are placed side by side (8.3.77–81).

σάρχα ("flesh").[213] This serves to recall the sins of the Watchers and the Sodomites (vv 6-7).

"They are destroyed" (φθείρονται) recalls the fate of all three previous examples in vv 5-7, and emphasizes the point that Jude is making: since the sectarians and their behavior resemble the sinners and sins of the examples, they will experience a similar judgment. Whereas the judgment of the examples is cited after each, this last phrase in v 10 is the only reference to the judgment of the sectarians in vv 8-10 and serves as a pointed conclusion.

The Second Proof (vv 11-13)

The traditional woe formula and the three aorist verbs representing the semitic use of a prophetic perfect indicate v 11 is a prophecy.[214] As the transitional phrase οὗτοι εἰσιν beginning v 12 denotes, vv 12-13 are the application of the prophecy to the sectarians. The stylistic use of transplacement employing the same topic unite prophecy and application: πλάνη ("error") in v 11 and πλανῆται ("wandering") in v 13.

The structure of vv 11-13 is very similar to that of vv 5-10: first examples from the Old Testament are presented (vv 5-7, 11), then application is made to the sectarians (vv 8-10, 12-13). As the application in vv 8-10 contained an additional text (*T. Mos.* in v 9), vv 12-13 contain several allusions to other texts.[215] Both applications establish that the sectarians are sinners, and conclude with explicit reference to their judgment. However, whereas the sins of the sectarians are merely compared with those of Old Testament examples in vv 5-10, the behavior of the sectarians is described using Old Testament related examples of sinners and images of sin in vv 11-13. Thus there is a heightening of accusation and specificity, a rhetorically effective development similar to refining.

The prophetic oracle of v 11 may either derive from Jude himself or from earlier Christian prophecy.[216] In the *narratio*, Jude's description of what follows as οἱ πάλαι προγεγραμμένοι gives indication that this prophecy may not derive from him. If this is the case, then the prophecy functions as an artificial,

---

[213] 4 Ezra 8:29-30 is a similar comparison of sin with the behavior of animals.

[214] Jude 11 is a woe oracle. This form developed both within and without the OT into a prophetic judgment on sinners. The woe oracle in its fullest form contained: 1) the exclamation "Woe," 2) specification of the sins of the wicked, and 3) a pronouncement of judgment. Often a ὅτι clause follows the exclamation to explain it and usually provides either the sin or the judgment. See D. E. Garland, *The Intention of Matthew 23*, NovTSup 52 (Leiden: E. J. Brill, 1979) 72-80; Bauckham, 77-78; David E. Aune, *Prophecy in Early Christianity and the Ancient Mediterranean World* (Grand Rapids: Eerdmans, 1983) 96-97, 116-17. Jude 11 contains the ὅτι clause and it provides both the sins and judgments.

[215] Ezek 34:2; Prov 25:14; Isa 57:20; *1 Enoch* 80:6.

[216] E. Earle Ellis, *Prophecy and Hermeneutic in Early Christianity* (Grand Rapids: Eerdmans, 1978) 224.

inductive proof based on example[217] of the type called judgment,[218] of the subtype constituted by supernatural oracles.[219] As such the comparison is of the like[220] and the parallel complete.[221] As a prophecy, v 11 possesses a supernatural ethos.

Since Jude usually prefaces the quotations of others which are used in proof (cf. vv 14, 17), this prophecy may derive from Jude himself. If so, then the prophecy functions as an artificial, deductive proof based on a testimony. In this case, the prophecy would not be external to the matter at hand, but be derived from it.[222] Prophecy is particularly effective in proof because it was commonly used in the Jewish-Christian as well as the Greco-Roman tradition.[223]

If Jude is not perceived to be the source of the prophecy, then the ethos of his proof is increased because of the respect for authoritative statements in the Greco-Roman world,[224] especially for prophetic statements in Jewish-Christian circles. If he himself is seen as the source, then his own ethos is boosted as well. In either case, God or Christ himself is conceived as the ultimate source of the prophecy, and divine ethos sustains the ethos of both Jude and his proof.

The traditional woe forumla beginning v 11 is an example of *exclamatio*,[225] and is designed to elicit pathos.[226] With it, Jude is able to express great emotion precipitated by the severity of the audacity of the sectarians described in vv 8–10 and try to elicit the same emotion from his audience. Within the confines of prophecy, v 11 presents three Old Testament examples of sinners who caused others to sin. There is not enough evidence to show that Cain, Korah, and Balaam were traditionally cited as a set of three examples of sinners.[227] However, in early Christian literature Korah and Balaam were used as examples of false teachers in the church.[228] Jude is using traditional and paradigmatic examples

[217] For a discussion of example, see ch. 1.

[218] Cic. *Inv.* 1.30.48; Quint. 5.11.36–44.

[219] Quint. 5.11.42–44. See the discussion of the nature of oracles as proof, ch. 1, p. 17, n. 143.

[220] *Rhet. ad Alex.* 8.1429a.20ff.; Cic. *Inv.* 1.30.49; Quint. 5.11.1–7.

[221] Quint. 5.11.5–7.

[222] Quintilian argues, against opposition, that authoritative sources are always external to the case and must be applied to the case at hand. Therefore, they must be considered artificial proofs (5.11.43–44). However, according to Quintilian's own understanding, prophecy which speaks directly to a case and is not found in tradition must be considered an inartificial proof because it is not external to the case. This is the understanding of Cic. *Part. Or.* 2.6 that divine oracles given directly to a case are inartificial proofs.

[223] Cf. Quint. 5.11.36–37, 42.

[224] Quint. 5.11.36–44.

[225] *Exclamatio* is a figure of thought in which an exclamation is artfully, not genuinely made (Quint. 9.2.26–27). Cf. Cic. *Or.* 39.135; Her. 4.15.22. For further discussion, see Lausberg, 1:399, §809; Martin, 282; Bullinger, 927–28.

[226] Quint. 9.2.26; 9.3.97.

[227] *T. Sota* 4:9 is an example of the use of this trio.

[228] Rev 2:14 (Balaam); 2 Tim 2:19 (Korah—quoting Num 16:5); *1 Clem.* 51:3–4 (Korah—quoting Num 16.33).

from post-biblical Jewish tradition which increase the effectiveness of his rhetoric. These examples are all historical[229] and compare like with like,[230] and the parallel between the example and point proven is complete rather than partial.[231] Using a triple expression which is accumulation employing διαλλαγή,[232] he amplifies the sinfulness of the sectarians.

The first example, that of Cain, is used in the metaphor "walk in the way of Cain." In post-biblical tradition Cain was typically presented as the archetypal sinner[233] and one who taught and enticed others to sin.[234] By using the example of Cain and the metaphor of walking describing an ethical pattern, Jude claims that the sectarians infiltrating the church are sinners and instructors in sin.[235] He further develops the topic of walking in vv 16, 18.

Although the biblical account claims that Balaam refused to curse Israel for monetary reward,[236] a post-biblical Jewish tradition assumed he did just the opposite.[237] He was considered a man of greed who persuaded Balak to entice Israel to sexual sin and idolatry.[238] By using this example, Jude claims that the sectarians lead the audience into sexual immorality and receive monetary reward for their teachings. His use of this example is particularly appropriate because the sectarians, like Balaam in tradition, may have claimed to be prophets receiving visions.[239]

The Balaam and Cain examples incorporate a play on words. While the sectarians walk in the way of Cain, they also abandon themselves to Balaam's

---

[229] Ar. *Rhet.* 2.20.1393a.2–1393b.4; *Rhet. ad Alex.* 8.1429a.20; 1430a.5ff.; Cic. *Inv.* 1.30.49; Quint. 5.11.1, 8, 15–16.

[230] *Rhet. ad Alex.* 8.1429a.20ff.; Cic. *Inv.* 1.30.49; Quint. 5.11.1–7.

[231] Quint. 5.11.5–7.

[232] Quint. 8.4.26–27; 9.2.103; 9.3.49. For further discussion, see ch. 1, p. 27, n. 270.

[233] *T. Benj.* 7:5; Philo, *Det.* 32, 78; 1 John 3:ll; *1 Clem.* 4:7; cf. Wis 10:3–4.

[234] Jos. *Ant.* 1.52–66; Philo, *Post.* 38–39.

[235] Jude may be alluding here to a Targumic tradition that Cain was the first heretic. All Targums, except Onqelos, include a haggadic expansion at Gen 4:8 which portrays Cain's murder of Abel as the outcome of an argument about the justice of God's governing of the world and the possibility of judgment. Cain indulges in wickedness because of his skepticism concerning divine justice and future judgment. This tradition may date from the first century. G. Vermes, "The Targumic Versions of Genesis 4:3–16," in *Post-Biblical Jewish Studies,* SJLA 8 (Leiden: E. J. Brill, 1975) 92–126; P. Grelot, "Les Targums du Pentateuque: Étude comparative d'après Genèse, IV, 3–16," *Sem* 9 (1959) 59–88; Bauckham, 79–80. If this tradition was known to Jude's audience, not only would Cain's wickedness be ascribed to the sectarians, but also his false teaching that there is no future judgment.

[236] Num 22:18; 24:13; cf. Deut 23:4; Neh 13:2.

[237] *Tgs.* Num 22:7; Philo, *Mos.* 1.266–68; *Mig.* 114; *'Abot R. Nat.* 1.29; *Num. Rab.* 20:10.

[238] Philo, *Mos.* 1.295–300; Jos. *Ant.* 4.126–30; *Bib. Ant.* 18:13; *Tg. Ps.-J.* Num 24:14, 25; 31:8; *y. Sanh.* 10:28d; *b. Sanh.* 106a; cf. Num 25:1–3; Rev 2:14.

[239] Jude 8; cf. v 19. Cf. *Tgs.* Num 22:5; *Bib. Ant.* 18:2; *Num. Rab.* 20:7; *b. Sanh.* 106a.

error of leading others from the way of truth.[240] In the application and amplification of v 11 in v 13, this topic of wandering from the way is reiterated in the designation of the sectarians as ἀστέρες πλανῆται ("wandering stars"), stars having wandered from their proper dwelling (v 6).

The example of Korah, who led rebellion against the authority of Moses,[241] became the classic paradigm of an antinomian heretic.[242] His judgment of being swallowed up by the earth (Num 26:10) was used in Jewish and Christian literature as a warning example of divine judgment. By his use of Korah to portray the sectarians and their fate, Jude subtlely claims they are rebelling against the law and are subject to judgment.

The example of Korah is out of biblical chronological order.[243] According to Quintilian, unless there is a reason, material should be presented in its natural order.[244] Jude seems to have two reasons for his unnatural order. First, the judgment of Korah in the Old Testament and in tradition was the most striking. He and his company were considered to have been swallowed by the earth to have gone down alive to Sheol,[245] and were to be destroyed on the last day.[246] Second, Korah's judgment serves best for analogy with that of the Watchers (v 6), the wandering stars (v 13) who are kept in nether gloom until judgment. In the preceding phrase, the sectarians are said to be guilty of Balaam's "wandering," and Korah's judgment in juxtaposition develops the topic. Thus, the order adopted allows Jude to end on a strong note of judgment and develop the topic of wandering. Emphasis is effected in the last word, the aorist ἀπώλοντο, "they have been destroyed," which is equivalent to the prophetic perfect. The entire emphasis is accentuated through amplification by accumulation,[247] employing three examples.

Jude 12-13 is the application of the prophecy of v 11 to the sectarians, serving to amplify the sinful nature of the sectarians, to decrease their ethos, and to increase negative pathos. This is accomplished with a series of six metaphors,

---

[240] Herbert Braun, "πλανάω," *TDNT* 6:249–50.

[241] Num 16:1–35; 26:9–10; cf. Ps 106:16–18; Sir 45:18–19.

[242] Jewish exegetical tradition interpreted Korah's rebellion in Numbers 16 in connection with the law of the fringes in Num 15:37–41. Korah and party made the tassels of their garments all blue rather than merely the cord of the tassel. Korah's rebellion was thus modifying the Torah. (*Bib. Ant.* 16:1; *Tg. Ps.-J.* Num 16:1–2; cf. *Num. Rab.* 18:3, 12). Jewish and Christian exegetical tradition also portrayed Korah as schismatic. (*Tg. Neof.* Num 16:1; 26:9; *Tg. Ps.-J.* Num 26:9; 2 Tim 2:19 [quoting Num 16:5]; *1 Clem.* 51:1–4; cf. *Num. Rab.* 18:2; Jos. *Ant.* 4:15–21).

[243] Cf. the correct chronological order of Cain, Korah, Balaam in *T. Sota* 4:9.

[244] Quint. 9.4.23.

[245] Num 26:10; Ps 106:17; Sir 45:19; *Bib. Ant.* 57:2; Jos. *BJ* 5.566; *1 Clem.* 4:12; 51:4; *Prot. Jas.* 9:2.

[246] *Bib. Ant.* 16:3; cf. *'Abot. R. Nat.* 36:2; *Num. Rab.* 18:13.

[247] Quint. 8.4.26–27. For more details, see ch. 1.

literature,[248] and considered faulty style by the handbooks.[249] This series serves as an elaborate denunciation, being metaphors drawn from what is mean for the purpose of depreciation.[250] The series constitutes amplification by accumulation using the figure διαλλαγή in which similar and different things are accumulated.[251] As is typical, here διαλλαγή is aided by asyndeton to make the things listed seem more numerous.[252] This series also exhibits *enargeia,* that is, vivid illustration or representation to create mental pictures and invigorate style.[253] It is particularly useful in arousing pathos,[254] and here supports the negative pathos heightened by the *exclamatio* of v 11. *Enargeia* is aided by giving accompanying circumstances ("carried along by the wind," "in late autumn"), the use of metaphor appealing to the sense of sight ("wild waves of the sea"), and metaphors making the inanimate, animate (waves as "casting up the foam of their own shame").[255]

Jude appeals to pathos by characterizing the sectarians with the metaphor "dangerous reefs" in the agape meal. The imagery of shipwreck and its danger, and the need to steer clear, would flash across his audience's minds, serving to dissuade them from association with the sectarians.[256] The behavior of the sectarians at the agape meal is characterized as "feasting without reverence." Probably, in accordance with their sensuality (v 10), the sectarians treat the agape as a mere meal to satisfy their hunger.[257] This serves as an explanation for why the sectarians are dangerous reefs and severely decreases their ethos. This first metaphor may be intended to make explicit a topic connected with the preceding example of Korah, that is, the danger of affiliation.[258]

---

[248] Cf. the series of similes in Wis 5:9-12, 14; Ep. Jer. 70-71; 1QH 3:6-7; the series of metaphors for the writer's enemies in 1QH 5:6 8; and the accumulated imagery in 4 Macc 7:1-5 and Jas 3:2-8.

[249] The handbooks advise that metaphors not be crowded together (Demetr. *Eloc.* 2.78). To frequent use of metaphor or metaphors in a continuous series are said to obscure language, making it "allegorical and enigmatic" (Quint. 8.6.14). Excessive use of metaphor is considered especially bad if the metaphors are all of one species (Quint. 8.6.16). Longinus advises that no more than three metaphors be used in a row (*Subl.* 32.1).

[250] Ar. *Rhet.* 3.2.1405b.13.

[251] Quint. 8.4.26-27; 9.2.103; 9.3.49. For further discussion, see ch. 1.

[252] Quint. 9.3.50. Asyndeton is a figure of speech in which there is an absence of connecting particles (Demetr. *Eloc.* 5.268; Cic. *Or.* 39.135; Her. 4.30.41; Quint. 9.3.50, 62). For further discussion, see Lausberg, 1:353-55, §709-11; Martin, 299-300; Bullinger, 137-48.

[253] Ar. *Rhet.* 3.10.1410b.6; 11.1411b.1-1412a.4; Long. *Subl.* 15; Demetr. *Eloc.* 4.209-20; Quint. 4.2.63; 6.2.29-33; 8.3.61-71, 88-89; 9.2.40-44; cf. 4.2.123-24; Lausberg, 1:399-407, §810-19; Martin, 288-89; Bullinger, 444-45.

[254] Quint. 6.2.29-30.

[255] Ar. *Rhet.* 3.11.1411b.1-4; Demetr. *Eloc.* 4.217-18; Quint. 8.3.70.

[256] For similar imagery, cf. 1 Tim 1:19; Barn 3:6. Cf. the more common metaphor of the rock of stumbling—Isa 8:14-15; Matt 13:41; 16:23.

[257] Cf. 1 Cor 11:20-22, 33-34.

[258] Num 16:24, 26-27, 34; cf. *Bib. Ant.* 16:7.

Jude continues with the common metaphor for leadership, calling the sectarians "those who shepherd themselves."[259] Jude is probably alluding to Ezek 34:2 which castigates Judah's leadership for enjoying the material benefits of leadership, but failing to aid the people, saying, "Ho, shepherds of Israel who have been feeding yourselves! Should not shepherds feed the sheep?"[260] In effect, Jude is warning that although the sectarians proclaim to be leaders, they have no real interest in the audience's welfare, but only in their own.

Jude then moves to four metaphors drawn from nature which all relate to the sectarians' claim to leadership. These metaphors probably derive from the same four metaphors in *1 Enoch* 2:1–5:4 and 80:2–8. *1 Enoch* 2:1–5:4 is a comment on 1:9 directed to the wicked, and as it closes in 5:4 it returns to the theme of 1:9. These four metaphors are in close literary proximity to 1:9 and to 5:4, being found in 2:1, 3 and 5:1, 4. In *1 Enoch* 2:1–5:4, the topic is that nature conforms to the laws of God ordained for them, whereas the wicked transgress God's laws. The topic is illustrated with the four natural phenomena that Jude takes up. Jude reverses the illustration so they describe nature transgressing the laws which God laid down for it; something the wicked also do. Jude shifts from contrast to comparison. In *1 Enoch* 80:2–8 these images from nature (with the exclusion of the sea) are found in a prediction that in the last days nature will cease to obey the laws God set for it and will go astray. Here the nature images parallel the behavior of the wicked (*1 Enoch* 80:2, 3, 6), and knowledge of it may have prompted Jude to emphasize the parallel, not the contrast, when using *1 Enoch* 2:1–5:4.[261] As such, vv 12–13 use traditional metaphors from an authoritative source, enhancing the persuasiveness of the rhetoric.

The metaphor, "waterless clouds," is a possible allusion to Prov 25:14: "Like clouds and wind without rain is a man who boasts of a gift he does not give." The metaphor further decreases the ethos of the sectarians for it implies that, although their teaching may sound promising, it does not deliver.

The metaphor, "fruitless trees," draws upon the traditional image of a tree and its fruit, and its many nuances.[262] Of particular note is Matt 7:16–20 where false prophets are known by their evil fruit.[263] Like trees that should bear means for sustenance, the sectarians do not provide benefit for the community. It was

---

[259] The metaphor of the shepherd is commonly used in Jewish and early Christian literature to signify human leadership and the leadership of God and Christ. It also was often used regarding Christian leadership (John 21:16; Acts 20:28; 1 Cor 9:7; Eph 4:11; 1 Pet 5:2; Ign. *Phld.* 2.1; Rom 9.1. Joachim Jeremias, "ποιμήν," *TDNT* 6:486–88, 491–99.

[260] Cf. *Asc. Isa.* 3:24: ". . . and many elders will be lawless and violent shepherds to their sheep and will become ravagers (of the sheep), since they have no holy shepherds."

[261] Bauckham, 79, 90–91.

[262] Ps 1:3; Jer 17:6, 8; Wis 4:3–5; Sir 6:3; *1 Enoch* 80:2–3; Matt 3:10 par. Luke 3:9; 13:61; Jas 3:12; Herm. *Sim.* 4.

[263] Cf. Matt 12:33 par. Luke 6:43–44.

traditional to extend the tree metaphor with a pronouncement of judgment,[264] and, unlike the previous metaphors, this metaphor ends with such a pronouncement. The sectarians are said to suffer the second death of the wicked after judgment on the Last Day.[265] Thus, the movement from sin to sin and judgment occurs in v 12 as it does in v 11, and like v 11, reaches its climax in the worst judgment: the second death. Again, as in v 11, the judgment is pronounced in the aorist as the equivalent of a prophetic perfect. This tense increases ethos and rhetorical effectiveness by implication that Jude has prophetic insight and the matter of judgment is divinely decreed and certain.

In v 13 the metaphor of the wild waves of the sea casting up the foam of their own shame is probably based on Isa 57.20, ". . . the wicked are like the tossing sea; for it cannot rest, and its waters toss up mire and dirt."[266] The metaphor is broken, for the shame belongs to the sectarians, not the waves. Jude increases the intensity of this attack on his opponents' ethos, for this metaphor, unlike the previous two, points to the results of the sin produces, that is, shame.

In the metaphor of the wandering stars, Jude is probably alluding to *1 Enoch* and, as in v 6, compares the sectarians with the Watchers of Gen 4:1-6. In *1 Enoch*[267] the Watchers are represented as wandering stars that disobeyed God,[268] were cast from heaven like falling stars[269] into the dark abyss,[270] and were bound there[271] to remain until the last judgment when they will be cast into the fiery abyss.[272]

Jude may be alluding specifically to *1 Enoch* 80 and be making a more poignant characterization and accusation. *1 Enoch* 80 describes the lawlessness of nature, 80:6 reading, "Many of the chiefs of the stars shall make errors in respect to orders given to them; they shall change their courses and functions and not appear during the seasons which have been prescribed for them." *1 Enoch* 80:7 goes on to describe how the wandering stars lead people astray. If Jude alludes to *1 Enoch* 80, then he is making the point that the sectarians have strayed from the path of obedience and lead others astray.[273] The example of transplacement, πλανῆται ("wandering," v 13) and πλάνη ("wander," v 11),

---

[264] Trees cut down—Matt 3:10 par. Luke 3:9; Matt 7:19; Luke 13:9. Uprooted—Ps 52:5; Prov 2:22; Wis 44:4; Matt 15:13.

[265] Rev 2:11; 20:6, 14; 21:8.

[266] Isa 57:20 is also the basis of the metaphor of the wicked as wild waves in 1QH 2:12-13 (". . . they have roared like turbulent seas, and their towering waves have spat out mud and slime.") and 8:15 (". . . they cast up their slime upon me."). Cf. the wicked as wild waves—1QH 2:27-28; 6:23. *T. Jud.* 21:9 predicts false prophets like storms at sea.

[267] *1 Enoch* 18:13-16; 21:3-6; 83-90, esp. 88:1-3.

[268] *1 Enoch* 18:13-16; 21:3-6.

[269] *1 Enoch* 86:1-3.

[270] *1 Enoch* 10.

[271] *1 Enoch* 88:1, 3.

[272] *1 Enoch* 90:24; cf. 10:6, 13; 21:7-10. Whereas the fiery abyss is the eternal fate of the Watchers, in Jude their eternal fate is the darkness.

[273] Bauckham, 90.

establishes a topical connection linking Balaam to the wandering stars, both of which lead astray and are compared to the sectarians.

Being based on traditional material, this metaphor is effective. The πλανάω word group was traditionally used to describe the activity of false prophets and teachers of the last days, and thus πλανῆτῆς ("wandering") contributes to the denunciation.[274] The punishment of eternal confinement in darkness described is also a traditional negative image.[275] As in both vv 11 and 12, there is a movement in v 13 from a metaphor emphasizing sinful behavior to one emphasizing judgment as well. Concluding a series of metaphors by emphasizing judgment of opponents for their activity is especially effective in deliberative rhetoric for dissuading an audience from association and similar activity. The six metaphors of vv 12-13 provide a powerful series of mental images and associations which seriously diminish the ethos of the sectarians especially with regard to their leadership and teaching roles, and elicit much negative pathos against them.

The Third Proof (vv 14-16)

In vv 14-16 Jude quotes the prophecy of *1 Enoch* 1:9 (vv 14-15), and makes an application to the sectarians (v 16).[276] Verses 14-16 function as an artificial proof drawn from example[277] of the type called a κρίσις or authoritative statement.[278] The κρίσις itself is of the type known as a supernatural oracle.[279] Jude proves that the sectarians are to be identified with the ungodly of the prophecy and are subject at the parousia to the judgment described.

In the formula introducing the prophecy, the verb προεφήτευσειν ("prophesy") indicates that Jude holds the prophecy of *1 Enoch* 1:9 to be inspired by God. As a good rhetor, Jude is using a κρίσις of the highest authority and persuasive impact in the eyes of his audience, for as a prophecy of divine origin, it carries God's ethos.

This section works out the propositions of the *narratio*. In v 4, Jude states that long ago certain ungodly persons were designated for condemnation, and now he supplies a prophecy which long ago did just this (vv 14-15). Supposedly, in the seventh generation from Adam, Enoch prophesied the judgment of the

---

[274] Matt 24:4-5, 11, 24; Mark 13:5, 22; Luke 21:8; 1 Tim 4:1; 2 Tim 3:13; 1 John 4:6; 2 Pet 2:15, 18; 3:17; Rev 2:20; 13:14; cf. 2 Tim 4:3-4. Herbert Braun, "πλανάω," *TDNT* 6:241-42, 246-50.

[275] Tob. 14:10; *1 Enoch* 46:6; 63:6; *Pss. Sol.* 14:9; 15:10; cf. Matt 8:12; 22:13; 25:30.

[276] That Jude is making a formal quotation is indicated by the use of a standard formula of introduction. Cf. the formulas of introduction in 4QpIsa[b] 2:7; 4QFlor. 1:16; Acts 2:16; 4:11. Application is again indicated by οὗτοι.

[277] For a detailed discussion of example, see ch. 1.

[278] Cic. *Inv.* 1.30.48; Quint. 5.11.36-44.

[279] Quint. 5.11.42-44. See ch. 1, p. 17, n. 143 for a discussion of the nature of a supernatural oracle.

ungodly for all their deeds and words against the Lord. In the prophecy in v 15, the repetition of the stem ἀσεβ- (ἀσεβεῖς twice, ἀσεβείας, ἠσέβησαν) repeats the topic of ungodliness from the *narratio* (v 4) where ἀσεβεῖς is a general characterization of the sectarians. It is likewise the figure of transplacement and amplification by use of repetition[280] that serves to amplify the sectarians' sinful nature. Also in v 15, the harsh things spoken against the Lord reiterates the topic of the *narratio* of denying the Lord. Verse 16 further explicates the proposition of the *narratio* that the sectarians deny Christ and his authority (as do vv 8, 10, 11) and are licentious (as do vv 7, 8, 18).

Jude's use of the prophecy of *1 Enoch* is governed by rhetorical concerns.[281] First, it was a typical Christian technique in proof to modify texts which originally spoke of the eschatological coming of God so that they referred to Christ's parousia.[282] Here *1 Enoch* 1:9, which originally spoke of God's coming in apocalyptic terms, is made, by the insertion of κύριος, to refer to Christ's parousia. This aspect of proof in Christian rhetoric is unusual, for rhetorical handbooks assume that, for the sake of persuasion, examples from history and literature would be utilized with the traditional understandings familiar to their audience.[283] However, since Jude's audience is probably familiar with the Christian use of examples in proof, Jude is not without rhetorical warrant in veering from Greco-Roman convention.

Secondly, whereas *1 Enoch* 1:9 speaks of God coming for three purposes, to judge, destroy, and convict, Jude speaks only of judgment and conviction, omitting destruction. With respect ot rhetoric, it seems at first that Jude would have retained reference to destruction in order to pick up this topic from vv 5–7, 10. However, he probably omitted it because the object of such destruction in *1 Enoch* 1:9 is "all flesh." Such omission provides better application to the sectarians and avoids the misconception that the audience will be destroyed at the parousia along with the sectarians.

Thirdly, Jude may have inserted the πάντων before τῶν σκληρῶν ("harsh things") in v 15. It is not found in the Ethiopic or Greek version of *1 Enoch.* If so, Jude sought to amplify the topic of rebellion against the Lord (vv 4, 5, 8–10, 11) by stressing that *all* things spoken against the Lord will be judged. Also, πάντων implies the harsh things are numerous, an implication serving to decrease the opponent's ethos. Whether or not this universal adjective was part of the text from which Jude quotes, the fourfold occurrence of πᾶς in the quotation is an effective use of pleonasm[284] and transplacement to amplify

---

[280] Cic. *Part. Or.* 15.54.

[281] For Jude's use of *1 Enoch* 1.9, see Carroll D. Osburn, "The Christological Use of *1 Enoch* 1.9 in Jude 14, 15," *NTS* 23 (1976/77) 334–41.

[282] Isa 40:10 (Rev 22:12); Isa 63:1–6 (Rev 19:13, 15); Isa 66:15 (2 Thess 1:7); Zech 14:5 (1 Thess 3:13; *Did.* 16:7).

[283] Quint. 5.11.36ff.

[284] Pleonasm can be either a fault of style or a figure of speech. As a fault, it is the overloading of a style with a "superfluity of words" (Quint. 8.3.53). As a figure of speech

by repetition[285] the thorough and complete scope of judgment upon the sectarians.

In parallel clauses, the prophecy speaks of both the deeds and words of the ungodly as necessitating judgment. The interpretation of v 16 explicates the sin of both the rebellious words and the licentious deeds of the sectarians, making it clear how easily the sectarians can be identified with the ungodly of the prophecy. Verse 16, containing as it does a list of various words and phrases, constitutes amplification by accumulation, here formed by διαλλαγή supported by asyndeton.[286] The initial two designations constitute the related figure called comma,[287] and both διαλλαγή with asyndeton and comma give style vigor and make the negative characteristics seem more numerous.[288] Such a listing of the evil traits of the sectarians is very effective in gaining audience recognition of their ungodliness, decreasing their ethos, and increasing negative pathos against them.

In v 16 Jude weaves his *probatio* together, designating the sectarians as grumblers (γογγυσταί) and malcontents (μεμψίμοιροι). Γογγυσταί is a traditional designation for the Israelites in the wilderness,[289] both for the incident at Kadesh referred to in v 5,[290] and of Korah's rebellion referred to in v 11.[291] In the New Testament, it is used to describe disputes regarding Jesus' authority.[292] Jude provides a further proof of the claim of the proposition of the *narratio* that the sectarians dispute divine authority.

Jude also claims of the sectarians that "their mouths speak huge (ὑπέρογχα) words." The Aramaic fragment of *1 Enoch* 1:9 (4QEn^c 1:1:17) from Qumran says the wicked spoke "great and hard things" (וקשין רבן [ורבן). If Jude relied on this version, he omitted "great" from his quotation in vv 14–15 and puts it here in the interpretation. Also, *1 Enoch* 5:4 (4QEn^a 1:2:13), which reiterates the topic of 1:9, reads, ". . . you have transgressed and spoken slanderously grave and harsh words with your impure mouths against his (God's) greatness."[293] In his

---

it is "language fuller than is absolutely required" (Quint. 9.3.46). Thus, if pleonasm is unnecessarily redundant, it is a fault (Quint. 9.3.53–55), but it is used for emphasis, it is a figure (Quint. 8.3.54; 9.3.46–47). For further discussion, see Lausberg, 1:251, §462; 427, §859; Martin, 276, 299, 301ff.; Bullinger, 405–18.

[285] Cic. *Part. Or.* 15.54.

[286] Quint. 8.4.26–27; 9.2.103; 9.3.49–50. For further discussion, see ch. 1, p. 27, n. 270.

[287] Comma is a figure of speech ". . . when single words are set apart by pauses in staccato speech" (Her. 4.19.26). For further information, see Lausberg, 1:465–67, 3935–40; Martin, 319–20.

[288] Demetr. *Eloc.* 2.61; Her. 4.19.26; 4:30.41; Quint. 9.3.50.

[289] Exod 15:34; 16:2, 7–9; 4 Ezra 1:15–16; 1 Cor 10:10.

[290] Num 14:2, 27, 29, 36; Deut 1:27; Ps 106:25; CD 3:8.

[291] Num 16:11.

[292] John 6:41, 43, 61; 7:12, 32. Karl Rengstorf, "γογγύζω," *TDNT* 1:728–35.

[293] Cf. *1 Enoch* 101:3.

interpretation, Jude may be tying prophecy and interpretation together, either by withholding a word from the former and using it in the latter, or, by quoting the prophecy of *1 Enoch* 1:9 proper and then using the reiteration of it (*1 Enoch* 5:4) to make the application. The intervening material of *1 Enoch* 2:1-5:3 has already been used to supply the metaphors of vv 12-13. As in *1 Enoch* 5:4, 101:3, the arrogant words are likely directed toward God (or Christ), like those of Nebuchadnezzar (*2 Apoc. Bar.* 67:7), Antiochus Epiphanes (Dan 7:8, 20; 11:36), and the Antichrist (Rev 13:5). As such, the sectarians' ethos would be severely reduced in the eyes of Jude's audience as the topic of rebellion and denial is continued.

Finally, the accusation that the sectarians are "showing partiality for the sake of benefit" casts doubt upon their integrity. The phrase may refer to teaching,[294] in which case the teaching of the sectarians is accused of being partial for financial gain.

The Peroratio *(vv 17-23)*

Verses 17-23 comprise Jude's *peroratio*.[295] The *peroratio* contains the twofold division and purpose of recapitulation or *repetitio* and emotional appeal of *adfectus*. In the *repetitio*, the rhetor seeks to recapitulate the main points of the *probatio* in summary fashion so as to place the whole case before the audience and refresh their memory.[296] For the *adfectus*, the rhetor appeals to the audience's emotion, arousing positive ones for himself and his case and negative ones for the opponent and his case.[297] Amplification is central to the *peroratio* as the rhetor strengthens his case and weakens the case of the opposition, expanding for the purpose of arousing the emotions of the audience.[298] Jude's *repetitio* comprises vv 17-19 and his *adfectus* comprises vv 20-23.

The division given above is independently corroborated on other than rhetorical grounds. The transition from body-middle to body closing within a letter is often begun with the vocative,[299] sometimes with the imperative form of the disclosure formula using the verb "to know,"[300] and often with a responsibility statement in which the addressor summons the addressee not to neglect but be concerned about something within the body of the letter.[301] Also, anywhere within the body of the letter the vocative signals a transition.[302]

[294] Mic 3:5, 11; Mal 2:9; Luke 20:21.

[295] For more on the *peroratio*, see ch. 1.

[296] For more on *repetitio*, see ch. 1.

[297] For more on *adfectus*, see ch. 1.

[298] Ar. *Rhet.* 3.19.1419b.1; Cic. *Part. Or.* 15.52-17.58; *De Or.* 1.31.143; Her. 2.30.47.

[299] White, 15-16. This is also true of the transition from letter opening to body-opening, and from body-opening to body-middle as in v 3.

[300] White, 3-5, 27. This is not common.

[301] White, 7-9, 41.

[302] White, 15-16.

The transition from body-middle to body-closing in Jude occurs in v 17, initiated by the vocative phrase ὑμεῖς δέ, ἀγαπητοί. The imperative μνήσθητε is an imperative form of the disclosure formula, being here a verb "to remember," and is related to the verb "to know" which is commonly used.[303] The remainder also functions as a responsibility statement summoning the audience not to neglect the predictions they had received from the apostles, predictions epitomizing the content of the body of the letter to this point. In v 20, the vocative phrase ὑμεῖς δέ, ἀγαπητοί, repeated from v 17, marks a transition within the body-closing.[304]

The two main and often intermingling functions of the body-closing provide ". . . a means of finalizing the principle motivation for writing (by accentuating and reiterating what was stated earlier in the body)" and ". . . a means of forming a bridge to further communication."[305] It often contains expressions urging responsibility for the matters discussed, usually without reference to the harm or benefit to befall for heeding or not heeding the request, but it also can hold out threat or promise.[306] These two functions correspond to those of recapitulation and emotional appeal which characterize the *peroratio*. It can be safely concluded that just as the body-opening and body-middle correspond to the *exordium-narratio* and *probatio* respectively, the body closing corresponds to the *peroratio*. On this analogy, v 17 marks the transition from *probatio* to *peroratio*, and v 20 marks the transition from recapitulation to emotional appeal within the *peroratio*.

The Repetitio (vv 17-19)

Recapitulation is needed in deliberative rhetoric only when there is a conflict of opinion.[307] Although Jude's audience is not of a differing opinion with regards to the sectarians, some doubt (v 22), and some former members have joined the sectarians (vv 19, 23). The *exordium* states it is necessary to contend for the faith and the *narratio* says the sectarians entered through stealth. Both imply the audience is not fully aware of the nature of the sectarians, and their opinion regarding them may be rather shapeless. These factors may explain Jude's use of recapitulation in his deliberation.

Cicero lists four types of recapitulation in the *peroratio*. In the first and usual method, each point of the *probatio* is touched on briefly by way of summation. The second states the propositions from the *partitio* and reviews the reasoning by which each was proven. In a third, the audience is asked if they want any more proof, a tactic which makes them review the argument and decide if it is complete. Fourthly, arguments can be posed against those of the opposition and

---

[303] Cf. the fuller disclosure formula, the infinitive ὑπομνῆσαι, which begins the body-middle, the *probatio*, in v 5.

[304] Cf. v 3 where ἀγαπητοί marks the transition from letter-opening to body-opening.

[305] White, 25.

[306] White, 28.

[307] Ar. *Rhet.* 3.13.1414b.3. Cic. *Part. Or.* 17.59 states recapitulation is seldom needed in deliberative rhetoric.

the latter shown to be refuted.[308] Jude takes the usual method of recapitulation, that of brief summation.

Jude's recapitulation (vv 17–19) is composed of an artificial proof based on an example[309] drawn from a κρίσις an authoritative judgment.[310] Being a summary of numerous predictions of Christ and the apostles, it is an "opinion of . . . distinguished citizens," as a κρίσις is defined,[311] but it is more specifically the subtype of a κρίσις, the supernatural oracle.[312] As a proof, it might be suspected that vv 17–19 should be part of the *probatio*. For reasons discussed above and reiteration of the topics discussed below, vv 17–19 are better seen as recapitulation within the *peroratio*. The case hinges on two interrelated propositions, and one, that the sectarians are ungodly, receives two of Jude's three proofs in the *probatio* (vv 5–10, 11–13). It is an effective way to recapitulate by presenting another such proof. Also, it is noteworthy that Cicero advises the rhetor to "reserve one's outstanding resources to the actual peroration,"[313] and considering Jude's audience, the prophecy of Christ and the apostles is the most outstanding resource Jude uses. In recapitulation, Cicero also advises that the rhetor can sum up in his own person or ". . . can bring on the stage some person or thing and let this actor sum up the whole argument."[314] This may in fact be what Jude is doing, allowing the apostles to sum up his case for him. Verse 18 is a summary of prophetic material from the preaching of the apostles who addressed the church(es) Jude admonishes[315] and is similar to numerous prophetic, apostolic teachings regarding false teachers or prophets in the last day.[316] The participle προειρημένων in the introductory formula in v 17 indicates that v 18 is considered prophecy by Jude and his audience. The proof is therefore strengthened by both apostolic and divine ethos.

In v 18 Jude continues to work out the topics of his previous rhetoric. The recurrence of the root ἀσεβ- (τῶν ἀσεβειῶν) reiterates the topic of ungodliness from the *narratio* (v 4) and the quotation from *1 Enoch* 1:9 in the *probatio* (vv 14–15). Ungodliness is a summary term encompassing many specific words

---

[308] Cic. *Inv.* 1.52.98–100. *Rhet. ad Alex.* lists calculation, proposal of policy, a question, or an enumeration as methods of recapitulation (20.1433b.30ff. for all three species of rhetoric, and 36.1444b.21ff. for judicial rhetoric only).

[309] for more on example, see ch. 1.

[310] Cic. *Inv.* 1.30.48; Quint. 5.11.36–44.

[311] Quint. 5.11.36.

[312] Quint. 5.11.42–44. For further discussion, see ch. 1.

[313] Cic. *De Or.* 2.77.314.

[314] *Inv.* 1.52.99–100.

[315] That Jude gives a summary, and not a quotation from a written source, is indicated by the use of vocabulary found elsewhere in Jude.

[316] Matt 7:15; 24:11, 24; Mark 13:22; Acts 20:29–30; 1 Tim 4:1–3; 2 Tim 4:3–4; 1 John 2:8; 4:1–3; 2 Pet 3:3; *Did.* 16:3; *Apoc. Pet.* A 1; *Sib. Or.* 2:165–66.

and deeds explicated throughout the *probatio*. The phrase τὰς ἑαυτῶν ἐπιθυμίας πορευόμενοι τῶν ἀσεβειῶν develops the topic of walking. In v 11 the sectarians are said to walk in the way of Cain, and this phrase in v 18 gives another facet of such a walk. More importantly, the topic of following ungodly desires is expressed in virtually the same form in v 16: κατὰ τὰς ἐπιθυμίας ἑαυτῶν πορευόμενοι. This is an example of reduplication,[317] a figure of speech used for amplification through repetition.[318] It serves well here to meet the *peroratio*'s need to arouse negative emotion towards the sectarians. The addition of τῶν ἀσεβειῶν in the repetition of v 18 accentuates the undesirable nature of the desires of the sectarians. In addition, the title "scoffers" (ἐμπαῖκται) indicates the attitude behind the sectarians' denial of Christ (v 4), rejection of authority (v 8), their reviling of angels (v 8) and whatever they do not understand (v 10), their reveling (v 11), and their speaking against Christ (v 15). It is an extremely derogatory term in Judaism, designating mockery by word, attitude, or act,[319] and further decreases ethos.

In v 19 Jude applies the prophecy of apostolic preaching to the sectarians, while continuing to reiterate topics. As is his custom, Jude amplifies the evil nature of the sectarians using a triple expression constituting accumulation using διαλλαγή, here emboldened with asyndeton[320] and the figure comma in the first two designations. The use of asyndeton makes the negative characteristics of the false teachers seem more numerous.[321]

The sectarians are said to create divisions (ἀποδιορίζοντες), a verb which harks back to the example of Korah (v 11), one who likewise created factions within the community. In the designation "worldly people, devoid of the Spirit" (ψυχικοί, πνεῦμα μὴ ἔχοντες), ψυχικός is clearly defined by πνεῦμα μὴ ἔχοντες.[322] Here the figure of refining is used which allows Jude to repeat himself saying virtually the same thing so as to amplify by repetition.[323] Jude decreases the ethos of the sectarians by countering their claim to possession of the Spirit, a claim which probably underlay their visionary experience (cf. v 8). By claiming them to be ψυχικός. Jude reiterates the critique of v 8 that these sectarians are dreamers, false prophets. In his application Jude implicitly argues that immoral

---

[317] Reduplication is a figure of speech constituted by ". . . the repetition of one or more words for the purpose of Amplification or Appeal to Pity . . ." (Her. 4.28.38). Cf. Quint. 9.3.28–29 for a similar definition. For further discussion, see Lausberg, 1:314–15, §619–22; Martin, 301–2; Bullinger, 251–55.

[318] Cic. *Part. Or.* 15.54.

[319] Georg Bertram, "παίζω," *TDNT* 5:630–36.

[320] Quint. 8.4.26–27; 9.2.103; 9.3.49–50. For further discussion, see ch. 1.

[321] Quint. 9.3.50.

[322] Ψυχικός is used only three other times in the New Testament. In 1 Cor 2:14 and 15:44 it is used in contrast to and refers to physical life in this world without the gift of the Holy Spirit. In Jas 3:15 it describes an aspect of worldly wisdom as opposed to wisdom from above.

[323] Cic. *Part. Or.* 15.54.

behavior (v 18 – "following their own ungodly passions") is evidence that the sectarians are not filled with the Spirit.

Because the teaching of the apostles referred to the last days and Jude applies the teaching to the sectarians, he clearly assumes that he and his audience are living in the last days. This adds to pathos, to the sense of urgency and need for action that Jude maintains throughout each segment of the epistle.[324] Such pathos greatly serves the purpose of deliberative rhetoric in which a decision on the issue at hand is sought.

The Adfectus (vv 20-23)

As noted above, ὑμεῖς δέ, ἀγαπητοί in v 20 marks another major transition. Verses 20-23 comprise the second section of the *peroratio*: the *adfectus*, the emotional appeal. Jude has proven to his audience that the sectarians are ungodly, licentious, and rebellious, and that they are the subject of previous prophecy (vv 5-16). He has reiterated his message (vv 17-19). In light of who the sectarians are, Jude now appeals to audience emotion to dissuade them from similar activity and to persuade them to work against the sectarians' influence in their own lives and the lives of others.

As is characteristic of the *peroratio* and the *exordium*, there is a greater use of pathos than elsewhere in the rhetoric.[325] The *peroratio* seeks to elicit the same pathos from the audience that the *exordium* does, but of much greater intensity.[326] Having appealed to emotion in the *exordium* mainly for the purpose of gaining the audience's attention and goodwill, Jude now increases his appeal so attention will be augmented by decision and action, desired ends of deliberative rhetoric. The appeal to contend for the faith found in the *exordium* is continued here in vv 20-23 with greater specificity and intensity. It is noteworthy that as identified, the *adfectus* and the *exordium* begin in similar fashion: Ἀγαπητοί ... ἐπαγωνίζεσθαι ... τοῖς ἁγίοις πίστει (v 3) and ἀγαπητοί, ἐποικοδομοῦντες ἑαυτοὺς τῇ ἁγιωτάτῃ ὑμῶν πίστει (v 20).

The *peroratio*'s attempt to elicit greater pathos from the audience requires a fuller treatment than in the *exordium*. To achieve this, the *adfectus* is generally composed of two sections, the *indignatio*[327] and the *conquestio*.[328] In the *indignatio* the rhetor seeks to elicit negative pathos for the opponent and his

---

[324] Especially in vv 3, 4, 14-15, 23.

[325] Quint. 6.1.51-52; cf. Cic. *De Or.* 2.77.311; *Part. Or.* 8.27.

[326] Quint. 4.1.28; 6.1.9-10, 12, 51-52; cf. Cic. *De Or.* 2.77.311; *Part. Or.* 1.4.

[327] *Indignatio* (Cic. *Inv.* 1.52.98). For further discussions on how to achieve this, see Ar. *Rhet.* 3.19.1419b.1; *Rhet. ad Alex.* 36.1445a.10ff.; Cic. *Inv.* 1.53-54; Her. 2.30; Quint. 6.1.9-20.

[328] *Conquestio* (Cic. *Inv.* 1.52.98), *commiseratio* (Her. 2.30.47; 2.31.50). For further discussions on how to achieve this, see Ar. *Rhet.* 3.19.1419b.1; *Rhet. ad Alex.* 36.1444b.35ff.; Cic. *Inv.* 1.55-56; Her. 2.31; Quint. 6.1.21-35.

case, and in the *conquestio* he seeks to elicit the opposite for himself and his case. In Jude, the *indignatio* is not a clearly defined section, for all of vv 17–23 functions like the *indignatio*. The *indignatio* may be so pervasive because, as Quintilian notes, appeal to emotion is ". . . specially required if the accused be a man of violent, unpopular or dangerous character,"[329] as in Jude.

The recapitulation of vv 17–19, inasmuch as it contains a very negative portrayal of the sectarians, functions like an *indignatio*. The *indignatio* can utilize the topics of confirmation, but emphasizes the negative.[330] These topics include those of person and action, and two topics of person are manner of life and habit.[331] Jude has utilized these topics in the recapitulation, calling the opposition scoffers who follow their own ungodly passions (v 18) and worldly people devoid of the Spirit who set up divisions (v 19).

Verses 20–23 take another approach to building negative emotion: arousing fear.[332] The exhortation to "save some, by snatching them out of the fire" (v 23) implies that fellow Christians under the influence of the sectarians are in danger of the punishment of eternal fire (v 7) about to befall those condemned at the coming parousia. Jude even exhorts his audience to work in fear (φοβός) of contamination by sin while trying to save their brethren (v 23).

Besides the more general topics discussed above, the *indignatio* has several topics it particularly uses for amplification.[333] Jude uses several of these. One is the topic of authority in which it is shown how the matter at hand has been of great concern to the gods, ancestors, and other authoritative groups.[334] Jude shows that ungodly behavior in the last days was a concern of the apostles (vv 17–19), and, by showing what God and Christ will do to prevent the audience itself from falling into such behavior (vv 20, 21, 24), he makes it clear that divine authority is likewise concerned. Of course, that Jude himself (or his pseudonymous counterpart) is concerned implicitly uses this topic of authority.

Another topic used to amplify the *indignatio* is the consideration of who is affected by the matter on which the charges rest, whether all persons, superiors, or peers.[335] This topic is implicit in Jude's *peroratio*. He has previously stressed that he and his audience share a common faith (v 3) and his *peroratio* shows how the sectarians affect his audience as peers in the faith.

---

[329] Quint. 6.1.12.

[330] Cic. *Inv.* 1.53.100. For a list of topics of confirmation, see Cic. *Inv.* 1.24–28.

[331] Cic. *Inv.* 1.25.35, 36.

[332] Quint. 6.1.14. Appeal to fear is part of the *exordium* as well (4.1.20–22), as in the case of Jude.

[333] Cic. *Inv.* 1.53.100–54.105 gives fifteen. Her. 2.30.47–49 reproduces the first ten of Cicero. *Rhet. ad Alex.* 36.1445a.12–29 and Quint. 6.1.14–20 gives several. These topics are applied to judicial oratory, but Her. 3.5.9 states that the perorations of judicial and deliberative rhetoric are virtually the same.

[334] Cic. *Inv.* 1.53.101; Her. 2.30.48.

[335] *Rhet. ad Alex.* 36.1445a.14ff.; Cic. *Inv.* 1.53.101; Her. 2.30.48.

Jude 20-23 is the *conquestio*.[336] Concerning amplification, particularly in the *peroratio*, Cicero advises that in exhortations (which is central to deliberative rhetoric) ". . . enumerations and instances of things good and evil will have the most effect."[337] This *conquestio* of Jude's *peroratio* has such a content, containing references to faith, prayer, God's love, Christ's mercy, eternal life, and salvation on the positive side, and punishement by fire and contamination by sin on the negative side. This enumeration is a decidedly persuasive factor, amplifying the positive help and benefits of contending for the faith, and the negative results of abandoning it.

The *conquestio* begins with four injunctions common to primitive Christian catechism and parenesis[338] in which Jude advises the audience how to meet the exigence for itself and further develops his topics. The first, third, and fourth injunctions represent the triad faith, love, and hope. The second, third, and fourth injunctions present the triad Holy Spirit, God, and Christ which brings the three-in-one authority to bear on the exigence. The use of these two triads would be rhetorically effective since they are based on tradition and invoke divine authority. Also, these four injunctions exhibit asynedeton[339] which makes them seem more numerous,[340] and adds vigor to the style so as to elicit emotions.[341]

The first exhortation, "build yourselves up on your most holy faith" (v 20) reiterates the topic of faith from the *exordium*. Whereas in v 3 Jude desires his audience to contend for the faith, here he desires them to build on it. The exhortation uses the metaphor of building common to early Christian tradition.[342] The metaphor may not have faded, for τῇ πίστει may be a dative indicating the foundation on which to build and not merely be an instrumental dative.[343] The designation of the audience's faith as "most holy" may contain the inherent comparison of their faith with the sectarians' "least holy" faith. The "building of the faithful" (ἐποικοδομοῦντες) contrasts the "creation of divisions" (ἀποδιορίζοντες) by the sectarians in v 19, constituting antithesis and helping to make a break between *repetitio* and *adfectus*.

---

[336] For a list of topics suitable for arousing emotion for the rhetor and his cause, see *Rhet. ad Alex.* 36.1444b.35-1445a.29; Cic. *Inv.* 1.55.106-56.109; Her. 2.31.50; Quint. 6.1.13, 21-25; cf. 4.1.20-21. These are given in the context of judicial rhetoric, but are applicable to deliberative as well (Her. 3.5.9).

[337] Cic. *Part. Or.* 17.58.

[338] This material may be derived from the apostles who ministered to the church (vv 3, 5, 17).

[339] This is a case of brachylogy, figure of speech, a subtype of asyndeton, in which nothing more is said than is absolutely necessary by using only essential words to achieve brevity (Her. 4.54.68; Quint. 8.3.82; 9.3.50).

[340] Quint. 9.3.50.

[341] Demetr. *Eloc.* 2.61; Her. 4.30.41; Quint. 9.3.50.

[342] Matt 16:18; Acts 9:31; 15:16; 20:32; Rom 14:19; 15:2, 20; 1 Cor 3:9-15; 8:1; 10:23; 14:3-5, 12, 17, 26; 2 Cor 10:8; 12:19; 13:10; Gal 2:18; Eph 2:18, 20-22; Col 2:7; 1 Thess 5:11; 1 Pet 2:5; *Barn.* 16:8-10; Ign. *Eph.* 9:1; Pol. *Phil.* 3:12; 12:2.

[343] Bauckham, 108, 113.

In early Christian literature, the phrase ἐν (τῷ) πνεύματι often means "under the inspiration or control of the Holy Spirit," and with reference to prayer often indicates prayer in which the Holy Spirit supplies the words.[344] Jude's second exhortation to his audience to "pray in the Holy Spirit" (v 20) develops the topic of the Spirit by forming a contrast to the sectarians' claim to possess the Spirit (vv 8, 19) when in fact they are devoid of the Spirit (v 19). This antithesis is reinforced with transplacement in the repetition πνεῦμα (v 19)—πνεύματι (v 20).

Jude's third exhortation to "keep (τηρήσατε) yourselves in the love (ἀγάπη) of God" reiterates the topics of love and keeping from the epistolary prescript (or quasi-*exordium*) of vv 1-2 where the audience is designated as "beloved (ἠγαπημένοις) of God the Father and kept (τετηρημένοις) for Jesus Christ" and it is wished that love (ἀγάπη) be multiplied to them. The specific topic of keeping (cf. v 24) also contrasts this topic in vv 6 and 13 where it is said that the sectarians have not kept their proper position and will be kept for nether gloom. Overall, these verses have the impact of antithesis.

The fourth exhortation, "wait for the mercy of our Lord Jesus Christ unto eternal life" (v 21), is based upon the hope of those addressed and carries great ethos. It reiterates this topic from the quasi-*exordium* (v 2) where Jude wishes his audience mercy multiplied. Since "mercy" refers to the eschatological hope of God's people and "waiting" to eschatological expectation,[345] this exhortation also relates to vv 14-15 and the quotation from *1 Enoch* 1:9 applied to Christ's return. All these passages carry the message that at his coming Christ will either bestow mercy (vv 2, 21) or judgment (vv 14-15). The very presence in the church of sectarians who were previously predicted would come in the last days indicates that the parousia is near and the "waiting for eternal life" short. Action must be taken. Pathos is heightened.

In vv 22-23,[346] Jude's exhortation shifts from what the audience can do for

---

[344] Matt 22:43; Mark 12:36; Luke 2:27; 4:1; Acts 19:21; Rom 8:9; 1 Cor 12:3; Rev 1:10; 4:2; *Barn.* 9:7; *Asc. Isa.* 3:19; cf. *Did.* 11:7-12. J. D. G. Dunn, *Jesus and the Spirit* (Philadelphia: Westminster, 1975) 239-40. Dunn affirms: "A reference to charismatic prayer, including glossolalic prayer, may therefore be presumed for Jude 20" (245-46).

[345] Ἔλεος as eschatological hope: *Pss. Sol.* 7:10; 8:27-28; 10:4, 7; 14:9; 17:45; *1 Enoch* 1:8; 5:6; 27:4; *2 Apoc. Bar.* 78:7; 82:2; 4 Ezra 14:34; Matt 5:7; 2 Tim 1:18; *1 Clem.* 28:1; Herm. *Vis.* 3:9:8; *Sim.* 4:2; Rudolph Bultmann, "ἔλεος," *TDNT* 2:484. "Waiting" as eschatological expectation—προσδέχεσθαι: Mark 15:43; Luke 2:25, 38; 12:36; 23:51; Acts 24:15; Titus 2:13; *2 Clem.* 11:2; προσδοκᾶσθαι: Matt 11:3; Luke 7:19-20; 2 Pet 3:12-14; *1 Clem.* 23:5; Ign. *Pol.* 3:2; ἐκδέχεσθαι: Heb 11:10; *Barn.* 10:11; *2 Clem.* 12:1; ἀπεδέχεσθαι: Rom 8:23; 1 Cor 1:7; Gal 5:5; Phil 3:20; Heb 9:28; ἀναμένειν: 1 Thess 1:10; *2 Clem.* 11:5; Friedrich Büchsel, "δέχομαι." *TDNT* 2:56, 57-58.

[346] Verses 22-23 have numerous textual variants. The variants generally refer to either two or three parties. The text adopted here is the three party text of ℵ, A adopted by the UBS text, 3d ed. This text is chosen because it conforms to Jude's predilection for triple expression and transplacement. For further details, see Metzger, 727-29; J. N. Birdsall, "The Text of Jude in p^72," *JTS* 14 (1963) 394-99; W. Beider, "Judas 22F: οὓς δὲ ἐᾶτε ἐν

itself to what it can do for those who have strayed. In vv 22-23 Jude uses epanaphora[347] in the οὕς μὲν . . . οὕς δὲ . . . οὕς δὲ structure which amplfies and emphasizes the exhortations.[348] Also, there are many topical links between vv 22-23 and the *probatio* in vv 7-9 which will be discussed below.

The first admonition, "Have mercy on (ἐλεᾶτε)[349] those who dispute (διακρίνω)" in v 22, refers back in part to v 9 where διακρίνω, in a quotation from the *T. Mos.* derived from the vision of Zech 3:1-5, is used to amplify the bellicose nature of the sectarians. The admonition is part of the further development of the topic of mercy. As the quasi-*exordium* wishes God's mercy to the audience (v 2), so the *peroratio* uses transplacement in vv 21-23 to exhort that the mercy (ἔλεος) the audience waits to receive at the parousia judgment (v 21), they should exhibit (ἐλεᾶτε) toward those under the grasp of the sectarians in an effort to save them from judgment (vv 22-23).

The second admonition, "snatch some from the fire" (v 23), is the second allusion to Zech 3:1-5.[350] It develops the topic of judgment by fire, the same fire to accompany the imminent judgment of the parousia (vv 10, 12, 13, 14-15). The exhortation is an example of the figure of thought called emphasis which reveals a deeper meaning than is actually expressed,[351] and is used for amplification.[352] Jude's appeal is amplified and made urgent, for the full meaning of the exhortation is to save fellow Christians from the doctrine and practice of the sectarians before they perish in eternal fire about to befall the sectarians at the imminent parousia.[353] The verb ἁρπάζω ("snatch") indicates that there is little time to act.

φόβῳ," *TZ* 6 (1950) 75-77; Carroll D. Osburn, "The Text of Jude 22-23," *ZNW* 63 (1972) 139-44; Bauckham, 108-11.

[347] Epanaphora is a figure of speech which ". . . occurs when one and the same word forms successive beginnings for phrases expressing like and different ideas . . ." (Her. 4.13.19). Cf. Demetr. *Eloc.* 5.268; Cic. *De Or. 3.54.206; Or.* 39.135; and Quint. 9.3.30 for similar definitions. For further discussions, see also Demetr. *Eloc.* 3.141; Lausberg, 1:318-20, §629-30; Martin, 296, 303; Bullinger, 199-205.

[348] Demetr. *Eloc.* 3.141; Her. 4.13.19; Quint. 9.3.30.

[349] Some mss. read ἐλέγχετε, "convince," for ἐλεᾶτε, "have mercy." I have adopted the reading ἐλεᾶτε because 1) ἐλέγχετε is explained as an attempt to differentiate the statement from the third admonition of this trio which also begins with ἐλεᾶτε, and 2) ἐλεᾶτε has the best mss. evidence (א B C²) and conforms to Jude's penchant for transplacement. For further discussion, see Metzger, 728.

[350] Jude may have noted this passage because the quotation from *T. Mos.* in v 9, "May the Lord rebuke you," derives from Zech 3:2, and there Joshua the high priest is called "a brand plucked from the fire."

[351] Her. 4.53.67; Quint. 8.3.83; 9.2.64; cf. Cic. *Or.* 40.139; Quint. 9.3.67. For further discussion, see Her. 4.53.67; Quint. 8.3.83-86; Lausberg, 1:298-99, §578; 450-453, §905-6; Martin, 254-55; Bullinger, 165-66.

[352] Quint. 9.2.3.

[353] Admonitions to rebuke and warn erring brothers and sisters are common: Matt 18:15-17; Luke 17:3; Gal 6:1; 2 Thess 3:15; 1 Tim 5:20; Titus 3:10; Jas 5:19-20; *Did.* 2:7; 15:3.

The third admonition, "have mercy with fear, hating even the garment spotted by the flesh" (v 23), refers back to vv 8, 12. Because the sectarians are dangerous reefs at the agape meal where they and their followers meet together with irreverence (ἀφόβως, v 12), Jude exhorts his audience to meet with the followers while remaining fearful (ἐν φόβῳ, v 23) of being influenced by them.

"Hating even the garment spotted by the flesh" is the third allusion to Zech 3:1-5.[354] The imagery here is strong, usually referring to undergarments defiled by human excrement.[355] This is hyperbole[356] which, for the purpose of amplification,[357] graphically depicts the severity of even the smallest amount of exposure to sin and the foul nature of contamination by sin. The phrase repeats this topic from v 8 where the sectarians are said to defile the flesh. The entire admonition is a warning to avoid the tempting sins of the flesh practiced by the sectarians (vv 6, 7, 8, 10, 16, 18), a warning eliciting strong pathos with its reference to fear and contamination.

The Doxology or "Quasi-Peroratio" (vv 24-25)

Jude ends his epistle, not with an epistolary postscript as one might expect, but with a doxology[358] which is seemingly more appropriate to end spoken rhetoric. The doxology brings his *peroratio* and the entire letter to an emotional climax. By ending his appeal with a focus upon God, Christ, and their future hope, his audience is ever more persuaded to act as Jude advises. It is an effective way to end deliberative rhetoric, and far more effective for emotional appeal than an epistolary postscript.

As the doxology begins, it functions almost as a prayer and serves to increase Jude's ethos, exhibiting his concern that his audience not fail to see the consummation of their hopes. In this regard the doxology functions like the *conquestio* section of the *adfectus* in the *peroratio*. It is noteworthy that the topics of keeping (vv 1, 6, 13, 21), ethical purity (vv 4, 6, 7, 8, 10, 12, 13, 15, 16, 18, 19, 20, 23), and the authority of God and Christ (vv, 4, 5, 8-10, 11, 15, 18, 22) are all reiterated. In this regard the doxology functions very much like the *repetitio* of the *peroratio*.

---

[354] In Zech 3:3-4, Joshua the high priest is said to be "clothed with filthy garments."

[355] Compare *sô'im* "filthy" of Zech 3:3-4 which is associated with *s'ām* and *sō'āh* which often refer to human excrement in the OT (Deut 23:14; 2 Kgs 18:27; Prov 30:12; Isa 36:12; Ezek 4:12). In Isa 28:8, *sō'āh* refers to a drunk's vomit, and in Isa 4:4 it is figurative for wickedness.

[356] Hyperbole is a trope, ". . . a manner of speech exaggerating the truth, whether for the sake of magnifying or minifying something" (Her. 4.33.44). Cf. Long. *Subl.* 38.6; Cic. *De Or.* 3.53.203; Quint. 8.6.67 for similar definitions. For further discussion, see Long. *Subl.* 38.1-6; Demetr. *Eloc.* 2.124-27; Quint. 8.6.67-76; Lausberg, 1:299-300, §579; 454-55, §909-10; Martin, 264; Bullinger, 423-28.

[357] Quint. 8.6.67. According to Quint. 8.4.29, hyperbole was once considered a specific form of amplification (as in Long. *Subl.* 11.2).

[358] Cf. *Mart. Pol.* 20:2 for a similar doxology ending a letter.

Stylistically, the doxology is masterful rhetoric. It ends with a triple expression of time. There are two traditional metaphorical expressions: "keep you from stumbling"[359] and the sacrificial metaphor "present you without blemish."[360] It contains, by its very nature, amplification using subject matter of great importance concerning the heavenly and divine.[361] It also amplifies by accumulation using διαλλαγή[362] when blessing God with glory, majesty, dominion, and authority. This serves to end the letter with an overwhelming sense of divine power.

Figure 1 is a rhetorical outline of Jude which takes account of the preceding discussion, particularly of invention and arrangement. For matters of style, see appendix 3.

FIGURE I
A RHETORICAL OUTLINE OF JUDE

I. Epistolary Prescript (Quasi-*Exordium*) - vv 1-2
II. *Exordium* - v 3
III. *Narratio* - v 4. Main propositions: 1) the sectarians within the church are ungodly and subject to judgment; 2) the sectarians are the ungodly whose presence and judgment in the last days has been foretold.
IV. *Probatio* - vv 5-16
    A. First Proof - "The sectarians within the church are ungodly and subject to judgment." An artificial proof based on examples drawn from history. vv 5-10.
        1. Three historical examples of sinners and their condemnation - vv 5-7.
        2. Comparison with the sectarians - v 8.
        3. Amplification by comparison - vv 9-10.
    B. Second Proof - "The sectarians within the church are ungodly and subject to judgment." An artificial (or inartificial) proof based on examples drawn from judgments of the subtype of supernatural oracle. vv 11-13.
        1. The prophecy - v 11.
        2. Application to the sectarians - vv 12-13.

---

[359] Used in the Psalms of God keeping one from disaster: Pss 38:16; 56:13; 66:9; 73:2; 91:12; 116:8; 121:3. Perhaps also inherent here is the metaphor of the wicked trying to trip the righteous or lay traps for them: Pss 140:4-5; 141:9; 142:3. ῎Απταιστος is a NT *hapax legomenon*, but cf. the metaphorical use of πταίεν in Rom 11:11; Jas 2:10; 3:2 and 2 Pet 1:10. Cf. the metaphor of 3 Macc 6:39 — ἀπταίστους αὐτοὺς ἐρρύσατο.

[360] 1 Thess 3:13; Eph 5:27; Col 1:22.

[361] Cic. *Part. Or.* 16.56.

[362] Quint. 8.4.26-27; 9.2.103; 9.3.49. For further discussion, see ch. 1.

C. Third Proof - "The sectarians are the ungodly whose presence and judgment in the last days has been foretold." An artificial proof based on an example drawn from a judgment of the subtype of supernatural oracle. vv 14–16.
1. The prophecy of *1 Enoch* 1:9 - vv 14–15.
2. Application to the sectarians - v 16.
V. *Peroratio* - vv 17–23
A. *Repetitio* - "The sectarians are the ungodly scoffers of apostolic testimony." An artificial proof based on an example drawn from a judgment of the subtype of supernatural oracle. vv 17–19.
B. *Adfectus* - vv 20–23.
VI. Doxology (Quasi-*Peroratio*) - vv 24–25.

EVALUATION OF THE RHETORIC

The following evaluation of the rhetoric of the epistle of Jude focuses first upon the degree of Jude's adherence to conventional rhetorical principles of invention, arrangement, and style. Secondly, the evaluation attempts to determine as nearly as possible how effectively Jude's rhetoric meets the needs of the exigence it seeks to modify.

As far as rhetorical conventions are concerned, Jude's rhetoric conforms to its best principles. In matters of arrangement, the elements of *exordium, narratio, probatio,* and *peroratio* are found, are in proper sequence, and are executing their individual and related functions. In matters of invention, the *narratio* contains two propositions, and the *probatio* provides concise, sufficient proofs for both. Not only are proofs from logos (example) effectively employed, but also those of ethos and pathos as well.

Since Jude's form of proof is almost solely the inductive proof of example, he might be faulted for not mixing induction with deduction and varying the method of proof.[363] However, his restrictive use of the inductive proof from example may be explained by two factors. First, ethos and example are the usual method of proof in deliberative rhetoric.[364] Second and more importantly, because Jude's exigence is concerned with ungodly behavior and past prophecy, proof from example is the most suited to his inventional needs.

The proofs make use of typical Jewish-Christian modes of argumentation, topics, authoritative sources, and constraints. There are numerous allusions to and citations of traditional figures and images. Particularly noteworthy in this regard are the conventional metaphors evoking strong imagery and emotion. The rhetoric is amplified throughout, but the method lacks variation, being most often amplification by accumulation.

[363] Cic. *Inv.* 1.41.76.
[364] Ar. *Rhet.* 1.9.1368a.40; 2.20.1394a.8; 3.17.1418a.5; *Rhet. ad Alex.* 32.1438b.29ff.; Quint. 3.8.12–13, 34, 66; cf. 5.11.8.

With regard to style,[365] Jude conforms most closely to the middle style.[366] It exhibits a variety of figures of speech and thought, and like the middle style, the majority of figures are those of speech.[367] The metaphor, most frequently used in the middle style, is present in abundance.[368] More importantly, Jude does not use the style simply for ornament, but rather, as the analysis shows, style aids invention.

It might be contended that Jude's rhetoric is deficient, for, unlike a Paul or a 2 Peter, he does not make any attempt to counter the arguments posed by the sectarians. These arguments obviously have proven convincing to the members of the audience who follow the sectarians (vv 19, 22–23). This lack of refutation may be partially explained by appeal to the intended length of epistle. A more fitting explanation is that Jude's response is conditioned by eschatological concerns. He perceives the sectarians as fulfillment of the prophecy. Their very presence in the church is a sign of the parousia (vv 14–15, 18; cf. v 4), and they are subject to its accompanying judgment (vv 4, 10, 12, 13, 15; cf. v 23). Such a conviction makes the need to identify the sectarians primary, and refutation of their doctrine and practice secondary.

The rhetoric of Jude should meet the needs of the exigence. To counter the sectarians' word and deed, Jude must convince his audience that the sectarians are ungodly and headed for judgment, and are the ungodly whose presence and judgment were previously predicted. He ostensibly addresses his rhetoric to those still loyal to apostolic doctrine and practice, bringing constraints to bear which should be persuasive to an early Christian audience. He chooses deliberative rhetoric which, of the three species of rhetoric, is best suited to move the audience to refrain from affiliation with the sectarians. Deliberative aims at persuasion and dissuasion, and its end is the advantageous and harmful. The heavy use of epideictic rhetoric supports the deliberation, helping to prove the proposition that the sectarians are ungodly, to decrease their ethos, and to elicit negative pathos; all with the intent of dissuading the audience from falling prey to their teaching and practice.

It can be affirmed that the author of Jude is skilled in the rhetoric of his time. The origin of this skill, whether gained from daily interaction with verbal and written culture and/or from formal training is impossible to determine. However, clearly to do justice to its content, the epistle must be interpreted in light of the conventions of Greco-Roman rhetoric. It must be viewed as a reasoned rhetorical attempt to counter a specific exigence experienced by a particular audience.

[365] For a sample of evaluations of Jude's style from grammarians and commentators, see F. H. Chase, "Jude, Epistle of," in *HDB*, ed. James Hastings, 5 vols. (New York: Charles Scribner's Sons and Edinburgh: T.& T. Clark, 1906) 2:800, col. 1– 802, col. 2; Bigg, 310–12; Mayor, lvi–lxvii; Bauckham, 6–7; Turner, 139–40.

[366] For a discussion of the three basic styles, see ch. 1.

[367] Cic. *Or.* 27.95.

[368] Cic. *Or.* 27.92–94; Quint. 12.10.60.

3
The Epistle of 2 Peter:
A Rhetorical Analysis

THE RHETORICAL UNIT

The entire epistle of 2 Peter will be the subject of the following analysis. There is debate concerning the integrity of 2 Peter, whether or not it is an original unity or a composite work. This issue will be addressed in chapter 4 in light of the following analysis and ancient rhetoric in general. Preliminary analysis demonstrates that 2 Peter is a rhetorical whole in its present state, and it will be treated below as such.

THE RHETORICAL SITUATION

The situation which prompted the author[1] of 2 Peter is decidedly rhetorical in nature and conforms well to Bitzer's definition of rhetorical situation.[2] Let us examine the three constituents of a rhetorical situation in relation to 2 Peter: the exigence, the audience, and the constraints.[3]

The exigence[4] of 2 Peter is the presence in the church of false teachers (2:1)

---

[1] In agreement with the current consensus of most scholars on the subject, I am assuming that 2 Peter is pseudonymous. For discussions of authorship, see Bauckham, 158–62; Tord Fornberg, *An Early Church in a Pluralistic Society: A Study of 2 Peter,* trans. Jean Gray, ConB 9 (Lund: CWK Gleerup, 1977) 15–19; Fuchs and Reymond, 30–37; Kelly, 235–47; Johann Michl, 156–58; Schelkle, 179–81; Schrage, 122, 126–27; Sidebottom, 99–100; Spicq, 191–93. Cf. E. M. B. Green, *2 Peter Reconsidered* (London: Tyndale Press, 1961) for a defense of Petrine authorship. I will hereafter refer to the author of 2 Peter simply as 2 Peter.

[2] Bitzer, 6.

[3] Bitzer, 6.

[4] For further discussion of the opponents and exigence faced by 2 Peter, see Bauckham, 154–57; H. C. C. Cavallin, "The False Teachers of 2 Pt as Pseudo-prophets," *NovT* 21 (1979) 263–70; Frederick W. Danker, "The Second Letter of Peter," in *Hebrews, James, 1 and 2 Peter, Jude, Revelation,* ed. Gerhard Krodel, PC (Philadelphia: Fortress, 1977) 82–85; Fornberg, 35–148, esp. 111–30; Fuchs and Reymond, 27–29; Kelly, 227–31; Jerome Neyrey, "The Apologetic Use of the Transfiguration in 2 Peter 1:16–21," *CBQ* 42 (1980) 504–19; Jerome Neyrey, "The Form and Background of the Polemic in 2 Peter" Ph.D. dissertation, Yale University, 1977) 11–162; Jerome Neyrey, "The Form and Background of

who apparently are backslidden Christians (2:15, 20–22). These false teachers have gathered a following to their practice and teaching (2:1–3a, 14, 18), particularly from among those who are weak or new in faith (2:14, 18). Their proselyzing continues to be a danger even to those of a mature faith (3:17).

Eschatological skepticism underlies the false teachers' doctrine. They had expected the parousia of Christ during the lifetime of the first generation of Christians, but that generation had passed away and the parousia had not yet materialized (3:4; cf. 3:9a). Consequently, they claim that the apostolic proclamation of the parousia is a myth (1:16a) and that Old Testament prophecies used to support that doctrine are not inspired, but rather, are the product of the prophets' own interpretation of their dreams and visions (1:20–21).

Along with their denial of Christ's parousia, these false teachers deny the reality of the judgment that was expected to accompany it (2:3b; cf. 3:10). Judgment is also based upon a belief that the world has never experienced divine intervention, but has always continued uninterrupted (3:4; cf. 2:3b; 3:5–7). The major outgrowth of the denial of judgment was a justification of moral libertinism (2:10, 19) which is outlined in detail in the stunning denunciation of 2:10b–22. This libertinism might also have arisen from a misinterpretation of Pauline doctrine (3:16).

2 Peter clearly perceives the exigence to be severe. The teaching and practice of the false teachers is the very antithesis of that which should characterize the Christian life (1:3–11; 3:11, 14–15a, 18). He considers their doctrine and deeds equivalent to a denial of Christianity, a return to the bondage to sin (2:2, 15, 19–22), and a guarantee of destruction (2:1, 3, 4–10a, 12; 3:7, 16; cf. 2:17). The exigence is particularly severe because many in the congregation(s) are following the false teachers down this road to destruction (2:1–3a, 14, 18; cf. 3:17). The audience certainly must also perceive the exigence within its midst, but what interest they have in it, what quality they ascribe to it, and what they see as the consequences of it, are impossible to determine from the content of the epistle.

The exigence is expected to remain. It is a precursor of the parousia of Christ and the judgment of the world, and will remain until they occur. The false teachers will experience the judgment (2:1, 3, 12, 17; cf. 3:10–13, 16) and their destruction will come swiftly (2:1). The very presence of the false teachers and their scoffing is a sign of the last days (3:3–4). The audience will also witness Christ's return in judgment (3:11–14).

However, the effects of the exigence can be minimized by the modification of the situation. 2 Peter desires his audience to strive for Christian maturity in accordance with traditional doctrine (1:3–11; 3:11–12, 14–15a, 17–18). He refutes the false teachers' charges against the doctrines of Christ's parousia (1:16–21; 3:1–4, 8–13) and judgment (2:3b–10a; 3:1–13). He exposes the false teachers' activity and doctrine and their consequences for the evil they really are (2:1–22). In doing so, he utilizes the authoritative memory and teachings of the Old Testament prophets (1:20–21; 3:2), the apostles (1:16–19), Paul (3:15–16), Jude (2:1–18; 3:1–3), Jesus himself (3:2), and Petrine tradition (1:12–19; 3:1). In this way 2 Peter hopes to put an end to the influence of the false teachers, save the audience from sharing their fate, and guide them toward Christian maturity.

The fact that 2 Peter is pseudonymous and stresses apostolic teaching may indicate that the exigence is more severe than it initially seems. The author does not choose to address the congregation under his own authority, but chooses rather to make his address under the authority of the apostle Peter, carefully grouping him with the other apostles (1:16–19; 3:2–4), especially Paul (3:15–16). Was it the case at that time that the leaders of the congregation, leaders of the second generation (3:4), did not have the ethos required to confront the false teachers? Or is our author a layman who has no ethos and must use a pseudonymous ploy because the church leadership is unwilling to respond? Or were the false teachers virtually the only leadership in the congregation, and the author, not having sufficient authority to alter the situation, chose to use that of the apostle Peter?

If a truly rhetorical audience consists of "those persons who are capable of being influenced by discourse and of being mediators of change,"[5] then 2 Peter's audience is such an audience.[6] It is an unspecified congregation(s) once addressed by 1 Peter (3:1) and by Paul (3:15). The audience is influenced by false teachers (2:1), has lost some of its members to their wiles (2:1–3a, 14, 18) and their spiritual well-being is threatened (3:17). However, they themselves have not yet been convinced by the false teachers (1:12; 3:17). This audience is thus subject to the exigence and capable of modifying it as 2 Peter advises. In fact, he fully assumes that they can respond as advised (1:3–11; 3:11–18).

Rhetorical constraints[7] have the power to direct the decision and action needed to modify the exigence. The numerous constraints operative within 2 Peter are rhetorical in nature. Beliefs and attitudes are major constraints. The belief system, the synopsis of doctrine, which begins 2 Peter (1:3–11) is the standard by which all else in the epistle is measured. The false teachers' doctrine and practice is judged accordingly and the audience is admonished to live according. Concerning attitudes, by associating the false teachers with characters traditionally abhorrent to Christians and to Jews, 2 Peter relies upon associated attitudes to prevent his audience from also becoming associated in kind. Examples of such associations are the perverse generation of Noah (2:5),

---

[5] Bitzer, 8.

[6] For further discussion on the audience of 2 Peter, see Fornberg, 111–30; Fuchs and Reymond, 29; Michl, 71–73; Schlekle, 177–78; Schrage, 126–27.

[7] For a list of rhetorical constraints, see Bitzer, 8, and ch. 2, p. 31.

the evil cities of Sodom and Gomorrah (2:6), and the prophet Balaam (2:15), all of which elicit negative attitudes. Resistive attitudes are also elicited by the numerous traditional negative descriptions which are used in the *digressio* (2:10b-22) to portray the false teachers' character and activity.

Documents, facts, and tradition act as constraints in 2 Peter. Cited documents do not play a direct role as constraints, but the mention of 1 Peter (3:1) and the letters of Paul (3:15-16) suffice to bring their content to bear indirectly on the exigence. Regarding facts, to those in the audience who have not yet been convinced by the false teachers, the doctrines 2 Peter espouses would be perceived as fact. For them, the doctrine of the parousia, the judgment, and Christian maturity would be readily accepted as constraints. More importantly, tradition plays an enormous constraining role in 2 Peter. This tradition includes the contents of the homily (1:3-11), Synoptic tradition (1:17-18), Old Testament prophetic tradition (1:19-21), Old Testament and Jewish tradition (2:4-7, 15-16, 22; 3:5-6), and Christ's and the apostolic tradition (1:16-18; 3:1-3, 15-16), all of which support the rhetoric of 2 Peter and/or offer deterents.

Positive and negative images are constraints. There are the positive images of entering the eternal kingdom (1:11), new heavens and a new earth in which righteousness dwells (3:13), and being found by Christ at his parousia without spot or blemish (3:14). These images surely act as constraints because the audience will not want to jeopardize their share in these. There are also the numerous negative images of swift destruction (2:1), destruction that is not asleep (2:3), casting into hell and being committed to pits of nether gloom to be kept until judgment (2:4), the fate of Sodom and Gomorrah (2:6), being kept under punishment until the day of judgment (2:9), slavery to corruption and defilement (2:19, 20), a dog turning back to its own vomit (2:22), a sow in the mire (2:22), and the fire of judgment (3:7, 10, 12). These images constrain the audience from behaving in such a manner that these fates become their own.

Interests and motives act as constraints. On the positive side, it is surely in the audience's interest to inherit eternal life (1:11) and to live holy and godly lives so as to hasten the parousia and participate in the new heavens and new earth (3:12). On the negative side, to be found at Christ's return without spot or blemish (3:14) and not suffer corruption (2:18-22), judgment and destruction (2:1, 3, 9, 12; 3:7, 10, 12, 16) is advantageous as well. 2 Peter mentions that the main motive of the false teachers is greed (2:3, 14) which results in the audience being exploited (2:3), falsely enticed (2:14), and enslaved (2:19). The audience should be constrained by the natural desire not to be made the fool, merely serving someone else's ends. 2 Peter's motives appear to be the spiritual health of the audience (1:3-15; 3:1-2, 11-18). Such pure motives engender goodwill which is itself a constraint.

The major constraint, and one which the pseudonymous author clearly wanted to employ, is the ethos of the apostle Peter. Anything that a revered apostle like Peter said would serve as a constraint to those who still considered his teachings to be authoritative. Pseudonymity indicates that 2 Peter believed the teaching of the apostle Peter enjoyed great authority with the audience. The refutation of the false teachers' doctrine (1:16-21; 2:3b-10a; 3:3-13) by an apostle would be an effective constraint, severely weakening its credibility. 2 Peter also relies upon the ethos of the prophets (1:20-21; 3:2); the apostles (1:1, 16, 18; 3:2), especially Paul (3:15-16); and Jesus Christ (3:2), drawing upon their testimony in his proof and refutation. In themselves, 2 Peter's proofs in rebuttal and counteraccusation are well-constructed, reasoned, and serve as constraints. If given credence, the doctrines which they undermine would obtain less adherence and those which they support would obtain more adherence.

THE SPECIES OF RHETORIC, THE QUESTION, AND THE STASIS

Before discussing the species, question, and stasis, the genre of 2 Peter must be briefly identified. 2 Peter is not only an epistle, but also a testament as well.[8] The content of the testament is twofold. First, the dying individual provides a summary to his community of the principal ethical and religious doctrines which are to be adhered to after his death. Second, he prophesies concerning the destiny of his community, often prompted by apocalyptic revelations of the end-days. Both the doctrine and the prophecy are bases of eschatological admonitions.[9] Throughout the analysis, aspects of the testament will be discussed in relation to the rhetoric.

2 Peter is to be classified as deliberative rhetoric.[10] First, it is clearly intended to advise and dissuade the audience with regard to a particular way of thinking and course of action.[11] This purpose is shared with the testament genre itself, and is indicated by the use of the reminder topic (1:12, 13, 15; 3:1-2) and the emphasis upon teaching (1:3-11) and exhortation (3:11-18). Second, as in deliberative, the time reference in 2 Peter is mainly future.[12] 2 Peter looks forward to future

---

[8] 2 Peter is one of several Christian testaments: Acts 20:17-34; 2 Timothy; *Acts Pet.* 36-39; *Acts John* 106-7; *Acts Thom.* 159-60.

[9] A. B. Kolenkow, "The Genre Testament and Forecasts of the Future in the Hellenistic Jewish Milieu," *JSJ* 6 (1975) 57-71; Otto Knoch, *Die "Testamente" des Petrus und Paulus: Die Sicherung der apostolischen Überlieferung in der spätneutestamentlichen Zeit*, SBS 62 (Stuttgart: KBW Verlag, 1973); J. Munck, "Discours d'adieu dans le Nouveau Testament et dans la litterature biblique," in *Aux Sources de la Tradition Chrétienne, M. Goguel Festschrift* (Neuchâtel: Delachaux and Niestlé, 1950) 155-70; Ethelbert Stauffer, *New Testament Theology*, trans. John Marsh (London: SCM Press, 1955) 344-47. With special reference to 2 Peter, see Bauckham, 131-35; Otto Knoch, "Das Vermächtnis des Petrus: Der zweite Petrusbrief," in *Wort Gottes in der Zeit, K. H. Schelkle Festschrift*, eds. H. Feld and J. Nolte (Düsseldorf: Patmos Verlag, 1973) 149-50 = *Die "Testamente" des Petrus und Paulus*, 65-81; Neyrey, *Form and Background*, 99-105.

[10] For more on deliberative rhetoric, see ch. 1.

[11] Ar. *Rhet.* 1.3.1358b.3; *Rhet. ad Alex.* 1.1421b.17-23; Cic. *Inv.* 1.5.7; *Part. Or.* 24.83ff.; Her. 1.2.2; Quint. 3.4.6, 9; 3.8.1-6, 67-70; cf. Cic. *De Or.* 1.31.141.

[12] Ar. *Rhet.* 1.3.1358b.4; 1.4.1359a.1-2; 2.18.1392a.5; Quint. 3.4.7; 3.8.6; cf. Cic. *Part. Or.* 3.10; 20.69.

Christian growth (1:3–11), heavenly rewards (1:11; 3:13), the parousia (1:16; 3:10, 12–13), the judgment (2:1, 3, 9, 12; 3:7), and the consummation (1:11; 2:9; 3:7, 10, 12–13, 18). It is in the very nature of the testament genre to look forward to the time after the death of the testator. Third, the fact that the question behind 2 Peter involves what is advantageous, necessary, and expedient, and their opposites, also indicates it is deliberative rhetoric.[13]

However, 2 Peter also contains concentrated sections of judicial and epideictic rhetoric. Judicial rhetoric[14] is clearly the proper designation of 1:16–2:10a and 3:1–13 where 2 Peter refutes and counteraccuses the claims of his opponents.[15] The time reference is clearly past, as characterizes judicial rhetoric,[16] for both the teaching denied and the denial itself occurred in the past. The section 2:10b–22 is to be designated as epideictic rhetoric.[17] It is a barbed denunciation of the false teachers based upon their teachings and deeds aimed at decreasing audience assent to both.[18] The time referent is present as is typical of epideictic.[19]

In his effort to persuade his audience to adhere to the knowledge and promises of Christ and to dissuade them from believing and behaving like the false teachers, 2 Peter relies upon judicial rhetoric to refute his opponents' claims and to bolster his own, and he relies upon epideictic rhetoric to lessen his opponents' ethos. This is a good example of the fact that all three types of rhetoric rely upon each other to be effective.[20] It also illustrates that epideictic rhetoric often constitutes extensive parts of deliberative,[21] since what deliberative advises and dissuades, epideictic praises and blames.[22]

There is only one question[23] behind 2 Peter's rhetoric. Therefore it is a simple rather than a complex case.[24] The question is, "Is the doctrine of the parousia and the judgment adequately supported, and are moral restraints and Christian growth essential?" This question is rational rather than legal because it does not involve written law,[25] and it is definite rather than indefinite because it involves

[13] Ar. *Rhet.* 1.3.1358b.5; *Rhet. ad Alex.* 1.1421b.21ff.; 6.1427b.39ff.; Cic. *Inv.* 2.4.12; 2.51.155–58.176; *Part. Or.* 24.83–87; *Top.* 24.91; Her. 3.2.3–5.9; Quint. 3.8.1–6, 22–35; cf. Cic. *De Or.* 2.82.333–36; Quint. 3.4.16.
[14] For more on judicial rhetoric, see ch. 1.
[15] Ar. *Rhet.* 1.3.1358b.3; *Rhet. ad Alex.* 4.1426b.22ff.; Cic. *Inv.* 1.5.7; Quint. 3.4.6–7, 9.
[16] Ar. *Rhet.* 1.3.1358b.4; 2.18.1392a.5; Cic. *Part. Or.* 20.69; cf. Cic. *Part. Or.* 3.10.
[17] For more on epideictic rhetoric, see ch. 1.
[18] Ar. *Rhet.* 1.3.1358b.5; *Rhet. ad Alex.* 3.1426b.36–39; Cic. *Inv.* 2.4.12; 2.51.155–56; *Top.* 24.91; Her. 3.6.10; cf. Quint. 3.4.16.
[19] Ar. *Rhet.* 1.3.1358b.4; cf. Cic. *Part. Or.* 3.10; 20.69.
[20] *Rhet. ad Alex.* 5.1427b.31ff.; Quint. 3.4.16.
[21] Her. 3.8.15; cf. Quint. 3.4.11.
[22] Quint. 3.7.28.
[23] For more on question, see ch. 1.
[24] Cic. *Inv.* 1.12.17; Quint. 3.10.1–2; cf. Quint. 7.2.8.
[25] Cic. *Inv.* 1.12.17; Quint. 3.5.4–5.

facts and persons.[26] A reconstruction of the conflicting causes giving rise to the question underlying the stasis would resemble the following:

Cause 1: The false teachers and their followers would assert that the apostolic teaching concerning the parousia of Christ is a cleverly devised myth (1:16a) based on personal interpretation of prophecy (1:20-21a). It is clearly proven false by the fact that those expected to witness it, the first generation Christians, have died (3:4), and God's dealing with creation does not include intervention in history (3:4). Therefore, be free from moral constraints.

Cause 2: 2 Peter would assert that the apostolic teaching concerning parousia of Christ is not a cleverly devised myth, but is rather based on eyewitness accounts of the Transfiguration and upon Old Testament prophecy. Thus, prophecy is inspired (1:16a-18) and not personal interpretation (1:19-21). The delay of the parousia does not invalidate the parousia doctrine, but is rather the result of God's mercy (3:8-9). Also, God's activity in history is one of intervention in judgment, not non-interference (3:5-7, 10). Therefore moral restraint and Christian growth are essential to escaping judgment and sharing in the new heavens and new earth.

Question: Is the doctrine of the parousia and the judgment adequately supported, and are moral restraints and Christian growth essential?

As typical of deliberative and epideictic rhetoric, the stasis is one of quality.[27] It concerns the nature of a thing. In this case, the question is whether it is apostolic doctrine or the doctrine of the false teachers that is correct.

INVENTION, ARRANGEMENT, AND STYLE

The following is a detailed consideration of 2 Peter's use of invention, arrangement, and style in the enablement of his audience to modify the exigence facing them. The reader is referred to figure 2 at the conclusion of this chapter which reflects the results of this analysis and will be useful to guide the reading. The inventional topics of 2 Peter are outlined in appendix 2, and the figures are outlined in appendix 4.

The Exordium (1:3-15)

Dismissing the epistolary prescript for a moment, we will discuss the *exordium* of 2 Peter. The *exordium* is the first part of arrangement in which the

---

[26] Cic. *Inv.* 1.6.8; *De Or.* 1.31.138; 2.10.42; 2.19.78; 3.28.109; *Or.* 14.46; *Part. Or.* 1.4; *Top.* 21-22; Quint. 3.5.4-18.

[27] Quint. 3.8.4; 7.4.1-3; cf. 3.7.28. For more on the stasis of quality, see ch. 1.

rhetor seeks to prepare the audience for what follows.[28] This epistle, as deliberative rhetoric, need not have an *exordium* per se,[29] but its opening must have some resemblance to one, even if it is no more than a mere heading.[30] Deliberative may have an *exordium* for the rhetor's own sake, or on account of the opponents, or if the audience attaches too much or too little importance to the question (in the rhetor's opinion). In this latter case he must remove prejudice and magnify or minimize the importance of the subject.[31]

In general, the *exordium* can be dispensed with if the audience is fully aware of what the rhetor will say, and, if such is the case, a short summary of the case is more than adequate.[32] The length of the *exordium* is also determined by the case. A simple case requires only a short *exordium*, and a complicated, suspect, or unpopular case requires a longer one.[33]

Although deliberative rhetoric and a simple case, 2 Peter provides a lengthy *exordium* of 13 verses (in 1:3-15). The length of the *exordium* is largely explained by the fact that 2 Peter is using the testament genre which possesses introductory standard features which are discussed below. However, it is probable that other factors are also at work. The length of 2 Peter's *exordium* may indicate that his audience is not fully aware of or prepared for what he has to say. Perhaps too, his audience does not perceive the exigence negatively or fully understand its gravity, and so he is trying to magnify its importance by setting up the standard of Christian growth for comparison (1:3-11).

There are five kinds of cause which may underlie the *exordium*: the honorable, the mean, the doubtful or ambiguous, the extraordinary, and the obscure.[34] 2 Peter's *exordium* is prompted by the honorable cause which wins the approval of the audience by its very nature.[35] "A cause is regarded as of the honorable kind when we either defend what seems to deserve defence by all men, or attack what all men seem in duty bound to attack . . ."[36] 2 Peter's cause is honorable because it is defending the teaching of the apostles (1:3-11; 1:16-2:10a; 3:1-13), including the teaching of Peter (3:1) and Paul (3:15-16), against attack. The audience holds this teaching in great respect (1:1, 12; 3:17) and its defense is sure to win their approval.

There are two types of approach to take in the *exordium*: the *principium* or the *insinuatio*.[37] 2 Peter takes the *principium* which, directly and in plain

---

[28] For more on the *exordium*, see ch. 1.

[29] Ar. *Rhet.* 3.14.1415b.12; Cic. *Part. Or.* 4.13.

[30] Ar. *Rhet.* 3.14.1415b.8; Quint. 3.8.6, 10; cf. Cic. *Part. Or.* 4.13.

[31] Ar. *Rhet.* 3.14.1415b.12.

[32] Ar. *Rhet.* 3.14.1415b.8; Quint. 4.1.72.

[33] Quint. 4.1.62.

[34] For references and further discussion of these five causes, see ch. 2, p. 35.

[35] Cic. *Inv.* 1.15.20; Her. 1.3.5; Quint. 4.1.41.

[36] Her. 1.3.5.

[37] For references and further discussion of these two approaches, see ch. 2, p. 35-36.

language, makes the audience well-disposed, receptive, and attentive.[38] With the honorable cause, such as that of 2 Peter, no *exordium* is really needed[39] because it wins approval by its very nature. However, the *principium* characterizes an honorable cause when an *exordium* is used.[40] When the *principium* is used with an honorable cause, the rhetor must show why the cause is honorable, briefly announce what will be discussed, and/or use the topics designed to produce goodwill so as to increase the advantage which already exists.[41] 2 Peter does this. The homily of 1:3-11 introduces numerous topics used throughout the rhetoric to support his insistence upon both avoiding the false teachers' words and deeds and living a life according to the way of truth. As shown below, 2 Peter also utilizes the topics designed to produce goodwill so as to increase his advantage.

The *exordium* of 2 Peter performs its three main functions of making the audience attentive, receptive, and well-disposed.[42] 2 Peter makes his audience attentive[43] by stressing the importance of what he is to discuss. These matters pertain to life and godliness, and ultimately to entrance into the eternal kingdom (1:3-11); they are the truth in which the audience is established (1:12), and are worthy of being recalled during Peter's lifetime (1:12-13) and even after his death (1:15). The testament genre itself clues the audience that matters of crucial importance are contained within. It is the nature of the testament to deliver crucial doctrine and prophetic insight, both for this life and for the next.

The welfare of the audience and the proper worship and relationship to God are clearly dependent upon what follows, because it pertains to life and godliness (1:3), escape from worldly corruption (1:4), Christian growth (1:5-10), and eternal reward (1:11). By placing the doctrine so central to his deliberation first in the *exordium* (1:3-11), and then emphasizing that such matters are to be remembered in both the present and in the future (1:12-13, 15), 2 Peter is clearly bidding audience attention. Attention is also sought by dwelling on the hopes of every Christian, especially eternal life (1:11), and by admonitions and entreaties recurring throughout the homily (1:5-7, 10).

Ethos plays a very large role in gaining attention in 2 Peter. The epistle begins in 1:1 with a reference to Simon Peter, the revered apostle, whose ethos pervades the epistle. The intimation of death, and the concern expressed that the audience be kept informed, bolsters ethos (1:12-15). This is discussed below in greater length.

Receptivity follows naturally from gaining audience attention[44] and by

---

[38] Cic. *Inv.* 1.15.20; Her. 1.4.6; Quint. 4.1.42.

[39] Cic. *Inv.* 1.15.21; Her. 1.4.6; cf. *Rhet. ad Alex.* 29.1437b.33ff.

[40] Cic. *Inv.* 1.15.21; Her. 1.4.6.

[41] Cic. *Inv.* 1.15.21-16.23; Her. 1.4.6-5.8.

[42] For more on the functions of the *exordium*, see ch. 1.

[43] For a complete list of procedures for gaining audience attention, and the ancient references, see ch. 2, p. 36.

[44] Her. 1.4.7; Quint. 4.1.34.

providing a brief summary of the case.[45] The homily (1:3-11)[46] is a brief summary, but not so much of the case as it is of the threatened doctrine which spurs 2 Peter to deliberate in the first place. His audience likely agrees with what he says in the homily because it probably derives from Peter (3:1) and the apostles (3:2, 15 16; cf. 1:16ff.). The homily, therefore, would facilitate receptivity for the remainder of the rhetoric.

To obtain audience goodwill, the rhetor can concentrate on the facts of the case itself, and on the persons connected with the case, including the rhetor himself, the audience, and the opposition.[47] In the *exordium*, 2 Peter does not even mention the opposition, and touches only indirectly on the facts of the case – the challenge to orthodox doctrine. He concentrates mainly upon Peter and to some extent upon the audience. 2 Peter's concentration upon Peter is not unexpected, for in deliberative rhetoric it was common for the rhetor to refer to himself or his opponents.[48] Also, reference to self was intrinsic to the introduction of the testament genre.

As previously discussed, there are several ways to elicit goodwill connected with the person of the rhetor.[49] 2 Peter exhibits several of these techniques. If being perceived as a good man is the strongest influence for obtaining goodwill,[50] then 2 Peter has done well in utilizing the apostle Peter. Clearly Peter was perceived as a good man, or our pseudonymous author would not have utilized him for his rhetoric. This perception is heightened by 2 Peter's grouping of Peter with the apostles (1:1, 16-18) and by implying that he has escaped the world of corruption through the promises (as indicated by the shift from the first person plural in 1:1-4 to the second person plural in 1:5ff.). This maneuver suggests that the apostles are considered sanctified by the author, and presumably by his audience, and enhances Peter's ethos.

Peter also is presented as having undertaken the case out of a sense of duty to a friend, because of a serious moral consideration, and because of an honorable reason. The underlying tone of 1:12-15 is that Peter must leave a summary of authoritative teaching for the benefit of his audience. The serious moral consideration is the fact that the audience, although believers, could fail to utilize the knowledge and promises of God (1:3-4) and fall prey to worldly corruption (1:4), fail to supplement their faith (1:5-7), and become ineffective and unfruitful, blind, and not confirm their call and election (1:8-10). The honorable reason motivating the writing is to provide the audience with a reminder of the essence of their faith.

---

[45] Ar. *Rhet.* 3.14.1415a.6; Cic. *Inv.* 1.16.23; Quint. 4.1.34; 10.1.48.

[46] For an explanation of the designation "homily," see below, p. 96.

[47] Ar. *Rhet.* 3.14.1415a–1415b.7; Cic. *Inv.* 1.16.22; *De Or.* 2.79.321-22; *Part. Or.* 8.28; Her. 1.4.8–5.8; Quint. 4.1.6-15.

[48] Quint. 3.8.8 after Ar. *Rhet.* 3.14.1415a.7.

[49] For a list of these methods, and the ancient references, see ch. 2, pp. 37-38.

[50] Quint. 4.1.7; Aug. *De Doct. Chr.* 4.27; cf. Ar. *Rhet.* 1.2.1356a.3 4; 3.14.1415a.7.

2 Peter portrays Peter referring without arrogance to his own acts and services. The section 1:12–15 is masterful in this regard. In 1:12, Peter states that his purpose in providing the homily is merely to remind his audience of its content. In the same sentence he qualifies this service with the phrase "though you know them and are established in the truth that you have," abrogating any impression that he speaks down to the audience since he clearly acknowledges their knowledge. Besides, the testament genre itself portrays leaders dutifully leaving a legacy, and in it arrogance played no part.

Peter also entreats with a humble spirit. He exhorts his audience to supplement their faith (1:5) and be zealous to confirm their call and election (1:10). The motivation is purely for his audience's sake to assure that they not be ineffectual and unfruitful in the knowledge of Christ (1:8), that they never fall (1:10), and that they be provided an entrance into the eternal kingdom (1:11).

In order to obtain goodwill, Peter is also portrayed as one dwelling on the difficulties yet to befall him, making it clear that he is about to die just as Jesus told him (1:13–15). Peter also gives the impression that his words are presided over by God, for it was understood of the testament genre that the dying hero's words were inspired. Here Peter has been shown his own future by Jesus himself and this vision has in part prompted his words.

Methods for obtaining goodwill connected with the audience have been enumerated above.[51] Of these, 2 Peter does not show excessive flattery, for it is assumed that the audience has yet to achieve the spiritual maturity that he outlines in 1:3–11. However, he does show his audience esteem by acknowledging that they have things pertaining to life and godliness (1:3), divine promises (1:4), and know the contents of the homily and are established in the truth that they have (1:12).[52] 2 Peter skillfully uses his praise to further his case by acknowledging his audience's establishment in the truth before he deliberates to persuade them to remain established in that truth.

Cicero writes of goodwill derived from the person of the opponents,

> Good-will is acquired from the person of the opponents if they are brought into hatred, unpopularity, or contempt. They will be hated if some act of their is presented which is base, haughty, cruel, or malicious; they will become unpopular if we present their power, political influence, wealth, family connexions, and their arrogant and intolerable use of these advantages, so that they seem to rely on these rather than on the justice of their case. They will be brought into contempt if we reveal their laziness, carelessness, sloth, indolent pursuits or luxurious idleness.[53]

All these methods of obtaining goodwill are to be employed throughout the rhetoric.[54] 2 Peter does not acquire goodwill from his opponents in the *exordium*

---

[51] See ch. 2, p. 37.

[52] Compare Jude's use of a similar sentiment in his *exordium* (v 3) where he states that the audience already has the precepts of faith and only needs to contend for them.

[53] Cic. *Inv.* 1.16.22. Similar instruction is given in Cic. *Part. Or.* 8.28 and Her. 1.5.8; cf. Cic. *De Or.* 2.79.321; Quint. 4.1.6.

[54] Ar. *Rhet.* 3.14.1415b.9 (attention only); Cic. *De Or.* 2.79.323; Her. 1.7.11.

itself. However, the above advice could just as well have guided his description of his opponents in chapter 2 where he does everything possible to destroy the goodwill enjoyed by the false teachers. The homily of 1:3–11 acts as a foil for their behavior. It is an asset which 2 Peter later capitalizes on to obtain goodwill for himself and to take goodwill from his opponent.

The *exordium* should briefly indicate the points which the rhetor purposes to address, points which serve the purposes of the *probatio*[55] and are reiterated in the *peroratio*.[56] Thus, there should be a close connection between *exordium*, *probatio*, and *peroratio*. This was the case for Jude and is even more evident in 2 Peter. The homily of 1:3–11 contains several topics developed further in the *probatio* and reiterated in the *peroratio*.

With bold affirmation, 1:3 introduces the topic of the power (δύναμις) of Christ. In the *probatio* in 1:16 the power (δύναμις) of Christ is affirmed against the false teachers' belittling of the doctrine of Christ's parousia. More central, the topic of godliness (εὐσέβεια) is introduced in 1:3, 6, 7 as a mark of Christian maturity. In the *probatio*, the fate of the godly (εὐσεβής, 2:9) is contrasted with that of the ungodly (ἀσεβής, 2:5, 6; ἀσεβέω, 2:5). Later in the *probatio* the topic is reiterated in an exhortation to live godly lives in keeping with eschatological realities (εὐσέβεια, 3:11). Also, the topic is expressed in terms of spots and blemishes (σπίλοι καὶ μῶμοι, 2:13), in the *peroratio* the audience is admonished to be found at the parousia without spot or blemish (ἄσπιλοι καὶ ἀμώμητοι, 3:14). Closely related to the topic of godliness is the topic of the way which is developed in the *probatio*. The false teachers are said to revile the way of truth (ἡ ὁδὸς τῆς ἀληθείας, 2:2), forsake the right way (εὐθεῖαν ὁδόν, 2:15), and turn from the way of righteousness (τὴν ὁδὸν τῆς δικαιοσύνης, 2:21).

In 1:4 the topic of Christ's promises (ἐπαγγέλματα) is first presented. These promises enable the Christian to escape worldly corruption and become partakers of the divine nature. In the *probatio*, 2 Peter refutes the scoffers' ridicule of Christ's promises (ἐπαγγελία) to return (3:4) by affirming that the promise (ἐπαγγελία) is slow to be fulfilled to allow for repentance (3:9). The topic if further developed in the affirmation of the promise (ἐπάγγελμα) of a new heavens and earth (3:13). As references above show, the *probatio* in 3:11–13 ties the topic of godliness and promises together, making the point that godliness is the result of participation in the promises.

The *exordium* introduces the topic of knowledge (ἐπίγνωσις) which plays a central role in 2 Peter. The knowledge (ἐπίγνωσις) of God and Jesus (1:2), or simply Jesus (1:3 [probably], 8), is the knowledge of the godhead obtained at conversion which forms the basis of Christian growth. Knowledge (γνῶσις) is to be gained from Christian growth (1:5, 6).[57] In the *probatio*, the knowledge

---

[55] Cic. *De Or.* 2.80.325; Quint. 4.1.23–27; cf. Cic. *De Or.* 2.79.320.

[56] See ch. 1.

[57] Ἐπίγνωσις (1:2, 3, 8; 2:20) and the verb ἐπιγινώσκειν (2:21, twice) refer to the fundamental knowledge of Christ essential to Christian conversion. This is indicated by their objects: ἐπίγνωσις has Christ as object, and ἐπιγινώσκειν has "the way of righteousness" as object.

(ἐπίγνωσις) of Christ is said to have enabled the Christian to escape the defilements of the world (2:20). The audience is also exhorted to know (γινώσκειν) certain doctrine (1:20; 3:8). This state is contrasted with the worse state of having known (ἐπιγινώσκω, twice) the way of righteousness, but to have turned from it (2:21). In the *peroratio*, the audience is admonished to grow in the knowledge (γνῶσις) of Christ (3:18).

In 1:4 the topic of escaping worldly corruption is also introduced, a topic closely related to the topics of knowledge and promise. Here in the *exordium*, 2 Peter affirms that the promises of Christ enable the Christian to escape worldly corruption (ἀποφυγόντες τῆς ἐν τῷ κόσμῳ ἐν ἐπιθυμίᾳ φθορᾶς). This topic is reiterated in slightly different terms in the *probatio* in 2:20 where it is the knowledge of Christ that enables the Christian to escape the defilements of the world (ἀποφυγόντες τὰ μιάσματα τοῦ κοσμοῦ). This state is contrasted with failure to heed the knowledge of Christ only to become entangled in worldly defilements (2:20–22).[58] Also in the *probatio*, in 2:12, using the same key term φθορᾷ, the topic of 1:4 is presented antithetically. Whereas in 1:4 the promises afforded the Christian enable escape from corruption, in 2:12 the false teachers' misuse of their Christian lives has made them the prey of worldly corruption. In 1:9 forgetting one's baptism is akin to backsliding and a return to worldly corruption. This topic is developed in the *probatio* in 2:20–22 where backsliding is discussed with reference to the topics of knowledge of Christ and worldly corruption.

The topic of being "established" is introduced in 1:12 where the audience is said to be established (στηρίζω) in truth. In the *probatio* in 2:14 the false teachers are not established, but are unstable (ἀστήρικτος) souls. In the *peroratio* 2 Peter reiterates and develops this topic by making the contrast more clearly, calling the false teachers unstable (ἀστήρικτος, 3:16), and by reaffirming the audience's stability (στηριγμός, 3:17). The entire epistle is evidence of 2 Peter's concern that his audience not loose their stability by following those who are unstable.

The *exordium* (and *peroratio*) should elicit the pathos desired from the audience more than elsewhere in the rhetoric.[59] In the *exordium* positive pathos is elicited for the person of Peter and for the Christian hope, pathos which will facilitate the desired negative response of the audience to the false teachers and their doctrine. In the *exordium* it is sometimes necessary to frighten the audience to gain objectives.[60] Expressions of wishing, detestation, entreaty, or anxiety can

---

It contrasts γνῶσις (1:5, 6; 3:18) and γινώσκειν (1:20; 3:8) or knowledge gained through experience. Rudolph Bultmann, "γινώσκω," *TDNT* 1:701–8; Picirelli, "The meaning of 'Epignosis,'" *EvQ* 47 (1975) 85–93; Bauckham, 169–70; Mayor, 171–74.

[58] Cf. 2:19 where the followers of the false teachers are described as those who have barely escaped (ἀποφεύγω) those who live in error.

[59] Cic. *De Or.* 2.77.310–11; *Part. Or.* 8.27.

[60] Quint. 4.1.20–21.

be used to elicit fear.[61] The exhortation in 1:5-7, 10-11 serves as entreaty and is strengthened by the emotive words σπουδή, "eagar," and σπουδάζω, "be zealous," used to describe the approach to take towards Christian maturity (1:5, 10; cf. 3:14). The testament genre by its very nature, as the dying words of a revered figure, instills anxiety and fear in the audience, the anxiety aroused with the awareness of the impending loss of a key member of the community. Here the anxiety is over the past experience of the death of Peter.

As noted above, the *exordium* can be faulty on a number of counts.[62] It is tempting to classify 2 Peter's *exordium* as "vulgar," for it could be used in a number of different cases. The entire *exordium*, both the homily of 1:3-11 and most of the personal material of 1:12-15, could just as easily be used to head an epistle of Paul aimed at libertines, for example Galatians. However, this is in the nature of the exigence. 2 Peter's *exordium* should not be classified as vulgar because, as previously demonstrated, he has subtlely woven topics and doctrine that he wishes to expound in the *probatio* into the *exordium*.

The question arises, "Has 2 Peter's conformity to the testament genre exposed his *exordium* to the criticism that it produces results different from those the case requires"? The testament genre requires this initial doctrinal section, but, although it does contain the doctrine and deeds which 2 Peter wishes the audience to note, it only indirectly relates to the doctrinal and ethical disputes which characterize the *probatio*. The *exordium* has been forced by the genre to be a positive presentation of the Christian faith, whereas the *probatio* and *peroratio* are mainly a negative rebuttal of charges made against the faith. This negative aspect should be found in the *exordium* to prepare for what follows, but it is lacking. In this respect the *exordium* produces only half the results that the case requires, and so is faulty.

Before leaving this section, it should be noted that 1:12-15 is the body-opening of the letter. The reminder topic is akin to the full disclosure formula "I wish you to know that."[63] There is a compliance statement referring to previous instruction,[64] a responsibility statement using μέλω,[65] a reassurance of continued allegiance,[66] and a given motivation for writing.[67] Like the body-opening, this section gives the principle occasion of the letter and proceeds from a common basis by allusion to subject matter shared by both parties.[68] In this last regard, the body-opening of the letter most closely functions like the *exordium* of the testament.

---

[61] Quint. 4.1.33; cf. 4.1.20-21.

[62] For a listing of the faults of the *exordium*, see ch. 2, p. 40.

[63] White, 2-5, 40.

[64] White, 24-25, 41. Here, however, the instruction is not that of the addressor.

[65] White, 7-9.

[66] White, 5-7.

[67] White, 3-5.

[68] White, 18-19, 39.

The Epistolary Prescript or "Quasi-Exordium" (1:1-2)

As in the analysis of Jude, it is appropriate now to return to the epistolary prescript. The prescript is necessitated by the decision to send the work as an epistle, and it is constituted of standard formulae and theological designations. However, it shares several rhetorical aims with the *exordium*: making the audience attentive, well-disposed, and ready to receive instruction; establishing desired ethos and pathos; and introducing points to be developed in the *probatio*.

The self-designation of Peter as "Simon Peter, a servant and apostle of Jesus Christ," and his speaking as a member of the apostolate immediately establishes his ethos. He has the authority of one of the Twelve, one chosen by Christ as apostle, witness to Christ's life and minsitry, and commissioned to continue his ministry in an authoritative role. This ethos pervades the entire epistle. As previously stated, the ethos of the rhetor is central to gaining audience attention and receptivity.[69]

Concerning obtaining goodwill from the person of the rhetor,[70] the rhetor perceived as a good man is the strongest influence in the case.[71] Also important is giving the impression of being a reliable witness,[72] and as an apostle, Peter's witness is surely perceived as reliable. As an apostolic message, there is automatically the impression that the words are presided over by the "gods."[73] The writing of an apostle would be understood by the audience as motivated by a sense of duty to a friend[74] and serious moral considerations.[75] By designating himself as servant of Jesus Christ,[76] and his addressees as "those who have obtained a faith of equal standing with ours," he shows that he shares a status with his addressees and lessens the possibility of offending his audience by seeming to speak from an aloof position.[77] The blessing naturally functions to obtain goodwill.[78]

In the course of obtaining goodwill from the person of the audience[79] by affirming that they "have obtained a faith of equal standing with ours in the righteousness of our God and Savior Jesus Christ," 2 Peter shows the honorable esteem in which the audience is held.[80] This faith is held by Peter and the

[69] Ar. *Rhet.* 3.14.1415a.7.

[70] For a listing of methods for obtaining goodwill from the person of the rhetor, and for the ancient references, see ch. 2, pp. 37–38.

[71] Quint. 4.1.7; Aug. *De Doct. Chr.* 4.27; cf. Ar. *Rhet.* 1.2.1356a.3–4.

[72] Quint. 4.1.7.

[73] Quint. 10.1.48.

[74] Cic. *Part. Or.* 8.28; Quint. 4.1.7.

[75] Quint. 4.1.7.

[76] On the nature of δοῦλος, see ch. 2, p. 41, n. 83.

[77] Cic. *Inv.* 1.16.22; Quint. 4.1.10.

[78] Cic. *Inv.* 1.16.22 states prayer and entreaty obtain goodwill.

[79] For discussion of obtaining goodwill from the audience, see ch. 2, p. 37.

[80] Cic. *Inv.* 1.16.22; Her. 1.5.8. Compare the wording of Jude's *exordium*: "Being very eager to write to you of our common salvation" (v 3).

apostles,[81] and is God-given.[82] This praise is linked to the furtherance of the case[83] since persuading the audience to uphold their faith and remain righteous is central to 2 Peter's deliberative rhetoric (1:3–11; 3:11–14, 17–18). The theological characterization of the recipients is part of the epistolary style and has the formal function of establishing a common ground between the rhetor and the audience[84] and increasing positive pathos.[85]

The prescript also briefly indicates topics which 2 Peter proposes to address in the *probatio*.[86] As discussed above, the topic of knowledge is introduced here. In order to describe the nature of faith, the typical binitarian formula "from God our Father and the Lord Jesus Christ" has been altered by 2 Peter to "in the knowledge (ἐπίγνωσις) of our God and Jesus Christ." Also, in 1:1, 2 Peter introduces the topic of righteousness (δικαιοσύνη). In the *probatio* he compares the righteous (2:5, 7, 8) with the unrighteous (ἄδικος, 2:9) who have forsaken the way of righteousness (2:15, 21) and will not partake of the new heavens and earth in which righteousness dwells (3:13).

Rhetorical Features of the Testament Genre (1:3–15)

Being of the testament genre, the *exordium* exhibits several genre specific features which are rhetorically effective. Section 1:3–11 constitutes a "miniature homily" presenting the essence of apostolic preaching. It conforms to the standard homiletic pattern found in Jewish and early Christian literature. First (a) there is an historical theological section which reiterates the acts of God in salvation history (1:3–4). Second (b) there are ethical exhortations based on (a) which anticipate (c) (1:5–10). Finally (c) there is an eschatological section in which salvation is promised or judgment threatened (1:11). The homily is intended to present the essence of the dying individual's message as he intended it to be remembered after his death (cf. 1:12 15).[87] In 2 Peter the ethical and eschatological teaching of the homily forms a conceptual background for the refutation of the doctrine and deeds of the false teachers.

As the opening words of verses 3 (ὡς), 5 (καὶ αὐτὸ τοῦτο δὲ), 8 (ταῦτα γάρ), 9 (γάρ), 10 (διὸ μᾶλλον), and 11 (οὕτως γάρ) indicate, the homily is closely

---

[81] Ἡμῶν probably refers to the apostles as do other references in the first person plural (1:16–19; 3:15).

[82] Λαγχάνειν - "to obtain a lot or divine will"; BAGD, 462; H. Hanse, "λαγχάνω," *TDNT* 4:2.

[83] Quint. 4.1.16.

[84] Rom 1:6–7; 1 Cor 1:2; Titus 1:4; 1 John 1:3; Jude 3; Rev 1:9.

[85] Cic. *De Or.* 2.77.311; *Part. Or.* 8.27.

[86] Cic. *De Or.* 2.80.325; Quint. 4.1.23–27; cf. Cic. *De Or.* 2.79.320.

[87] Klaus Baltzer, *The Covenant Formulary*, trans. David E. Green (Oxford: Basil Blackwell, 1971); Karl P. Donfried, *The Setting of Second Clement in Early Christianity*, NovTSup 38 (Leiden: E. J. Brill, 1974) 41–48; Bauckham, 173–75. Cf. 4 Ezra 14:28–36 and *Acts John* 106–7 which exhibit this pattern and are also farewell discourses.

reasoned. In fact, vv 3-11 constitute a complex enthymeme.[88] Verses 3-4 provide a premise to which vv 5-7 provide a conclusion. The justification for the exhortation to virtue (vv 5-7) is the benefits afforded the Christian (vv 3-4). Thus, in themselves vv 3-7 constitute an enthymeme. This close relationship between these verses is indicated not only by the phrase καὶ αὐτὸ τοῦτο beginning v 5, but also by the fact that faith is the basis of the virtues listed in vv 5-7, and the benefits of vv 3-4 are received by faith.

Verses 8-9 provide further reasons for heeding the exhortation of vv 5-7 as the introductory words ταῦτα γάρ (v 8) and γάρ (v 9) indicate. They present two antithetical responses to the exhortation to supplement faith. Together with vv 5-7 they constitute an enthymeme. Verses 8-9 related closely to v 3 with its reference to the potential of a godly life in knowledge. Here knowledge can be made effective and fruitful through the supplementation of faith, or it can remain dormant.

As clearly indicated by the initial words διὸ μᾶλλον, v 10 functions as a conclusion, while vv 3-9 serve as the premises. The content of v 10 echoes that of v 5 in stressing that effort be exerted toward Christian maturity (σπουδή, v 5; σπουδάζω, v 10).

Verse 11 provides amplification of vv 3-10 using augmentation.[89] It is the climax of their forward progression, holding out the ultimate hope of every Christian: entrance into the eternal kingdom. The highly emotive adjective πλουσίως ("richly") is used to describe the entrance. To the Christian who adds (ἐπιχορηγήσατε) virtue to his faith (1:5), Christ will richly add (ἐπιχορηγηθήσεται) entrance into the kingdom (1:11).

The entire section builds toward a climax. It begins by giving the benefits of the Christian life, benefits which need ethical development (vv 3-4), then it progresses to explain that ethical development (vv 5-7), describe the benefits of developing the gifts and the detriment of not developing them (vv 8-9), and exhort to Christian living (v 10). It concludes with a description of the ultimate reward (vv 10-11).

The rhetorically effective structure of the homily is supplemented by numerous rhetorical devices. In vv 3-4, synecdoche[90] is found in τῆς θείας δυνάμεως αὐτοῦ, an attribute of God standing for God himself. The portrayal of divine power granting matters pertaining to life and godliness is personification of the type attributing certain behavior to a thing.[91] The phrase ζωήν καὶ εὐσέβειαν

---

[88] For more on enthymeme, see ch. 1.

[89] Cic. Part. Or. 15.54; Quint. 8.4.3-9.

[90] Synecdoche is a trope ". . . making us realise [sic] many things from one, the whole from a part, the genus from a species, things which follow from things which preceded . . ." and vice versa (Quint. 8.6.19). See Cic De Or. 3.42.168; Her. 4.33.44-45; Quint. 8.6.28; 9.3.20 for similar definitions. For further discussion, see Lausberg, 1:295-98; §572-77; Martin, 306-7; Bullinger, 613-56.

[91] Personification is a figure of thought which ". . . consists in representing an absent

is an example of hendiadys,[92] and is best translated "godly life." Τοῦ καλέσαντος ἡμᾶς is an example of antonomasia[93] of the type referring to an act or striking characteristic of an individual.[94] Verses 3–4 also exhibit transplacement, for the repetition δεδωρημένης-δεδώρηται links as dual divine gifts things pertaining to life and godliness to previous and very great promises.

The rhetorical features of vv 5–7 are numerous. It is a fine example of climax, the figure of speech in which ". . . the speaker passes to the following word only after advancing by steps to the preceding one . . ."[95] Here 2 Peter relies upon Jewish-Christian catechetical practice and material, laying out the virtues of the Christian life beginning with faith and ending with love, the crowning virtue in such lists.[96] The climax exhibits five special stylistic features: homoeoptoton,[97] isocolon,[98] polysyndeton, reduplication, and transplacement. Isocolon gives balance, homoeoptoton aids the building effect, polysyndeton adds vigor to style[99] and a sense of importance[100] and reduplication and transplacement amplify the virtues through repetition.[101]

---

person as present, or in making a mute thing or one lacking form articulate, and attributing to it a definite form and a language or a certain behaviour appropriate to its character . . ." (Her. 4.53.66). Cf. the definition in Quint. 9.2.30–31. For further discussion, see Demetr. *Eloc.* 5.265–66; Her. 4.53.66; Quint. 9.2.29–37; Lausberg, 1:407–13, §820–29; Martin, 292–93; Bullinger, 861–69.

[92] Hendiadys occurs when two words are employed, but only one thing or idea is meant (Bullinger, 657).

[93] Antonomasia is a trope which ". . . substitutes something else for a proper name . . ." (Quint. 8.6.29). See Her. 4.31.42 for a similar definition. For further discussion, see Quint. 8.6.29–30; Lausberg, 1:300–2, §580–81; Martin, 263; Bullinger, 682–83.

[94] The other type of antonomasia is substitution of an epithet (Quint. 8.6.29). Cf. Her. 4.31.42.

[95] Her. 4.25.34. Cf. Cic. *Or.* 39.135; Quint. 9.3.55; Aug. *De Doct. Chr.* 4.7.11 for similar definitions. For further discussion, see Her. 4.25.34–35; Quint. 9.3.54–57; Lausberg, 1:315–17, §623–24; Martin, 303; Bullinger, 256–59.

[96] Bauckham, 174–76; Henry A. Fischel, "The Uses of Sorites (*Climax, Gradatio*) in the Tannaitic Period," *HUCA* 44 (1973) 132–43.

[97] Homoeoptoton is a figure of speech occurring ". . . when in the same period two or more words appear in the same case, and with like terminations . . ." (Her. 4.20.28). Cf. Cic. *Or.* 39.135. Quintilian also defines homoeoptoton as "use of similar cases," but, unlike Cornificius, does not restrict the case endings to identical appearance (9.3.78). For further discussion, see Her. 4.20.28; Quint. 9.3.78–79; Lausberg, 1:363–64, §729–31; Martin, 311; Bullinger, 177.

[98] Isocolon is a figure of speech which is ". . . composed of colas . . . which consist of a virtually equal number of syllables" (Her. 4.20.27). Cf. the definition of Quint. 9.3.80 and the definition of equality of members under symmetrical members in Demetr. *Eloc.* 1.25. For further discussion, see Lausberg, 1:359–61, §719–24; Martin, 310–11.

[99] Demetr. *Eloc.* 2.63; Quint. 9.3.54.

[100] Demetr. *Eloc.* 2.54.

[101] Cic. *Part. Or.* 15.54.

In v 8, "unfruitful" (ἄκαρπος) depends upon the metaphor of fruit for good works or ethical qualities.[102] In v 9, τυφλός and μυωπάζων are two of many metaphors in antiquity for the inability or unwillingness to see the truth.[103] *Homoeopropheron*[104] characterizes vv 10-11 with its proliferation of π: ποιεῖσθαι . . . ποιοῦντες . . . πταίσητε ποτε . . . πλουσίως. In v 10, the first two words of the preceding chain form transplacement and paronomasia of the type in which a word occurs in different cases.[105] The verb πταίω, "stumble" or "fall," forms a metaphor for not attaining salvation.[106] In v 11, "entrance" into the eternal kingdom stands for eternal status in heaven, not merely the literal entrance, and constitutes synecdoche.

In 1:12-15, a traditional element having a highly rhetorical function is the topic of reminding or remembering, a standard feature in farewell discourses.[107] The purpose of the testament letter is to serve as a reminder of proper doctrine during the remainder of the author's life (cf. v 14) and in the future when his voice is silent (cf. v 15).[108] The reminder topic occurs three times in 1:12-15: v 12 ὑπομιμνήσκειν, v 13 ὑπομνήσει, and v 15 μνήμην ποιεῖσθαι in what effects paronomasia. It is reiterated in the secondary *exordium* of 3:1-2: ὑπομνήσει v 1, and μνησθῆναι v 2. In large part the reminder topic refers the audience back to the apostolic teaching in 1:3-11 (1:12) and in 1 Peter (3:2) which they know. Before debate begins with the false teachers, the topic indicates that Peter's message is aligned with both their own and with the apostles. It thus increases the ethos of his rhetoric.

Peter is portrayed intending his letter to serve as a constant reminder of "orthodox" doctrine. The future tenses μελλήσω . . . ὑπομιμνήσκειν (1:12) and

[102] Prov 19:22 LXX; Matt 3:8, 10; 21:43; Mark 4:20; Luke 13:6 9; John 15:2-8; Gal 5:22; Eph 5:9; Col 1:10; Titus 3:14; Heb 2:11; Jas 3:18; Herm. *Sim.* 4; 9:19:2; Friedrich Hauck, "χαρπός," *TDNT* 3:614-16.

[103] The metaphor of blindness: Matt 15:14; 23:16, 24; Luke 6:39; John 9:40-41; 12:40; Rom 2:19; 2 Cor 4:14; 1 John 2:11; Rev 3:17; *1 Clem.* 3:4; *Gos. Thom.* 28; cf. *T. Sim.* 2:7; *T. Dan* 2:4; *T. Jud.* 18:3, 6; 19:4. Wolfgang Schrage, "τυφλός," *TDNT* 8:275-79, 281-82, 284-86, 291-93.

[104] *Homoeopropheron* is ". . . the repetition of the same letter or syllable at the beginning of two or more words in close succession" (Bullinger, 171, i.e., modern alliteration). For further discussion, see Her. 4.12.18; Lausberg, 1:478, §975; Martin, 323; Bullinger, 171-75.

[105] Quint. 9.3.66.

[106] Cf. this metaphor using ἄπταιστος in Jude 24. Karl Schmidt, "πταίω," *TDNT* 6:883-84.

[107] *Jub.* 22:16; *2 Apoc. Bar.* 84:7-8; *Bib. Ant.* 19:5; 24:3; Josephus, *Ant.* 4.318; John 14:16; Acts 20:31; 2 Tim 2:8, 14; *Act. Verc.* 36.

[108] A. Vögtle, "Die Schriftwerdung der apostolischen Paradosis nach 2 Petr 1, 12-15," in *Neues Testament und Geschichte: Historisches Geschehen und Deutung im Neuen Testament,* eds. H. Baltenweiler and B. Reicke (Zurich: Theologischer Verlag/Tübingen: J. C. B. Mohr, 1972) 298-300. *T. Mos.* 10:11; *T. Sim.* 7:3; *T. Dan* 6:9.

σπουδάσω (1:15), and the adverb ἀεί, indicate that 2 Peter wants the epistle read more than once in the future in order for it to fulfill its role as a reminder. Such an intention greatly increases the ethos of his epistle. It has apostolic authority, contains apostolic teaching already received, and is intended for posterity as an authoritative statement of such teaching.

In obtaining goodwill from the person of the rhetor, the reminder topic also has the advantage of not offending the audience, for it in no way connotes their ignorance or implies that Peter is superior because he possesses knowledge they do not have.[109] To be urged to recall is not threatening, and is somewhat complimentary because it implies that the rhetor recognizes that the audience possesses knowledge. As noted above, the reminder topic's role in goodwill is enhanced by the explicit phrase "though you know them and are established in the truth that you have."[110] Also, being reminded of doctrine they already know enables the audience to use its own knowledge as a personal basis of truth confirming the deliberation to follow.

Stylistically, this section (1:12-15) relies heavily upon metaphor. Στηρίζω, "establish," in v 12 is a common Christian metaphor for stability in the Christian life.[111] In vv 13-14, the two occurrences of σκήνωμα, "tent," are examples of the metaphor for the body.[112] In v 14, ἡ ἀπόθεσις, "the divesting," is a metaphor for taking off clothes,[113] and together with σκήνωμα, creates a mixed metaphor for death.[114] This mixed metaphor for death is reinforced in v 15 by ἔξοδος, "end," "departure", another metaphor for death.[115] By ancient standards the mixed metaphor is a stylistic fault,[116] and all these metaphors are too crowded, the language allegorical, and the style faulty.[117]

In general, the testamentary epistle has two other rhetorically effective aspects. First, the one who is about to die and is giving his last words was considered to have special revelation. The revelation implied by the use of the

---

[109] Cic. *Inv.* 1.16.22; Quint. 4.1.10.

[110] Compare Jude's use of similar sentiment in his *exordium* (v 3) where he states that the audience already has the precepts of faith and only need contend for them.

[111] Luke 22:32; Acts 18:3; Rom 16:25; 1 Thess 3:2; 2 Thess 3:3; 1 Pet 5:10; *2 Clem.* 2:6; *Ep. Apost.* 1. Günther Harder, "στηρίζω," *TDNT* 7:656.

[112] Wis. 9:15; *Paral. Jer.* 6:6-7; Tatian, *Oratio* 15; *Diogn.* 6:8; *Apoc. Paul* 15; Eusebius, *Hist. Eccl.* 2.25.6; 3.31.1-2. Cf. 2 Cor 5:1, 4 where σκῆνος is used as a metaphor for the body. Wilhelm Michaelis, "σκηνή," *TDNT* 7:381-84. The repetition σκηνώματι-σκηνώματος constitutes transplacement.

[113] 2 Macc 8:35; Acts 7:58.

[114] These metaphors are also mixed in *Asc. Isa.* 9.8; 2 Cor 5:3-4. Both metaphors were probably weak.

[115] Wis 3:2; 7:6; Jos. *Ant.* 4.189; Luke 9:31; *Apoc. Paul* 14; Justin, *Dial.* 105.3, 5; Eusebius, *Hist. Eccl.* 5.1.36, 55; 5.2.3; Irenaeus, *Adv. Haer.* 3.1.1. Wilhelm Michaelis, "ὁδός," *TDNT* 5:103-9.

[116] Quint. 8.6.50.

[117] Demetr. *Eloc.* 2.78; Quint. 8.6.14; cf. Long. *Subl.* 32.1.

testament genre serves as a major source of authority for the epistle, as well as goodwill,[118] and for enhancing the ethos of the message. Secondly, since the message is presented as written by Peter during his lifetime and intended to serve the needs of future readers, and yet, describes present conditions, it would be perceived by the audience as foretold and currently applicable to them. They can conceive of themselves as those for whom the prophecy and teachings were specifically written. The audience is thereby made attentive, receptive, and well-disposed.

The Probatio (1:16–3:13)

The next element of rhetorical arrangement, the *probatio*, encompasses 1:16–3:13. In the *probatio*, the rhetor attempts to persuade the audience of the legitimacy of his case through a presentation of propositions and corresponding proof and refutation.[119] These propositions may be implicit or explicit in the *narratio*,[120] be contained in the *partitio* in which they are specifically listed,[121] and/or be given at the beginning of every proof.[122]

2 Peter does not contain a *narratio* or a *partitio*. The propositions are found at the beginning of each proof. These propositions are either the denial of the opponents' charge or the opponents' charge itself restated for rebuttal. The initial denial of a charge of the false teachers is often stated using the formula οὐ . . . ἀλλά (1:16, 21; 3:9).[123]

The proofs 2 Peter utilizes to verify his propositions and refute those of his opponents are both inartificial and artificial.[124] Proof in deliberative rhetoric is usually example and comparison of example,[125] and ethos.[126] However, although 2 Peter is classified as deliberative rhetoric, example does not play a large role in the argumentation, being found only in the proof of 2:3b–10a. First, 2 Peter uses judicial rhetoric to refute the objections of the false teachers lodged against apostolic preaching of Christ's parousia and judgment (1:16–2:10a; 3:3–13). After refutation he uses deliberative rhetoric to persuade his audience to forsake the

---

[118] Quint. 10.1.48.

[119] For more on the *probatio*, see ch. 1.

[120] Quint. 3.9.7; 4.2.54, 79, 86; cf. 4.4.9.

[121] Quint. 4.5.1–25. For more on the *partitio*, see ch. 1.

[122] Quint. 4.4.1.

[123] Neyrey, *Form and Background*, 18–19, 22, 24. Two times the formula is used merely in the refutation of a charge, not in its initial statement or denial. These are 2:4–5 and 3:9b. The possibility that οὐ . . . ἀλλά is an apologetic form has to be established for each occurrence. Compare Stanley Stowers, *The Diatribe in Romans*, SBLDS 57 (Chico, CA: Scholars Press, 1981) 125–28, for the use of ἀλλά in the diatribe to introduce a formal objection to opponents.

[124] For more on the basic types of proof, see ch. 1.

[125] Ar. *Rhet*. 1.9.1368a.40; 2.20.1394a.7–8; 3.17.1418a.5; *Rhet. ad Alex*. 32.1438b.29ff.; Quint. 3.8.34, 66; cf. 5.11.8.

[126] Quint. 3.8.12–13.

doctrine and practice of the false teachers that is based on their objections. Therefore, as is typical of judicial rhetoric, 2 Peter relies mainly upon enthymemes in his proof in the *probatio*.[127] Unlike Jude, 2 Peter does not utilize radical Christian rhetoric.[128] In fact, even the *exordium* and the *digressio* incorporate enthymemes.

First Accusation and Refutation (1:16-19)

As the *probatio* begins, 1:16a is an implicit charge of the false teachers and 1:16b-18 contains 2 Peter's first proof and refutation of it. The charge of the false teachers implicit in 1:16a is that the apostolic proclamation of the parousia of Christ is a cleverly devised myth. That 2 Peter is refuting an objection of opponents, rather than making a charge against them, is indicated by the polemic formula οὐ . . . ἀλλά[129] and a similar charge by the false teachers in 3:4.

2 Peter refutes the charge of 1:16a with an inartificial proof of eyewitness testimony (1:16b-18).[130] As often is the case in the testament genre, so here a revelation of the future is given the hero.[131] Peter and the apostles witnessed the Transfiguration of Jesus which was a proleptic vision of God's installation of Jesus as his eschatological viceregent. Therefore, the parousia hope is not false: it only remains for Jesus to exercise this authority.[132] It was a common apologetic against attacks on Christian doctrine to stress apostolic eyewitness testimony to historical events.[133]

Supporting the inartificial proof of eyewitness testimony are an unnecessary sign[134] and ethos. The Transfiguration is treated as a sign of the parousia and thus as a probable proof of its reality. This is an example of the use of an unnecessary sign to strengthen proof.[135] The shift to the first person "we" in 1:16-18 groups Peter with the apostles, the underlying assumption being that the apostles all preached the same message. Like John and James, Peter witnessed the Transfiguration, and his account like those of John and James and the other apostles after them, is the same. Thus, the refutation of 2 Peter relies heavily upon proof from the ethos of both the rhetor and his message.[136] The proof is

---

[127] Ar. *Rhet.* 1.9.1368a.40; 3.17.1418a.5; *Rhet. ad Alex.* 6.1428a.5ff.

[128] Kennedy, *New Testament Interpretation*, 7-8.

[129] Neyrey finds all the occurrences of the οὐ . . . ἀλλά formula in Philo and Diodorus of Sicily in contexts defending the truth of scriptures or oracles against the charge that they are fabricated myths. Neyrey, "Apologetic Use of the Transfiguration," 506-9.

[130] For more on this type of proof, see ch. 1.

[131] *1 Enoch* 93; *2 Apoc. Bar.* 81:4; *T. Levi* 2-5, 8; *Adam and Eve* 25-29; *2 Enoch* 39:2; *Bib. Ant.* 28:4.

[132] Bauckham, 211-12, 215-21.

[133] John 19:35; 1 Cor 15:3-8; 1 John 1:1-3; 4:14; *Gos. Pet.* 7:26-27; 14:59-60; D. E. Nineham, "Eyewitness Testimony and the Gospel Tradition III," *JTS* 11 (1960) 254-64.

[134] For more on unnecessary sign, see ch. 1.

[135] Quint. 5.9.8-11.

[136] For more on ethos, see ch. 1.

amplified by reasoning from antecedent circumstances,[137] here the Transfiguration, and by discussion of important matters, here the wonders of earth and sky.[138]

The related topics of leading-following, error, and the way are introduced here in 1:16 in the false teachers' accusation that the apostles follow (ἐξακολουθέω) cleverly devised myths, that it, error rather than the way of truth (cf. 2:2, 15, 21). In 2:2 a portion of the audience is said to follow (ἐξακολουθέω) the licentiousness (a facet of error, cf. 2:18) of the false teachers, and revile the way (ὁδός) of truth. In 2:15 the false teachers are accused of wandering (πλανάω) from the straight way (ὁδός) to follow (ἐξακολουθέω) the way (ὁδός) of Balaam (i.e., error), and in 2:18 they are accused of enticing (i.e., leading) into licentiousness (a facet of error) new converts who had just escaped error (πλάνη). In the *peroratio* in 3:17, the audience is exhorted not to be led (συναπάγω) into error (πλάνη), that is, leave the way (cf. 2:2, 15, 21).

The style of 1:16–18 greatly aids in the proof. μεγαλειότητος-μεγαλοπρεποῦς in 1:16–17 constitutes paronomasia of the type using words with some resemblance and similar meaning.[139] In 1:17, μεγαλοπρεποῦς δόξης is metonymy[140] making a substitution for the name of God, and the repetition δόξαν-δόξης forms transplacement. Together these figures imply that the majesty and glory of Christ witnessed by the apostles has its origin in God, the "Majestic Glory," not in the imagination of the apostles. The transplacement, φωνῆς ἐνεχθείσης-φωνὴν ἐνεχθεῖσαν, in 1:17–18 is part of refining which amplifies through repetition[141] the fact that the voice which the apostles heard giving honor and glory to Christ was of divine origin. It was from heaven (1:17) and God himself (1:18), not merely the apostolic imagination.

Whereas the false teachers accused the apostles of following "cleverly devised myths" (σεσοφισμένοις μύθοις, 1:16a), 2 Peter in his first countercharge accuses the false teachers of exploiting the audience with "false words" (πλαστοῖς λόγοις, 2:3). The association of μῦθος with πλάσσειν and πλάσμα is common in Philo to refer to other religions.[142] Μῦθοι carries the connotation that the doctrine is not true or lacks historical verifiability.[143] Σεσοφισμένοι, "concocted slyly" or "devised craftily,"[144] clearly implies deceit and stealth.[145] It would be interesting

---

[137] Quint. 8.4.18.

[138] Cic. *Part. Or.* 16.55–56.

[139] Her. 4.22.30.

[140] Metonymy is a trope ". . . which draws from an object closely akin or associated an expression suggesting the object meant, but not called by its own name" (Her. 4.32.43). Cf. Cic. *De Or.* 3.42.167; *Or.* 27.93; Quint. 8.6.23 for similar definitions. For further discussion, see Cic. *De Or.* 3.42.167–68; Her. 4.32.43; Quint. 8.6.23–28.

[141] Cic. *Part. Or.* 15.54.

[142] G. Stählin, "μῦθος," *TDNT* 4:785 n. 139; Herbert Braun, "πλάσσω," *TDNT* 6:259, 262; Neyrey, "Apologetic Use of the Transfiguration," 507.

[143] Stählin, "μῦθος," *TDNT* 4:784–86, 789–91.

[144] BAGD, 767.

[145] Ulrich Wilckens, "σοφία," *TDNT* 7:527–28.

to know whether the phrase σεσοφισμένοι μύθοι was the actual terminology used by the false teachers to designate apostolic teaching of the parousia, or is the language chosen by 2 Peter to portray their argument. If the former, then the false teachers' charge has some rhetorical finesse of its own to decrease ethos and elicit negative pathos. If the latter, 2 Peter is stating the false teachers' claim as strongly as possible so as to use it against them in 2:3 where he designates their teaching as πλαστοὶ λόγοι, "fabricated words."

The second refutation of the false teachers' charge that the apostolic teaching of the parousia is a myth (1:16a) is found in 1:19. 2 Peter uses an inartificial proof of a document in his refutation.[146] He points out that the apostolic teaching is dependable because it is reliant upon Old Testament prophecy.[147] The comparative can be given its comparative force and be translated "more certain," in which case 1:19a can be taken to mean that Old Testament prophecy has been made more reliable by the Transfiguration. However, it is better to take βεβαιότερον in a superlative sense, as it often is in Koine, meaning "very firm,"[148] and 1:19a be taken to mean that Old Testament prophecy provides firm support for the apostolic doctrine of the parousia.

An artificial proof based on the ethos[149] of Peter is also provided by 1:19. 2 Peter is confident enough of the reality of the parousia to portray Peter as offering its near coming as a proof of its reality. He affirms that at the parousia, "the dawning day"[150] when "the morning star rises,"[151] the apostolic preaching of the parousia will be proven true to his audience. His confident hope in the parousia, his affirmation of its imminence, and his expectation that his audience will experience it underlie other portions of the *probatio* (3:1-4, 10, 11-13, 14) and act as constraints. The audience would be reluctant to abandon apostolic

---

[146] For more on this type of proof, see ch. 1.

[147] Τὸν προφητικὸν λόγον refers to all of, or the prophetic portion of, the Old Testament. 1) All known occurrences of the phrase refer to the Old Testament (except *2 Clem.* 11:2 which refers to an apocryphon). 2) 2:1a refers to false prophets of the Old Testament period. Like the word "scripture" it can refer to specific passages (Philo, *Leg. All.* 3.43; *Sob.* 68; Justin *Dial.* 56.6; 77.2; 110.3) or several passages (Philo, *Plant.* 117–19) or the Old Testament generally (Justin, *Dial.* 128.4). Our author may have specific Old Testament prophecies in mind (e.g., Ps 2:9; Dan 7:13–14; Num 24:17), but does not specify. Bauckham, 224.

[148] *BDF*, 32–34, §60–61; Neyrey, "Apologetic Use of the Transfiguration," 515; Bauckham, 223.

[149] For more on this type of proof, see ch. 1.

[150] Ἕως οὗ ἡμέρα διαυγάσῃ is probably a symbol of the eschatological age (cf. Rom 13:12; 2 Pet 3:18: ἡμέραν αἰῶνος).

[151] Φωσφόρος ἀνατείλη refers to Christ's parousia. It is an allusion to Num 24:17 LXX (ἀνατελεῖ ἄστρον ἐξ Ἰακωβ), which was interpreted messianically in Judaism (*T. Levi* 18:3; *T. Jud.* 24:1; 1QM 11:6–7; 4QTestim. 9–13; CD 7:18–20; *y. Ta'an.* 68d). In *T. Levi* 18:3–4 and *T. Jud.* 24:1 the image of star and sunrise are associated. Cf. Rev 22:16 which calls Jesus ὁ ἀστὴρ ὁ λαμπρὸς ὁ πρωϊνός "the bright morning star." Here φωσφόρος is antonomasia substituting an epithet for the name Jesus it replaces (Quint. 8.6.29; cf. Her. 4.31.42).

doctrine and take the risk of not being ready at the parousia. The importance of this proof is underscored by the phrase "You will do well to pay attention to this as to a lamp shining in a dark place." This is amplification of the type which states what is advantageous to humankind![152] It is also the use of a similitude to embellish, vivify, and clarify![153]

The section of the *probatio*, 1:16–19, is reiterated in the *peroratio* in the *adfectus*. The day (ἡμέρα) that is awaited (1:19) is the anticipated eternal day (ἡμέραν αἰῶνος, 3:18). The glory (δόξα) awarded the Son by the Father (1:17) is expected to remain with him until he returns (3:18).

Second Accusation and Refutation (1:20–21)

A statement of the second charge of the false teachers in combination with 2 Peter's refutation is provided by 1:20–21![154] That a charge is here being refuted is indicated by the οὐ . . . ἀλλά formula of 1:21a, although the charge underlies 1:20 as well![155] The charge of the false teachers that implicitly lies behind 1:20–21 is that the Old Testament prophecy upon which the apostles base their teaching of the parousia is a matter of the prophet's own interpretation and impulse, not the inspiration of the Holy Spirit. Their charge is akin to attacking a document used in inartificial proof by calling it a fraud![156]

The introductory phrase τοῦτο πρῶτον γινώσκοντες of 1:20 (repeated in 3:3) is an indication that a proposition is being presented![157] 2 Peter here uses an artificial proof, an enthymeme![158] the conclusion being 1:20 and the supporting premise being 1:21. He argues that Old Testament prophecy used to support the parousia must be inspired because all prophecy is inspired.

Stylistically, 2 Peter effectively utilizes transplacement in these verses. In 1:21, two forms of φέρω occur: ἠνέχθη and φερόμενοι. These are part of a larger transplacement, for in 1:17 and 1:18 we find two forms of ἐνφέρω: ἐνεχθείσης and ἐνεχθεῖσαν respectively. Transplacement serves other than stylistical concerns, for by using forms of the root φερ- to describe the origin of the words of the Transfiguration and of Old Testament prophetic interpretation as coming from God, 2 Peter ties both the apostolic and prophetic messages to their divine source and thereby increases their ethos.

---

[152] Cic. *Part. Or.* 16.56.

[153] Her. 4.45.59; Quint. 8.3.72–78; cf. Quint. 5.11.22. The similitude can incorporate antithesis between word groups as here (Quint. 9.3.81). Λύχνη is often used as a simile or metaphor for the Old Testament; Ps 119(118):105; Wis 18:4; *2 Apoc. Bar.* 17:4; 59:2; 77:16; *Bib. Ant.* 9:8; 15:6; 19:5.

[154] For further discussion on 1:20–21, see John T. Curran, "The Teaching of II Peter 1:20 on the Interpretation of Prophecy," *TS* 4 (1943) 347–68.

[155] Neyrey, "The Apologetic Use of the Transfiguration," 518.

[156] Quint. 5.5.

[157] Cf. similar phrase in Luke 12:39; Gal 3:7; 2 Tim 3:1; Heb 13:3.

[158] For more on enthymeme, see ch. 1.

It should be noted that this type of argumentation and the words and phrases utilized within it were standard in the discussion of prophetic inspiration in Hellenistic Judaism and early Christianity.[159] Thus, it would be an effective artificial proof because the traditional nature of its form and and content would make it virtually a self-evident truth.

Counteraccusation (2:1-3a)

In ch. 2,[160] 2 Peter turns from defending apostolic teaching against charges of the false teachers to counteraccusing the false teachers and their own teaching. In 2:1-3a, the charges leveled against the apostles in 1:16-21 are turned against the false teachers. The apostles do not proclaim "cleverly devised myths" based upon false prophecy (1:16a, 20-21), but rather, the false teachers are those standing in the succession of the false prophets with their "destructive heresies" (2:1) and "false words" (2:3). This counteraccusation contains the additional element that the false teachers will be judged (2:1, 3).

The refutation of 1:16-21 and the counteraccusation of 2:1-3a are creatively interconnected in a chiastic structure:[161] 1) the apostles' words (1:16-18), b) the Old Testament true prophets (1:19-21), b') the Old Testament false prophets (2:1a), and a') the false teachers' words (2:1b-3a). This chiastic structure is reinforced by *inclusio*. Whereas the false teachers accuse the apostles of "following cleverly devised myths" (σεσοφισμένοις μύθοις ἐξαχολουθήσαντες, 1:16), 2 Peter accuses the audience of "following the licentiousness" of the false teachers

---

[159] 2 Peter used the standard terms of Hellenistic Judaism to describe the divine origins of the Old Testament prophecy. Ἰδίας is a technical term in such argumentation to deny the human origin of prophecy (Ezek 13:3 LXX; Philo, *Quis Her.* 259; *Mos.* 1.281, 286; *Spec. Leg.* 1.65; 4.49; *Quaest. Gen.* 3.10; Jos. *Ant.* 4.121. Ἐπιλύσεως (ἐπίλυσις and ἐπιλύειν) is a technical term for the divinely inspired interpretation of a prophet or seer's vision by the prophet or seer (Aquila Gen 40:8; 41:8, 12; 4 Ezra 10:43 (Greek version); Herm. *Sim.* 5:3:1-2; 5:4:2-3; 5:5:1; 5:6:8; 5:7:1; 8:11:1; 9:10:5; 9:11:9; 9:13:9; 19:16:7). Ὑπὸ πνεύματος ἁγίου φερόμενοι recalls θεοφόρος, θεοφόρητος, θεοφορείσθαι and πνευματοφορός used in Hellenistic Judaism to describe prophetic inspiration (Philo, *Mos.* 1.283; *Quis Her.* 266; *Spec. Leg.* 1.65; 4.49; Jos. *Ant.* 4.119; Justin, *1 Apol.* 33, 36, 37). Compare the Old Testament polemic (Jer 14:13; 18:21-22. 26; 23:16-22; Ezek 13:1-7) that a true prophet as opposed to a false prophet does not speak his own words, but the word of God. Bauckham, 228-35.

[160] At this point, 2 Peter begins to rely upon Jude (Jude 4-13, 16-18 = 2 Pet 1-18; 3:1-3). The reasons behind this dependence are unknown, but, from a rhetorical standpoint, it is probably best to assume that Jude was held authoritative by 2 Peter and his audience, and/or, being dependent upon traditional material and manner of argumentation to meet a similar exigence, Jude met the needs of 2 Peter's polemic. Both reasons explain the rhetorical effectiveness of using Jude. See ch. 4, pt. 2 for a detailed discussion of the relationship of Jude and 2 Peter from a rhetorical standpoint.

[161] Chiasm is a rhetorical device common to ancient literature, but is not discussed in ancient handbooks. For further discussion, see Lund, *Chiasmus in the New Testament,* and Kennedy, *New Testament Interpretation,* 28-29.

(ἐξακολουθήσουσιν, 2:2), and the false teachers of greedily exploiting with false words (πλαστοῖς λόγοις, 2:3). The chiastic structure and *inclusio* makes a correlation and contrast between the apostles, the genuine prophets and their teaching, and the false teachers, the false prophets, and their teaching. Such a correlation serves to enhance the ethos of Peter, the apostles, and their teaching, especially of the parousia that is defended in the preceding section (1:16-21). All this is accomplished at the expense of the ethos of the false teachers and their teaching.

Like false prophets, the false teachers do not speak with divine authority,[162] as the prefix ψευδο- implies. Rather, they proclaim a false message of peace and security against the true prophetic (and apostolic) message of judgment.[163] Also like the false prophets, the false teachers will be condemned to punishment by God.[164] All the negative pathos and images the audience has regarding false prophets will, by association, be brought to bear against the false teachers.

The testament genre usually includes predictions of the last times,[165] and in early Christian testaments the appearance of false teachers in the church is the main element of prediction.[166] 2 Peter is here dependent upon the preaching of the apostles which did include prophecies and predictions of false teaching and false prophecy in the last days.[167] He may also be dependent upon a genuine tradition of Peter's preaching of false teachers in the last time, although this is impossible to determine. The prediction and counteraccusation of 2:1-3a enjoy the ethos of the apostles, Peter, and that of an inspired prediction within a testament.

As a prophecy within a testament, 2:1-3a functions like an artificial proof based on an example,[168] of the type of example called a judgment,[169] and the type of judgment called a supernatural oracle,[170] the application of the example to the false teachers is not explicitly made, but is left to the audience to make as a natural consequence of reading a testament describing their current situation.

In this counteraccusation of 2:1-3a, 2 Peter employs strong words to achieve amplification[171] and introduces several important topics. In 2:1, the switch from ψευδοπροφῆται to ψευδοδιδάσκαλοι within isocolon is not merely paronomasia,[172]

[162] Deut 18:20; Jer 14:14; 23:21, 32; Ezek 13:2-7.
[163] Jer 4:10; 6:14; 14:13, 15; 23:17; 27:9, 16-18; Ezek 13:10; Mic 3:5, 11.
[164] Jer 14:15; 23:15; 28:16-17.
[165] Tob 14:4-7; *T. Mos.* 5-10; *Jub.* 45:14; *T. Levi* 1:1; 4:1; 10:1-5; 14:1-18:14; *T. Jud.* 18:1; 21:6-25:5; *T. Iss.* 6:1-2; *T. Zeb.* 9:5-10:3; *T. Dan.* 5:4-13; *T. Napht.* 4:1-5; 8:1-3; *T. Gad* 8:2; *T. Asher* 7:2-7; *T. Benj.* 9:1-5.
[166] Acts 20:29-30; 2 Tim 3:1-5; 4:3-4; cf. *T. Jud.* 21:9.
[167] Jude 17-18; Matt 7:15; 24:11, 24: Mark 13:22; Acts 20:29-30; 1 Tim 4:1-3; 2 Tim 4:3-4; 1 John 2:8; 4:1-3; *Did.* 16:3; *Apoc. Pet.* A 1; *Sib. Or.* 2.165-66.
[168] For more on example, see ch. 1.
[169] Cic. *Inv.* 1.30.48; Quint. 5.11.36-44.
[170] Quint. 5.11.41-42.
[171] Cic. *Part. Or.* 15.53; Quint. 8.4.1-3.
[172] It is paronomasia using words lacking close resemblance, but yet are not dissimilar in meaning (Her. 4.22.30).

but serves to distinguish two different classes![173] It is an example of amplification by strong words within a comparison![174]

In the phrase, "bring in destructive heresies," although παρεισάγειν simply means "to bring in," it can often have the connotation of something under-handed or surreptitious![175] Αἱρέσεις ἀπωλείας, "destructive heresies," is prejorative. It gives the result of the false teacher's teaching in its very designation, that is, destruction at the eschaton, as the further development of this topic in 2 Peter makes clear. This is probably the figure of irony,[176] for the very judgment the false teachers deny is the very judgment they incur![177]

The topic of eschatological destruction (ἀπώλεια, ἀπόλλυμι) occurs again in 2:1 in the phrase ταχινὸς ἀπώλεια, "imminent destruction," which describes the results of denying Christ. Together, παρεισάξουσιν αἱρέσεις ἀπωλείας and ἐπάγοντες . . . ταχινὴν ἀπώλειαν constitute paronomasia[178] and transplacement and serve to amplify the fate of the false teachers by repetition![179] Ταχινὸς ἀπώλεια, "imminent destruction," anticipates the charge of the false teachers found in 2:3b that destruction is asleep, and in 3:4, 9 that Christ is slow about his coming in judgment. This is probably another use of irony, for the "slow" coming is really "imminent" destruction. This topic of eschatological destruction occuring in 2:1 occurs again in 2:3, is found in 3:6, 7, 9 in the further development of the *probatio* in the defense against the accusations of 3:4, 9, and also in 3:16 in the *repetitio* of the *peroratio* in a reaffirmation of the destruction of the false teachers.

---

[173] Apparently 2 Peter's opponents did not claim prophetic inspiration, but rather, in contrast to the apostles (1:16), were teaching false words based on human invention rather than words based on authoritative prophecy and eyewitness experience.

[174] Quint. 8.4.2–3.

[175] It is used of heretics by Hegesippus, *ap.* Eusebius, *Hist. Eccl.* 4.22.5; Hippolytus, *Ref.* 5.17.13; 7.29.1; Wilhelm Michaelis, "παρεισάγω," *TDNT* 5:824–26.

[176] Irony can be either a trope or a figure of thought. In both cases, something understood is opposite of what is actually said. As a trope, irony confesses that it implies something opposite of what it actually says, whereas as a figure, it is apparent, but not confessed that such is the case. In the trope, the conflict is verbal, whereas in the figure of thought the meaning conflicts with the language (Quint. 9.2.44–46). Here in 2:1, irony is a figure. For further discussion, see *Rhet. ad Alex.* 21; Lausberg, 1:302–3, §582–85; 446–50, §902–4; Martin, 263–64; Bullinger, 807–15.

[177] 2 Peter may be alluding to the traditional agraphon: "There will be divisions and heresies," ἔσονται σχίσματα καὶ αἱρέσεις. Justin, *Dial.* 35:3; phps also referred to in 1 Cor 11:18. J. Jeremias, *Unknown Sayings of Jesus,* trans. R. H. Fuller (New York, Macmillan, 1957) 59–61; Cf. Justin, *Dial.* 51:2: γενήσεσθαι αἱρέσεις ψευδοπροφήτας ἐπὶ τῷ ὀνόματι αὐτοῦ, "heresies and false prophets would arise in his name;" *Asc. Isa.* 3:22: ἔσονται αἱρέσεις πολλαί, "there will be many heresies."

[178] This is paronomasia with and is the type using works lacking a close resemblance, yet having similar meaning (Her. 4.22.30): παρεισάγω - ἐπάγω.

[179] Cic. *Part. Or.* 15.54.

In 2:1, the phrase "denying the Master[180] who bought them" is a metaphor of a slave master who purchased slaves, a common metaphor for Christ's work in redemption.[181] It is probably borrowed from Jude 4, but by adding that the master is the "one having bought them," 2 Peter has shown why the master is owed allegiance and has in essence called the false teachers renegade slaves, apostate Christians.

As noted above, 2:2 develops the topic of following (ἐξακολουθέω) introduced in 1:16. Whereas in 1:16 the apostles are accused of following cleverly devised myths, here in 2:2 a portion of the audience is accused of following the licentiousness of the false teachers. In addition, in 2:15 the false teachers are accused of following the way of Balaam. The related topic and metaphor of the way is introduced here in 2:2 in the accusation that the audience is in danger of reviling the way of truth (ἡ ὁδός τῆς ἀληθείας).[182] Elsewhere in the *probatio*, the false teachers are said to have forsaken the straight way (εὐθεῖαν ὁδόν, 2:15), although having once known "the way of righteousness" (τὴν ὁδὸν τῆς δικαιοσύνης, 2:21). The "way" was a common metaphor in Jewish-Christian traditions for ethical life and behavior.[183]

Probably 2:2b is an allusion to Isa 52:5 (LXX): δι᾽ ὑμᾶς διὰ παντὸς τὸ ὄνομα μου βλασφημεῖται ἐν τοῖς ἔθνεσιν, "because of you my name is continually reviled among the nations." It was commonly alluded to or quoted in early Christian literature in the context of exhorting Christians not to offend the Gentiles with immoral living.[184] The seriousness of the behavior of the false teachers and their followers is thus highlighted by authoritative tradition.

In 2:3, πλαστοί λογοί, "fabricated words," is an expression for deceitful speech.[185] The exploitation with false words is said to be motivated by greed (πλεονεξία). This topic of greed introduced here is developed in the *digressio* in 2:14-15 where the false teachers are said to be trained in greed (πλεονεξία) and to be followers of Balaam who loved dishonest gain (μισθὸς ἀδικία). The accusation of greed was typical in polemics.[186]

---

[180] Δεσπότης is an example of metonymy and antonomasia of the type substituting an epithet for the name it replaces (Quint. 8.6.29; cf. Her. 4.31.42).

[181] 1 Cor 6:20; 7:23. Cf. Acts 20:28; Rev 5:9; 14:3-4; 1 Pet 1:18; Rom 6:17-18. I. H. Marshall, "The Development of the Concept of Redemption in the New Testament," in *Reconciliation and Hope, L. Morris Festschrift*, ed. R. Banks (Exeter: Paternoster; Grand Rapids: Eerdmans, 1974) 153-69.

[182] LXX Ps 118:30; Wis 5:6; *1 Clem.* 35:5; CD 3:15; 1QS 4:2; Tob 1:3; *1 Enoch* 104:13 (Gk).

[183] Christianity as the way—Acts 9:2; 19:9, 23; 24:14, 22; Eusebius, *Hist. Eccl.* 5.1.48; Wilhelm Michaelis, "ὁδός," *TDNT* 5:50-64, 69-96.

[184] 1 Tim 6:1; Titus 2:5; *1 Clem.* 47:7; *2 Clem.* 13:2; Ign. *Trall.* 8:2; Pol. *Phil.* 10:3; Herm. *Sim.* 6:2:3. In such allusions to Isa 52:5; the phrase τὸ ὄνομά μου is frequently replaced by some other term, as here where we find "the way of truth" replacing "my name."

[185] Herod 1.68; Soph. *Aj.* 148; *T. Reub.* 3:5; Braun, "πλάσσω, *TDNT* 6:262.

[186] 2 Cor 2:17; 1 Tim 6:5; 2 Tim 3:2; Titus 1:7, 11; 1 Pet 5:2; Did 11:5-6, 9, 12: Herm. *Mand.* 11:12.

Third Accusation and Refutation (2:3b–10a)

A marked shift occurs in the *probatio* at 2:3b. Prior to this point, in 2:1–3a, 2 Peter has given a counteraccusation in the form of a prophecy of the false teachers in the future tense, according to the conventions of the testament genre. However, starting at 2:3b and continuing through the rest of ch. 2, he turns to the present tense when further refuting their charge. This same tense shift occurs in ch. 3 where a prophecy of false teachers and their charge is given in the future in 3:3–4 and then their charge is refuted in the present in 3:5–10.

It has sometimes been argued that 2 Peter has naively neglected the genre he is using and that these tense shifts are "slips of the pseudonymous ploy."[187] It must be conceded that it is difficult for 2 Peter to refute the false teachers in the future, that is, as prophecy *ex eventu*. Recently, Bauckham has proposed that these tense shifts are part of 2 Peter's pedagogical method. The prophecy of false teachers in the future is juxtaposed with the refutation of their doctrine in the present so as to make the audience aware that prophecy is currently being fulfilled in the persons and teachings of the false teachers in their midst![188]

For the most part I agree with Bauckham, but I oppose his underlying assumption that the audience of 2 Peter knew by the tense shifts that the epistle was pseudonymous, and was aware that these shifts are merely a teaching tool. From a rhetorical standpoint, it is clear that 2 Peter makes a great effort to portray himself as the apostle Peter, and depends heavily upon the ethos of Peter (1:1, 12–19; 3:1–2, 15–16). It seems unlikely that he expects his pseudonymous nature to be perceived, for if that were so, his efforts at using Peter's ethos are unexplainable. He could just as well have juxtaposed prophecy and fulfilment with only general reference to the apostles and their teaching, in effect arguing, "the apostles once prophesied . . . now observe. . . ."

These tense shifts can be explained by rhetorical considerations as products of literary skill, rather than lapses of memory or a detectable teaching tool. In 2:3b–10b, the present tense can be legitimately used with a prophecy of false teachers to describe their judgment because the judgment active in both the past and the present is the same judgment the false teachers of the future will experience. However, the present tense predominantly occurs in 2:10b–22, the entire *digressio*. The *digressio* in 2 Peter is a denunciation of the false teacher's behavior aimed at undercutting their ethos and eliciting negative pathos from the audience against them. As shown below, 2:10b–22 utilizes many forms of amplification to achieve these aims, any one of which has greater impact in the present tense. Since the false teachers are present in the audience portraying them

---

[187] J. C. W. Wand, *The General Epistles of St. Peter and St. Jude,* WC (London: Methuen, 1934) 132. Mayor writes, "If the former epistle is a product of the second century, the writer may have used the future tense to give it versimilitude, while falling at times into the present from inadvertence" (xxiii).
[188] Bauckham, 134–35, 245.

in the present makes them more readily identifible. Possibly for these reasons, 2 Peter utilizes the futuristic use of the present. "In confident assertions regarding the future, a vivid, realistic present may be used for the future."[189] With regard to prophecies, this usage is occasionally found in classical Greek and is very frequent in the New Testament.[190]

This section begins in 2:3b with the denial of the charge of the false teachers that "divine condemnation is idle and divine destruction is asleep." The same claim of the false teachers underlies 3:4, 9.[191] This charge is similar to that of pagan skeptics who mocked the inactivity of the gods in the affairs of the world,[192] and to several Old Testament passages aimed at God's seeming ineffectiveness.[193] The use of synonymy[194] within isocolon serves to reiterate the denial of the false teachers' charge before it is refuted, and constitutes amplification by repetition.[195] The personification of condemnation and destruction highlights the affirmation of their activity.

Section 2:4–10a constitutes an elaborate, one sentence proof for the proposition of 2:3b that the condemnation and destruction of judgment has not been idle or asleep, but rather, has been active from long ago. The proof takes the form of an extended conditional, 2:4–8 being the apodosis and 2:9–10a the protasis. The proof is artificial and based upon examples.[196] The use of example and comparison of example, especially historical examples as here, is characteristic of deliberative rhetoric.[197] These examples are all from things like,[198] and the parallel is partial,[199] concerning the fact of punishment for sin, not the specific

---

[189] *BDF,* 168, §323.

[190] A similar shift of tenses is found in the testament of 2 Tim 3:1–9 within a prophecy of future profligates. Some of the prophecy is given in the future (3:1–5, 9) and some in the present (3:6–8).

[191] Neyrey, *Form and Background,* 27–30, and "Form and Background," 415–16.

[192] Cic. *Nat. Deor.* 1.21–22; cf. Oenomaus of Gadara, *ap.* Eusebius, *Praep. Evan.* 5.19.2; Celsus, *ap.* Origen, *C. Cels.* 6.78.

[193] 1 Kgs. 18:27– a taunt that God is asleep; Ps 44:23– a request to God to awaken and bring judgment; Ps 121:4 (120:4 LXX)—God neither slumbers nor sleeps; Isa 5:27– the nations executing God's judgment neither slumber nor sleep.

[194] Synonomy is a figure of speech which ". . . does not duplicate the same word by repeating it, but replaces the word that has been used by another of the same meaning" (Her. 4.28.38). It occurs when ". . . the beginnings and the conclusions of sentences are made to correspond by the use of other words with the same meaning" (Quint. 9.3.45). For further discussion, see Lausberg, 1:329–32, §649–56; Martin, 306–7; Bullinger. 324–38.

[195] Cic. *Part. Or.* 15.54.

[196] For more on the proof from example, see ch. 1.

[197] Ar. *Rhet.* 1.9.1368a.40; 2.20.1394a.8; 3.17.1418a.5; *Rhet. ad Alex.* 32.1438b.29ff.; Quint. 3.8.34, 66; cf. 5.11.8.

[198] *Rhet. ad Alex.* 8.1429a.20ff.; Cic. *Inv.* 1.30.49; Quint. 5.11.1–8.

[199] Quint. 5.11.5–7.

sin and punishment itself. The common topic employed is that of past and future fact.[200]

Three Old Testament examples of sinners who were judged are found in 2:4–6. They are prophetic types or acted prophecies of the eschatological judgment awaiting the false teachers plaguing the church. Rhetorically, 2:3b and supporting proof is a very effective unit, for the judgment denied by the false teachers is vividly proven to be both active in the past and affirmed for the present. These three examples of judgment are part of the traditional parenetic schema also used by Jude to affirm final judgment.[201]

The first example of judgment is the casting of the Watchers into Tartarus and their confinement to pits of nether gloom until judgment (Gen 6:1–4). Using *regressio*, the fact of the judgment is reiterated and distinctions drawn for emphasis: God did not spare, but he cast and confined. The topic of keeping (τηρέω) for judgment is worked out throughout the *probatio*. It occurs again in the conclusion of this proof in 2:9, in the denunciation of the *digressio* in 2:17, and in continued refutation in the *probatio* in 3:7. The latter is in a section where these judgments are explicitly cast as eschatological. Stylistically, this example is adorned with the metaphor "fetters of nether gloom."

The second example of past judgment serving as a sign of future judgment, the Flood, is found in 2:5. It is connected to the previously example by the use of epiphora,[202] for οὐκ ἐφείσατο concludes the opening phrase of both and serves to amplify by repetition[203] the fact that sinners were not spared judgment. In Judeo-Christian tradition, the Flood was considered a prototype of the eschatological judgment.[204] 2 Peter is using righteous Noah, who survived the flood, as a type of the faithful Christian who will survive the judgment of the parousia. The rhetorical force of this verse is reinforced by the allusion to Gen 6:17 (LXX): ἐπάγω τὸν κατακλυσμὸν ὕδωρ ἐπὶ τὴν γῆν, "I am bringing the flood of water upon the earth." In 2:5 is introduced the antithesis of righteous-ungodly (δικαιοσύνη-ἀσεβῆς) which is reiterated in 2:6–8 (δίκαιος-ἄθεσμος) and 2:9 (εὐσεβής-ἄδικος). Such antithesis is enhanced by the use of synonyms for each repetition.

Topically connected are 2:5 and 3:7. Whereas 2:5 speaks of the universal judgment by water upon the world (κόσμος) to punish the ungodly (ἀσεβῶν), 3:7 speaks of this, but compares it to the eschatological universal judgment by fire upon the world (γῆ) to punish the ungodly (ἀσεβῶν). As stated above, the Flood was considered a prototype of the eschatological judgment. Here is a good

---

[200] Ar. *Rhet.* 1.3.1359a.8; 2.18.1391b.3; 1392b.16–1393a.25.

[201] For further discussion of this schema, see ch. 2, p. 51.

[202] Epiphora (or *conversio*) is a figure of speech which repeats the last word in successive phrases (Her. 4.13.19). Cf. Cic. *Or.* 39.135; *De Or.* 3.54.206; Quint. 9.3.30 for similar definitions, but without the figure being identified. For further discussion, see Lausberg, 1:320–21, §631–32; Martin, 304; Bullinger, 241–43.

[203] Cic. *Part. Or.* 15.54.

[204] *1 Enoch* 1–16; 1QH 10:35–36; Matt 24:37–39; 2 Pet 3:5–7.

example of the *probatio* building upon previously presented material and developing it further.

The third example of judgment, the destruction of Sodom and Gomorrah, is presented in 2:6-7. It is described as a ὑπόδειγμα, a "warning example,"[205] something the destruction of Sodom and Gomorrah was often portrayed as.[206] The Flood and Sodom and Gomorrah were sometimes traditionally linked together as the two major examples of divine judgment,[207] or the two prototypes of eschatological judgment.[208] They exemplify eschatological destruction by water and fire mentioned in 3:5-7, which further develops this topic. That Sodom and Gomorrah especially serve as examples of the fiery judgment of the wicked at the parousia is indicated by the phrase ὑπόδειγμα μελλόντων ἀσεβέσιν, "example of those being wicked," a reference to the false teachers and their followers.[209] This example would be particularly effective if 2 Peter and his audience believed that Sodom and Gomorrah were still burning, as was believed by many of the era.[210] This series of three examples of sinners and their judgment constitutes amplification by accumulation. Climax is reached by the mere amassing.[211]

Like 2:5, 2:7-8 is a further example of the rescue of the righteous to form an antithesis with the ungodly of the preceding verse. Here Lot is compared with his ungodly contempories. Verse 8 is an example of the figure of speech called parenthesis,[212] and serves as amplification by reasoning.[213] The description of Lot's plight in 2:8 serves to magnify his spiritual distress over licentiousness mentioned in 2:7. This extended description of Lot and his plight portray Lot's situation in a way with which 2 Peter's audience can empathize: they too are probably distressed at surrounding evil, particularly exploitation, as 2:3a indicates. Possibly the synecdoche "day after day," suggesting the extended

---

[205] E. K. Lee, "Words Denoting 'Pattern' in the New Testament," *NTS* 8 (1961/62) 168-69; *BAGD* 844.

[206] Deut 29:22-28; 3 Macc 2:5; Wis 10:6-8; Matt 10:15; 11:23-24; Luke 10:12; *1 Clem.* 11:1-2; Just. *Apol.* 1.53.8-9.

[207] *Jub.* 20:5; *T. Napht.* 3:4-5; cf. Jos. *BJ* 5.566; J. Schlosser, "Les jours de Noé et de Lot: A propos de Luc XVII, 26-30," *RB* 80 (1973) 13-14, 23-24; Luhrmann, "Noah und Lot (Lk 17$^{26-30}$)—ein Nachtrag," *ZNW* 63 (1972) 130.

[208] Luke 17:26-30.

[209] Lee, 167-69.

[210] Wis 10:7; Philo, *Mos.* 2.56; Jos., *BJ* 4.483.

[211] Quint. 8.4.26-27; cf. Long. *Subl.* 12.2.

[212] Parenthesis is a figure of speech which ". . . consists in the interruption of the continuous flow of our language by the insertion of some remark" (Quint. 9.3.23). 2 Pet 2:8 is part of the fourth conditional clause in the extended conditional comprising 2:4-10a. The fact that 2:8 extends the clause to double the length of the others, and 2:7 could function alone as a unit in the sentence, indicates that 2:8 is a parenthesis. For further information on parenthesis, see Quint. 9.3.23-26; Lausberg, 1:427-28, §860; Martin, 266, 299; Bullinger, 470-71.

[213] Quint. 8.4.15-26.

period of Lot's oppression, is placed here because it describes the duration of the audience's oppression by false teachers. Negative pathos is engendered towards the false teachers as the audience identifies with Lot in his plight with the ungodly of Sodom and Gomorrah.

The proposition that the examples of 2:4–8 prove is stated in 2:9, the beginning of the apodosis of the conditional sentence 2:4–10a: the Lord will rescue the righteous and judge the ungodly. The proposition is given in the form of an antithesis which draws the dual emphasis of the righteous and ungodly of the examples together. The trial the righteous will be rescued from is the afflictions the righteous suffer in an evil world, trials with which the audience can probably identify. Rhetorically it is very effective to put the fate of the righteous first and end with the fate of the ungodly applied to the false teachers, especially when this fate parallels the fate of the Watchers (2:4).

The phrase of 2:10a functions as amplification of 2:9. It mentions for the first time the sins of the three examples of 2:4–8 which had not been previously specified, that of indulging in lust and despising authority, and applies them to the false teachers. Ὀπίσω σαρκὸς . . . πορευομένους echoes LXX[214] which implies that the flesh is a master or god that the false teachers follow. While 2:10a summarizes 2:4–8, it also reiterates the topic of licentiousness from 2:2 and denying authority from 2:1, thus tying this counteraccusation and proof of 2:3b–10a to the counteraccusation of 2:1–3a.

The entire proof of 2:3b–10a is woven together using a variety of figures, all of which reiterate topics, amplify through repetition,[215] and tie examples and their antitheses together in the prodosis (2:4–8) and to the apodosis (2:9–10a). There is the epiphora previously noted in 2:4–5; transplacement in 2:5–6 (ἀσεβῶν-ἀσεβέσιν) and 2:7–9 (δίκαιον-ἐρύσατο, δίκαιος-ἡμέραν-ἡμέρας-δικαίαν, ῥύεσθαι-ἀδίκους-ἡμέραν); and paronomasia in 2:6–7 (κατακλυσμόν-καταστροφῇ-κατεκρίνω-καταπονούμενον-ἀναστροφῆς and ἀσεβέσιν-ἀθέσμων-ἀσελγείᾳ) and 2:8–9 (δικαίαν-ἀδίκους).[216]

The Digressio *(2:10b–22)*

This section, 2:10b–22, constitutes a *digressio* within the *probatio* of 1:16–3:13. The *digressio*[217] is ". . . the handling of some theme, which must however have some bearing on the case, in a passage that involves digression from the logical order of our speech."[218] Digressions are of various kinds,

[214] LXX Deut 4:3; 6:14; 28:14; 3 Kgdms 11:10; Hos 11:10.
[215] Cic. *Part. Or.* 15.54.
[216] This is paronomasia of the type in which words do not closely resemble one another, yet are not dissimilar (Her. 4.22.30), and the change of a preposition with which a verb is compounded (Quint. 9.3.71).
[217] Παρέκβασις (Quint. 4.3.12), *egressio* (Quint. 4.3.12), *egressus* (Quint. 4.3.12), *digressio* (Quint. 9.1.28 = Cic. *De Or.* 3.53.203), *digressus* (Quint. 10.1.49), *excursus* (Quint. 4.3.12).
[218] Quint. 4.3.14.

dealing with a variety of topics. Some examples are the praise or blame of persons or places, the description of regions, the narration of historical or legendary occurrences, or the display of emotion.[219] A *digressio* may be found in any of the standard parts of arrangement, and is especially suited to amplifying or abridging a topic, making an emotional appeal, or using topics to add elegance[220] or brilliance to style.[221] The more important the case, the greater the role of digressions.[222]

The *digressio* of 2 Peter is a loosely structured series of denunciations of the false teachers based in part upon Jude 8-12. Such a *digressio* serves to amplify topics related to the ungodliness of the false teachers, increase negative pathos towards them, decrease their ethos and the ethos of their teaching, and add brilliance to style. The length of the *digressio* is indicative of the seriousness of the case. The heavy reliance upon traditional, authoritative material enhances the ethos of the *digressio*.

2 Peter begins the *digressio* in 2:10b with asyndeton and comma in the word pair τολμηταί, αὐθάδεις, "bold, arrogant," which gives style a vigorous thrust forward.[223] It readies the audience to anticipate an explanation for these abrupt and grammatically disconnected words. 2 Peter immediately gives one explanation that the false teachers revile evil angels.

In 2:11 he makes his denunciation more striking by contrasting this behavior with that of good angels who, even though more powerful than the evil angels, would not revile them. His comparison is embellished by the synonymous word pair ἰσχὺς καὶ δύναμις which emphasizes the greater might of the good angels, and makes more striking the contrast between their hesitation and the false teachers' lack of hesitation in reviling evil angels. This is the topic of degree,[224] and amplification by reasoning[225] in which the magnification of the position of the good angels in respect to the evil angels correspondingly magnifies the weakness and folly of the false teachers' reviling of evil angels.

The next section, 2:12-14, is a denunciatory description of the false teachers consisting of a series of short phrases exhibiting asyndeton. 2 Peter is using amplification by accumulation,[226] emphasis being obtained by the amassing of characteristics, with asyndeton making things seem more numerous.[227] This amplification greatly contributes to decreasing the ethos of the false teachers.

---

[219] Quint. 4.3.12-13, 15.

[220] Cic. *De Or.* 2.77.311-12; Quint. 4.3.12, 15.

[221] Quint. 9.1.28 = Cic. *De Or.* 3.53.203.

[222] Cic. *De Or.* 2.77.312.

[223] Demetr. *Eloc.* 2.61; Her. 4.19.26; Quint. 9.3.50.

[224] Ar. *Rhet.* 1.2.1358a.21; 1.3.1359a.9; 2.18.1391b.4; 2.19.1393a.26-27; Cic. *De Or.* 2.40.172; *Part. Or.* 2.7 (an interpolation); Quint. 5.10.86-94.

[225] Quint. 8.4.15-26.

[226] Quint. 8.4.26-27; cf. Long. *Subl.* 12.2. For a discussion of accumulation, see ch. 1.

[227] Quint. 9.3.50.

The topic of "reviling," introduced in 2:10b, continues through 2:12 and is interconnected by the use of transplacement: βλασφημοῦντες (2:10), βλάσφημον (2:11), and βλασφημοῦντες (2:12). In 2:12 the false teachers are said to revile that of which they are ignorant. 2 Peter claims that such reviling shows the false teachers to be functioning "like irrational animals, creatures of instinct, born to be caught and killed." This similitude[228] amplifies by means of comparison,[229] and clarifies and vivifies[230] the irrationality of their reviling. The phrase, "like irrational animals, creatures of instinct," is itself an example of *regressio* and by nature amplifies through repetition.[231]

Also in 2:12, 2 Peter develops the topic of destruction, using the combination of transplacement and paronomasia:[232] φθοράν . . . φθορᾷ . . . φθαρήσονται. The false teachers, although presuming to be able to pronounce a reviling judgment upon the evil angels as if from a superior position, will in fact suffer their judgment of destruction (cf. 2:4),[233] like a mere animal born for that purpose. The ironic implication is that the false teachers, like the evil angels, are immoral and subject to impending destruction. The topic of destruction is amplified in 2:13a in the phrase ἀδικούμενοι μισθὸν ἀδικίας. This is a play on words using transplacement, stating a *jus talionis:* the false teachers will suffer wrong in recompense for the wrong they have done.

In 2:13b, 2 Peter accuses the false teachers of reveling in the daytime, of reveling in deceitful pleasure while feasting with the audience. This has considerable denunciatory effect because such behavior was considered a standard mark of degeneracy.[234] This behavior is amplified through repetition,[235] repetition being effected in the paronomasia τρυφήν and ἐντρυφῶντες[236] which structures the repeated charge. The charge is ornamented with *homoeopropheron:* ἡδονὴν ἡγούμενοι τὴν ἐν ἡμέρᾳ.

Reveling makes the false teachers σπίλοι καὶ μῶμοι, "blots and blemishes." This synonymous word pair and metaphor conjures up the imagery of animals not suitable for sacrifice (Lev 1:3) or a man unfit for priestly duties (Lev 21:21). The audience becomes aware that because the false teachers are among them, they are not a holy and pleasing sacrifice to God. In the *peroratio* in 3:14, 2 Peter

---

[228] This is simulitude based on an abridged comparison (Her. 4.47.60).

[229] Quint. 8.4.9–14.

[230] Her. 4.45.59; Quint. 8.3.72ff.; cf. 5.11.22.

[231] Cic. *Part. Or.* 15.54.

[232] This type of paronomasia is not explicitly found in the handbooks, but compares to types listed in Her. 4.21.29, 30 and Quint. 9.3.66.

[233] Οἷς, which refers to the evil angels or glories of 2:10–11, is the nearest antecedent of αὐτῶν and thus φθορᾷ αὐτῶν is most likely a reference to the destruction of the evil angels, not the animals.

[234] Eccl 10:16; Isa 5:11; *T. Mos.* 7:4; Juvenal 1.103.

[235] Cic. *Part. Or.* 15.54.

[236] This type of paronomasia is not specifically listed in the handbooks, but compares with elements of those given in Her. 4.21.29 and Quint. 9.3.71.

makes this topic more explicit by holding up the absence of spots and blemishes before God (ἄσπιλοι καὶ ἀμώμητοι) as the ideal of audience (cf. 1:3-7).

2 Peter may incorporate an ironic pun in 2:13b.[237] He may have changed Jude's reference to the ἀγάπαις, "love feast" (v 12), to the similar sounding ἀπάταις, "deceits." The phrase, "while they feast with you" (συνευωχούμενοι ὑμῖν), would suggest the agapes to the audience, regardless of their knowledge of Jude. The irony is that what is supposed to be an ἀγαπή is more appropriately called an ἀπάτη because of the reveling of the false teachers.

In 2:14, 2 Peter accuses the false teachers of having "eyes full of an adultress" (ὀφθαλμοὺς ἔχοντες μεστοὺς μοιχαλίδος), that is, of always looking for someone with whom to commit adultery. This is an example of *enargeia* or vivid representation used to arouse pathos.[238] *Enargeia* here uses the figure of thought called emphasis which reveals something deeper than is actually expressed.[239] The emphasis is produced by hyperbole,[240] and both emphasis and hyperbole amplify.[241] As is rhetorically advantageous, 2 Peter may rely upon a well-known maxim that a shameless man does not have κόρας ("pupils" or "maidens" — a pun) in his eyes, but πόρνας ("harlots").[242] He further amplifies this charge by adding that the false teachers' desire for sin is insatiable (ἀκαταπαύστος).

Another charge of 2 Peter in 2:14 is that the false teachers "entice unsteady souls," δελεάζοντες ψυχὰς ἀστηρίκτους. The charge relies on the metaphor of fishing and snaring with bait underlying the verb δελεάζω,[243] a metaphor creating a vivid mental picture.[244] In conjunction with the metaphor of snaring and the description of the victims of the false teachers as unsteady (ἀστήρικτοι), the audience envisions the false teachers preying on the vulnerable among them, a vision eliciting negative pathos. Regarding the topic of stability, in the *exordium* 2 Peter designates his audience as those steady in the truth (ἐστηριγμένα, 1:12, cf. 3:17). The description of others as unsteady (ἀστήρικτοι) affirms the audience that they themselves are considered stable by Peter, an affirmation which elicits positive pathos.

Yet another charge of 2:14 is that the false teachers possess "hearts trained

---

[237] This would be an example of irony as a figure, for it is not confessed that the meaning is opposite of what is actually said (Quint. 9.2.44-46).

[238] Quint. 6.2.29-36.

[239] This is emphasis of the type meaning more than it actually says (Quint. 8.3.83; cf. 9.2.3).

[240] Her. 4.53.67. This is hyperbole used for magnification and exaggeration (Her. 4.33.44; Quint. 8.6.67), of the type giving more than the actual facts (Quint. 8.6.68). Her. 4.53.67 notes hyperbole is often used with the figure emphasis.

[241] Quint. 9.2.3 notes that emphasis is a type of amplification. Cf. Quint. 8.4.29 which notes that hyperbole itself was once considered a type of amplification.

[242] Plut. *Mor.* 528E; the reverse of a chaste man is attributed to Timaeus in Long. *Subl.* 4.5.

[243] A metaphor used in Philo, *Praem.* 25.

[244] Cic. *De Or.* 3.40.160-61; Her. 4.34.45.

in greed." This is another example of the figure called emphasis,[245] here produced by hyperbole,[246] and the metaphor of athletic training in the verb γυμνάζω.[247] The metaphor, hyperbole, and their combination in emphasis provide amplification.[248] The charge implies effort was expended and practice performed to become effective in being greedy, and forms a contrast to ἀστήρικτος. Whereas the victims of the false teachers are unsteady, the false teachers themselves are throughly trained and dedicated in greed and know how to exploit that unsteadiness.

Finally, 2:14 ends with the exclamation κατάρα τέκνα, "Accursed children!" Besides being an example of metonymy, this is an example of *exclamatio* which intensifies the emotion[249] created by the amplification by accumulation begun in 2:12. It effectively summarizes the consequences of the behavior described both before and after it in the *digressio:* becoming accursed by God and coming under his judgment. It is strategically located to break up the bombardment of the denunciation and to summarize it in a fashion which still constitutes denunciation. The *exclamatio* is formed by analogy with similar phrases found in the LXX[250] and Christian usage.[251]

In 2:15, 2 Peter relies on the comparison of the two ways, first stating of the false teachers: "Leaving the straight way they have gone astray." The accusation is an example of the figure of thought called refining, the reiteration inherent in the figures serving to amplify the charge through repetition.[252] His accusation contains three metaphors for embellishment.[253] "Straight way" (εὐθὺς ὁδός) is a common metaphor for obedience to God,[254] and "leaving" and "going astray" are complementary metaphors. The metaphor of "going astray" in the verb πλανάω introduces the topic recurring again in 2:18, in the accusation that the false teachers entice new converts who just escaped error (πλάνη), and in 3:17 in the *peroratio,* where the audience is exhorted not to fall prey to the error (πλάνη) of the false teachers.

---

[245] This is emphasis of the type meaning more than it says (Quint. 8.3.83–84; cf. 9.2.3).

[246] This is hyperbole for magnification and exaggeration (Her. 4.33.44; Quint. 8.6.67) of the type giving more than the actual facts (Quint. 8.6.68). Her. 4.53.67 discusses the interaction of hyperbole and emphasis.

[247] Albrecht Oepke, "γυμνός," *TDNT* 1:775.

[248] Long. *Subl.* 32.5–6 and Her. 4.34.45 discuss metaphor's use in amplification. Quint. 8.4.29 notes that hyperbole was once a type of amplification. Quint. 9.2.3 confirms emphasis is used for amplification.

[249] Quint. 9.2.26–27; 9.3.97.

[250] Isa 57:4 τέκνα ἀπωλείας; Hos 10:9 τέκνα ἀδικίας.

[251] Eph 2:3; 5:8; 1 Pet 1:14; *Barn.* 7:1; 9:7; 21:9; Ign. *Phld.* 2:1; G. Adolf Deissmann, *Bible Studies,* trans. Alexander Grieve, 2d ed. (Edinburgh: T. & T. Clark, 1903) 161–66.

[252] Cic. *Part. Or.* 15.54.

[253] Demetr. *Eloc.* 2.78; Her. 4.34.45; Quint. 8.6.6.

[254] Ὁδὸς εὐθεία—LXX 1 Kgdms 12:23; Ps 106:7; Prov 2:16; Isa 33:15; *1 Clem.* 7:3. ὁδοὶ εὐθειαί - LXX Prov 2:13; Hos 14:10; Acts 13:10. ὁδὸς ὀρθή - Herm. *Mand.* 6:1:2; Philo, *Det.* 22; *Agr.* 101.

2 Peter 2:15b-16 is an example of the use of the figure called exemplification, here used to amplify the charge of 2:15a, by embellishing, clarifying, and vivifying.[255] At the same time it is developing the four interrelated topics of the way (2:2, 15a, 21), leading-following (1:16, 2:2; 3:17), greed (2:3a, 14), and wrongdoing (2:13a), most all of which are found together in the immediate context and in the counteraccusation in 2:2-3a. The exemplification uses the traditional metaphor[256] and narrative[257] of Balaam's way as an example of one who left the right way because of greed, something the false teachers are now doing. The phrase "loved a reward of wrongdoing" (μισθὸν ἀδικίας ἠγάπησεν) further explains this topic from 2:13a where the false teachers are said to be destined to "suffer wrong as a reward of wrongdoing" (ἀδικούμενοι μισθὸν ἀδικίας).

2 Peter enhances his amplification in 2:15b-16 by calling Balaam the son of Bosor. Bosor is an otherwise unattested form of the name of Balaam's father Beor,[258] and is probably a play on the Hebrew word *bāśār,* "flesh."[259] This clues the audience that the way of Balaam is opposed to God, as the connotations of *bāśār* indicate. The designation ὃς μισθὸν ἀδικίας ἠγάπησεν, "who loved unjust gain," may not only refer to what Balaam hoped to gain from Balak for cursing Israel, but may also be meant as irony, referring to the reward of judgment Balaam received from Israel's God. Jewish exegesis contains similar irony when discussing how Balaam was killed along with the Midianite kings (Num 31:8) because he had gone to them to receive the reward Balak promised him for his cursing of Israel.[260]

Verses 2:15b-16 are closely linked to 2:12. Having compared the false teachers to ἄλογα ζῷα, "irrational animals" (2:12), having identified the false teachers as followers of Balaam, and now having shown that Balaam's madness was refuted by an ass which proved more rational,[261] 2 Peter has indirectly led his audience to the conclusion that the false teachers, like Balaam, are less rational than the irrational ass. A similar thought concerning Balaam is expressed in Philo, *Mos.* 1.272: "For the unreasoning animal (ἀλόγου ζῴου) showed a superior power of sight to him who claimed to see not only the world but the world's Maker." Stylistically, 2:16 exhibits paronomasia in the words παρανομίας, "transgressing," and παραφρονίαν, "madness," which respectively end

---

[255] Her. 4.49.62; cf. 4.45.59.

[256] Num 22:32 LXX.

[257] Num 22:21-35.

[258] *b 'ōr,* LXX βεωρ.

[259] It is noteworthy that in *b. Sanh.* 105a, *b 'ōr* (Beor) is associated with *b 'îr* (beast) in order to accuse Balaam of bestiality.

[260] *b. Sanh.* 106a; *Num. Rab.* 22:5; *Sipre Num.* 157; Bauckham, 268; Neyrey, *Form and Background,* 92-93.

[261] Although in the text of Num 22:21-35 the ass does not rebuke Balaam (the angel does later), 2 Peter here relies upon Jewish haggadic tradition in which the ass does speak (Targums to Num 22:30- *Tg. Ps.-J; Tg. Neof.*). These same texts refer to Balaam's madness as do Philo, *Mut.* 203; *Mos.* 1.293.

each clause, and in ἄφωνον and φωνῇ which form antithesis.[262]

In 2:17, 2 Peter continues his denunciation using two metaphors reliant upon traditional imagery of religious teaching as sustainer of spiritual life, as water is sustainer of natural life.[263] Both metaphors are used to clarify[264] and create a vivid mental picture.[265] The first metaphor of "waterless springs" was traditional.[266] The second metaphor, "mists driven by a storm," has no known ancient counterpart, but is appropriate, for it signifies the coming of hot, dry weather rather than rain.[267] Both metaphors drive home the point that the false teachers, although seeming to promise life-giving doctrine, as a well or clouds promise life-giving water, offer only empty promise. In the metaphor of mists driven by a storm, the mists have no will of their own, but are subject to the wind. Another point may be that like the mists, the false teachers are not free. In 2:19–20, where they are slaves to corruption and defilement of the world, this is clearly the case.

At the close of 2:17, 2 Peter asserts that the judgment of "nether gloom of darkness" (ὁ ζόφος τοῦ σκότους) is reserved for the false teachers. This phrase refers back to the Old Testament example of the Watchers used in 2:4, 9 where the topic is developed that since the Watchers were kept in nether gloom (σειραῖς ζόφου ταρταρώσας) until judgment, the false teachers will also be kept until judgment. This verse makes it explicit that the punishment of the false teachers is the very same as that of the Watchers.

As the conjunction γάρ beginning 2:18 indicates, 2:18–19 functions as the premise of 2:17, and together with 2:17 forms an artificial proof, an enthymeme.[268] The false teachers can be characterized as spiritually empty of promise, lacking freedom, and headed for nether gloom (2:17) because they speak haughty futility and entice new converts with promises of moral freedom, although they themselves are really only slaves of corruption (2:18–19).

In 2:19 is given the empty message with which the false teachers ensnare the new Christians (2:18) and which renders them liable to judgment (2:17). The antithesis of freedom-slavery is used in irony to charge that, while the false teachers promise freedom from eschatological judgment, they themselves are in slavery to its destruction.[269] Φθορά is personified and portrayed in the common imagery of a victor in war who seizes those defeated as slaves and booty. The

---

[262] Both are paronomasia of the type in which letters are modified so similar words express dissimilar things (Her. 4.21.29; cf. Quint. 9.3.69, 72–74).

[263] Prov 13:14; Sir 24:25–26; CD 6:4; cf. Jer 2:13.

[264] Demetr. Eloc. 2.82; Cic. De Or. 3.38.155–39.157; Quint. 8.6.5–6.

[265] Cic. De Or. 3.40.160–61; Her. 4.34.45.

[266] Jer 2:13.

[267] Ar. Meteor. 1.346B; Theophr. De Signis 4; cf. Prov 25:14.

[268] For more on enthymeme, see ch. 1.

[269] This is irony as a trope, which confesses that it implies something opposite of what it actually says (Quint. 9.2.44–46).

sentence, "Whatever overcomes a man to that he is enslaved," in 2:19 is a maxim[270] common to antiquity,[271] and ends the sentence as convention dictates.[272] As a maxim it increases the rhetor's ethos[273] and lends authority to the accusation.[274]

It is noteworthy that in 2:19, the verb ἐπαγγέλλομαι, used of the false teachers' promise of freedom, anticipates the argument in 3:4, 9 where 2 Peter relates the false teachers' scoff that Christ's promise (ἐπαγγελία) of the parousia is "as yet" unfulfilled. Before specifying such scoffing, he points out that it is the false teachers who are guilty of making promises "already" shown unfulfilled.[275]

The premise of 2:18-19 elaborates four topics from 2:3ff.: the false teachers speak falsely (2:3), they are immoral (2:2, 10a, 14, 20-22), they ensnare others in their sin (2:14; cf. 3:17), and they will be destroyed (2:3, 9, 12). The use of the terms ἀσέλγεια (2:2, 18), ἐπιθυμία (2:10a, 18), δελεάζω (2:14, 18), and φθορά (2:12, 19) interrelate these topics. Of particular note is the similarity of 2:14 and 2:18. In both, immorality is the charge made against the false teachers. The metaphor of fishing, expressed by the metaphorical verb δελεάζω, is used of the proselyzing practices, and the victims are designated as unsteady Christians (2:14 – ψυχὰς ἀστηρίκτους; 2:18 – τοὺς ὀλίγως ἀποφεύγοντας τοὺς ἐν πλάνῃ ἀναστρεφομένους).

Serving as a strong deterent to those who would follow or have followed the false teachers, 2:20-22 describes how drastic a step is taken when following their lead. In 2:20 there is reference back to the *exordium* in 1:3-4 where it is clear that becoming a Christian means escaping the world through the knowledge of God and Jesus Christ. Using antithesis and the common topic of degree,[276] 2 Peter now makes the point that to leave this state has the tragic consequences of being in a worse state. He supports his assertion with a verbatim rendering[277] of a

---

[270] A maxim is a figure of speech, ". . . a saying drawn from life, which shows concisely either what happens or ought to happen in life . . ." (Her. 4.17.24). Cf. Ar. *Rhet.* 2.21.1394a.2; Quint. 8.5.1-2 for similar definitions. Maxims were considered true to the observation and experience of all humankind, or a subgroup within it (Ar. *Rhet.* 2.21.1394a.2; 1395a.11; 1395b.15; Her. 4.17.25; Quint. 8.5.1-2). For further discussion, see Ar. *Rhet.* 2.21; Her. 4.17.24-25; Quint. 8.5; Lausberg, 1:431-34, §872-79; Martin, 122-24, 257-58; Bullinger, 778-803. The maxim here is embellished with homoeoteleuton in ἥττηται and δεδούλωται; which respectively end the two clauses, and it is tied by the paronomasia δοῦλοι and δεδούλωται and to the preceding part of the sentence.

[271] Cf. Hippolytus, *In Dan.* 3.22.4: ᾧ γὰρ ἄν τις ὑποταγῇ τούτῳ καὶ δεδούλωται; *Clem. Rec.* 5.12; Origen, *In Exod. Hom.* 12; cf. Rom 6:16; John 8:34.

[272] Quint. 8.5.2. Ar. *Rhet.* 2.21.1394b.7 states that the maxim can either begin or end a sentence.

[273] Ar. *Rhet.* 2.21.1395b.16.

[274] Ar. *Rhet.* 2.21.1395a.11; 2.21.1395b.15; Her. 4.17.25.

[275] Neyrey, "Form and Background," 419.

[276] Ar. *Rhet.* 1.2.1358a.21; 1.3.1359a.9; 2.18.1391b.4; 2.19.1393a.26-27; Cic. *De Or.* 2.40.172; *Part. Or.* 2.7 (an interpolation); Quint. 5.10.86-94.

[277] Only substituting αὐτοῖς for τοῦ ἀνθρώπου ἐκείνου.

saying of Jesus[278] concerning the return of the unclean spirit: γίνεται τὰ ἔσχατα τοῦ ἀνθρώπου ἐκείνου χείρονα τῶν πρώτων. It should carry great authority therefore and serve as a constraint.[279]

This section of 2:18–20 echoes the *exordium* of 1:3–4. In 1:3–4, the essential content of Christianity is presented positively and in 2:18–20 the content of apostasy is presented negatively. This is part of a larger antithesis. In 1:3–4, the knowledge (ἐπιγνώσις, 1:3) of God is the medium of the things pertaining to life and godliness. The promises of God (ἐπαγγέλμα, 1:4) enable escape (ἀποφεύγω, 1:4) from corruption in the world (ἐν τῷ κόσμῳ . . . φθορᾶς, 1:4) because of passion (ἐπιθυμία, 1:4). In 2:18–20 the knowledge of Christ (ἐπιγνώσις, 2:20) enables the escape (ἀποφεύγω, 2:20) from worldly defilements. Those who had escaped (ἀποφεύγω, 2:18) error (πλάνη, 2:18) are lured by the promises (ἐπαγγέλομαι, 2:19) of the false teachers to slavery and corruption (δοῦλοι, φθορά, 2:19; cf. 2:10), because of licentious passions of the flesh (ἐν ἐπιθυμίαις σαρκὸς ἀσελγείαις, 2:18; cf. 2:10), a return to the corruption of the world (μιάσματα τοῦ κόσμου, 2:20).

Using comparison, 2:21 amplifies 2:20[280] again using the topic of degree. It reiterates its content in different form using refining.[281] Like 2:20, it looks back to the *exordium* in 1:3–4 and the topic of the knowledge of God and Christ (ἐπεγνωκέναι, cf. Jude 3). It utilizes this topic within the antithesis of the state of the faithful and of the apostate Christian.[282] In this amplification, 2 Peter further works out the topic of the "way" found in 2:2, 15. Here the common metaphor of the ethical life, the way of righteousness (τὴν ὁδὸν τῆς δικαιοσύνης) is used[283] in the antithesis with its equivalent, the synecdoche[284] "holy commandment" (ἁγία ἐντολή). The verb form παραδοθείσης, "delivered," should remind the audience that this Christian instruction was delivered by the apostles and is therefore authoritative, as assumed in 3:2. The whole verse has been written in the form of a *Tobspruch,* a proverbial form expressing the idea of one state being "better than" another, a form widely used in early Christianity to emphasize the terribleness of a certain action.[285]

The amplification of the state of apostasy (2:20–21) of the false teachers is made in 2:22 using what is specifically identified as a proverb, a παροιμία. The

---

[278] From either Matt 12:45 par. Luke 11:26, Q, or oral tradition.

[279] The saying is also applied to backsliding in Herm. *Mand.* 5:2:7; 12:5:4.

[280] Quint. 8.4.9–14.

[281] This is refining of the type repeating the idea in different form (Her. 4.42.54).

[282] Verse 2:21 also uses transplacement in ἐπεγνωκέναι-ἐπιγνοῦσιν.

[283] LXX Job 24:13; Prov 21:16, 21; *Jub.* 23:26; *1 Enoch* 82:4; Matt 21:32; *Barn.* 1:4; 5:4. Cf. also, plural: LXX Prov 8:20; 12:28; 16:31; Tob 1:3; *1 Enoch* 91:18–19; 94:1; 99:10; 1QS 4:2. "The righteous way": LXX Job 24:4, 11; 28:4; Ps 2:12; *2 Clem.* 5:7; *Barn.* 12:4.

[284] This is synecdoche suggesting the whole from the part.

[285] G. F. Snyder, "The *Tobspruch* in the New Testament," *NTS* 23 (1976/77) 117–20; Matt 5:29, 30; 18:6, 8, 9; 26:24; Mark 9:42, 43, 45, 47; 14:21; 1 Cor 7:9; 1 Pet 3:17; *1 Clem.* 46:8; Ign. *Rom.* 6:1.

maxim lends 2 Peter's argument and identification authority.[286] The adjective ἀληθής in the phrase τῆς ἀληθοῦς παροιμίας is really redundant, for proverbial material is by definition held to be true to observable experience.[287] The use of ἀληθής draws attention to the authority of this supporting material and ultimately the entire argument.

Dogs and pigs were often joined in proverbs symbolizing immorality in gentile life.[288] Here in 2:22 two separate proverbs have been joined. The first half of the proverb concerning dogs is derived from Prov 26:11.[289] The second half of the proverb concerning the pig's delight in wallowing in mud is traditional to the ancient world.[290] 2 Peter relies on a proverb from *Ahikar*.[291] The reference to getting dirty after cleaning (λούω) refers to apostasy, possibly a reference to post-baptismal sin (cf. καθαρισμός in 1:9). The entire proverb works out the topic that although the Christian has been cleansed from old sins (1:9), like unreasoning animals (2:12) the false teachers return to soil themselves in sin.

Within the *digressio,* the four maxims found successively in 2:19–22 make the style faulty. Maxims are not to be placed too close together or to be too numerous, or their contribution to ethos and argumentation is lost and style becomes discontinuous.[292] The ancients warned that concentration on maxims makes it seem that the rhetor is preaching morals rather than pleading the case.[293] Since the rhetorical situation of 2 Peter centers in the church, not the courtroom, some relaxation of this last restriction would be expected.

Also, within the *digressio* in 2:13–22, there are eleven metaphors. Too frequent use of metaphor was also considered faulty style, making the language obscure.[294] Too frequent use of metaphor was especially bad if they were all of one species,[295] and three metaphors in a series was considered the limit.[296] These faults are all found in the *digressio* of 2 Peter, with even all the metaphors but

---

[286] Ar. *Rhet.* 2.21.1395a.11; 1395b.15; Her. 4.17.25.

[287] Ar. *Rhet.* 2.21.1394a.2; 1395a.11; 1395b.15; Her. 4.17.25; Quint. 8.5.1–2.

[288] Horace, *Ep.* 1.2.26; 2.2.75; Pap. Oxy. 840, lines 33–34; Matt 7:6; cf. Rev 22:15.

[289] Cf. *Gos. Truth* 33.15–16 dependent upon 2 Peter.

[290] G. S. Kirk (ed.), *Heraclitus, The Cosmic Fragments* (Cambridge: Cambridge University Press, 1954) 76–80; M. Aubineau, "La thème du 'bourbier' dans la littérature grecque profane et chrétienne," *RSR* 33 (1959) 201–4. E.g., Sextus Empiricus, *Hypot.* 1.14.56; cf. Clem. Alex. *Protr.* 10.92.4; *Strom.* 1.1.2.2; 2.15.68.3.

[291] 8:18 (Syriac): "My son, thou hast been to me like the swine that had been to the baths, and when it saw a muddy ditch, went down and washed in it, and cried to its companions: Come and wash." 8:15 (Arabic): "O my son! Thou hast been to me like the pig who went into the hot bath with people of quality, and when it came out of the hot bath, it saw a filthy hole and it went down and wallowed in it" (*APOT* 2:772).

[292] Quint. 8.5.26–29, 32–34.

[293] Her. 4.17.25.

[294] Quint. 8.6.14.

[295] Quint. 8.6.16.

[296] Long. *Subl.* 32.1.

two (2:17) being of the same species substituting the inanimate for the inanimate.[297]

The Transitio (3:1–2)

The second part of the *probatio* proper is constituted by 3:1–13. Like its counterpart in 1:16–2:10a, 3:1–13 is preceded by 2 Peter, under the guise of the testament genre, exhorting his audience to remember apostolic witness and Old Testament prophecy concerning the reality of the parousia and the judgment (1:12–15; 3:1–2). As in 1:16–21, in 3:8–13 he seeks to defend the teaching of the parousia. As in 2:3b–10a, in 3:4–7 he defends the teaching of the judgment.[298]

2 Peter provides a transition within the body-middle of the letter in 3:1–2. This transition is indicated by the reminder topic (which is akin to the full disclosure formula, "I wish you to know that"),[299] a given motivation for writing,[300] a compliance statement referring to previous instruction,[301] a reference to past writing using the standard form of the past tense of γράφω, use of the unemphatic form of the personal pronoun, a given object of the correspondence using ὅτι,[302] and the vocative ἀγαπητοί.[303]

This transition is necessitated by rhetorical considerations. After a lengthy *digressio*, a transition back to the *probatio* proper is needed. Two methods of accomplishing this are the use of the figures of thought called *aphodos* and *transitio. Aphodos* is a brief transitional statement after a *digressio* which is used to return to the main subject.[304] *Transitio* briefly recalls what has been said and briefly sets forth what follows.[305] Recapitulation was prescribed for the end of a division of a rhetorical work and for the end of the work as a whole to serve

---

[297] Quint. 8.6.9–10.

[298] It should be noted that probably 3:4–13 is partially derived from a Jewish apocalyptic source or standard type of argumentation which tried to explain the delay of the inbreaking of God in judgment in history. See D. von Allmen, "L'apocalyptique juive et le retard de la parousie en II Pierre 3:1–13," *RTP* 16 (1960) 256–58; Bauckham, 283–84. *1 Clem.* 23:3–4 and *2 Clem.* 11:2–4 use the same apocalyptic source.

For further discussion of the apologetic of ch. 3, see Anton Vögtle, *Das Neue Testament und die Zukunft des Kosmos.* KomBeiANT (Dusseldorf: Patmos, 1970) 121–42; Joseph Chaine, "Cosmogonie aquatique et conflagration finale d'apres la secunda petri," *RB* 46 (1937) 207–16.

[299] White, 2–5, 48, 51.

[300] White, 3.

[301] White, 24–25.

[302] White, 33–34, 38, 41.

[303] White, 15–16, 38, 41.

[304] Cic. *Or.* 40.137; *De Or.* 3.53.203 = Quint. 9.1.28. For further discussion, see Lausberg, 1:187, §340; Martin, 91.

[305] Her. 4.26.35; Quint. 9.3.98. For further discussion, see Lausberg, 1:422–23, §849–50; Bullinger, 908.

as reminders.[306] One method of doing so is to propose a line of action beginning with a phrase like "You must bear in mind. . . ."[307]

After the lengthy *digressio* and denunciation of 2:10b-22, 2 Peter needs a transition to bring the audience's attention back to the pattern of refutation ceased at 2:10a. *Aphodos, transitio,* and recapping by proposing a line of action beginning with a phrase like "You must bear in mind" are found in 3:1-2. Here, 2 Peter returns to the main subject, setting forth that what will be discussed is the predictions of the prophets, of Jesus, and of the apostles. The reminder topic proposes a line of action which the audience must "bear in mind." The reminder topic is here repeated in the paronomasia,[308] ὑπομνήσει μνησθῆναι, for amplification through repetition[309] of the need "to bear in mind." The reference to this being a second letter intended as a reminder recalls 1 Peter and 2 Peter 1:12-15, and serves to revitalize the pseudonymous ploy.

Any portion of the speech can have the force of an *exordium,* especially when it seeks to gain attention and goodwill from the audience.[310] Quintilian writes, "Even in the proof there are many passages which perform the same functions as an *exordium.*"[311] Also, narrative should serve in other places in the rhetoric besides in the *narratio.*[312] This section, 3:1-2, functions as a mini-*exordium.*[313] Noteworthy is the similarity to the *exordium* in 1:12-15 with the use of the reminder topic and reference to what is known of Peter.

This section helps to renew the audience's attention, receptivity, and goodwill,[314] all of which may have become strained under the severity and length of the denunciation. Attention is gained largely from the ethos of Peter,[315] and receptivity naturally follows.[316] The effort to obtain goodwill concentrates on the persons of the rhetor and audience.[317] From the person of the rhetor, goodwill

---

[306] *Rhet. ad Alex.* 20.1433b.30ff.; 21.1434a.30ff. Cf. Her. 2.30.47 which advises that conclusions, or *epilogoi,* occur in four places in a rhetorical work: the *principium,* after the *narratio,* after the strongest argument of the *probatio,* and in the *peroratio.*

[307] *Rhet. ad Alex.* 20.1434a.3ff.

[308] This paronomasia is not specifically discussed in the handbooks, but corresponds in part to several. Cf. Her. 4.21.29; Quint. 9.3.69, 71.

[309] Cic. *Part. Or.* 15.54.

[310] Ar. *Rhet.* 3.14.1415b.9; Quint. 4.1.73-75.

[311] Quint. 4.1.75.

[312] Ar. *Rhet.* 3.16.1417b.11.

[313] Quint. 4.3.9 discusses using a second *exordium* after the *digressio* that sometimes accompanies the *narratio.* Here the *exordium* follows the *digressio,* although it is within the *probatio,* not after the *narratio.*

[314] For more on the *exordium,* see ch. 1.

[315] Ar. *Rhet.* 3.14.1415a.7.

[316] Her. 1.4.7; Quint. 4.1.34.

[317] Ar. *Rhet.* 3.14.1415a.7; Cic. *Inv.* 1.16.22; *De Or.* 2.79.321-22; *Part. Or.* 8.28; Her. 1.4.8-5.8; Quint. 4.1.6-15. For a list of methods for eliciting goodwill from the audience and the rhetor, see ch. 2, pp. 37-38.

is elicited by a non-arrogant reference to Peter's past service, that is, Peter's previous letter of 1 Peter, and, as in the main *exordium* of 1:12-15, by the reminder topic. Although a feature of the testament genre, the reminder topic serves to avoid the impression that Peter thinks himself in any way superior in his knowledge of the issues addressed. The topic assumes that the audience is familiar with the facts of the case and only needs to be reminded of them. This prevents the appearance of arrogance.[318]

2 Peter also gains goodwill from the audience[319] by referring to their understanding as "pure" (εἰλικρινής) in a moral sense. This is effective for two reasons. First, it distinguishes the audience from the false teachers whose understanding is corrupted by passion (3:3) and twisted (3:16), showing in what esteem they are held.[320] Secondly, it appeals to the audience's own knowledge as a source of authority that they can bring to bear on the issue to be refuted, and appeals ultimately to the source of their knowledge: the apostles, prophets, and 1 Peter. This links audience praise to the furtherance of the case.[321]

In 3:1-2, 2 Peter appeals to the same two authorities as in 1:16-21 to support the teaching of the parousia and the judgment: the Old Testament prophets and the apostles. Before further refutation of the opponents is given, it is worthwhile to remind the audience of the authorities which they are to remember so that the teaching will be upon their mind. It is noteworthy that the Old Testament prophets and the apostles are deemed on par. This same phenomenon occurs in 1:16-21 and 3:15-16, and indicates the regard 2 Peter and this audience have for the apostles.[322] The double possessive genitive "the commandment of the Lord and Savior[323] through your apostles" gives added authority to the commandment which the apostles gave the audience by pointing to Christ as its co-possessor and originator. The phrase "your apostles" emphasizes that the commandment is derived from the apostles who founded the audience in their faith and was accepted freely from those apostles, and even from Paul (3:15). This accentuates the ethos of the commandment for its use in proof. Finally, the reference to the commandment (ἐντολή) forms an antithesis with 2:21. Whereas the false teachers have forgotten the holy commandment (2:21), the audience is exhorted to remember it (3:2).

Fourth Accusation and Refutation (3:3-13)

The phrase τοῦτο πρῶτον γινώσκοντες, "know this first," which also begins a crucial point in the *probatio* in 1:20-21, opens 3:3. It gains audience attention

---

[318] Quint. 4.1.10, 33.

[319] Cic. *Inv.* 1.16.22; *Part. Or.* 8.28; Her. 1.5.8.

[320] Cic. *Inv.* 1.16.22; Her. 1.5.8.

[321] Quint. 4.1.16.

[322] Some passages coupling the Old Testament prophets and the apostles, or the Old Testament prophets and the gospel are *2 Clem.* 14:2; Ign. *Phld.* 5:1-2; Pol. *Phil.* 6:3; 9:1-2; 3 Cor 3:36.

[323] This is an example of synecdoche also found in 2:21.

and readies them to receive instruction, because it alerts them that what is about to be stated is very important in the eyes of the rhetor.[324]

On the surface, 3:3-4 functions as a prophecy of Peter concerning the presence of scoffers in the church in the last days.[325] As such 3:3-4 functions like an artificial proof based on example,[326] the type of example called a judgment,[327] and the type of judgment called a supernatural oracle.[328] The application of the example to the false teachers is left to the audience. Secondly, from the perspective of a pseudonymous author and his audience in an age when scoffers exist, 3:3-4 also functions as a necessary sign of the parousia.[329] It can clearly be seen that the scoffers currently in the church are those once predicted would come in the last days. Thus, ironically, the false teachers who deny the parousia are themselves a sign of its imminence.[330] They are a necessary sign because their nature as scoffers, and their presence according to prophecy, cannot be denied. The scoffers' charge of the non-materialization of the parousia is thus minimized by their very presence. Thirdly, 3:4 is also a proposition of the false teachers.

This section, 3:3-4, employs amplification by strong words[331] which serves to decrease the ethos of the false teachers. Ἐμπαίκτης is a derogatory term for the one who despises and ignores religion and morality.[332] Besides being an example of paronomasia,[333] the phrase ἐμπαιγμονῇ ἐμπαῖκται, "scoffers scoffing," is a Septuagintalism, imitating the use of a cognate noun with a verb to translate the Hebrew infinitive absolute for amplification through repetition.[334]

The topics of following (ἐξακολουθέω) and desire (ἐπιθυμία) are further developed and tied together. Previously, the apostles are accused of following cleverly devised myths (1:16), those following the scoffers are said to revile the way of truth (2:2), and the scoffers themselves to have forsaken the right way and

---

[324] Compare Luke 12:39; Gal 3:7; 2 Tim 3:1; Heb 13:3.

[325] The nominative case of τοῦτο πρῶτον γινώσκοντες indicates that 3:3-4 is not closely tied to 3:2 which refers to Old Testament prophecy. There were prophecies of scoffers who mock the delay of divine judgment in Old Testament prophecy (Amos 9:10; Mal 2:17; cf. Ezek 12:22; Zeph 1:12) and prophecies of false teachers in the last days in early Christian teaching (Matt 7:15; 24:11, 24; Mark 13:22; Acts 20:29-30; 1 Tim 4:1-3; 2 Tim 4:3-4; 1 John 2:8; 4:1-3; Did. 16:3; Apoc. Pet. A 1; Sib. Or. 2.165-66. Here, however, in the context of a testament, 2 Peter probably expects the audience to understand the prediction as that of Peter.

[326] For more on example, see ch. 1.

[327] Cic. Inv. 1.30.48; Quint. 5.11.36-44.

[328] Quint. 5.11.41-42.

[329] For more on necessary sign, see ch. 1.

[330] Fornberg, 61.

[331] Cic. Part. Or. 15.53; Quint. 8.4.1-3.

[332] Georg Bertram, "παίζω," TDNT 5:635-36.

[333] This paronomasia is not specifically discussed in the handbooks, but corresponds in part to several. Cf. Her. 4.21.29; 4.22.30; Quint. 9.3.69.

[334] Cic. Part. Or. 15.54.

to be following the way of Balaam (2:15). Also, it was previously noted that the desire of the world can be escaped by Christians (1:4), but is fully indulged by the false teachers (2:10, 18). Now it is affirmed that the false teachers follow after their own desires (3:3).

In 3:4, 2 Peter presents the proposition of the false teachers: "Where is the promise of his coming? For ever since the fathers fell asleep, all things have continued as they were from the beginning of creation." This proposition is in the form of a rhetorical question,[335] ποῦ ἐστιν being a standard form of introduction to rhetorical questions of scoffers of God in the Old Testament.[336] 2 Peter has probably fashioned this rhetorical question[337] to frame the false teachers' charge in a mode reminiscent of the "scoffer tradition" of the Old Testament and of known apostolic prophecy (possibly even an apocalyptic source).[338] As such, their own charge is stated to make it contribute to the decrease of their ethos.

Promise, ἐπαγγελία, refers back to the *exordium* in 1:4, to the promises (ἐπαγγέλματα) of Jesus. These promises are probably those which seem to temporally limit the parousia to the lifetime of Jesus' contemporaries (cf. 3:13).[339] The false teachers are shown to be denying the parousia because a fundamental of the faith which the apostles delivered to the original congregation, namely, that Christ would come within their lifetime, failed to materialize. As the polemic of 3:5-7 indicates, the false teachers also base their denial of the parousia upon the belief that world history has not witnessed the intervention of God.

The refutation of the false teachers' claim of 3:4 constitutes 3:5-13.[340] This refutation deals with the two parts of the charge in reverse order. The claim of the latter part of 3:4, that all things have continued undisturbed, is refuted in 3:5-7. The main charge of 3:4, that the promise of Christ's coming is mute because the parousia did not come during the lifetime of first generation

---

[335] Rhetorical Question is a figure of thought in which a question is asked ". . . not to get information, but to emphasise [sic] our point" (Quint. 9.2.7). Cf. Quint. 9.1.29 = Cic. *De Or.* 3.53.203 and the unnamed figure of thought defined in Cic. *Or.* 40.137 for similar definitions. For further information, see Quint. 9.2.6-16; Lausberg, 1:379-81, §767-70; Martin, 284-88; Bullinger, 944-56.

[336] LXX Ps 41:4, 11- of the psalmist's enemies; Pss 78:10; 113:10; Joel 2:27; Mic 7:10)— of Gentile nations when God does not aid his people; Mal 2:17- of those who doubt God's judgment. Cf. Jer 17:15 — of those doubting the fulfilment of God's word. Examples of eschatological skepticism arising from non-fulfilment of prophecy— Exod 12:22; Sir 16:22; *b. Sanh.* 97b.

[337] 2 Peter's hand is observed in the metaphor "fell asleep" for death which is in line with the two metaphors of "putting off" and "departure" for death in 1:14-15.

[338] Von Allmen, 256-64; Bauckham, 283-85. Cf. *1 Clem.* 23:3 and *2 Clem.* 11:2 for similar doubts expressed about eschatological hopes.

[339] Matt 16:28 par. Mark 9:1 par. Luke 9:27; Matt 24:34 par. Mark 13:30 par. Luke 21:32; John 21:22-23; cf. Matt 10:23.

[340] On the tense shift, see above, pp. 110-11.

Christians, is refuted in 3:8-13.

The opening phrase of 3:5, "when they maintain this, it escapes their notice,"[341] implies that the false teachers can only maintain the position of 3:4 by ignoring the facts that follow in 3:5-13. Rhetorically, it functions well to destroy the credibility of the preceding charge by stating that it does not account for the facts, and by presenting the arguments that follow as essential information refuting the charge.

The false teachers' charge of 3:4 that "all things have continued as they were from the beginning of creation" is the starting point of 3:5-7. 2 Peter first establishes the premise that by God's word water was stored for world judgment at the Flood (3:5-6) and then establishes the premise that by God's word fire is stored for world judgment at the parousia (3:7).[342] The conclusion is left implicit that God therefore has and will intervene in judgment in world history. He thus uses an artificial proof of enthymeme.[343] The first premise is necessary, and the second is unnecessary since it can be contested by the opposition.[344] The premises are intricately interwoven with transplacement: οὐρανοί-γῆ-ὕδατος-ὕδατος-λόγῳ (3:5), ὕδατι-ἀπώλετο (3:6), οὐρανοί-γῆ-λόγῳ-ἀπωλείας (3:7).

The affirmation in 3:7 that the world is stored up for destruction "by the same word" (τῷ αὐτῷ λόγῳ), indicates that 2 Peter believes himself to be drawing this information from prophecy in which God has revealed such. This prophecy may be the Jewish apocalyptic source he may be using and/or the Old Testament texts.[345] As such, 3:7 in itself is an artificial proof drawn from an example[346] of the type of a judgment[347] based primarily on a supernatural oracle,[348] and

---

[341] The phrase λανθάνει γὰρ αὐτοὺς τοῦτο θέλοντας can also be translated "for they deliberately ignore this fact" which points to the material that follows and does not connect 3:4 and 3:5 as directly as the translation given. However, the position of τοῦτο indicates it is probably the object of θέλοντας, thus supporting the translation given. Even if the alternative translation is correct, the phrase functions rhetorically as stated above, but not as pointedly.

[342] Since Jewish apocalypses correlated the Flood and the eschatological conflagration, with the exception of the transitional phrase of 3:5a, 3:5-7 gives further support that a Jewish apocalyptic source underlies 3:4-13. See von Allmen, 260-61. Cf. *1 Clem.* 27:4 — "By a word of his majesty did he establish all things, and by his word can he destroy them." *1 Clement* is thought to use this same Jewish apocalyptic source and its contains this rare reference to both creation and destruction by the word of God. Whereas creation by God's word is a common idea (Gen 1:3-30; Pss 33:6; 148:5; Wis 9:1; 4 Ezra 6:38, 43; *Sib. Or.* 3:30; Heb 11:3; *1 Clem.* 27:4; Herm. *Vis.* 1:3:4), destruction of the world by God's word is not (*1 Clem.* 27:4; *Apoc. Pet.* E 4 dependent on 2 Pet 3:5, 7).

[343] For more on enthymeme, see ch. 1.

[344] Ar. *Rhet.* 1.2.1357a.14.

[345] Old Testament texts like Deut 32:22 (quoted in Justin in a similar context in *1 Apol.* 60:8); Isa 34:4 LXX (to which 2 Pet 3:10, 12 allude); Mal 3:19 (cf. *2 Clem.* 16:3); Isa 66:15-16; Zeph 1:18.

[346] For more on example, see ch. 1.

[347] Cic. *Inv.* 1.30.48; Quint. 5.11.36-44.

[348] Quint. 5.11.41-42; cf. Cic. *Part. Or.* 2.6.

secondarily, upon the popular beliefs it fostered.[349]

The argument and topics of 3:5-7 continue to work out those of 2:5-6. It is maintained in 2:5 that the judgment of the ungodly (ἀσεβῶν) in the Flood clearly illustrates God's judgment is active in history, and this is reaffirmed in 3:7. Also, it is maintained in 2:6 that the judgment of the ungodly (ἀσεβῶν) will be in fire, like Sodom and Gomorrah, and this is here reaffirmed for the ungodly (ἀσεβῶν). In addition, the topic of keeping is being worked out. In 2:4 the Watchers are said to be kept (τηρέω) by God until judgment, and in 2:9 the unrighteous are said to be kept (τηρέω) for judgment. Now in 3:7 the world is kept (τηρέω) for judgment of ungodly men. These judgment arguments and topics of 2:5-6 are now further substantiated by the assertation that judgment is tied up in the fate of the world itself.

The second part of the refutation of the false teachers' claim of 3:4, that the promise of Christ's coming is mute because the world neither has nor will be interrupted by God's judgment, begins in 3:8. That 3:8 is part of the larger refutation begun in 3:5 is indicated by the opening phrase, "do not ignore this one fact," which is similar to the opening phrase of 3:5. Both verses begin by drawing the audience's attention to the following material in an emphatic way. In 3:5a the false teachers are accused of overlooking an important fact and in 3:8a the audience is urged not to overlook one.

In 3:8, 2 Peter reworks Ps 90:4 (LXX 89:4) which reads, "For a thousand years in thy sight are but as yesterday when it is past, or as a watch in the night." For stylistic reasons, 2 Peter's version supplements the content of the psalm by repeating it in reverse order, creating antimetabole[350] using antithesis.[351] He presents a comparative, inartificial proof[352] drawn from a document, here Scripture, that human and divine time perspectives vary, and that the delay of the parousia is not delay from God's perspective. The basic mode of this proof concerning divine-human time perspectives was traditional.[353]

In 3:9, 2 Peter explicitly takes up the main point of 3:4 that God is slow about his promises. That this is the intent of 3:9 is indicated by the use of the verb βραδύνω, "to be slow" (cf. 3:4), and the οὐ . . . ἀλλά formula which 2 Peter uses to reject the false teachers' charges.[354] He presents an artificial proof in an enthymeme[355] based upon a reason subjoined to a dissimilar proposition, the

---

[349] Quint. 5.11.37–41.

[350] Antimetabole is a figure of speech in which "two discrepant thoughts are so expressed in transposition that the latter follows from the former although contrary to it" (Her. 4.28.39). For further information, see Quint. 9.3.85; Lausberg, 1:395–97, §800–803; Bullinger, 301–3.

[351] Antimetabole often uses antithesis (Quint. 9.3.85).

[352] For more on inartificial proof, see ch. 1.

[353] Sir 18:9–11; 2 Apoc. Bar. 48.12–13; Bib. Ant. 19:13a, the latter two in eschatological contexts and clearly inspired by Ps 90:4.

[354] Neyrey, Form and Background, 18–19; 2 Pet 1:16, 21.

[355] For more on enthymeme, see ch. 1.

most effective form of enthymeme according to Quintilian.[356] 2 Peter is employing paronomasia[357] in the rebuttal of the charge with the words βραδύνει and βραδύτητα. This serves to amplify the false teachers' charge through repetition.[358] Also, he uses the figure of speech called distinction in which similar things are distinguished,[359] here slowness and forbearance; a figure which serves his inventional needs well.

2 Peter's proof in 3:9 is very heavily dependent upon traditional apologetic. It contains an allusion to Hab 2:3: "For still the vision awaits its time; it hastens to the end—it will not lie. If it seems slow, wait for it; it will surely come, it will not delay." Habakkuk 2:3 was the *locus classicus* for reflection in Judaism on the problem of the delay of God's judgment.[360] To this traditional apologetical material, 2 Peter has added the concept of divine forbearance.

It is important to note that in 3:9 2 Peter changes the stasis of the argument. The false teachers are claiming that the promise of the parousia had a time limit—the lifetime of the apostolic generation. To most adequately answer this charge, 2 Peter needs to explicitly address the issue of the limited time in which the parousia was expected to occur, but failed to materialize. Rather, he affirms the eventual fulfilment of the parousia hope. The stasis is shifted from one of fact to one of definition.[361] The fact of the delay of the parousia is admitted, but it is denied that it is to be interpreted as it has been. The delay does not indicated forfeited promise, but divine forbearance. In light of the historical circumstances (the expected time had elapsed), this was about the only thing 2 Peter could do to refute the false teachers.

The argument that judgment is delayed because of God's forbearance and provision for repentance is a traditional argument,[362] and was often associated with eschatological judgment.[363] Since it provides traditional argumentation to explain the delay, 3:9 should be very persuasive to the audience. This is part of the broader ethical scheme in 2 Peter encompassing 3:9-12. Whereas

---

[356] Quint. 5.14.4.

[357] This example of paronomasia is not a variety found in the discussions of the handbooks, but compare similar ones in Her. 4.21.29 and Quint. 9.3.69.

[358] Cic. *Part. Or.* 15.54.

[359] For further information on distinction, see Quint. 9.3.82; Lausberg, 1:333-35, §660-62; 373-74, §749; Martin, 306, 315; Bullinger, 238-40.

[360] 1QpHab. 7:5-12; Heb 10:37; *2 Apoc. Bar.* 20:6; 48:39; *b. Sanh.* 97b. A. Strobel, *Untersuchungen zum eschatologischen Verzögesungsproblem auf Grund der spätjüdisch-urchristlichen Geschichte vom Habakuk 2,2ff,* NovTSup 2 (Leiden: E. J. Brill, 1961) chs. 2-3. Unlike the MT, in the LXX and Aquila the subject is "he" (i.e., God in his eschatological coming), not "it."

[361] For more on stasis, see ch. 1.

[362] Joel 2:12-13; Jonah 4:2; Rom. 2:4; Herm *Sim.* 8:11:1; 9:14:2; 10:4:4; *Clem. Hom.* 11:7:2; cf. Jonah 3:10; Wis 11:23.

[363] *1 Enoch* 60:5; Ign. *Eph.* 11:1; Justin, *1 Apol* 28; *Clem. Hom.* 9:19:1; 16:20; Syriac *Apoc. Bar.* 11:3; 12;4; 21:20-21; 24:2; 48:29; 59:6; 85:8; cf. 4 Ezra 3:30; 7:33, 74; 9:21.

unrepentance defers the parousia (3:9), repentance and good works hasten it (3:12). This argument is further discussed below.

Being a striking affirmation of the fact of the parousia and the judgment, 3:10 is primarily an artificial proof based upon the ethos of the apostle Peter.[364] In the opening phrase, ἥξει, "will come," is placed first for emphasis. It helps affirm that although the parousia delays, it will surely come. Δέ is adversative and indicates that the position to follow is in refutation of the one previously stated, here the false teachers' charge underlying 3:9 that the Lord is slow about his promise. In 3:10, 2 Peter may be continuing the allusion to Hab 2:3 from 3:9, for Aquila's version reads, ἐρχόμενος ἥξει καὶ οὐ βραδυνεῖ, "he will surely come and will not be slow."

The simile[365] of the thief likely derives from Jesus' parable of the thief.[366] It is found in Matt 24:43–44 par. Luke 12:39–40, 1 Thess 5:2, Rev 3:3; 16:15, and except for the gospel references, is stated as a simile as here. Since 2 Peter is familiar with a Pauline corpus (cf. 3:15–16), and among the New Testament uses of the thief, only 1 Thess 5:2 applies it to the parousia, direct dependence upon 1 Thess 5:2 for this simile is not impossible. However, in light of the fact that he not only knows, but also uses gospel tradition in 1:16–18, it seems likely that his source is gospel tradition. Thus, the assertation of 3:10 is also an artificial proof based on example[367] of the type called a judgment,[368] of the subtype of judgment called popular belief and saying.[369] The simile is quite effective in conveying not only the unexpectedness, but also, in view of the accompanying judgment, the threat of the parousia. It should serve well to dissuade the audience not to abandon Christian teaching and morality as a consequence of a denial of the parousia, and, if the audience includes those already following the false teachers (2:14, 18), it should encourage repentance in the face of unexpected judgment.

The image of 3:10 of heaven and earth passing away is used in the Gospels,[370] and the idea is attested in other sources.[371] Using the transplacement

---

[364] For more on ethos as proof, see ch. 1.

[365] A simile is a figure of thought, ". . . the comparison of one figure with another, implying a certain resemblance between them" (Her. 4.49.62). Cf. Ar. *Rhet.* 3.4.1406b.1–2; 3:10.1410b.3; Demetr. *Eloc.* 2.80; Quint. 5.11.24 for similar definitions. For further information, see Ar. *Rhet.* 3.4; 3.11.1412b.11–1413a.13; Demetr. *Eloc.* 2.80, 89–90; Quint. 5.11.22–31; Martin, 253, 262; Bullinger, 726–33; McCall; Caird, 144–71.

[366] A. Smitmans, "Das Gleichnis vom Dieb," in *Wort Gottes in der Zeit: Festschrift Karl Schelkle zum 65 Geburtstag,* ed. H. Feld and J. Nolte (Dusseldorf: Patmos, 1973) 43–68. R. J. Bauckham, "Synoptic Parousia Parables and the Apocalypse," *NTS* 23 (1976/77) 162–76.

[367] For more on example, see ch. 1.

[368] Cic. *Inv.* 1.30.48; Quint. 5.11.36–44.

[369] Quint. 5.11.37–39.

[370] Matt 5:18; 24:35; Mark 13:31; Luke 16:17; 21:33; cf. *Did.* 10:6.

[371] *1 Enoch* 91:16; Rev 21:1; *Clem. Rec.* 2:68:3.

λυθήσεται (3:10), λυομένων (3:11), λυθήσονται (3:12), 2 Peter amplifies the dissolution through repetition.[372] Ῥοιζηδόν, "with a roar," is an onomatapoeic[373] word describing the eschatological conflagration in terms of the noise.[374] Also, God's voice in theophany announcing his coming as a warrior is associated with thunder and roaring.[375] Thus, ῥοιζηδόν may not merely describe cosmic destruction, but the Judge's voice as well.

The description of the resulting state of the earth as εὑρεθήσεται, "discovered," is extremely effective.[376] The intervening heavens will be burned away, and the works of the human race will become quite visible to God and vulnerable to his wrath. That the parousia judgment of the wicked is here in view, and not merely cosmic conflagration, is indicated by the context, for part one of this refutation of 3:4 ends with this referene (3:7). Such a picture provides an ironic contrast to the Old Testament picture of the wicked trying vainly to hide from God's impending eschatological judgment.[377]

The three results of the parousia given in 3:10 are found in tricola exhibiting parisosis[378] and homoeoteleuton,[379] both of which serve to unite the proof and enhance style. All of 3:10 exhibits *enargeia* or vivid representation, here achieved in part by giving accompanying circumstances and onomatopoeia ("with a loud noise") and by making the inanimate animate by using a simile

---

[372] Cic. *Part. Or.* 15.54.

[373] Onomatopoeia is a trope in which one would ". . . designate with a suitable word, whether for the sake of imitation or expressiveness, a thing which either lacks a name or has an inappropriate name" (Her. 4.31.42). For further information, see Demetr. *Eloc.* 4.220; Quint. 8.6.31-32; 9.1.3-5; Lausberg, 1:281, §547-48; Martin, 261, 262, 269. Cf. Quint. 8.3.30-37.

[374] *Sib. Or.* 4.175; 1QH 3:32-36; *Apoc. El.* 3.82.

[375] Pss 18:13-15 (LXX 17:14-16); 77:18 (LXX 76:19); 104:7 (LXX 103:7); Amos 1:2; Joel 4:16 (EVV 3:16); cf. 4 Ezra 13:4; 1 Thess 4:16.

[376] There are several textual variants here. Εὑρεθήσεται and οὐκ εὑρεθήσεται are the two major contenders. The former has the superior external evidence, being found in אBKP, but is usually questioned on internal evidence. How can the world "be found"? The latter reading is considered because in context of eschatological dissolution, the world "not found" makes better initial sense. However, because εὑρεθήσεται is the more difficult reading and can be a theological passive used in conjunction with εὑρεθῆναι in 3:14, and οὐκ εὑρεθήσεται can be explained as an ancient attempt to clarify, εὑρεθήσεται is the preferred reading. For a meticulous discussion, see Bauckham, 316-21; Metzger, 705-6; Frank Olivier, "Une Correction au Texte du Nouveau Testament: II Pierre III 10," *RTP* 8 (1920) 237-78.

[377] Isa 2:19; Hos 10:8; Amos 9:1-6; Rev 6:15-17.

[378] Parisosis is a figure of speech involving parallelism of structure. For further information, see Ar. *Rhet.* 3.9.1410a.9; 1410b.10; *Rhet. ad Alex.* 27; Quint. 9.3.75-76; Lausberg, 1:359-61, §719-24; Martin, 310-11.

[379] It is typical for homoeoteleuton to be used with tricola (Quint. 9.3.77), and parisosis (Ar. *Rhet.* 3.9.1410a.9; 1410b.10). Here it is composed of παρελεύσονται . . . λυθήσεται . . . εὑρεθήσεται.

("the day of the Lord will come like a thief").[380]

Eschatological parenesis is common to two literary genres, the epistle[381] and the testament,[382] and such parenesis is found in 3:11-13. The first verses, 3:11-12, constitute *exclamatio* or *epiphonema:* "an exclamation attached to the close of a statement or a proof by way of climax."[383] After having refuted the false teachers' charge against the integrity of the parousia teaching (3:5-10), 2 Peter attaches an exclamation to the last proof (3:10) to emphasize the behavior appropriate in light of the certainty of the parousia, and to intensify emotion.[384] It is closely tied thematically with 3:10. Whereas in 3:10 the present heavens will melt and the earth and its works will be discovered, in 3:11-13 the heavens and heavenly bodies will melt,[385] and new heavens and new earth will exist in which righteousness dwells.

The new element in 3:11-13 is the assumption that godly lives will hasten the parousia (3:11-12a). This is a corollary of the enthymeme in 3:9 which claims that God delays the parousia to allow for repentance. This stands in stark contrast to the argument of the false teachers that the delay implies the void of the promise and gives sanction to ungodly behavior. 2 Peter claims the opposite: godly behavior not only has a ground in the delayed parousia hope, but also can hasten its fulfillment.

In the *exordium* it is merely stated that through divine power, Christians are given all things necessary for life (ζωή) and godliness (εὐσέβεια, 1:3), that through the promises they can escape the world's corruption (1:4), and therefore they should be zealous to confirm their call and election so as to enter the eternal kingdom (1:10-11). In 3:11-13 the audience is admonished to lead lives of holiness and godliness (ἐν ἁγίαις ἀναστροφαῖς καὶ εὐσεβείαις, 3:11), that is, confirm their call and election, and be fit for a new heavens and a new earth where righteousness dwells (3:13), that is, the eternal kingdom. Thus 3:11-13 is not merely *epiphomena,* but functions further to develop central topics introduced in the *exordium.*

Whereas in the *probatio* the false teachers consider the parousia hope a myth (1:16) because of its delay (3:4), and no longer live as though it will come, in this section and in the *peroratio,* using transplacement, the audience is admonished strongly to wait for the parousia (προσδοκέω, 3:12, 13, 14). This topic of waiting is probably carried on from the quotation in 3:9 from Hab 2:3 which

---

[380] Demetr. *Eloc.* 4.220; Quint. 8.3.70. Cf. Ar. *Rhet.* 3.11.1411b.2-3 on metaphor.

[381] 1 Cor 15:58; Gal 5:7-10; Eph 5:10-16; Phil 4:5; Col 4:5; 1 Tim 6:14; 2 Tim 4:1-5; 1 Pet 5:1-10.

[382] *1 Enoch* 91:3-19; 94:1-5; *Jub.* 36:3-11; *2 Apoc. Bar.* 84-85; *Bib. Ant.* 33:1-3.

[383] Quint. 8.5.11; Lausberg, 1:434, §879. It is a use of the figure of thought called *exclamatio.*

[384] Quint. 9.2.26-27; 9.3.97.

[385] There is parisosis in 3:12b in the description of the fate of the heavens and earth.

claims that the response to eschatological delay is to "wait for him."[386]

The last clause of 3:12, στοιχεῖα καυσούμενα τήχεται, is probably derived from Isa 34:4 LXX (B, Lucian): ταχήσονται πᾶσαι αἱ δυνάμεις τῶν οὐρανῶν, "all the powers of the heavens will melt," and is repeated from 3:10 with slight variation in order to prepare for the antithesis of a new heaven and a new earth in 3:13. Whereas in 3:10 the phrase helps refute the claim of the false teachers, in 3:12 it serves as eschatological motivation for ethical exhortation. Its recurrence is reduplication, amplifying a topic through recapitulation of consequences[387] and repetition.[388]

In 3:13 the promise of the parousia is reaffirmed with an artificial proof of pathos,[389] consisting of a positive affirmation with a supporting reason:[390] "But according to his promise we wait for a new heavens and a new earth in which righteousness dwells." This reiterates the topic of the promises from the *exordium* in 1:4, which states that Christ has given his promises, from 3:4, where the false teachers deny the promise of the parousia, and also from 3:9, where it is affirmed that Christ's promise is not slow. The content of the promise of 3:13 is derived from Isa 65:17 and 66:2, was common to Jewish apocalyptic,[391] and was adopted by early Christianity.[392] The proof is embellished with personification; righteousness being said to dwell in the new heavens and new earth.[393]

The Peroratio *(3:14–18)*

The *peroratio* of 2 Peter is constituted by 3:14–18. As previously discussed, the *peroratio* contains the twofold division and purpose of recapitulation or *repetitio* and emotional appeal or *adfectus*.[394] In 2 Peter the *repetitio* constitutes 3:14–16 and the *adfectus* comprises 3:17–18. This division is supported on other grounds. In 3:14 the transition to body-closing is indicated by the vocative ἀγαπητοί[395] and a responsibility statement.[396] In 3:17 a transition within the body closing is indicated by the vocative ἀγαπητοί,[397] the fuller disclosure

---

386 LXX: ὑπομείνον αὐτόν; A προσδέχον αὐτόν. Cf. *2 Apoc. Bar.* 83:4; *b. Sanh.* 97b; *1 Clem.* 23:5.

387 Cic. *Part. Or.* 16.55.

388 Cic. *Part. Or.* 15.54.

389 For more on the proof from pathos, see ch. 1.

390 Quint. 5.12.9–13.

391 *Jub.* 1:29; *1 Enoch* 45:4–5; 72:1; 91:16; *Sib. Or.* 5:212; *2 Apoc. Bar.* 32:6; 44:12; 57:2; 4 Ezra 7:75; *Bib. Ant.* 3:10; *Apoc. El.* 3:98.

392 Matt 19:28; Rom 8:21; Rev 21:1.

393 Righteousness is similarly personified in Isa. 32:16 LXX - δικαιοσύνη ἐν τῷ καρμήλῳ κατοικήσει.

394 For a discussion of the *peroratio,* its component parts, and special features, see ch. 2, pp. 67–76 passim.

395 White, 15–16, 38.

396 White, 7–9, 28–29, 41.

397 White, 15–16, 38.

formula using a form of the verb γινώσκω,[398] the imperatival form of the disclosure formula,[399] and a responsibility statement.[400] Like the body-closing, 3:14-16 finalizes the motivation for writing by reiterating what was stated earlier in the letter, and urging responsibility in the matters of the epistle,[401] that is, recapitulation. Also, like the body-closing, 3:17-18 hold out a threat to encourage responsibility in the matters discussed,[402] that is, appeals to the emotion.

The Repetitio (3:14-16)

Of the four basic types of recapitulation that can be used in the *peroratio*,[403] 2 Peter's recapitulation is most akin to the usual type which briefly summarizes each point of the *probatio*.[404] Recapitulation is needed in deliberative rhetoric only when there is a conflict of opinion[405] as here in 2 Peter. Also, this conflict has necessitated a heavy reliance upon judicial rhetoric, and judicial rhetoric requires recapitulation.

An enthymeme is constituted by 3:14-15a. The premise is, "Since you wait for these," that is, the new heavens and new earth in which righteousness dwells (3:13), and the conclusion is, "be zealous to be found by him without spot or blemish, and at peace and count the forbearance of our Lord as salvation." This is eschatological parenesis, and, considering the exigence and genre of 2 Peter, is well suited to recapping the arguments of the *probatio*.

This enthymeme of 3:14-15a recapitulates topics of the proof of 3:8-13 of the *probatio*. Whereas in 3:8-9, 2 Peter contends that the Lord is not slow to fulfill his promise of the parousia but, in fact, is forbearing (μακροθυμία), desiring repentance, in 3:15 he reiterates that the Lord's forbearance (μακροθυμία) is to be conceived as salvation. Whereas, in 3:10, 2 Peter contends that the Lord will come as a thief, and the earth and its work will be discovered for what they are (εὑρεθήσεται), in 3:14 he admonishes his audience to be zealous to be discovered (εὑρεθῆναι) without spot or blemish and at peace by the Lord when he comes. As in 3:12 and 3:13, in 3:14 the audience is again exhorted to wait (προσδοκέω) for the new heavens and new earth.

The enthymeme of 3:14-15a recapitulates other topics as well; topics contingent upon the antithesis between the spiritual condition of the false

---

[398] White, 2-5.

[399] White, 3-5, 27, 40.

[400] White, 7-9, 28-29, 41.

[401] White, 5, 7-9, 25, 28-29, 40-41.

[402] White, 28-29.

[403] For a discussion of these four types of recapitulation and for references, see ch. 2, pp. 68-69.

[404] Cic. *Inv.* 1.52.98-99; *Rhet. ad Alex.* 36.1444b.21ff.; cf. 20.1433b.30ff.

[405] Ar. *Rhet.* 3.13.1414b.3. Cic. *Part. Or.* 17.59 states that recapitulation is seldom needed in deliberative rhetoric.

teachers and the audience. First, whereas the false teachers are spots and blemishes (σπίλοι χαὶ μῶροι, 2:13), the audience is admonished to be found by Christ at the parousia without spot or blemish (ἄσπιλοι χαὶ ἀμώμητοι, 3:14). This is traditional terminology which is often found in eschatological contexts, frequently referring to the state the Christian or church ought to be in at the time of the parousia.[406] Ἄσπιλος, "without spot," and ἄμωμητος, "blameless," can describe sacrificial animals, and the combination is probably intended as a metaphor to describe Christians as a pure sacrifice for God at the parousia.[407] The metaphor clarifies[408] the idea of being morally blameless. Secondly, in the *exordium* the audience is exhorted to exert effort (σπουδή) to supplement their faith (1:5) and to be zealous (σπουδάζω) to confirm their call and election (1:10). Now in 3:14 they are exhorted to be zealous (σπουδάζω) to be found at the parousia without spot or blemish.

In 3:15b-16, 2 Peter makes his last attempt to bolster the authority of his whole case. With the phrase "so also our beloved brother Paul wrote to you according to the wisdom given him," he associates Peter with the apostles[409] as a friend of Paul and, more importantly, with Paul as one having the same message for the audience. The phrase χατὰ τὴν δοθεῖσαν αὐτῷ σοφίαν, "according to the wisdom given him," probably equals πνευματιχῶς. Δοθεῖσαν is a theological passive with God as agent. Σοφία is often portrayed as a gift of God,[410] and can be associated with the Holy Spirit.[411] The whole phrase deems Paul's letters to be inspired and on par with scripture. By claiming that the false teachers twist Paul's letters like they do the rest of scripture (αἱ λοιπαὶ γραφαί), Paul's letters are again portrayed as on par with the authoritative scripture.[412] 2 Peter thus implies his message is analogous to Paul's inspired epistle which is ranked with scripture itself.

2 Peter states that Paul's epistles are hard to understand (δυσνόητος). However, he does not mean Paul is obscure, but is implying that correct interpretation comes in light of his own and apostolic teaching (3:15b-16a). The false teachers, identified as the ignorant and unstable,[413] are said to twist or torture

---

[406] Eph 1:4; 5:27; Phil 1:10; 2:15; Col 1:22; 1 Thess 3:13; 5:23; Jude 24; *1 Clem.* 63:1; Ign. *Trall.* 13:3; Herm. *Vis.* 4:3:5; *Sim.* 5:6:7; cf. also 1 Cor 1:8.

[407] Cf. 2 Pet 1:19 where within a simile ἀμώμος χαὶ ἀσπῖλος describes Christ as a sacrificial lamb, and Heb 9:14 where ἀμώμος describes him as a pure sacrifice. Albrecht Oepke, "ἄσπιλος," *TDNT* 1:502; F. Hauck, "μῶμος," *TDNT* 4:829–31.

[408] Demetr. *Eloc.* 2.82; Cic. *De Or.* 3.38.155–39.157; Quint. 8.6.5–6.

[409] Ἡμῶν probably refers to the apostles as do the other references in the first person plural (1:1, 16–19).

[410] Ezra 7:25; Dan 1:19; Wis 7:7; 9:17; Mark 6:2; Eph 1:17; Col 1:9; Jas 1:5.

[411] Acts 6:3, 10; 1 Cor 2:13.

[412] Αἱ λοιπαὶ γραφαί – the article implies that the technical sense of scripture, and λοιπάς, "remaining," implies that Paul's writings are ranked with Scripture.

[413] This identification constitutes metonymy based on a vice (Cic. *De Or.* 3.42.168).

(στρεβλόω) Paul's epistles and the Old Testament to support their views.[414] This emphasis downplays the ethos of the false teachers and their message by portraying them as uninstructed and unstable "exegetes," and their message as a twisted aberration from recognized interpretation.

The section 3:15b-16 reiterates several topics. The identification of the false teachers as "ignorant" (ἀμαθεῖς) and "unstable" (ἀστήρικτοι) recapitulates both these topics. 2 Peter has already claimed that his audience has knowledge (1:2, 3, 5, 6, 20; 2:20, 21; 3:8, 18) and the false teachers are ignorant (ἀγνοέω, 2:12; λανθάνω, 3:5). He has also already claimed that his audience is stable (ἐστηριγμένοι, 1:12) in the truth and the followers of the false teachers are unstable (ψυχαὶ ἀστήρικτοι, 2:14). This topic of instability (ἀστήρικτος) is found again in the next verse, 3:17, which begins the *adfectus*. There the audience's stability (στηριγμός) is said to be threatened. This repetition of the topic constitutes paronomasia[415] and helps bridge the *repetitio* and the *adfectus*. Whereas in 2:1 the false teachers are accused of destructive heresies (αἱρέσεις ἀπωλείαι), in 3:16 they are accused of twisting scripture, a practice leading to destruction (ἀπώλεια). The destruction mentioned throughout the *probatio* is the judgment of ungodly behavior justified by the misuse of authoritative tradition (ἀπώλεια, 2:1, 3; 3:7; cf. φθορά, 2:12, 19).

The Adfectus (3:17-18)

As previously stated, 3:17-18 is the *adfectus*. Having defended his case, refuted his opponents, and recapitulated his case, 2 Peter makes an appeal to his audience's emotions to dissuade them still further from the doctrine of the false teachers, and to persuade them to puruse a Christian walk according to the provisions given. Usually the same pathos elicited in the *exordium* is sought in greater intensity in the *peroratio*.[416] However, this is not entirely true in 2 Peter. The *peroratio* can also elicit negative emotion by arousing fear.[417] Whereas the *exordium* exhorts Christian behavior solely within the context of its rewards (such as escaping corruption and sharing the divine nature [1:4], and entering the eternal kingdom [1:11]), the *peroratio* exhorts Christian behavior primarily within the context of the fear of being drawn away from such behavior by the false teachers. The audience is admonished to "beware lest you be carried away

---

[414] The parts of Paul's misinterpreted may include: 1) imminence of the parousia (Rom 13:11-12; 16:20; 1 Cor 7:29; Phil 4:5; 1 Thess 4:15) which the false teachers reject for lack of fulfilment; 2) passages which could support antinomianism (Rom 4:15; 5:20; 8:1; 1 Cor 6:12) which the false teachers twist to offer freedom (2:19; cf. Rom 8:2; 2 Cor 3:17). Paul himself faced this problem (Rom 3:8; 6:15; Gal 5:13); and 3) both, since eschatology sanctions ethics. (Bauckham, 332).

[415] This is the type of paronomasia in which letters are changed and added so that similar words express dissimilar things (Her. 4.21.29). Cf. Quint. 9.3.69, 72-74.

[416] Quint. 4.1.28; 6.1.9-10, 12, 51-52; cf. Cic. *De Or.* 2.77.311; *Part. Or.* 1.4.

[417] Quint. 6.1.14.

by the error of lawless men and lose your own stability." The inherent warning is that those who so err will suffer the fate of the false teachers, that is, destruction (2:1, 3, 12; 3:7, 16) and will loose their reward (1:11; 3:11-13). The *peroratio*'s attempt to elicit greater pathos is especially required if the opponent is of dangerous character[418] as is the case in 2 Peter's rhetorical situation.

The *adfectus* of 2 Peter cannot be divided precisely into *conquestio* and *indignatio*.[419] However, 3:17 functions primarily as the *indignatio*, and 3:18 as the *conquestio*. The *indignatio* can use the topics of confirmation, but will emphasize the negative.[420] These topics include those of person and action. Two topics of person are manner of life and habit,[421] both of which 2 Peter uses. He designates the false teachers as lawless (ἄθεσμος) and in error (πλάνη). He bases his designation on the habitual words and deeds characterizing their manner of life in order to elicit negative pathos from his audience.

Besides these more general topics, the *indignatio* utilizes several specific topics for amplification.[422] One is the topic of authority in which it is shown that the case greatly concerns the gods, ancestors, and other authoritative groups.[423] 2 Peter naturally uses this topic since the matters discussed in the epistle are portrayed as being of great concern to the apostle Peter, and by implication, to Paul, the apostles, and God himself.

Three other topics are: the consideration of who is affected by the matters upon which the charges rest, whether all persons, superiors, or peers;[424] the showing of what happens if another emulates the act spoken against;[425] and expressing indignation, especially pointing out that the act is at variance with law.[426] 2 Peter makes it very clear that the matter affects the audience, because it is they who are subject to the error of the false teachers and stand to falter in their Christian lives. He also makes it clear that emulating the error of the false teachers that he speaks against leads to the loss of stability. This warning functions as indignation toward the acts of the false teachers, specifically the reference to their activity as lawless (ἄθεσμον).

Turning to the *conquestio*, προγινώσκοντες, "knowing beforehand, beware . . .," resumes the fiction of Peter's prophecy from 2:1-3 and 3:3-4, and serves to remind the audience of Peter's predictions of false teachers. It elicits

[418] Quint. 6.1.12.

[419] For more on the *conquestio* and *indignatio*, and for references, see ch. 2, pp. 71-76 passim.

[420] Cic. *Inv.* 1.53.100. For a list of topics of confirmation, see Cic. *Inv.* 1.24-28.

[421] Cic. *Inv.* 1.25.35, 36.

[422] Cic. *Inv.* 1.53-54 provides fifteen. Her. 2.30.48-49 reproduces the first ten of Cicero. *Rhet. ad Alex.* 36.1445a.12ff. and Quint. 6.1.14-20 give several. These topics are applied to judicial rhetoric, but Her. 3.5.9 states that the *peroratio* of judicial and deliberative rhetoric are virtually the same.

[423] Cic. *Inv.* 1.53.101; Her. 2.30.48.

[424] Cic. *Inv.* 1.53.101; Her. 2.30.48; cf. *Rhet. ad Alex.* 36.1445a.14ff.

[425] Cic. *Inv.* 1.53.101; Her. 2.30.48.

[426] Cic. *Inv.* 1.53.102.

positive emotion for Peter as rhetor, for it gives evidence that Peter is concerned enough for the welfare of the audience to warn them of the false teachers ahead of time.

There are several topics suitable to the *conquestio*,[427] but 2 Peter uses only one of those prescribed. In this topic, ". . . one recounts shameful, mean, and ignoble acts and what they have suffered or are likely to suffer that it unworthy of their age, race, former fortune, position, or preferment."[428] In 3:17 the shameful acts of the false teachers are described as the "error of lawless men," and what the audience is likely to suffer is given as being seduced by this error and losing stability. It is implied in 3:18 that this possible scenario is incongruous with the audience's position or preferment.

Several topics from elsewhere in 2 Peter are reiterated to some degree in 3:17-18a, giving evidence that 2 Peter combines some recapitulation in his emotional appeal. The interrelated topics of leading-following, error, and the way recur.[429] Whereas in the *probatio* in 2:15 2 Peter accuses the false teachers of going astray (ἐπλανάω) and following (ἐξακολουθέω) the way of Balaam, and in 2:18 of enticing immature Christians who had barely escaped error (πλάνη), here he warns his audience not to be led away (συναπάγω) with error (πλάνη). Not to be led away into error is not to follow cleverly devised myths (1:16). Whereas in the *probatio* in 2:7 the false teachers are compared with the lawless (ἄθεσμοι) men of Sodom and Gomorrah, here 2 Peter warns his audience not to be carried away with the error of lawless men (ἄθεσμοι). Whereas in the *exordium* in 1:12 2 Peter claims the audience is established (στηρίζω) in the truth, here he admonishes them to avoid error so as to maintain their stability (στηριγμός), a metaphor for moral steadfastness[430] providing clarity.[431] This topic of stability contrasts the portrayal of the false teachers and the Christians who follow them as unstable (ἀστήρικτοι, 2:14; 3:16).[432] This contrast is aided by the emphatic ὑμεῖς beginning 3:17 which distinguishes the audience as stable from the unstable false teachers in 3:16, doing much to elicit positive pathos. In 3:18a the phrase "grow in grace and in the knowledge of our Lord and Savior Jesus Christ" takes up the topic of the need to grow in the Christian life found in the epistolary prescript (1:2) and the *exordium* (1:5-10).

The letter closes in 3:18b with a doxology. Εἰς ἡμέραν αἰῶνος, "on the day of

---

[427] For a list of suitable topics for arousing emotion in the *conquestio*, see *Rhet. ad Alex.* 36.1444b.35-1445a.29; Cic. *Inv.* 1.55.106-56.109; Her. 2.31.50; Quint. 6.1.13, 21-25; cf. 4.1.20-21. These topics are presented with reference to judicial rhetoric, but can be used in deliberative and epideictic rhetoric as well (Her. 3.5.9).

[428] Cic. *Inv.* 1.55.107.

[429] For a full discussion of the interrelationship of these topics, see above, p. 103.

[430] See above, p. 100.

[431] Demetr. *Eloc.* 2.82; Cic. *De Or.* 3.38.155-39.157; Quint. 8.6.5-6.

[432] As previously noted, στηριγμοῦ in 3:17 is used in paronomasia with ἀστήρικτοι, and helps unite recapitulation and emotional appeal.

eternity," probably refers to the eschatological future as a day that will be ushered in at the parousia.[433] This phrase helps the *peroratio* reiterate the hope expressed in 1:19 of the day dawning (ἕως οὗ ἡμέρα διαυγάσῃ), and in 3:12 of the day of God (τοῦ θεοῦ ἡμέρας) as well as the parousia hope defended throughout (1:16-21; 3:8-13).

Figure 2 is a rhetorical outline of 2 Peter which takes account of the preceding discussion, particularly of invention and arrangement. For matters of style, see appendix 4.

FIGURE 2
A RHETORICAL OUTLINE OF 2 PETER

I. Epistolary Prescript (Quasi-*Exordium*) - 1:1-2
II. *Exordium* 1:3-15
   A. Miniature homily in the form of a complex enthymeme - 1:3-11
   B. Personal data - 1:12-15
III. *Probatio* - 1:16-3:13
   A. First Accusation and Refutation - 1:16-19
      1. Accusation "The apostolic proclamation of the parousia is a cleverly devised myth." 1:16a
      2. Refutation - 1:16b-19
         a. Inartificial proof based on eyewitness testimony - "The apostles witnessed the precursor of the parousia, the Transfiguration." 1:16b-18
         b. Inartificial proof based on a document - "The apostolic preaching of the parousia is dependable because it is based on OT prophecy." 1:19. Secondarily, an artificial proof based on the ethos of Peter.
   B. Second Accusation and Refutation - 1:20-21
      1. Accusation - "The OT prophecy upon which the apostles base their teaching of the parousia are matters of the prophet's own interpretation and impulse, not that of the Holy Spirit." 1:20b-21a
      2. Refutation Artificial Proof of enthymeme - 1:20-21
         a. Conclusion "Prophecy is not a matter of a prophet's own interpretation." 1:20
         b. Premise "Prophets are inspired by the Holy Spirit." 1:21

---

[433] The idea of a day of eternity may derive from Isa 60:19-20, "Your sun shall no more go down, nor your moon withdraw itself; for the Lord will be your everlasting light." It is noteworthy that Isa 60:22 is echoed in 2 Pet 3:12. The phrase ἡμέρα αἰῶνος, "day of eternity," occurs elsewhere only in Sir 18:10 which is based on Ps 90:4 as is 2 Pet 3:8 also.

C. Counteraccusation - "The teachers within the congregation are false teachers, immoral, corrupting, and destined for destruction." 2:1-3a

D. Third Accusation and Refutation - 2:3b-10a

    1. Accusation - "Divine judgment is 'idle' and 'asleep.' " 2:3b (cf. 3:9)

    2. Refutation - Artificial proof based on historical examples "If the wicked were punished and the righteous saved in history, then the same will occur at the future parousia and the judgment." 2:3b-10a

E. *Digressio* - denunciation serving to destroy the ethos of the opponents. 2:10b-22.

F. *Transitio* or "Secondary *Exordium*" - 3:1-2

G. Fourth Accusation and Refutation - 3:3-13

    1. Accusation - "The apostolic preaching of an imminent parousia is to be denied on the basis of the death of the first generation of Christians who were prophesied would experience it, and on the basis of the lack of divine intervention in history." 3:3-4

    2. Refutation - 3:5-13

        a. Artificial Proof of enthymeme - 3:5-7

            1. Premise 1 - "By God's word water was stored for world judgment at the Flood and it occurred." 3:5-6

            2. Premise 2 - "By God's word fire is stored for world judgment at the parousia." 3:7

            3. Implied conclusion - "Therefore, God has and will act in judgment in history."

        b. Inartificial Proof based on a document - "The seeming delay of the parousia is an illusion because divine and human time perspectives vary." 3:8

        c. Artificial Proof of enthymeme - 3:9

            1. Premise "The Lord forbears waiting for repentance." 3:9b

            2. Conclusion "The Lord is not slow about his promises." 3:9a

        d. Artificial Proof drawn from ethos - 3:10-13. Secondarily, an artificial proof based on example of the type of a judgment or popular belief and saying.

            1. Affirmation of the reality of the parousia using gospel tradition. 3:10

            2. *Epiphonema* - 3:11-12

        e. Artificial Proof of pathos - 3:13

IV. *Peroratio* - 3:14-18

  A. *Repetitio* - 3:14-16

  B. *Adfectus* - 3:17-18

    1. *indignatio* - 3:17

    2. *conquestio* - 3:18

EVALUATION OF THE RHETORIC

This evaluation of the rhetoric of 2 Peter will concentrate first upon the degree of its adherence to the conventions of Greco-Roman rhetoric in matters of arrangement, invention, and style. Secondly, the evaluation will attempt to ascertain the rhetoric's effectiveness in meeting the exigence that elicited it, and it in turn seeks to counter.

Regarding arrangement, 2 Peter contains the essential elements, and their subcategories, that should specifically characterize deliberative rhetoric, and presents these elements in correct order: *exordium*, *probatio*, and *peroratio*. As is generally true in the deliberative species, the *narratio* is missing, and there is a lengthy denunciatory *digressio* serving to destroy the ethos of the opponents in order to dissuade the audience from adopting their stance. As is proper, these elements of arrangement are all topically interwoven.

In the *exordium*, the miniature homily of 1:3–11 is a model of doctrine and deeds which 2 Peter hopes to persuade his audience to maintain. It also serves as a foil for the refutation of the doctrine and deeds of the false teachers from which 2 Peter is concerned to dissuade his audience. The homily is necessitated by the testament genre, and provides a synopsis of doctrine shared by the rhetor and his audience. The inclusion of the homily in the *exordium*, however, renders the *exordium* partially faulty. Although it contains topics found throughout 2 Peter, it does not relate directly to the refutation of the doctrinal and ethical position of the false teachers in the *probatio*. Thus the *exordium* suffers the fault of producing only part of the results the case requires.[434]

2 Peter's rhetoric is skillful where invention is concerned. Foremost, his adoption of the testament genre and the guise of the apostle Peter offers several advantages. It enables him to address the rhetorical situation in a post-apostolic period with Peter's ethos. He has the ability to mold the testament so that the arguments and behavior of the false teachers can be refuted specifically as if they had been prophesied. The latter scheme is enhanced by a futuristic use of the present which allows refutation of the false teachers' charges in the present. Finally, the testament genre, while maintaining the guise of prophecy, is generally deliberative, and is suited to the needs of the rhetorical situation which 2 Peter seeks to modify.

The arguments of the false teachers are presented and systematically refuted by using a variety of proofs, including both the inductive and the deductive proofs. Of the former there are the proofs of eyewitness testimony and document. Of the latter, at least one each from ethos, pathos, and logos is represented. Specifically from logos, at least one proof each from example and enthymeme is found. In other words, every type of rhetorical proof is represented at least one. 2 Peter has properly mixed deductive and inductive argument and their subtypes.[435] These proofs utilize many constraints, including the Old

[434] Cic. *Inv.* 1.18.26; Her. 1.7.11; cf. Cic. *De Or.* 2.78.319.
[435] Cic. *Inv.* 1.41.76.

Testament; Jewish, apostolic, gospel, and Pauline tradition; and foremost, the ethos of the apostle Peter.

Regarding style, 2 Peter is best classified as being in the grand style.[436] like the grand style, it is powerful in thought,[437] impressive words being carefully selected.[438] Style is vigorous,[439] containing much amplification.[440] There is an abundance of figures of speech and thought[441] (including hyperbole),[442] several of which are interrelated in complexes.

The three main styles have three corresponding faulty styles.[443] Akin to the grand style is the swollen style, characterized by turgid and inflated language, new or archaic words, clumsy metaphors, and diction more impressive than the theme demands.[444] Frigidity in any style originates in the use of compound or strange words; epithets that are either long, unseasonable, or too crowded; and metaphors that are too dignified, somewhat tragic, far-fetched, or obscure.[445] 2 Peter's style has characteristics of the swollen[446] and frigid style, containing

---

[436] For more on the grand style, see ch. 1. This classification of the style of 2 Peter corresponds to the analyses given by many commentators and grammarians: ". . . a general impression 2 Peter gives of aiming at ambitious literary effect" (Bauckham, 137). J. H. Moulton, *Word-Formation*, in *A Grammar of New Testament Greek*, gen. eds. James Hope Moulton and Nigel Turner, 4 vols. (Edinburgh: T. & T. Clark, 1906-76) 2 (1929) 6. For further evaluation of the style of 2 Peter, see Bauckham, 135-38; Bigg, 224-32; F. H. Chase, "Peter, Second Epistle of," in *HDB*, ed. James Hastings, 5 vols. (New York: Charles Scribner's Sons, 1906) 3:807, col. 1- 809, col. 1; Mayor, lvi-lxvii; Moulton, 2:28; B. Reicke, *The Epistles of James, Peter, and Jude*, AB 37 (New York: Doubleday, 1964) 146-47; Turner, 140-41.

[437] Cic. *Or.* 5.20.

[438] Her. 4.8.11. Several words and phrases seem to be chosen for the sake of euphony: εἰρήνη πληθυνείη ἐν ἐπιγνώσκει (1:2); μωπάζω (1:9); αὐχμηρός, φωσφόρος, διαυγάζω (1:19); ταρταρώσας παρέδωκεν (2:4); ἀστήρικτος (2:14; 3:16); καυσόω (3:10, 12); ῥοιζηδόν (onomatopoeia; 3:10). The use of παρανομίας and παραφρονίαν at the end of successive clauses in 2:16 may be an attempt at rhyme.

[439] Quint. 12.10.58-59; Aug. *De Doct. Chr.* 4.20.42.

[440] Quint. 12.10.62; cf. Cic. *Or.* 5.20 and Her. 4.8.11.

[441] Her. 4.8.11; Aug. *De Doct. Chr.* 4.20.42. See appendix 4.

[442] Quint. 12.10.62.

[443] Her. 4.10.15-11.16.

[444] Cic. *Brut.* 55.202; Her. 4.10.15. Cf. the advice of Quintilian: "An acceptable style is defined by Cicero [*Part. Or.* 6.19] as one which is not over-elegant . . . excess is always a vice" (8.3.42). Cf. Quint. 8, pr. 23-33 for a critique of style which abandons the common idiom.

[445] Ar. *Rhet.* 3.3.1406a.1-1406b.4. Demetrius applies this discussion from Aristotle to the elevated style (*Eloc.* 2.115-16).

[446] Cf. Turner's comment of 2 Peter's style: "Always there is the striving after the pompous phrase" (142).

inflated language, new and archaic words,[447] and compound and strange words.[448]

2 Peter is often classified as Asian rhetoric.[449] Asian rhetoric is described as "redundant and lacking conciseness,"[450] "empty and inflated. . .deficient alike in taste and restraint,"[451] and a "vainglorious style of eloquence."[452] According to Cicero,

> Of the Asiatic style there are two types, the one sententious and studied, less characterized by weight of thought than by the charm of balance and symmetry. . . . The other type is not so notable for wealth of sententious phrase, as for swiftness and impetuosity . . . combining with this rapid flow of speech a choice of words refined and ornate.[453]

2 Peter does exhibit a lack of restraint with regard to tropes and figures. It is redundant within the *digressio*, but not as a whole. It is not empty, but rather offers a reasoned approach to the exigence. 2 Peter does not fit exactly either of Cicero's definitions of Asianism. It is characterized by weight of thought, but

---

[447] New coinages consist of combining words together or making completely new words, expansion and inflexion, and derivatives from proper names. To be understood, coinages must have resemblance to established words. In the late first century it was always advised that new coinages be used sparingly. (Ar. *Rhet.* 3.2.1404b.6; Cic. *De Or.* 3.38.154; 52.201; *Or.* 24.81; Quint. 8.3.30–37).
In 2 Pet 2:16, παραφρονία may be a new coinage for the sake of euphony with παρανομία found earlier in the sentence, and in 3:3, ἐμπαιγμονή may be a coinage for ἐμπαίζω.

[448] 2 Peter contains 57 *hapax legomena* (see Bauckham, 135 for a complete list). Four are not found elsewhere in extant Greek literature: ψευδοδιδάσκαλος (2:1), ἀκατάπαστος (2:14), ἐμπαιγμονή (3:3), and παραφρονία (2:16). Bauckham writes, "The list of *hapax legomena* includes enough extremely rare words to show that the author is widely read, and fond of rather literary and poetic, even obscure words. They do not on the whole seem to be used arbitrarily where common words would suffice as well, but contribute to the author's literary and rhetorical effects" (136).

[449] Bauckham, 137; Green, *Second Epistle of Peter, and the Epistle of Jude*, 18, 41; Reicke, 146–47. Asian rhetoric was a development of early Hellenistic rhetoric fostered by the exposure of Greek rhetoric to new influences following Alexander's conquests. Cic. *Brut.* 13.51 and Quint. 12:10.16–17 give a brief account of this. An opposing position, Atticism arose in the first century B.C. and espoused a return to the ideals of the Attic Orators of the classical period. For further discussion of the Attic-Asian dispute, see Cic. *Opt. Gen.* 3.8ff.; Quint. 12.10.16ff.; U. von Wilamowitz-Moellendorf, "Asianismus und Attizismus," *Hermes* 35 (1900) 1–52; Norden, *Die antike Kunstprosa*, 126ff., 196ff., 218–22; Leeman, 1:91–111, 140–45; Grube, 122–23; Kennedy, *Art of Persuasion in Greece*, 301–3; *Roman World*, 97–100; Russell, *Criticism in Antiquity*, 48ff.

[450] Cic. *Brut.* 13.51.
[451] Quint. 12.10.16.
[452] Quint. 12.10.17.
[453] Cic. *Brut.* 95.325.

also by a swiftness and impetuosity combined with refined and ornate words. 2 Peter is not the best example of Asian style, but does possess several of its characteristics.

Rhetorical analysis of 2 Peter has shown that it conforms to the conventions of Greco-Roman rhetoric. It also has shown how the testament genre and the epistle themselves contain rhetorically effective features which contribute to the rhetoric. Whereas it is clear that both Jude and 2 Peter are skilled rhetors, 2 Peter's rhetoric seems much more the product of study. He outshines Jude, both in inventional and in stylistic finesse.

2 Peter is a fitting response to the exigence of the rhetorical situation. Using standard constraints and argumentation, the *probatio* refutes the doctrine which is used to justify immorality. The *digressio* castigates the immorality itself. All is backed by the ethos of the apostle Peter. It is reasonable to believe that the ethos of the false teachers, their doctrine, and their influence would be lessened, and that negative pathos would be aroused against them. There is reason to assume that those yet faithful to apostolic doctrine who are directly addressed, and the unfaithful who may be addressed, would find the rhetoric persuasive and respond as desired.

4
The Implications of
Rhetorical Criticism for Questions
of Literary Integrity and Dependency

This chapter concerns itself with the questions of the literary unity of 2 Peter and the nature of the literary relationship between Jude and 2 Peter. First, an overview of each question is provided. Second, general principles of ancient rhetoric will be used to identify tendences and to formulate a series of probabilities pertaining to each issue. Third, the findings of the preceding rhetorical analyses, in conjunction with identified tendences and formulated probabilities, will be applied to each question in an attempt to define and clarify rhetoric's contribution to the discussion.

THE QUESTION OF THE LITERARY INTEGRITY OF 2 PETER

The majority of New Testament scholars hold that 2 Peter is an original literary unity. However, numerous source-critical proposals have been advanced claiming that multiple letters, sources, and interpolations are constituent parts of 2 Peter. These proposals often seek to preserve some part of the epistle as genuinely Petrine in the face of weighty arguments of many scholars who claim pseudonymity and dependency upon Jude. These proposals are in part prompted by the following observations: 1) Jude and 2 Peter share material (Jude 4-13, 16-18 and 2 Peter 2:1-18, 3:1-3 exhibiting literary correspondence); 2) in 3:1 the author refers to a second epistle; 3) the epistle contains several abrupt transitions and a variety of theological materials which suggest diverse sources.

A noted proponent of this position, E. Iliff Robson, says of 2 Peter, "It is a thing of shreds and patches; it passes, by what seems to be happy-go-lucky sutures, from exhortation to narrative, narrative to prophecy, prophecy to apocalyptic."[1] It is the purpose of the first part of this chapter to review these proposals, offer traditional critique, and then show what rhetorical criticism contributes to the question.

---

[1] E. Iliff Robson, *Studies in the Second Epistle of St. Peter* (Cambridge: University Press, 1915) 3.

The Proposals for the Non-Literary Integrity of 2 Peter

We turn first to interpolation and combination theories,[2] and will deal with source theories momentarily. In 1641, Grotius asserted that chapters 1-2 and 3 originally constituted two distinct letters. He claimed that the author's statement in 3:1, "this is now the second letter that I have written to you," refers to the content of chapter 3, the previous letter being chapters 1-2.[3] In 1819, L. Bertholdt offered the hypothesis that chapter 2 of 2 Peter is a later interpolation based on Jude, chapters 1 and 3 constituting the original letter.[4] In 1879, W. F. Gess extended the proposed interpolation from Jude to include 1:20b–3:3a.[5] This trend of extension was continued in 1907 by J. V. Bartlet who asserted that the interpolation encompassed 2:1–3:7, 3:8–13 and 1:13–15 being reworked by an editor to align the interpolation with the rest of the letter. This interpolation is indicated by a sudden transition at 2:1.[6] A turn came in 1914 when Grosch proposed that Peter, upon hearing disturbing news, subsequently inserted chapter 2 and 3:15b–18 into an already completed letter awaiting to be sent.[7]

By far the most noted interpolation theory has been proposed by Ernst Kühl. He believed that 2 Peter 1 and 3:3–18 constituted the authentic letter, chapter 2 being later interpolated from Jude, and 3:1–2 being modified with addition of words to dovetail the interpolation into the original letter. In the original letter 1:21, with its reference to prophecy, was succeeded in 3:2 by ὑμεῖς δὲ, ἀγαπητοί, μνησθῆναι τῶν προειρημένων ῥημάτων ὑπὸ τῶν ἁγίων προφητῶν. . . .[8]

The interpolation theories of Kühl and others are usually criticized on the grounds of internal evidence. First, it is argued that the transition from 1:21 to 2:1 is natural, a reference to Old Testament prophecy leading to a reference to false prophets of the Old Testament era.[9] There is the related corollary that what is an abrupt transition to one person is not to another. Therefore, there is no

---

[2] For overall discussions, see "Peter, The Epistle of," in *Encyclopedia Biblica*, ed. T. K. Cheyne and J. Sutherland Black, 4 vols. (New York: Macmillan, 1903) 3: cols. 3684–85; James Moffatt, *An Introduction to the Literature of the New Testament*, 3d ed. (New York: Charles Scribner's Sons, 1923) 369–71; M. McNamara, "The Unity of Second Peter: A Reconstruction," *Scr* 12 (1960) 14–15; Michael Green, *The Second Epistle of Peter and the Epistle of Jude*, TNTC 18 (Grand Rapids: Eerdmans, 1968) 40–41; Donald Guthrie, *New Testament Introduction*, 3d ed. (Downers Grove: Inter-Varsity Press, 1970) 851–53.

[3] *Adnotationes in Actus Apostolorum et in Epistolas Catholicas*, Paris, 1641. This work, and the two cited below, are unavailable to this author.

[4] *Historischkritische Einleitung in sämmtliche kanonische und apokryphische Schriften des alten und neuen Testaments* (1813–1819), pp. 3157ff.

[5] *Das Apostolische Zeugniss von Christi Person*, II, ii, 1879, 412ff.

[6] *The Apostolic Age*, Epochs in Church History (New York: Charles Scribner's Sons, 1907) 518–21.

[7] *Die Eictheit das Zweite Briefes Petri Untersucht*. 2d ed. (Leipzig: Deichert, 1914).

[8] *Die Briefe Petri und Judä*. 6th ed., MeyerK 12 (Göttingen: Vandenhoeck and Ruprecht, 1897).

[9] Chase, "Peter, Second Epistle of," 799, col. 1; Bigg, 216; Moffatt, 370.

reason to assume that 2:1ff. is an interpolation.[10] Second, there is a uniformity of style throughout 2 Peter, something which weighs against later interpolation or addition.[11] Third, Bigg presents an often repeated argument that the repetition of certain words and topics throughout 2 Peter is "a strong guarantee of its unity."[12] Fourth, many interpolation theories fail to account for the shared material with Jude, so that proposed interpolations are made to encompass either more or less of the material shared with Jude.[13] Fifth, as part of the pseudonymous ploy, the first letter implied in 3:1 refers to 1 Peter, not chapters 1-2 as a separate letter. Finally, quite on his own, Robson argues that the reference to a second letter in 3:1 does not necessitate there being two actual letters. It "merely notes that the writer is resuming his pen after an interval. . . . It is 'second' in relation to what stands already written."[14]

M. McNamara in his article, "The Unity of Second Peter: A Reconsideration," brings the discussion of the unity of 2 Peter to the modern stage.[15] Looking first at 1:15, he notes that it is usually translated to the effect, "Yes, I will see to it that when I am gone you will keep this constantly in mind." This makes ἑκάστοτε, "always, constantly," qualify ἔξοδον, "departure," understanding it is the author's intent to enable the content of 1:3-11 to be recalled after his death. McNamara asserts that ἑκάστοτε syntactically can qualify either ἔξοδον or σπουδάσω, "I will see to it." He proposes that ἑκάστοτε qualify σπουδάσω with the resultant meaning, "I will see to it on every occasion that presents itself (i.e., before I die) that you remember these things when I am gone." The author is thus referring to sending further letters on as many occasions as possible before he dies.[16]

McNamara also scrutinizes chapter 3 and points out that the transition from 2:22-3:1 is abrupt. While 2:22 is a comparison of the condition of backsliders with that of dogs and swine, 3:1 reads,

> This is now the second letter that I have written to you, beloved, and in both of them I have roused your sincere mind by way of reminder that you should remember the predictions of the holy prophets and the commandment of the Lord and Savior through your apostles.

Section 3:1-2 is well suited to being the beginning of another letter. The wording δευτέραν . . . ἐπιστολήν "second letter," indicates a previous letter, and the adverb

[10] Cf. Guthrie, 852.
[11] Chase, "Peter, Second Epistle of," 799, col. 1; Bigg, 216; Guthrie, 852; cf. Moffatt, 369-70.
[12] Bigg, 226, also 216. Echoed in Moffatt, 369-70; Chaine, *Les Épîtres Catholiques,* 2d ed., EBib (Paris: Gabalda, 1939) 32; Guthrie, 852.
[13] Chase, "Peter, Second Epistle of," 799, col. 1; Moffatt, 369.
[14] Robson, 42-43; cf. 8.
[15] *Scr.* 12 (1960) 13-19.
[16] Ibid., 16-17.

ἤδη, "now" or "already," gives evidence that this previous letter was recently penned.

This other letter is believed by a vast majority of scholars to be 1 Peter, but McNamara disagrees with this traditional designation on two grounds. First, the time frame connoted by the adverb ἤδη implies that the other letter was very recent, and 2 Peter is the work of a considerable later author than that of 1 Peter. Second, the content and purpose of 1 Peter does not correspond to "predictions of the holy prophets and the commandment of the Lord and Savior through your apostles" which were previously given and are being reiterated for remembrance.[17]

McNamara concludes that the first letter recently received by the congregation is that of chapter 1. It could have been recently written as 3:1 implies and it corresponds to the purpose and content given in 3:1-2. Chapter 3 is one of the reminders the author promised to send in 1:15. Chapter 2 is another letter which borrows from Jude and was possibly written by the author of chapters 1 and 3. All three chapters circulated independently and were later combined by an editor who excised unnecessary salutations and conclusions.[18]

McNamara's proposal can immediately be perceived as deficient because it ignores the genre of 2 Peter. Since 2 Peter is a testament in epistolary form, several features should not be interpreted as he interprets them. First, the reminder theme found in 1:12, 14, 15 and 3:1, 2 is a standard element of testaments and refers to the content of the testament itself, not another letter the author intends to write. Second, as a pseudonymous genre, the testament can utilize particles like ἤδη in 3:1 without regard to chronological considerations. In fact, the pseudonymous author would want to place his own letter within the time frame of 1 Peter. Third, a pseudonymous testament does not need to consider whether or not references to a previous letter under the same name correspond exactly in purpose or content. The reference is part of the pseudonymous ploy, a "touch of authenticity." Fourth, the consistency of style, content, and vocabulary of 2 Peter argues against McNamara's proposal.[19] Fifth and finally, the material shared by Jude and 2 Peter is not restricted to 2 Peter 2, but is also found in 3:1-3, a fact which argues against 2 Peter 2 and 3 ever having been separate letters.

We now turn from interpolation and combination theories to source theories. In 1821, Ullmann proposed that chapter 1 of 2 Peter is a fragment of a lost, original letter of the apostle Peter.[20] In 1915, E. Iliff Robson offered a new source theory, proposing that 2 Peter is composed of four originally separate

[17] Ibid., 17–18.

[18] Ibid., 19.

[19] Spicq, 197 n. 1; Green, 41; Guthrie, 852. McNamara averts this critique by proposing that all three letters may be from the same hand or have been reworked by an editor; thus a uniform style (19).

[20] *Der zweite Briefe Petri, Kritisch Untersucht* (Heidelberg: A. Oswald, 1821).

sources: a moral fragment (1:5b-11), a personal statement and narrative (1:12-18), a prophetic discourse (1:20b-2:19), and an apocalyptic fragment (3:3b-13). These are homogeneous in thought, style, and vocabulary, and can be distinguished from their contexts in these regards. These may or may not be Petrine, but did bear Peter's *imprimatur*. These circulated independently, possibly becoming part of a collection of apostolic fragments which were combined together by a single editor to produce the current form of 2 Peter.[21]

Related in part to Robson's source proposal is that of von Allmen who proposes that 2 Peter 3:5-13 may be an adaptation from a Jewish apocalyptic source which dealt with the delay of God's inbreaking.[22] Bauckham modifies von Allmen's thesis, extending the source one verse to 3:4-13.[23] These correspond closely to Robson's apocalyptic source of 3:3b-13.

Very recently, B. Witherington has proposed that 3:1-3 and 1:16-2:3a, in this order, constitute a Petrine source from the same hand as 1 Peter. He bases his thesis on the grounds of the similarity of vocabulary between 1 Peter and 2 Peter 1:12-2:3a and 3:1-3, the chiastic structure of 1:16-2:3a, and the tense shift from the future to the present between 2:3a and 2:3b.[24]

The obvious objection to these source theories is that their diversity detracts from their basic claim to be able to isolate a source. This is not the case, however, with the apocalyptic source proposed by Robson and von Allmen which are virtually identical and has other evidence to support it. Second, both the theories of Robson and Witherington propose sources which violate the recognized bounds of the shared material with Jude: Robson's prophetic discourse includes 1:20b-21 and 2:19 and excludes 3:1-3, and Witherington's Petrine source attributes 2:1-3a and 3:1-3 to Peter, not Jude. As their sources are defined, both the thesis of Robson and Witherington necessitate adopting either Petrine priority or a common source theory to explain the verbal similarities between Jude and 2 Peter. Third, these two source theories do not posit enough editing to explain the current stylistic and topical unity of 2 Peter, something necessitated in light of these realities.

The Contribution of Rhetorical Criticism
to Questions of Literary Integrity

Rhetorical criticism contributes much to questions of interpolation, addition, and sources in the New Testament that has yet to be utilized. On the basis of invention, arrangement, and style, it offers arguments founded upon a known, standard, and highly conceptualized system. Argumentation on such questions generally has been based upon external textual evidence and internal

---

[21] *Studies in the Second Epistle of St. Peter.*

[22] *RTP* 16 (1966) 155-74, especially, 156-64.

[23] Bauckham, 283.

[24] Ben Witherington, "A Petrine Source in Second Peter," in *SBLSP*, ed. Kent Richards (Atlanta: Scholar's Press, 1985) 187-92.

stylistic and thematic evidence. It is contended here that argumentation from internal evidence can be greatly supplemented and enhanced by rhetorical criticism.

After a literary unit has been subjected to rhetorical criticism, then the species of rhetoric, the basic question(s), and the stasis have been identified. Each segment has been assigned to a part of the arrangement and is known to be in or be itself the *exordium, narratio, probatio,* or *peroratio.* The inventional aspects of propositions, topics, and types of argument in each part of arrangement have been explored and their interrelationships exposed. Style has been analyzed in part and in whole. Sections suspected of being interpolations, additions, or sources can then be examined against the rhetoric of the whole work to see what probability there is for and against their having been an original or non-original element of the rhetorical scheme.

Many questions pertaining to style can now be asked. Does the suspected unit exhibit the style chracteristic of the work as a whole? Does it exhibit the style characteristic of the species of rhetoric of the overall work? Is its style characteristic of the element of arrangement in which it now functions?

A number of questions arise from arrangement as well. Does the suspect unit violate the conventional order of the elements of arrangement by duplicating an element of arrangement out of turn? Does its elimination partially or completely eliminate an element of arrangement, or leave it unaffected? Does its content conform to the prescribed content of the element of arrangement in which it is found?

Many questions might be asked from invention. Is the suspect unit of the same species of rhetoric as the remainder of the work? If not, does its species work as prescribed to support the main species? Is the question(s) underlying it the same as that underlying the work as a whole? Is the same stasis being worked out? Does it further elaborate topics and proofs in progress, or offer those of a similar or supporting nature?

We turn now to formulate probabilities and improbabilities of interpolation and addition based upon conventions of Greco-Roman rhetoric. The same will be done for source theories momentarily. When a work like 2 Peter is so clearly a rhetorical unit in its current form, exhibiting both a uniform style and conventional arrangement and invention, and these are intricately interwoven, then without a corroborating source, there is no basis for positing interpolation or addition. All that can be brought to the defense of such a theory is a claim for extensive redaction of both the original work and the interpolation or addition by a redactor so that the rhetoric of the whole conforms to convention. For example, when style is uniform, one of several things may be indicated. First, the work may be an original unity. Second, secondary material in the same style as the original work may have been introduced. Third, secondary material may have been introduced and edited to coordinate its style to the original work. Without the source(s) from which interpolated or added elements have been borrowed, the formulation of probabilities or improbabilities of interpolation and addition must be based upon observable transgressions of rhetorical conventions of invention, arrangement, and style. The following are formulations of this nature.

The analysis from style offers several approaches to determining if a literary unit is an interpolation or an addition. If the style is inconsistent, there may or may not be evidence of interpolation or addition. The following must be brought to bear on the issue. First, all three basic styles, the grand, middle, and plain, are often used in a single work as purpose, occasion, audience, case or portion of a case requires.[25] Thus a shift in style may be necessitated by the exigence and rhetorical needs of that section of the work and need not indicate interpolation. If a shift in style cannot be adequately accounted for, interpolation or addition may be indicated.

Second, the embellishment or ornament must be suited to the species of rhetoric involved.[26] Epideictic uses every means of ornament[27] and is characterized by a more than average grandeur of style.[28] Deliberative rhetoric exhibits a certain loftiness and impetuosity of style,[29] and a more than average grandeur.[30] Judicial rhetoric is characterized by a less obvious ornament adapted to the matter at hand.[31] Thus a shift of style from the use of few to several figures may be necessitated by a shift from judicial to epideictic rhetoric within the work, as in a shift from the *probatio* to the *digressio*. If the style of a unit does not conform to the species of rhetoric of its context, interpolation or addition may be indicated.

Third, style should suit the parts of arrangement as well. The *exordium* should possess "little brilliance, vivacity or finish of style."[32] The *narratio* should be clear, credible, almost in the tone of everyday conversation,[33] yet graceful.[34] The style of the *probatio* should be as elevated as the subject's importance warrants.[35] Thus a shift from plain to grand style may be accompanied by a shift from the *exordium* to the *probatio*. If a unit does not exhibit style appropriate to the element of arrangement in which it is found, it may be secondary.

---

[25] Cic. *De Or.* 3.52.199–200; *Or.* 21.70–22.74; 35.123; Her. 4.11.16; Quint. 12.10.69–72; Aug. *De Doct. Chr.* 4.19.38; 4.22.51ff. Cf. Demetr. *Eloc.* 2.36. For discussions of how styles interrelate in a work, see Demetr. *Eloc.* 2.36; Cic. *Or.* 28.99; Her. 4.11.16; Aug. *De Doct. Chr.* 4.22–23.

[26] Quint. 8.3.11–14.

[27] Quint. 8.3.11–12.

[28] Cic. *De Or.* 2.82.337. For further details, see Cic. *Or.* 12.38.

[29] Quint. 8.3.14.

[30] Cic. *De Or.* 2.82.337–83.338, 340.

[31] Quint 8.3.13.

[32] Cic. *Inv.* 1.18.25. Similar sentiments are given in Cic. *Or.* 36.124; Her. 1.7.11; Quint. 4.1.55–60.

[33] Cic. *Or.* 36.124; Quint. 4.2.125–26; cf. 4.2.63–65.

[34] Cic. *De Or.* 3.53.202; Quint. 4.2.46, 63, 116.

[35] Cic. *Or.* 36.124–25.

Arrangement provides several probabilities and indications pertaining to interpolation and addition. First, if there is irregularity in the standard order of *exordium, narratio, probatio, peroratio,* that is, if a section is functioning as an element of arrangement unlike that of its context, interpolation or addition is indicated. For example, if a section of the *probatio* contains a detailed narration of facts, something more suited to the *narratio,* it may be secondary.

Second, if the excision of a suspected interpolation or addition eliminates a necessary element of arrangement, or leaves one disproportionate to the other elements of arrangement in the rest of the rhetoric, then the suspect material was probably original to the work. If the excision leaves arrangement unimpaired, then it is possibly secondary.

Third, an interpolation or addition is indicated if the suspect unit does not conform to the content or perform the task of the element of arrangement in which it is found, or relate particularly to the exigence and to the development of the rhetoric. Thus interpolation may be indicated by the following: 1) the suspect unit is in the *exordium,* but is not conducive to gaining audience attention, receptivity, or favor; 2) the suspect unit is in the *narratio,* but does not relate closely to the facts of the case or set out propositions to be developed in the *probatio;* 3) the suspect material is in the *probatio,* but does not aid in proof or refutation; 4) the suspect unit is in the *peroratio,* but does not recapitulate proofs and topcis of the previous rhetoric. If the suspect unit is in the *digressio,* there is little to indicated interpolation because the content and functions of the *digressio* are less rigidly prescribed than those of the other elements of arrangement.

Probabilities for interpolation based on invention are numerous. The following conditions are indications of interpolation from invention: 1) if the suspect unit does not relate to the exigence which prompted the work as indicated in the rest of the rhetoric; 2) if there is a change in the species of rhetoric used which cannot be explained by the reliance of the three rhetorical species on one another to further the rhetorical purpose of the work; 3) if it does not relate to the question(s) giving rise to the stasis, or exhibits a stasis different than the work as a whole or the subsection of the work in which it is a part; 4) if the suspect section does not develop topics and propositions anticipated and given in the *narratio* or *propositio,* developed in the *probatio,* or summed up in the *peroratio.*

Since each species of rhetoric has its own typical style of argumentation,[36] abrupt variation in the type of argument used may be indicative of addition or interpolation. However, this can be pressed only if the change in argumentative format is not furthering the development of proof central to the exigence, or is not explained by a shift to a subunit of another species of rhetoric. 2 Peter is a

[36] Epideictic prefers amplification and appeal to pathos, deliberative prefers example and comparison of example, and judicial prefers enthymemes and inartificial proof. See ch. 1 for further discussion and references.

good example of shifting styles of argumentation, and yet, all is related to the exigence and all is explained by shifts from one species of rhetoric to another.

Two important unknowns must always be considered in discussions of interpolation, addition, and rhetorical criticism. The first unknown is the skill of an editor to blend interpolated segments into the rhetoric of the work as a whole. Since rhetoric was well known in the ancient world, the editor could have taken the pains to assimilate an interpolation into a larger piece, observing rhetorical convention and making topical and stylistic alterations. The second unknown is the skill of the rhetor of the original work. Material suspected to be an interpolation on rhetorical grounds may be merely a departure from rhetorical conventions attributable to the rhetor's disregard for of ignorance of those conventions.

Regarding source theories, the following are general principles and probabilities derived from rhetorical criticism. First, the probabilities derived from style, arrangement, and invention stated above as applicable to interpolation and addition theories are also applicable to source theories.

Second, if the rhetoric is unified, without external corroboration it is highly improbable that a source can be isolated. In this case, the very postulation of a source also necessitates the postulation of extensive revision and editing to account for the interdependence of invention, arrangement, and style.

Third, since the *exordium, narratio,* and *peroratio* are situation specific, no source is likely to underlie them. Borrowing is most expected as part of the *probatio,* where argumentation of standard nature from other sources bearing on the case can be introduced, and the *digressio,* where there is freedom in the use of material. If the source postulated is contained within the bounds of the *probatio* or *digressio,* it is more probable than if it overlaps the *probatio* or *digressio* and a juxtaposed element of arrangement. For example, postulating a source as part of the *probatio* and *peroratio* seems unlikely due to the specific nature of the *peroratio.*

These observations must be made in conjunction with each other due to the adaptability of, and variations within the system of rhetoric in the classical world. The system was not rigid and monolithic, but flexible and multi-faceted. It allowed the exigence to determine the approach to take in any given case, or part of a case, and provided a variety of options for doing so. Taking any one of these observations in isolation is unwise.

The Contribution of Rhetorical Criticism to the
Question of the Literary Integrity of 2 Peter

Interpolation and combination theories regarding 2 Peter's non-original literary unity are basically: 1) that chapter 3 is a distinct letter; 2) that most of chapters 1 and 3 constitutes the authentic letter, 1:20b–3:7 or a smaller portion being interpolated from Jude; 3) that all three chapters circulated as separate letter. These theories will now be examined in light of probabilities and tendencies formulated from conventions of Greco-Roman rhetoric, and the previous rhetorical analysis of 2 Peter in chapter 3.

First to be considered is the argument from style. Each section of 2 Peter exhibits the same penchant for exaggerated style.[37] As stated above, uniformity of style offers no basis for positing interpolation or addition. Thus considerations must move to arrangement and invention.

On the basis of argumentation from invention and arrangement, it is improbable that chapter 3 was once a separate letter later added to chapters 1-2 (Grotius) or a later addition to chapters 1-2 before sending (Robson). As demonstated above in chapter 3, 3:1-2, although sounding like the beginning of a new letter (Grotius), or a new beginning after an interval (Robson), is easily explained as recapitulation necessitated by the length of the *digressio* of 2:10b-22. It is needed to introduce further proof and refutation closely related to that found earlier in the *probatio* in 1:16-2:10a. As previously argued, 3:1-2 is an example of the figures of thought called *aphodos* and *transitio* which recap after the *digressio,* and it functions as a secondary *exordium* renewing audience attention, goodwill, and receptivity.

Arguing from the vantage of arrangement, without chapter 3, chapters 1 and 2 constitute an *exordium* (1:1-15), a *probatio* (1:16-2:10a) with defense (1:16-21; 2:3b-10a) and counteraccusation (2:1-3), and a *digressio* (2:10b-22). Chapters 1-2 would be incomplete without chapter 3, lacking a return to the *probatio* after the *digressio* and a *peroratio.* "Miraculously" these are just the elements supplied by chapter 3.

Arguing from invention, the topics of the *exordium* and *probatio* of chapters 1 and 2 are continually refined in 3:1-13 and are recapitulated in 3:14-18. As fully shown previously, the topics and propositions in a rhetorical piece of this time are, in general, casually introduced in the *exordium,* sometimes stated explicitly in the *narratio,* developed in the *probatio,* and recapitulated and blended in an emotional appeal in the *peroratio.* If chapter 3 was once a distinct letter, it is startling that now functioning as a secondary *exordium* (3:1-2), as part two of the *probatio* proper (3:3-13), and as the *peroratio* (3:14-18) of 2 Peter, it should so perfectly serve the *exordium* and *probatio* of chapters 1 and 2.

As demonstrated in chapter 3, the invention, arrangement, and style of 2 Peter all conform to convention and are all interrelated. If chapter 3 was a distinct letter which was added later to chapters 1 and 2, then either chapter 3 or chapters 1 and 2 had to be extensively revised, and in places, completely rewritten in order that the rhetoric of all parts might work together effectively and according to convention as they do now. This is particularly true of the *peroratio* of chapter 3 which would of necessity have been made to serve as the *peroratio* of the entire letter.

Based upon the above argumentation, I conclude that there are two choices in this matter. Either chapter 3 must be considered an original part of 2 Peter, or it must be posited that a letter has been added to a defective letter to serve as the missing *probatio* and the *peroratio,* and both letters were extensively

[37] See ch. 3, pp. 144-46. See appendix 4 for a catalog of figures in 2 Peter.

revised. The former hypothesis, explaining everything in a single act of composition, is preferable as the simpler explanation. Redaction should not be assumed without compelling evidence, especially when the proposed redactional units are incomplete rhetorical units and their merging requires positing extensive redaction.

We turn now to the second proposal against literary unity, namely that 2 Pet 1:20b-3:7, or a smaller portion, should be considered an interpolation derived from Jude (Bertholdt, Gess, Bartlett, Kühl). From a rhetorical standpoint, it is preferable not to consider this section an interpolation, even if one believes that it derives from Jude. As it now stands, 1:20b-3:7 is an integral part of the *probatio* of 2 Peter. Verses 1:20b-21 form part of an artificial proof by enthymeme in 1:20-21, and 2:1-3a forms a counteraccusation linked closely with the *probatio* in 1:16-21 by means of vocabulary, topics, chiastic structure, and *inclusio*. In fact, as our analysis shows, 2:1-3a presents the broad outline of 1:16-21 in reverse order, and directs the charges of the false teachers back upon themselves. Verses 2:3b-10 provide another accusation and refutation which is a logical step from that of the preceding segment of the *probatio*, especially 1:16-21. Whereas 1:16-21 defends the message of the parousia, 2:3b-10a defends the message of the judgment which will accompany the parousia. Verses 2:10b-22 serve as a *digressio* aimed at amplification to destroy the ethos of the false teachers. Such a unit would be conspicuous by its absence in a subsection of judicial rhetoric such as that begun in 1:16. Verses 3:1-2 form a transition to the *probatio* after the *digressio*. Verses 3:3-4 are the accusation of the false teachers, and 3:5-7 are part of the refutation of 3:3-4 (which constitutes 3:5-13) and is itself an artificial proof by enthymeme.

From another angle, if 1:20b-3:7 or any smaller portion were removed, 2 Peter would still possess all the necessary elements of arrangement — *exordium, probatio,* and *peroratio*. However, major topics introduced in the *exordium* would find no development in the remaining *probatio* (3:8-13), and topics reiterated in the *peroratio* would have no earlier referent. Also, a *probatio* consisting only of 11 verses would be disproportionately short in comparison with an *exordium* of 13 verses and a *peroratio* of 5 verses. If 1:20b-3:7, or a smaller portion, is an interpolation, extensive revision of chapters 1 and 3 must be assumed to account for stylistic and inventional uniformity.

We are again left with two choices. Either the author incorporated 1:20b-3:7, or some portion thereof, in the original composition of his work because it suited his needs, or someone later interpolated it, extensively revising chapter 1 and 3:8-18. I conclude that 1:20b-3:7 is adequately explained as an original and integral part of 2 Peter, and that the hypothesis of a later interpolation is unnecessary.

It must be noted that among these interpolation theories, Kühl's is the most plausible. If any section could be excised from the standpoint of arrangement, it is 2:1-3:2. Without this section, no proof is left partial; the *probatio* is left with three proofs in 1:16-21 and a full accusation and refutation in five proofs in

3:3–13. However, from the standpoint of invention, if 2:1–3:2 was not original, then the topics introduced in the *exordium* and reiterated in the *peroratio* do not find counterparts in the *probatio*, nor is there a denunciatory *digressio* needed to counter a serious case and a dangerous opponent.[38]

The interpolation theory of Grosch, that upon hearing bad news Peter added chapters 2 and 3:15b–18 to an existing letter yet to be sent, must be rejected. Rhetorically the original letter would have lacked a suitable *peroratio*, for having only 3:14–15a, it would have lacked an *adfectus*. Also, if chapter 2 was inserted, the whole letter would of necessity have had to be rewritten by Peter and, if so, how can an interpolation now be isolated?

The argument of McNamara that chapters 1, 2, and 3 were originally separate letters must also be seriously questioned. According to this proposal, chapter 1 as it stands contains only an *exordium* (1:1–15) and *probatio* (1:16–21). If it were an independent letter which was later placed into its current place in 2 Peter, it would have had its *peroratio* excised and probably part of its *probatio* as well, for as it now stands, the *probatio* is far too short, comprising less of the letter than the *exordium*.

Chapter 2 as it stands contains a counteraccusation (2:1–3a), a *probatio* (2:3b–10a) and a *digressio* (2:10b–22). As such it has lost the *exordium*, the *narratio* (if it had used one), and the *peroratio*. Thus if it was once an independent letter, it has been considerably pruned on both ends.

Chapter 3 contains material which could originally have been an *exordium* (3:1–2), *probatio* (3:3–13), and *peroratio* (3:14–18). If chapter 3 was once a separate letter, it has probably not lost any major portion. It is only chapter that is a rhetorical whole, insofar as arrangement and invention are concerned.

If chapters 1, 2, and 3 were all originally independent letters, then the unity of invention, arrangement, and style demonstrated in all three chapters can only be explained by major editing of all three letters. This editing necessitated major reductions of chapters 1 and 2. We are again confronted with only two choices: either 2 Peter is an original unity, or it is the product of addition, extensive excision, and revision.

We turn now to source theories. Of all four presented above, that of von Allmen and Bauckham are rhetorically the most justified. If an apocalyptic source resides behind 3:5–13 (von Allmen), it provides the refutation of the false teachers' accusation of 3:4. If it resides behind 3:4–13) (Bauckham), then the standard argument of the scoffers in 3:4 is included with its refutation. This borrowing is feasible, since the scoffers' claim and the argumentation are traditional, and other sources provide similar argumentation and corroboration of

---

[38] Cic. *De Or.* 2.77.312. Cf. Quint. 6.1.12 which states that greater emotional appeal is required in the *peroratio* if the opponent is dangerous. This would naturally apply to the *digressio* as well.

borrowing.[39] Also, the source postulated is either the refutation of an accusation (3:5-13) or the accusation and its refutation (3:4-13), that is, definite rhetorical units. These units also do not overlap elements of arrangement, but constitute most of the second part of the *probatio* proper (3:3-13).

Robson proposes that 2 Peter is composed of four sources of a moral fragment (1:5-11), a personal statement and narrative (1:12-18), a prophetic discourse (1:20-2:19) and an apocalyptic fragment (3:3b-13). On the basis of rhetorical analysis, as it now stands, the moral fragment is part of the *exordium,* the personal narrative is part of the *exordium* and *probatio,* the prophetic discourse is part of the *probatio* and *digressio,* and the apocalyptic fragment is part of the *probatio.* Thus the personal narrative and prophetic discourse have been used to serve in two juxtaposed elements of arrangement serving different purposes. This is unlikely because of the different nature of each element of arrangement. The only way such overlap is probable is if the fragment is from such a cross-section of these elements of arrangement in another work. However, this is unlikely because all the elements of arrangement, except the *probatio,* are very situation specific and their content not very conducive to borrowing.

As stated earlier, Witherington proposes that 3:1-3 and 1:12-2:3a, in this order, once constituted a Petrine source. This theory has the advantage of recognizing the sectional bounds in 3:1-3, 3:1-2 being a secondary *exordium* and 3:3 being the introduction to the second half of the *probatio* proper. Clearly, the content of 1:16-2:3a is most suited to the *probatio* of any work, and 3:1-3 and 1:12-15 are most suited to an *exordium* or *narratio.* A major problem with this theory is that the Petrine source is ordered with the *exordium* sandwiched between two sections of the *probatio.*

If any of these sources of Robson and Witherington were once separate sources that have been edited together, then their interdependence in invention and arrangement, and their unity of style, must be the result of extensive editing. This being the case, it is hard to imagine that such sources can be identified in the first place. Either these portions of 2 Peter are original creations of the author to meet his exigence, or they are extensively edited to do the same. In either case they cannot be identified in the current work without external sources to corroborate the theory.

In summary, this examination has shown that rhetorical criticism has numerous implications for the question of the literary integrity of 2 Peter. It seriously questions all interpolation and addition theories, and all but two source theories. Regarding the latter, it supports the source theories of von Allmen and Bauckham that 3:5-13 or 3:4-13 could be based on an apologetic source. This examination strongly indicates that the current form of 2 Peter is also its original form. We turn now to the second and more central issue to be addressed in this chapter, the question of the literary relationship between Jude and 2 Peter.

[39] von Allmen, 156-64; Bauckham, 283-85; 290-91, 296-97.

THE NATURE OF THE LITERARY RELATIONSHIP
BETWEEN JUDE AND 2 PETER

The similarities of subject matter, order or ideas, and wording of Jude and 2 Peter have been noted and their significance has been debated for centuries. Upon even the most casual reading it is easily noted that Jude 4-13, 16-18 is similar to 2 Pet 2:1-18 and 3:1-3 in these regards. Although only one clause in Jude 13 and 2 Peter 2:17 is almost identical, verbal correspondance is close enough to warrant postulating a literary relationship between Jude and 2 Peter.[40]

The Proposed Explanations for the Literary
Relationship Between Jude and 2 Peter

There are three major explanations for the literary affinity between Jude and 2 Peter.[41] In brief outline these are: 1) Jude and 2 Peter are dependent upon a common source;[42] 2) Jude is dependent upon 2 Peter;[43] 3) 2 Peter is dependent upon Jude.[44]

---

[40] Reicke postulates an oral sermonic pattern can account for these verbal similarities (148, 189-90). Kelly suggests the possibility of a step-removed literary relationship, that is, the author of 2 Peter was familiar with Jude, but when writing was quoting from memory (227). However, neither theory explains the rare vocabulary of Jude and 2 Peter (Cantinat, 275).

[41] I am not dealing with the fourth position of common authorship which has little to commend it. One example is John A. T. Robinson who postulates that Jude the Lord's brother wrote both works (*Redating the New Testament* [Philadelphia: Westiminster, 1976] 192-95). The Palestinean Jewish character of Jude and the Hellenistic character of 2 Peter, as well as stylistic differences, rule against this position (Bauckham, 141).

[42] Robson identifies this source as a prophetic discourse underlying 2 Pet 1:20b-2:19 and shared portions in Jude. However, while the author of 2 Peter uses the source, he also consults Jude's editing of the source (52-59, esp. 59). Green identifies it as an anti-heretical tract (54-55; *2 Peter Reconsidered*, 10-11). Spicq, 197 n. 1, writes ". . . genre littéraire polémique et apologétique bien défini dans la littérature grecque et qumran-nienne."

[43] This position is generally espoused by older commentators who assume the authenticity of 2 Peter. Luther; Spitta, *Der zweite Brief des Petrus und der Brief des Judas* (Halle: Waisenhauses, 1885) 381-470; Falconer, "Is Second Peter a Genuine Epistle to the Churches of Samaria," *Exp* 6/6 (1902) 218-24; Theodor Zahn, *Introduction to the New Testament*, trans. M. W. Jacobus, et al., 2 vols. (Edinburgh: T. & T. Clark, 1909) 2:249-51, 265-67, 285; Bigg, 216-24; Guthrie, 919-27.

[44] Most commentators since Eichhorn and Herder. Bauckham, 141-43; Cantinat, 272-75; Chaine, 18-24; F. H. Chase, "Jude, Epistle of," 802, col. 2; Chase, "Peter, Second Epistle of," 814, col. 1; Danker, 89-90; Fornberg, 33f.; Fuchs and Reymond, 20-24; W. Grundmann, *Der Brief des Judas und der zweite Brief des Petrus*, THKNT 15 (Berlin: Evangelische Verlagsanstalt, 1974) 75-83, 102-7; J. E. Huther, *Kritisch exegetisches Handbuch über den 1. Brief des Petrus, den Brief des Judas und den 2. Brief des Petrus*, 5th ed., rev., MeyerK 12 (Göttingen: Vandenhoeck & Ruprecht, 1887) 254-60; Kelly, 225-27; Mayor, i-xxv; Michl, 153-55; Moffatt, 348-52; Neyrey, *Form and Background*, 119-67;

Position 1, that Jude and 2 Peter are dependent upon a common source, is unlikely for the following reasons. First, Jude 5-19 is composed of traditional material that Jude assumes his audience knows (v 5). It could be based on a common source shared with 2 Peter. However, the fact that Jude 4 is part of the shared material, as its parallel in 2 Pet 2:1-3 makes clear, and is not part of the traditional material designated in Jude 5, makes a common source unlikely.[45] Second, the author of 2 Peter could have rewritten the common source as easily as he could have rewritten Jude. The hypothesis does not explain the difference between Jude and 2 Peter any better than literary dependency theories.[46] Third, if Jude and 2 Peter are dependent upon a common source, then the literary affinities between them indicate that vv 4-13 and 16-18 of Jude are derived from the source. If this is the case, then Jude is little more than a plagarized work, Jude contributing only vv 1-3, 14-15, and 19-25. Jude thus has no real role as rhetor which is unrealistic in an urgent situation (v 3).[47]

Position 2, that Jude is dependent upon 2 Peter, is untenable for the following reasons. First, the same basic argument against the use of a common source applies in this case as well. If Jude borrowed so extensively, here from 2 Peter, why write at all?[48]

Second, it has been noted that 2 Pet 2:1-3 and 3:3-4, 17 speak of false teachers in the future tense, and 3:4 is an apostolic prediction of false teachers. Jude 4 mentions the condemnation of the sectarians as having been previously designated, and Jude 17-18 mentions previous apostolic predictions and gives one almost identical to that of 2 Pet 3:4. From these facts, it is argued that Jude presupposes 2 Peter and quotes from it. Otherwise, it is thought that 2 Peter was made up to supply these prophecies.[49] However, this is a highly speculative position. Jude 4 and 17-18 are very vague references, and are just as easily explained as references to tradition in general.[50] Also, the future tense of 2 Peter is a facet of the testament genre, not a real future tense which Jude could point out to show fulfillment of prophecy.

Robson, 52-59, although he believes 2 Peter 2 was a separate letter; Rowston, 129-39; Schelkle, 138-39; Schrage, 122-23; Schmid, 605-9; Sidebottom, 65-69; H. Windisch, *Die katholischen Briefe erklärt,* 3d ed., HNT 15 (Tübingen: J. C. B. Mohr, 1951) 91-92.

[45] Bauckham, 141-42. Compare my argument from rhetoric below, pp. 171-72 for a similar approach.

[46] Zahn, 2:226; Sidebottom, 67; Bauckham, 142.

[47] Kelly, 226; Sidebottom, 68; Rowston, 131; Guthrie, 920; Bauckham assumes Jude's main message is the exhortation of vv 20-23. Jude could have added vv 20-23 to a source and still accomplished his purpose (141-42). This would lessen the force of the argument. However, our analysis has shown that vv 5-16 is the central part of Jude's message.

[48] Huther, 255; Kelly, 226; Green, 52; Robinson, 192.

[49] Spitta, 145, 146; Bigg, 221; Zahn, 2:250-52, 266, 285-86; Guthrie, 922-23.

[50] Huther, 255, Mayor, xxiii, Chaine, 22; Green, 51-52; Bauckham, 143.

Third, and related to the last argument, since Jude speaks of the sectarians in the present tense and 2 Peter speaks of them primarily in the future tense (though sometimes in the present), Jude is said to be the later letter combating what was formerly predicted by 2 Peter.[51] Again, this argument can be decisively refuted by acknowledging that 2 Peter is of the testament genre which employs the future tense as a standard feature. 2 Peter's occasional use of the present indicates that the false teachers are as much present in his community as they are in the community to which Jude is addressed.

Position 3, that 2 Peter is dependent upon Jude, is by far the best position. Before progressing further, let us dispose of three arguments for this position that are untenable, but often given. First, it is argued that because 2 Peter presents the biblical examples like those in Jude in chronological order, whereas Jude presents them in a non-biblical order, 2 Peter redacts Jude and corrects his chronology.[52] This argument falters when one notes that the biblical examples of 2 Peter are chronological only because 2 Peter excises that which was not in chronological order in Jude, possibly in accordance with a traditional parenetic schema.[53] Thus no consciousness of chronology needs to be postulated for 2 Peter. It may just as well be the case that Jude inserted biblical examples into the framework of 2 Peter without regard for chronology.[54]

Second, it is often argued that because 2 Peter does not contain the pseudepigraphical references which are found in Jude,[55] the author redacted Jude at a later time when the canon was taking shape.[56] However, this argument can be used to support Jude's dependency upon 2 Peter as well. Writing in a setting where pseudepigrapha were still held in high esteem, Jude could have inserted quotations and allusions into the material he borrowed from 2 Peter, thus sharpening 2 Peter's material with reference to known sources.[57]

Third, arguments for priority based on conciseness or verbosity, which assume either that the more concise or the more verbose statement is the edited one, are highly subjective.[58] They ignore the fact that it is the need to meet an

---

[51] Guthrie, 924.

[52] Kelly, 227; Cantinat, 275. Suggested by Mayor, vi.

[53] See ch. 2, p. 51; ch. 3, p. 112.

[54] Bigg, 221–22.

[55] For example, Jude 14 quotes *1 Enoch* 1:9, and Jude 9 uses *T. Mos.*

[56] Mayor, ix; Kelly, 227; Cantinat, 274, 275; suggested by Rowston, 134; cf. Sidebottom, 68.

[57] Bigg, 222; Zahn, 2:285; Green, 52–53; Guthrie, 921–22.

[58] For example, Huther argues that 2 Peter is secondary because he simplifies and edits Jude (255); Bigg argues Petrine priority because Jude has taken out the repetitions of 2 Peter (226); Chase argues that Jude is prior because the style is more natural ("Jude, the Epistle of," 803, col. 2); Moffatt argues that Jude's style is forcible and terse and is the earlier one (351); Kelly argues the more verbose 2 Peter is secondary (226); Fuchs and Reymond argue that 2 Peter is better from a literary standpoint and this is the result of the editing of Jude (22).

exigence and the individuality of an author's style which determines the length.[59]

More lucid support for the priority of Jude is found in the following arguments. First, Jude 4–18 is carefully structured, whereas the corresponding parts of 2 Peter, especially 2:10b–18, are not as carefully structured. It is easier to see how the author of 2 Peter could use the material of Jude 8c–18 to construct a less structured denunciation of the false teachers, than how Jude could utilize 2 Pet 2:10b–18 to construct a tightly woven argument to show that the sectarians were predicted in prophecy.[60] Second, redaction criticism indicates that 2 Peter utilized Jude. Although redaction criticism cannot give a conclusive answer to the question of literary dependency here, by weighing the plausibility of dependency in each case of correspondance, Jude is usually concluded to be the most likely to have been redacted.[61] Third, 2 Peter is usually dated later than Jude on linguistic, historical, and theological grounds.

As the discussion turns to consider the contribution of rhetoric to this question of dependency, position 1, the common source theory, will be minimally considered because there is little evidence to support it, and because rhetorical criticism cannot address it extensively for lack of the source. The two major positions which posit literary dependency between Jude and 2 Peter will receive the bulk of further consideration.

The Contribution of Rhetorical Criticism
to the Questions of Literary Dependence
Between Jude and 2 Peter

In the effort to determine priority, the comparison of Jude and 2 Peter has always involved redactional considerations. However, situation and theological purpose have been considered virtually identical for both books, and the focus has been upon stylistic matters and authenticity. In recent years, redaction criticism has been used in the effort to determine the situation prompting the works, and the theological purpose of the authors.[62] These studies, especially those of Fornberg and Neyrey, although for the first time using redaction criticism fully and systematically, assume the priority of Jude, and thus focus on the redaction of Jude by the author of 2 Peter. On its own, redaction criticism has not been able to establish the priority it assumes.

I propose that redaction criticism can be more completely informed by rhetorical criticism. Currently such considerations as word choice, grammar, style, situation, purpose, and audience concern redaction criticism. Rhetorical conventions of invention, arrangement, style, situation, audience, and exigence

---

[59] Guthrie, 922, 924.

[60] Bauckham, 142.

[61] Fornberg, ch. 3; Neyrey, *Form and Background,* ch. 3; Cavallin, 263–70; Bauckham, 142–43; cf. Danker, 89–90.

[62] Fornberg, 33ff.; Neyrey, *Form and Background,* 119–67; cf. Danker, 89–90; Cavallin, 263–70; Rowston, 129–39.

include and excede these considerations as currently formulated, and can more fully inform redaction criticism. Bauckham writes,

> One may produce . . . a convincing interpretation of 2 Peter's use of Jude, but one cannot be sure that an equally convincing interpretation of Jude's use of 2 Peter is impossible. No one since Spitta and Bigg has attempted it, but the analogy with Synoptic criticism perhaps suggests that their view may be ripe for revival.[63]

I suggest going a step further than Bauckham proposes. While using rhetorical criticism to inform redaction criticism, let there be no assumption as to priority, so that each correspondence is evaluated on its own merits in the light of rhetorical convention. This way a more objective redactional reconstruction can be formulated using existing methodology and insights without the bias for priority.

The following is first a general and then a specific analysis of the verbal correspondence between Jude and 2 Peter in which the concerns and system of Greco-Roman rhetoric are utilized to inform a redactional analysis. Without assuming priority of either book, and on the basis of invention, arrangement, and style, the attempt is made to determine in broad outline, and in each instance of correspondence, which book was the redacted and which author was the redactor. All these probabilities are then weighed to determine the most likely direction of dependence. Of course, redactional and rhetorical probabilities are subject to a variety of opinions, and the conclusions to follow will be subject to challenge. It can be hoped, however, that supplementing redactional criticism with rhetorical criticism will increase objectivity and lead to a probable result providing supporting grounds for consensus. The following figure provides a diagram of the verbal correspondences between Jude and 2 Peter, and will be useful for reference throughout the discussion.

FIGURE 3
THE LITERARY CORRESPONDENCE BETWEEN JUDE AND 2 PETER

Jude	*2 Peter*
	2:1
	But false prophets also arose among the people (λαῷ), just as there will be false teachers among you
v 4	
For admission has been secretly gained (παρεισέδυσαν)	who will secretly bring in (παρεισάξουσιν)
by some who long ago (πάλαι) were designated for this	destructive (ἀπωλείας) heresies,

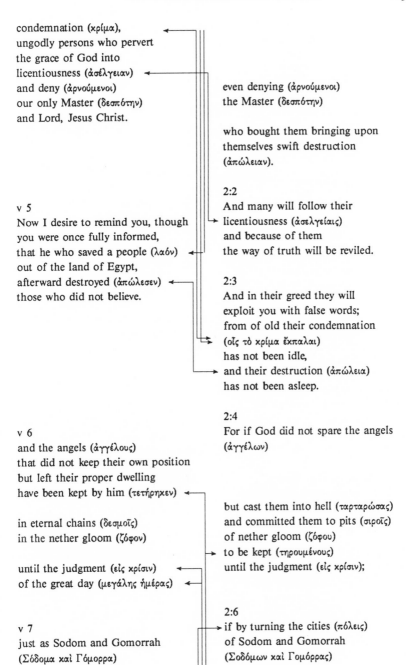

condemnation (κρίμα),
ungodly persons who pervert
the grace of God into
licentiousness (ἀσέλγειαν)
and deny (ἀρνούμενοι)
our only Master (δεσπότην)
and Lord, Jesus Christ.

even denying (ἀρνούμενοι)
the Master (δεσπότην)

who bought them bringing upon
themselves swift destruction
(ἀπώλειαν).

2:2

v 5
Now I desire to remind you, though
you were once fully informed,
that he who saved a people (λαόν)
out of the land of Egypt,
afterward destroyed (ἀπώλεσεν)
those who did not believe.

And many will follow their
licentiousness (ἀσελγείαις)
and because of them
the way of truth will be reviled.

2:3
And in their greed they will
exploit you with false words;
from of old their condemnation
(οἷς τὸ κρίμα ἔκπαλαι)
has not been idle,
and their destruction (ἀπώλεια)
has not been asleep.

2:4
For if God did not spare the angels
(ἀγγέλων)

v 6
and the angels (ἀγγέλους)
that did not keep their own position
but left their proper dwelling
have been kept by him (τετήρηκεν)

but cast them into hell (ταρταρώσας)
and committed them to pits (σιροῖς)

in eternal chains (δεσμοῖς)
in the nether gloom (ζόφον)

of nether gloom (ζόφου)
to be kept (τηρουμένους)

until the judgment (εἰς κρίσιν)
of the great day (μεγάλης ἡμέρας)

until the judgment (εἰς κρίσιν);

2:6

v 7
just as Sodom and Gomorrah
(Σόδομα καὶ Γόμορρα)

if by turning the cities (πόλεις)
of Sodom and Gomorrah
(Σοδόμων καὶ Γομόρρας)

and the surrounding cities (πόλεις) ◄┘
which likewise acted immorally
and indulged in unnatural lust,
(ἀπελθοῦσαι ὀπίσω σαρκὸς ἑτέρας) ◄────┐

serve as an example
(πρόκεινται δεῖγμα)
by undergoing a punishment of
eternal fire

to ashes he condemned them to
extinction and made them an
example (ὑπόδειγμα . . . τεθεικώς)

to those who were to be ungodly;

2:9
then the Lord knows how to rescue
the ungodly from trial
► and to keep (τηρεῖν)
the unrighteous under punishment
until the day of judgment
► (εἰς ἡμέραν κρίσεως)

2:10
and especially those who indulge
► in the lust (τοὺς ὀπίσω
σαρκὸς . . . πορευομένοις)

v 8
Yet in like manner
these men in their dreamings
defile the flesh
(σάρκα μὲν μιαίνουσιν),
reject authority (κυριότητα),

of defiling passion
(ἐν ἐπιθυμίᾳ μιασμοῦ)
and despise authority (κυριότητος)
► Bold (τολμηταί) and willful,

and revile the glorious ones
(δόξας δὲ βλασφημοῦσιν).

they are not afraid to revile
the glorious ones (δόξας οὐ τρέμουσιν
βλασφημοῦντες)

v 9
But when the archangel (ἀρχάγγελος)
Michael contending with the devil,
disputed about the body of Moses
he did not presume (ἐτόλμησεν) ◄──┐
to pronounce (ἐπενεγκεῖν)
a reviling judgment
(κρίσιν βλασφημίας)
upon him

2:11
Whereas angels (ἄγγελοι)

though greater in might and power

do not pronounce (φέρουσιν)
a reviling judgment
(βλάσφημον κρίσιν)
upon them

but said
"The Lord (κύριος) rebuke you."

before the Lord (παρὰ κυρίου).

v 10
But these men (οὗτοι δέ) revile
whatever they do not understand
(ὅσα μὲν οὐκ οἴδασιν βλασφημοῦσιν)
and by those things that they know
(ἐπίστανται)

2:12
But these (οὗτοι δέ)

like irrational animals
(ὡς ἄλογα ζῷα)
creatures of instinct (φυσικῶς)
born to be caught and killed (φθοράν),

by instinct (φυσικῶς)

as irrational animals do
(ὡς τὰ ἄλογα ζῷα),

reviling in matters of which
they are ignorant
(ἐν οἷς ἀγνοοῦσιν βλασφημοῦντες)
will be destroyed (φθαρήσονται)
in the same destruction with them
(ἐν τῇ φθορᾷ αὐτῶν).

they are destroyed (φθείρονται).

v 11
Woe to them!
For they walk in the way (ὁδῷ)
of Cain,
and abandon themselves
for the sake of gain (μισθοῦ)
to Balaam's error
(τῇ πλάνῃ τοῦ βαλαάμ)

[2:15]
Forsaking the right way
(εὐθεῖαν ὁδόν)

they have gone astray
(ἐπλανήθησαν),
they have followed the way of
Balaam (τῇ ὁδῷ τοῦ βαλαάμ)
the son of Beor,
who loved gain (μισθόν)
from wrongdoing (ἀδικίας)

and perish in Korah's rebellion.

2:13
suffering wrong for their
wrongdoing.
(ἀδικούμενοι μισθὸν ἀδικίας)
They count it a pleasure
to revel in the daytime.

These are blemishes (σπιλάδες)

on your love feasts
(ἐν ταῖς ἀγάπαις ὑμῶν)
as they boldly carouse together
(συνευωχούμενοι ἀφόβως),
looking after themselves;

waterless clouds (νεφέλαι ἄνυδροι)

carried along by winds
(ὑπὸ ἀνέμων παραφερόμεναι)
fruitless trees in late autumn,
twice dead, uprooted;

v 13
wild waves of the sea, casting up
the foam of their own shame;
wandering stars
for whom (οἷς)
the nether gloom of darkness
(ὁ ζόφος τοῦ σκότους)
has been reserved (τετήρηται)
for ever.

v 16
For these are grumblers,
malcontents, following their own
passions (ἐπιθυμίας), ←————————┐
loud-mouthed boasters
(ὑπέρογκα),
flattering people to gain advantage.└──►

They are blots and blemishes,
(σπίλοι καὶ μῶμοι)
reveling
in their dissipation
(ἐν ταῖς ἀπάταις αὐτῶν)
carousing with you
(συνευωχούμενοι ὑμῖν).

2:17
These are
waterless springs (πηγαὶ ἄνυδροι)
and mists (ὁμίχλαι)
driven by a storm
(ὑπὸ λαίλαπος ἐλαυνόμεναι);

for them (οἷς)
the nether gloom of darkness
(ὁ ζόφος τοῦ σκότους)
had been reserved (τετήρηται).

2:18
For uttering loud boasts
(ὑπέρογκα) of folly,
they entice with licentious
passions (ἐπιθυμίας) of the flesh
men who have barely escaped
from those who live in error

3:1
This is now the second letter
I have written to you beloved
┌─► (ἀγαπητοί) and in both of them
│   I have aroused your sincere mind
┌─► by way of reminder (ἐν ὑπομνήσει);

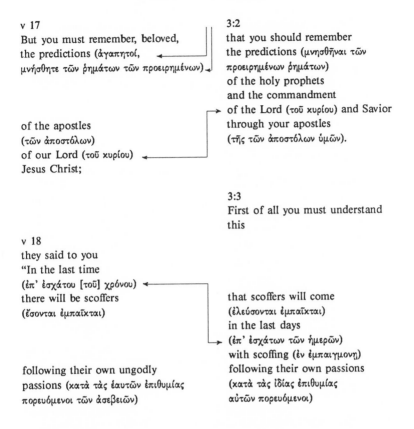

v 17
But you must remember, beloved,
the predictions (ἀγαπητοί,
μνήσθητε τῶν ῥημάτων τῶν προειρημένων)

of the apostles
(τῶν ἀποστόλων)
of our Lord (τοῦ κυρίου)
Jesus Christ;

3:2
that you should remember
the predictions (μνησθῆναι τῶν
προειρημένων ῥημάτων)
of the holy prophets
and the commandment
of the Lord (τοῦ κυρίου) and Savior
through your apostles
(τῆς τῶν ἀποστόλων ὑμῶν).

3:3
First of all you must understand
this

v 18
they said to you
"In the last time
(ἐπ' ἐσχάτου [τοῦ] χρόνου)
there will be scoffers
(ἔσονται ἐμπαῖκται)

that scoffers will come
(ἐλεύσονται ἐμπαῖκται)
in the last days
(ἐπ' ἐσχάτων τῶν ἡμερῶν)
with scoffing (ἐν ἐμπαιγμονῇ)

following their own ungodly
passions (κατὰ τὰς ἑαυτῶν ἐπιθυμίας
πορευόμενοι τῶν ἀσεβειῶν)

following their own passions
(κατὰ τὰς ἰδίας ἐπιθυμίας
αὐτῶν πορευόμενοι)

General Analysis

In general, it is unlikely that a document should be so constituted that its content can be used in sequence and still meet the requirements of rhetorical invention and arrangement needed to effectively counter the exigence facing another rhetor. The rhetor must invent arguments specific to the exigence, support these arguments with materials considered persuasive by a specific rhetorical audience, and arrange them in the most persuasive sequence. It is particularly unlikely that a document can be used with the basic argumentation intact and still be very persuasive to another audience facing a different or even a similar exigence.

The sequence of correspondences between Jude and 2 Peter is as follows: Jude v 4 = 2 Pet 2:1-3; v 6 = 2:4; v 7 = 2:6; v 8 = 2:10a; v 9 = 2:11; v 10 = 2:12; v 12 = 2:13; v 11 = 2:15; v 12 = 2:17; v 16 = 2:18; v 17 = 3:1-2; v 18 = 3:3. Clearly, with the exception of v 11 = 2:15, the correspondence is sequential and, from initial considerations, unlikely, regardless of the direction of the dependence. The discussion must turn to more specific considerations.

The material shared by Jude and 2 Peter is found in the *narratio* (v 4), *probatio* (vv 5–14, 16), and *peroratio* (vv 17–18) of Jude, and the *probatio* (2:1–10a; 3:1–3), and *digressio* (2:10b–18) of 2 Peter. Since the *narratio* and *peroratio* are by nature highly individual and situation specific, it is improbable that a rhetor would borrow material to compose them. The content of the *narratio* is supplied by the facts of the case, and contains the propositions needing proof to support the case. The content of the *peroratio* is conditioned by the same propositions in recapitulation, and by an appeal to the emotions deemed useful in eliciting the desired response from the audience. Jude's *narratio* (v 4) and part of the *peroratio* (vv 17–18) have counterparts in 2 Pet 2:1–3 and 3:1–3 respectively. Jude's borrowing from 2 Peter is unlikely on the grounds of invention, and the nature of the *narratio* and *peroratio*.

The *probatio* develops the propositions of the *narratio* through the construction of proofs. Material for proof is drawn from authoritative sources and molded in a variety of ways suited to the exigence and audience. Borrowing from another written source to construct proof would not be the least bit surprising, but borrowing almost solely from one source and borrowing in sequential order to construct proof is surprising. The fact that Jude's *probatio* (vv 5–16) finds virtually all of its content in 2 Pet 2:4–18, and in sequence, makes it unlikely that Jude is the dependent source.

Now, the possibility that Jude borrowed from 2 Peter cannot be entirely ruled out by rhetorical criticism. However, as rhetoric was understood in the Greco-Roman world, such extensive borrowing as Jude would have done, according to this scheme, is virtually inconceivable and contrary to all rhetorical convention. The specificity and detail of rhetorical handbooks concerning the composition, arrangement, and embellishment of a rhetorical piece indicate how completely contrary borrowing from one source is to the classical conception of rhetoric. If all Jude had to do was to add epistolary pre- and post-scripts, a one line *exordium,* and a portion of the *peroratio* to borrowed material, and modify what was borrowed, it is inconceivable, by ancient standards, that he would have achieved his purpose in countering the exigence. Such extensive borrowing by Jude becomes slightly conceivable in the unlikely case that the rhetorical situation addressed by Jude, and the aspect of the rhetorical situation addressed by the corresponding portions of 2 Peter, were virtually identical in kind. However, the remainder of 2 Peter demonstrates this is not the case. To a significant degree, then, the old argument that extensive borrowing on Jude's part is not likely because it diminishes his role as author recieves support from rhetorical considerations.

The use of Jude by the author of 2 Peter is considerably more probable than the use of 2 Peter by the author of Jude. Whereas the shared material would practically constitute Jude, it is found only as part of the *probatio* (2:1–10a; 3:1–3) and *digressio* (2:10b–18) of 2 Peter. In the *probatio,* the material functions as parts of a counteraccusation (2:1–3a), a proof (2:3b–10a; 3:3), and a transition (3:1–2). Borrowing from Jude on the part of 2 Peter is conceivable in ancient terms. The utilization of traditional and authoritative material in the *probatio,* such as historical examples, prophecy, and testimony, was expected and encouraged. Jude's use of standard Jewish and Christian tradition and apologetic makes it useful for 2 Peter's *probatio.* Elsewhere in 2 Peter, 1:12-21, 2:18-22, and 3:15-16 all show a conscious concern for authoritative oral and written tradition. It is even more easily explained why the author may have borrowed from Jude if Jude is considered to be the brother of James and Jesus.

Concerning the *digressio,* it is conceivable that the tightly woven argumentation of a *probatio* is the source of material for a loosely woven *digressio,* even when the material is used sequentially. The reverse is not readily conceivable. Jude's *probatio* in vv 8-16 corresponds to 2 Peter's *digressio* in 2:10b-18. It is easier to identify the source of the *digressio* of 2 Peter as Jude 8-16 than vice-versa. Virtually any material can be used to formulate a *digressio.* Jude's use of metaphor, historical example, and apostolic proclamation, which all dwell on sin and judgment, readily suit an extended denunciation.

For 2 Peter to have borrowed from Jude would have been standard practice of one aiming to persuade an audience. Since Jude is deliberative rhetoric, which by nature is intended to persuade and dissuade an audience with regards to persons or courses of action, and since Jude contains subunits of epideictic rhetoric, which by nature is intended to raise or lower the ethos of opponents in the eyes of the audience, all sections of Jude are well-suited to the needs of 2 Peter's *probatio* and *digressio.* 2 Peter would not be expected to use this material from these sources for his own *exordium, narratio,* or *peroratio* because these are situation specific, and, in fact, no borrowing is found in these sections.

The above argument could be challenged by observing that as with Jude, borrowing by 2 Peter is also sequential and therefore unlikely. However, this critique is less damaging in the case of 2 Peter than in the case of Jude. The borrowed material is spread throughout more of the content of 2 Peter and consists mainly of examples and designations of the opponents, whereas, in Jude it is concentrated and constitutes a major portion of the rhetoric. It is still the case that borrowing of sequential material is unlikely, if rhetorical conventions are carefully observed.

The theory that reliance on a common source explains the literary relationship between Jude and 2 Peter runs into several obstacles, from a rhetorical perspective. First, this borrowed material underlies the *narratio* (v 4) and *peroratio* (vv 17-18) of Jude. Again, these parts of arrangement are specific to the exigence, and therefore, it is improbable that their content is borrowed by Jude. Secondly, this supposed source practically constitutes Jude, as the use of the material in 2 Peter makes clear. Only the epistolary prescript (vv 1-2), the *exordium* (v 3), and part of the *peroratio* (vv 19-25) would derive from Jude. It is unlikely that a source would be so extensively used by Jude. The rhetorical situation of the source, and that of Jude, would have to be identical so that the argumentation would be persuasive to the audience of both works. Even if this remote possibility existed, it is unlikely that no more argumentation would be added by Jude. This presupposes that Jude forsook all personal effort at invention. What is even more improbable is that the content of a common source met the rhetorical needs of both Jude and 2 Peter, particularly in the order in which it was found.

Specific Analysis

Before turning to examine each correspondance between Jude and 2 Peter individually, major assumptions used in the analysis will be outlined here. First, stylistic considerations are a very limited tool in the question of literary dependency. Presence or absence of a device does not indicate either its purposeful addition or omission in editing. Considerations of style perform a supporting role when other factors of invention and arrangement provide insight into probability. For example, if on the grounds of invention a section can reasonably be assumed to be secondary to the corresponding section in another work, the presence of more rhetorically useful style is evidence of secondary enhancement. On the other hand, style inferior to that of the primary source would lessen the probability of the inventional argument.

Second, if topics introduced in the *exordium* and *narratio* are developed in the *probatio*, and reiterated in the *peroratio*, the chances are that, when they are found in parallel sections of Jude and 2 Peter, the book in which topics are central from the beginning is prior. This is especially indicated if the topics appear for the first time in the other work in the parallel section, possibly never to appear again.

Third, propositions of the work stated in the *narratio* and/or *propositio*, and reiterated in the *peroratio*, indicate the recurrences of these propositions are central to the rhetor's message from the start. If these propositions are found in parallel sections of Jude and 2 Peter, then the book in which the proposition occurs in the above mentioned contexts is likely to be primary.

Fourth, noting what is absent in each work also gives clues to priority. If absent material would clearly assist the rhetoric of a work, and do so consistently, then this work may very well be prior to the other work, the author being unaware of the material.

Fifth, if parallel material of one source can be shown to be part of an allusion or quotation of a third source, its priority is indicated at that juncture.

Jude 4–5 and 2 Pet 2:1–3

Jude 4 is the *narratio* of Jude and functions as the *propositio*. It clearly states that propositions to be proven in the *probatio*: that the sectarians in the church are ungodly, licentious, and rebellious, and are those whose appearance was foretold. Jude 5 begins the *probatio* and the artificial proof of historical example in vv 5–10, and is the first example of that proof. 2 Pet 2:1–3a is a counteraccusation. The accusations of the false teachers implicit in 1:16–21 (cf. 3:3–4, 9), that the apostolic message of the parousia is based on deceptions and false prophecy, is turned against them. 2 Pet 2:3b is a proposition countering the false teachers' claim that the judgment, which is expected to accompany the parousia, will not materialize. The priority of Jude is strongly indicated in this section.

As argued in the preceding section, it is unlikely, by the very nature of the *narratio* as specific to the rhetorical situation, that Jude would use any source to construct it. If he did, a *narratio* of another work is the most likely source. Jude's reliance on 2 Peter is especially unlikely here, where he would be borrowing scattered and unrelated words from a counteraccusation and a counterproposition which are specific to the exigence of 2 Peter.

As explained in chapter 3, 2 Pet 2:1-3 is the second part of a chiasm encompassing 1:16-2:3, a chiasm which is bounded by *inclusio* in 1:16 and 2:3. If 2 Peter borrowed from Jude, Jude 4-5 would have greatly influenced the content of 1:16-21. However, since 1:16-21 constitutes two charges of the false teachers (1:16a, 1:20b-21a) and their refutations (1:16b-18, 19, 20-21), it is unlikely that anything but the exigence of 2 Peter influenced their content. It is more probable that Jude was initially used by 2 Peter at 2:1 when he turned from proof-refutation to counteraccusation where the exigence is less of a determining factor.

In a related observation, two topics given previously in the *exordium* of 2 Peter occur in 1:16-21, and elsewhere in the rhetoric: knowledge (1:2, 3, 5, 6, 8, 20; 2:20, 21; 3:8, 18) and power (1:3, 16). Arrangement and invention indicate that these topics are central to 2 Peter's attempt to counter his exigence. In contrast, no topics introduced in the *exordium* appear in 2:1-3. Thus, it is likely that the content of 1:16-21 was largely determined by the exigence, and the content of 2:1-3, although designed to counter the exigence, is, in part, borrowed due to the greater freedom of counteraccusation.

In Jude 5, the fate of the disobedient people (λαός) in the wilderness is described as destruction (ἀπόλλυμι). 2 Pet 2:1 describes the false teachers as coming in among the people (λαός), their teachings as destructive (ἀπώλεια), and their fate as destruction (ἀπώλεια). In 2 Pet 2:3 destruction (ἀπώλεια) and judgment (κρίμα) are used in isocolon, destruction providing the content of judgment. 2 Peter's borrowing here would explain why this example of Jude 5 is not used to construct the proof of 2:4-10a, whereas the following examples in Jude 6-8 do appear.[64]

From another perspective, it seems unlikely that this limited verbal correspondence of "people" and "destruction" between Jude 5 and 2 Pet 2:1-3 suggested to Jude the example of the wilderness generation for use in proof. Rhetorically, this example of the wilderness generation is better explained as an independent use of an historical example in deliberative rhetoric, here an example used in a common Jewish-Christian parenetic schema in evidence in vv 5-7.[65]

[64] Suggested by Fornberg, 38.
[65] For more on this schema, see ch. 2, p. 51.

In contrast, borrowing by 2 Peter of what are cleverly two central, general terms from Jude to construct a counteraccusation and a counter-proposition within the *probatio* is more probable. Since in the *narratio* of v 4 Jude sets forth in negative terms the exigence he faces, and in v 5 he deliberates with a negative example, "destruction" is easily molded into counteraccusation and a counter-proposition which both require negative terminology.

Both Jude 4 and 2 Pet 2:1 contain the charge "denying the Master" (ἀρνούμενοι . . . δεσπότην). Whereas denying the Master in 2 Peter is a dogmatic denial of Christ's parousia,[66] in Jude it is a corollary of immorality. Thus in both Jude and 2 Peter the exigence determines the usage. In Jude, δεσπότης is an epithet, and in 2 Peter it is an example of antonomasia.[67] Either stylistic quality may have prompted its reuse by the other author. However, in 2 Peter, with the addition of the phrase τὸν ἀγοράσαντα αὐτούς "the one having bought them," δεσπότης is also used in a metaphor of a slavemaster purchasing slaves. This strong metaphor of purchase would suit the rhetorical needs of Jude since the sectarians' licentiousness is a denial of their Master who bought them. The absence of this effective metaphor in Jude weighs in favor of 2 Pet 2:1 as an enhanced version of Jude 4.

2 Pet 2:2b is suspected to be an allusion to Isa 52:5. Interestingly, no correspondence with Jude is found in this section and such correspondence is found in every part of 2:1-3. There is evidence here of Jude's priority, 2 Peter combining an allusion to Isaiah within his reworking of Jude.

Whereas the above evidence strongly indicates the priority of Jude, other verbal correspondences and redactional-rhetorical considerations in this section do not support the priority of either Jude or 2 Peter. For example, Jude 4 refers to the sectarians as long ago (οἱ πάλαι) the subject of prophecy concerning the judgment (κρίμα) he is about to expound in what follows.[68] 2 Pet 2:3 denies a claim of the false teachers that judgment for a long time (τὸ κρίμα ἔκπαλαι) has been idle and asleep. 2 Peter's proof of 2:3b, which follows in 2:4-10a, emphasizes the work of judgment in the past in order to counter the false teachers' claim that judgment has been inactive and will remain so. In both Jude and 2 Peter the vocabulary fits the exigence and nothing can be said regarding priority.

In Jude 4 and 2 Pet 2:3, the noun ἀσέλγεια, "licentiousness," is found. In Jude it is in the first accusation, namely that the sectarians turn God's grace into licentiousness, and it is moral connotations. In 2 Peter, ἀσέλγεια is in a prediction that believers will follow the licentiousness of the false teachers and revile the way of truth, and it has doctrinal as well as moral connotations. Whereas the exigence Jude faces is libertinism based upon a false interpretation of the

---

[66] Fornberg, 36–38; Neyrey, *Form and Background*, 129 n. 17.

[67] See the glossary for definitions of these terms.

[68] For a discussion of the controversy concerning κρίμα, see ch. 2, p. 33, n. 17.

implications of grace, that of 2 Peter is libertinism founded upon eschatological skepticism. Nothing can be said here regarding priority since both uses of ἀσέλγεια can be explained by the exigence involved.

In Jude 4 the verb παρεισεδύ(ν)ω, "slip in stealthily, sneak in,"[69] is found, and in 2 Pet 2:1 the verb παρεισάγω, " 'bring in' with the connotations of secrecy or maliciousness"[70] appears. In Jude παρεισέδυσαν describes the sectarians entering the church from outside, whereas in 2 Peter παρεισάξουσιν describes false teachers from within the chruch bringing in their teachings from outside. Jude's verb does not apply to the heavily doctrinal aspect of 2 Peter's exigence, and 2 Peter may be thought to substitute παρεισάγω, which is applicable to doctrine yet maintains the desirable negative connotations of παρεισεδύ(ν)ω.[71] 2 Peter's verb does not adequately describe the exigence of itinerant teachers and/or prophets faced by Jude's church, and Jude may have modified 2 Peter's verb to παρεισεδύ(ν)ω, which is applicable to his exigence and also maintains the negative connotations of παρεισάγω. Nothing can be said about priority at this juncture.

Jude 6-10 and 2 Pet 2:4, 6, 10-12

Jude 6-10 is part of an artificial proof from like historical examples which is composed of vv 5-10. Verses 6-7 belong to the series of three examples in vv 5-7, and v 8 is the explicit application of the examples to the sectarians. Verses 9-10 are an amplification of v 8, advancing a parallel for exaggeration. 2 Pet 2:4, 6, 10a are also components of an artificial proof from historical examples; a proof encompassing 2:4-10a. Verses 2:4 and 2:6 are part of a list of three examples in 2:4-8, and 2:10a is the amplification in the application to the false teachers in 2:9. The denunciatory *digressio* is the context of 2:10b-12.

It is more probable on the grounds of invention and arrangement that 2 Peter here relies on Jude than vice-versa. On the one hand, Jude's dependency would have to consist of borrowing from historical examples (2:4, 6), as well as from the amplification of their application (2:10a), in order to compose only examples. Also, in Jude the application of the examples (v 8) and their amplification (vv 9-10) would derive from denunciatory material in a *digressio* (2:10b-12). Suitable wording for the application and amplification of the examples would more likely be determined by the exigence than by 2 Peter's *digressio*.

On the other hand, 2 Peter's borrowing would consist of using two historical examples (vv 6-8) and their application (v 8), in order to compose a similar proof from historical example (2:4, 6), and to develop the amplification of it application (2:10a). Also, the negative application of Jude 8, which incorporates amplification by accumulation, and the negative amplification of the application in vv 9-10, would be borrowed to construct a denunciatory *digressio* relying

[69] *BAGD* 624.
[70] Ibid.
[71] Fornberg, 36; Neyrey, *Form and Background,* 128.

heavily on amplification. In essence, 2 Peter would properly use authoritative examples to construct a proof from historical example, and conveniently use negative, amplifying words to construct denunciation.

Jude 6–10 is part of the artificial proof composed of Jude 5–10, a proof which attempts to demonstrate that the sectarians within the church are sinners and will be condemned. This purpose is clearly anticipated in the statement of the case in the *narratio* of v 4 and, like the *narratio,* can reasonably be thought to derive from the exigence. The first proof, and its examples in vv 5–10, was thus more likely composed to meet the exigence than it was borrowed from another source. 2 Pet 2:4, 6, 10–12 are parts of the proof of 2 Pet 2:3b–10a, namely, that the judgment of the parousia is real, and are parts of the *digressio* of 2:10b–22. Neither is clearly indicated in the *exordium* of 1:3–15. 2 Peter's proof and *digressio,* since they are not indicated previously in the rhetoric, can more easily be accounted for as borrowings at a later time in the writing.

Arguing from topics, the topic of "keeping" is found in Jude 1, 6, 13, 21 (τηρέω) and v 24 (φυλάσσω). It is also found in 2 Pet 2:4, 9, 17 and 3:7 (τηρέω). Jude's priority is here indicated because the topic is touched on in the quasi-*exordium* (v 1), twice used in the *probatio* (vv 6, 13), and recapitulated in the *peroratio* (v 21, 24), that is, it seems to have been Jude's interest to develop this topic from the start. In 2 Peter this topic appears only in the *probatio* in 2:4 after its first parallel with Jude. Also, the topic of "judgment" is found in the *narratio* (κρίμα, v 4), *probatio* (κρίσις, vv 6, 15) of Jude, and in the *probatio* (κρίσις, 2:9) of 2 Peter. Again, Jude's priority is indicated by the use of the topic in the *narratio* and its development in the *probatio.*

For a closer look, Jude 8 and 2 Pet 2:10 share numerous verbal parallels. Jude 8 is the specific application to the sectarians of the three examples of vv 5–7, examples which are part of a traditional schema.[72] 2 Pet 2:10a forms the amplification of the conclusion of the proof of 2:4–9 in 2:9, and 2 Pet 2:10b forms the beginning of the *digressio.* From the standpoint of invention and arrangement, it would be amazing if material from 2 Peter's *probatio* (2:10a) and *digressio* (2:10b) can be used in the order in which it is found and supply a comparison of these three traditional examples to the sectarians. It is even more amazing when it is noted that the three-pronged comparison begins with a point corresponding to all three examples, continues with one corresponding to examples 2 and 3, and finishes with one common to example 3 only. In other words, the borrowed elements from 2 Peter can be used in order and even allow for a climax in Jude's comparison; the example with the worst judgment being applied last.

Jude twice bases his material on other literature. Verse 6 is dependent on *1 Enoch* 6–19,[73] and v 9 relies upon the storyline of *T. Mos.* No connection with such works is found in the parallels in 2 Pet 2:4 and 2:11 respectively. However,

---

[72] See ch. 2, p. 51.
[73] See ch. 2, p. 52.

it cannot be argued either that Jude added these allusions to material from 2 Peter or that 2 Peter excised these from Jude in the light of a developing canon.[74] The degree of authority given these works by the respective rhetors and their audiences is an unknown determining factor here.

As previously noted, both Jude 5-7 and 2 Pet 2:4-8 rely on a traditional parenetic schema that is also found in Sir 16:7-10, CD 2:17-3:12, 3 Macc 2:4-7, *T. Napht.* 3:4-5, and *m. Sanh.* 10:3.[75] 2 Peter has several features of the schema that are not found in Jude. These are: 1) the phrase οὐκ ἐφείσατο used in epiphora in 2:4, 5, is also found in Sir 16:18; 2) the historical examples are in chronological order; 3) 2 Pet 2:9-10a explicitly draws the lesson that the examples illustrate (Sir 16:6, 11-14; CD 2:16-17; 3 Macc 2:3-4a); 4) the example of the Flood (CD 2:20-21; *m. Sanh.* 10.3); 5) contrasting examples of the righteous who were saved when the wicked were punished, these being Noah and Lot (CD 3:2-4—Abraham, Isaac, Jacob; 3 Macc 2:7—Israel at the Exodus).[76] It cannot be argued either that such additional knowledge of the schema indicates 2 Peter elaborated Jude's version of it,[77] or that Jude redacted 2 Peter and, being less familiar with the schema or finding it less useful, made modifications. The use of these examples of Jude and 2 Peter is explained by their exigencies.

It is conceivable that Jude substituted the example of the wilderness generation for that of the Flood. Possibly, he rejected the example of the Noachian generation because it provided no specifics with which to compare the sectarians, whereas the example of the wilderness generation did. As the topic of "the lack of faith," found in the *exordium* (v 3) and here in the wilderness example in the *probatio* indicates, Jude is intent on this specific characteristic of the sectarians, a characteristic not prominent in the example of the Flood.

The example of the disbelieving Israelites in the wilderness is out of chronological order in Jude. As argued in the analysis,[78] this change may be for the sake of grouping the two examples of immorality together, or to create a climax based on an intensification of punishment, that is, amplification by augmentation. It cannot be assumed to be a rhetorical blunder excised by 2 Peter.[79] However, the bulk of evidence does point to 2 Peter's use of Jude.

First, the absence in 2 Peter of the example of the wilderness generation at this juncture is not surprising for two reasons. First, this example of disobedience and slow forty-year judgment does not serve his rhetorical needs. Although the relationship of disobedience judgment is central to his proof, the slow judgment of the wilderness generation over forty years is not analogous to the dramatic and sudden judgment of the false teachers at the parousia. In this

---

[74] So Bigg, 222. For an assertion to the opposite, see Mayor, ix, xxv.
[75] For more on this schema, see ch. 2, p. 51, n. 167.
[76] Bauckham, 246-47.
[77] Against Bauckham, 246.
[78] See ch. 2, p. 51; ch. 3, p. 112.
[79] Suggested by Mayor, vi; Fornberg, 46.

regard, the example of Noah and the Flood in 2 Pet 2:5, which currently corresponds here to the example of the wilderness generation, better serves the rhetorical needs of 2 Peter and may have been substituted by him.

Second, 2 Peter's exigence includes the oppression of his audience by the false teachers (2:3a), and he desires to assure them of eventual reward (2:9). Although in the example of the Israelites in the wilderness, the righteous Joshua and Caleb are not judged with the others and do enter Canaan, they do not illustrate those living among decadent sinners like the audience among the false teachers. Historical examples are useful in argumentation, particularly because their details can be related as the case demands,[80] and they are especially useful to deliberative rhetoric, as found here, because as what happened in the past, they relate what is likely to happen in the future.[81] They should be nearly equal to what they are compared.[82] 2 Peter may have substituted the example of the Flood for that of the wilderness generation because it is more conducive to these rhetorical requirements.

That the Flood example is more conducive to 2 Peter's rhetorical needs is further indicated by the fact that the example of the Flood is used in 2 Pet 2:5 as a type of the eschatological judgment. The destroyed world is given the cosmological reference "ancient world" (ἀρχαίου κόσμου) upon which God brought (ἐπάξας) a Flood. There is the implicit comparison with the judgment of the present world in 2:1 where the false teachers are described as bringing (ἐπάγοντες) swift destruction upon themselves, that is, the imminent destruction of eschatological judgment.

Also, in 2:5-8, the dual judgments of water and fire are given in the judgment of the world by the water of the Flood, and the judgment of Sodom and Gomorrah by fire, a traditional pairing. This pattern of destruction is reiterated in the proof of 2 Pet 3:5-7 in another eschatological context. In 3:6, the reference to the example of the Flood is found in the words, "the world that then existed (ὁ τότε κόσμος) was deluged with water and perished." In 3:7, this is coupled with the judgment of earth and heaven by fire. Thus the selection of the example of the Flood is likely prompted not only by traditional pairing, but also by the needs of the exigence to refute eschatological skepticism here and elsewhere in the rhetoric.[83]

2 Pet 2:1-3 speaks of the false teachers' exploitation of the audience, and exploitation motivated by greed. His example of judgment of the wicked in 2:4-8 include two references to the salvation of the righteous: Noah and Lot. As stated earlier, the suitability of such a contrast may have prompted the selection of the example of the Flood over that of the wilderness generation. These examples serve to meet the audience's concern that their trials among the ungodly were

---

[80] Quint. 5.11.15-16.

[81] Quint. 5.11.8; cf. Ar. *Rhet.* 2.20.1394a.8.

[82] Quint. 5.11.8-9.

[83] Bigg, 222; Mayor, vii; Fornberg, 41-42; Neyrey, *Form and Background,* 134.

shared by Noah and Lot. It shows that like Noah and Lot, they too will be spared for their endurance in righteousness.[84] In the recapitulation of 2 Pet 2:9, reference is made to the rescue of the godly in conjunction with 2 Peter's attempt to meet the concerns of his audience.

These contrasting examples do not serve Jude's exigence or proof, and it could be argued that he left them out when borrowing from 2 Peter. The exhortation of vv 20-23 and the doxology in vv 24-25 assume that the audience is not itself under trial, but need merely to buttress a faith in jeopardy by influence only. Also, Jude's proof seeks only to show that the wicked are punished, and not also that the righteous are saved. The proposition of the *narratio* and the remainder of the proof make this clear.

Shifting focus, verbal correspondence between Jude 6-10 and 2 Pet 2:4, 6, 10-12 is limited. Many verbal links are capable of supporting arguments for the priority of either book and thus offer no insight into priority. We will examine the few which offer more direct possibilities from rhetorical-redactional analysis.

Whereas Jude 7 considers the fate of Sodom and Gomorrah a δεῖγμα, "example,"[85] 2 Pet 2:6 labels it a ὑπόδειγμα, "example, model, pattern."[86] The latter is a stronger term, akin to a warning example. In these proofs from example, it is easier to see why 2 Peter would intensify δεῖγμα than Jude would weaken ὑπόδειγμα. Jude is concerned that some in the audience are following or will follow the sectarians (vv 3, 22-24), and the labeling of the example as a warning example would be appropriate to his exigence.

In 2 Pet 2:11 the false teachers are described by the synonymous word pair, ἰσχύς καὶ δυνάμις, in a comparison functioning as amplification by reasoning.[87] This very effectively emphasizes the folly of the false teachers' audacity in reviling evil angels when good angels, who are clearly in a superior position, do not do so. Jude 9 makes the point that the sectarians are audacious for reviling the angels of the law and the law itself, when Michael the archangel would not rebuke Satan in a matter of law (Satan accused Moses of murder), but deferred it to God's authority. It is more difficult to conceive of Jude's eliminating the "greater in might and power" comparison in 2 Peter when it would amplify his proof so well, than to conceive of its addition by 2 Peter to heighten the effect of the contrast.

2 Pet 2:12 is an effective piece of rhetoric, interweaving several important figures. Particularly noteworthy is the transplacement-paronomasia in φθοράν . . . φθορᾷ . . . φθαρήσονται, the *regressio* (like irrational animals, creatures of instinct), and the similitude with which it is synonymous. The similitude has a twofold point of comparison in 2 Peter: that the false teachers are totally irrational like animals, and that they will be destroyed like animals. In Jude 10,

---

[84] Fornberg, 48; Neyrey, *Form and Background*, 133.

[85] *BAGD* 172.

[86] *BAGD 844.*

[87] See ch. 3, p. 115.

only the similitude is found, emphasizing that the sectarians act on instinct like irrational animals, but they are not denied all understanding as in 2 Peter. The transplacement-paronomasia, the refining, and the expanded version of the comparison would be useful for Jude in amplifying his comparison, but are absent. It is difficult to believe that Jude used 2 Pet 2:12 and in the process composed a rhetorically inferior line which less effectively serves his desire for amplification of the fate and destruction of the sectarians than the borrowed material. It is easier to conceive that 2 Peter reworked the amplification of Jude 10, making it rhetorically more effective in amplifying the false teachers' character and fate, and thereby increased the denunciatory effect of his *digressio*.

Jude 11–13, 16 and 2 Pet 2:13, 15, 17–18

Jude 11–13 constitutes an artificial proof from example of the type called a judgment, and the type of judgment called a supernatural oracle. The proof demonstates that the sectarians in the audience are ungodly and subject to judgment. Verse 11 is the prophecy and vv 12–13 are its application and amplification through accumulation. Verse 16 is part of vv 14–16, an artificial proof of example of the same variety as vv 11–13. Verse 16 is the application to the sectarians of the prophecy of *1 Enoch* 1:9 used in vv 14–15. 2 Pet 2:13, 15, and 17–18, are parts of the *digressio* aimed at decreasing the ethos of the false teachers (2:10b–22). As the following argumentation shows, rhetorical-redactional considerations weigh more heavily in favor of the priority of Jude in the case of this correspondence.

First, it is improbable by the nature of prophecy and the *digressio*, that Jude would utilize the *digressio* of 2 Peter to construct two proofs from prophecy. This is surely true if the prophecy of Jude 11 derives from Jude himself. However, 2 Peter's borrowing of negative elements from Jude's proofs from prophecy to form a loosely constructed denunciatory *digressio* is probable.

Arguing from topics, this section develops two topics which are central to Jude's rhetoric: peace and love. In the quasi-*exordium* in v 2, he wishes peace be multiplied to the audience. This topic is developed here in the *probatio* in v 12, which speaks of disruptive activity during the love feast, and in v 16, where the sectarians are said to be grumblers and malcontents. In the *peroratio* in v 19, the topic is reiterated with reference to the sectarians being divisive. In the quasi-*exordium* in v 2 Jude wishes love (ἀγάπη) be multiplied to the audience, and in the *exordium* in v 3 he claims they are beloved of God (ἠγαπημένοις). This topic recurs in the *probatio* in v 12 in the reference to love feasts (ἀγάπαις), and is reiterated in the *peroratio* in v 21 in the exhortation to remain in God's love (ἀγάπη). These topics of peace and love are thus introduced in the quasi-*exordium* and *exordium*, developed in the *probatio*, and reiterated in the *peroratio*. This use and distribution of the topics indicates that they are central to Jude's exigence and his attempt to meet the rhetorical situation, not merely on-the-spot borrowings from 2 Peter.

As noted in the analysis above in chapter 2, Jude 11 is a prophetic oracle deriving either from Jude himself, or from the store of early Christian prophecy. Along with vv 12–13 it forms either an inartificial or an artificial proof, depending upon its origin.[88] Jude 11 finds a parallel in 2 Pet 2:15 (cf. 2:13a) which is both a denunciatory statement about the false teachers and part of its amplification in 2:15b–16.

Jude's reliance upon prophecy is in evidence elsewhere in vv 14b–15 and v 18. Such a reliance could indicate that Jude is dependent upon 2 Pet 2:15 to supply the prophecy of v 11. Within the testament of 2 Peter all of 1:16–3:13 functions as prophecy. However, that section contains less than one fourth of the wording of Jude 11, and its content is dissimilar, regardless of rewording. If Jude were quoting a prophecy to devise a proof, rhetorical considerations clearly indicate that it should be presented in standard form so that the audience would recognize it and give it proper ethos to lend support to the proof.

The more likely prospect is that 2 Peter has molded the woe formula of Jude 11 into the exclamation "accursed children" (2:14), utilized the prophecy's content to enhance topics found elsewhere in the rhetoric, and developed figures that would further decrease the ethos of the false teachers. One topic is the way (ὁδός), found in the counteraccusation in 2:2 and in the *probatio* in 2:21. As in 2:21, it is used here in a contrast of the two ways. A second topic is wandering or error (πλανάω, πλάνη). He uses ἐπλανήθησαν in a fine example of refining: "forsaking the right way they have gone astray." This amplifies by repetition the sin of the false teachers and helps work out the topic of the way. This topic of wandering or error recurs in the *probatio* in 2:18 and in the *peroratio* in 3:17. A third topic is following (ἐξαχολουθέω). 2 Peter accuses the false teachers of following (ἐξαχολουθέω) the way of Balaam, that is, error, as others follow (ἐξαχολουθέω) their error (πλάνη, 2:2; cf. 3:17). This use of the topic counters the false teachers' accusation in 1:16 that the apostles follow (ἐξαχολουθέω) error. The designation of Balaam as "son of βοσόρ" using an unattested form of Balaam's father's name, Beor, may be an ironical twist of the Hebrew word *bāśār*, "flesh." This irony, "son of the flesh" enhances the topic of immorality found elsewhere in 2 Peter (2:2, 10a, 14, 20–22). There is also the reiteration of the topic of greed from 2:3a, 14. Here, as in 2:13, there is reference to a reward of unrighteousness (μισθὸς ἀδικίας), which at this point ironically refers to monetary reward as well as eschatological judgment.

On the one hand, three of these topics in 2 Pet 2:15 are central to the rhetoric. The topic of the way (ὁδός) is introduced in the counteraccusation in 2:2, and is further developed in the *probatio* in 2:21 in a contrast of the two ways. The topic of greed is introduced in the counteraccusation in 2:3a and recurs in the *probatio* in 2:14. The topic of following (ἐξαχολουθέω) is found in the accusation of the false teachers in 1:16 and in the counteraccusation in 2:2. It might be

---

[88] For further discussion of these points, see ch. 2, pp. 57–58.

argued that such a distribution of topics is indicative of 2 Peter's priority. However, the nature of Jude 11 as a prophecy gives strong reason to say that 2 Peter created his counteraccusation of 2:1-3 in the light of Jude 11. Jude 11, being clearly a prophecy, provided 2 Peter with topics for his own prophecy of 2:1-3. He borrowed the topics of the way, greed, and following, planning to amplify them in the *digressio* in 2:15.

On the other hand, references to Cain and Korah in Jude 11, and the imagery associated with them, suit 2 Peter's exigence. Cain, being an example of those leading others to sin, would serve to amplify the reference to "enticing unsteady souls" in 2:14, 18 (cf. 2:2). Korah, being rebellious and a scoffer who was judged, would serve to amplify this topic from the rhetoric as a whole, particularly from 2:1, 10-12. If 2 Peter is dependent on Jude, then the exclusion of these references is difficult to explain. In this regard, the priority of 2 Peter is indicated.

Turning now to the correspondence Jude 12-13 — 2 Pet 2:13, 17, by its nature as the application of prophecy within an artificial proof, we can expect Jude 12-13 to correlate the preceding sins outlined in the prophecy to a description of the sins of the sectarians, a correlation which Jude would compose to be easily verified by his audience. With the contingencies of the propehcy (v 11) and the rhetorical situation, it is unlikely that Jude would resort to borrowing material. If he did, that material would need to be specific to his prophecy and his rhetorical situation. It would be remarkable if Jude used 2 Pet 2:13 to provide the specific wording needed for the application of the prophecy. This seems even more remarkable when it is noted that 2 Pet 2:13 does not directly relate to 2:15 which corresponds to the prophecy of Jude 11. If 2 Pet 2:13 were the application of 2 Pet 2:15 as Jude 12-13 is of Jude 11, then borrowing might be expected to some degree.

At this juncture, 2 Peter has fewer contingencies imposed by argument from logos than does Jude 12-13. 2 Pet 2:13 argues purely from ethos and pathos. Here, 2 Peter needs only to be sure that his designation of the false teachers is accurate so that his audience can clearly perceive his referent. 2 Pet 2:17-18 is part of the enthymeme constituted by 2:17-19, 2:17 being the conclusion and 2:18 being the first part of the premise of 2:18-19. Since 2:17 is the conclusion of a loosely reasoned enthymeme, there are fewer constraints upon it than there are for Jude 12-13 which must apply the prophecy of Jude 11 within an argument from example. In both the cases of 2:13 and 2:17-18, 2 Peter can freely borrow from Jude those elements which are useful to his exigence, and thus his dependence here is more likely.

On a more specific level, the most notable difference between Jude 12 and 2 Pet 2:13 is two verbal similarities. Whereas Jude has ἀγάπαις . . . σπιλάδες, "love feasts . . . dangerous reefs," 2 Peter has σπίλοι καὶ μῶμοι . . . ἀπάταις, "spots and blemishes . . . dissipation." In Jude, the sectarians are thus identified by metaphor as dangerous reefs in an agape meal, implying that close association may lead to shipwrecked faith. The verb σπιλόω occurs in the *peroratio* of

Jude (v 23) in an exhortation to avoid any association with immorality. In 2 Peter's account, σπίλοι and ἀπάταις are intimately connected and both words serve to decrease the ethos of the false teachers, the former aiming at their person and the latter at their actions. As stated in chapter 3, possibly ἀπάταις is part of a pun. The attached phrase συνευωχούμενοι ὑμῖν, "while they feast with you," would suggest the agape context, the irony being that what should be an ἀγάπη is more appropriatedly called an ἀπάτη. The nearly synonymous word pair σπίλοι καὶ μῶμοι is found in the negative in the *peroratio* in an exhortation to be found ἄσπιλοι καὶ ἀμώμητοι (3:14). It is often suggested that Jude's reading of σπιλάδες was changed by 2 Peter because it was obscure,[89] and ἀγάπαις was changed to ἀπάταις to create a pun. However, in both Jude and 2 Peter these readings are rhetorically effective, both here and later on in the works, and the priority of one book or the other cannot be argued from either word.

From the standpoint of invention, Jude's priority in the specific correspondence of Jude 12–13 and 2 Pet 2:17 is quite probable. The four metaphors from nature in Jude 12–13 most likely derive from *1 Enoch* 2:1–5:4 and 80:2–8.[90] In fact, the use of *1 Enoch* by Jude is quite certain for almost all of vv 12–15. 2 Pet 2:17 has two metaphors exhibiting elements similar to those of Jude's first metaphor "waterless clouds, carried along by winds." These metaphors are "waterless springs" and "mist driven by a storm."

Jude uses *1 Enoch* to compose parts of two proofs, vv 11–13 and vv 14–16, that is, two-thirds of the proofs of his *probatio*. To presume that Jude relied on 2 Peter is to presume that two-thirds of the proofs of Jude's *probatio* were suggested by two metaphors in 2 Pet 2:17. It is more likely that the urgent exigence (v 3) and the propositions of the *narratio* (v 4) influenced the selection of proofs.

From another perspective, the style of 2 Peter is heavily dependent upon metaphors.[91] These are concentrated mainly in the context of 2:17 where five are found (2:14, 15). Use of metaphor is to be expected in a *digressio* aimed at decreasing the ethos of opponents since metaphor plays a role in creating vivid mental pictures[92] and in magnifying and minifying.[93] In Jude, vv 12–13 constitute amplification by accumulation and would be helpful to 2 Peter's denunciation. Thus 2 Peter's use of all four metaphors from Jude would seem more likely than his selection of only one, and his dependence on Jude would seem less likely by their absence.

It could be argued to the contrary, that 2 Peter at this point follows the

---

[89] Cf. Mayor who suggests that the metaphor of reefs was too bold and was thus changed (xi).

[90] See ch. 2, p. 62.

[91] 1:8, 10, 13, 14(2), 15; 2:1, 2, 4, 13, 14(2), 15(3), 17(2), 21; 3:4, 14, 17.

[92] Cic. *De Or.* 3.40.160–61; Her. 4.34.45.

[93] Long. *Subl.* 32.5; Her. 4.34.45.

conventions of not crowding metaphors[94] in order not to obscure language,[95] of avoiding a series of metaphors of the same species,[96] and of avoiding using more than three metaphors in a row.[97] However, in 1:14, 15 and 2:14, 15, and in his overall pendantic style, he already demonstrates his lack of regard for stylistic conventions of moderation. A more likely explanation is that 2 Peter, desiring to create the enthymeme of 2:17-19, could not effectively utilize a series of metaphors. The metaphor that was borrowed was probably used because it could so easily be modified to suit the exigence. The metaphor of waterless springs emphasizes "boasts of folly" and "empty promises" (2:18, 19), and "mists driven by a storm," emphasizes the false teachers' lack of freedom due to slavery to passion (2:14, 18-20).

Jude 13 contains the traditional image of the wandering stars confined in nether gloom. In 2 Pet 2:17 it is the false teachers as mists and springs that are so confined, an image unparalleled in tradition. The easiest explanation for this untraditional imagery is that 2 Peter excised Jude's reference to wandering stars, but retained his reference to judgment because it suited his needs so well in countering his exigence.[98]

Regarding the correspondence of Jude 16 and 2 Pet 2:18, Jude 16 is part of an artificial proof based on example, here a supernatural oracle; a proof comprising vv 14-16. Verses 14-15 are the oracle of *1 Enoch* 1:9, and v 16 is its application to the sectarians. 2 Pet 2:18 is part of the enthymeme constituting 2:17-19, 2:17 being the conclusion, and 2:18-19 being the premise.

In Jude's *narratio* (v 4) it is clearly Jude's intention to prove that the sectarians are the ungodly (ἀσεβεῖς) whose judgment had been foretold. This quotation of *1 Enoch* 1:9 in vv 14-15 contains this topic of ungodliness, words with the ἀσεβ- root occurring three times, and it is clearly a prophecy foretelling the judgment of the ungodly. Also, the metaphors of vv 12-13 are found immediately after 1:9 in *1 Enoch*. All these factors point to the quotation and its application in v 16 as original to Jude's purpose. Thus v 16 is not likely to be in any way an on-the-spot borrowing from 2 Peter.

There is a complete lack of familiarity with *1 Enoch* 1:9 in 2 Peter. This is usually explained by the theory that the author of 2 Peter was working with a developing sense of canon, that he lacked familiarity with *1 Enoch*, or that *1 Enoch* 1:9 was unusuable since the prophecy is in the past tense and is not suited to proof regarding the future parousia.[99] However, there are topics in the quotation that 2 Peter could have gleaned, as he seems to elsewhere, if he had relied upon Jude. The topic of ungodliness and speaking against divine authority

---

[94] Demetr. *Eloc.* 2.78.
[95] Quint. 8.6.14.
[96] Quint. 8.6.16.
[97] Long. *Subl.* 32.1.
[98] Fornberg, 56.
[99] Fornberg, 47, 56.

are both central to 2 Peter, occurring prior to this point in 2:1-3, 9-16 and 2:1, 10-12 respectively. The lack of typical borrowing points in the direction of Petrine priority, Jude having inserted the prophecy in his work at this juncture.

In this case of correspondence, Jude 16 and 2 Pet 2:18, only two words are held in common: ὑπέρογκα and ἐπιθυμία. As would be expected in an application within an artificial proof of example, Jude 16 has verbal ties with the example itself so as to facilitate the application. 4QEnoch 1:1:17, the Aramaic fragment of *1 Enoch* 1:9, affirms that the ungodly uttered "great and hard things" *(rb)rbn wqs'n*. *1 Enoch* 5:4 reiterartes the theme of 1:9 after the four metaphors of nature found in 2:1-5:3 (as well as Jude 12-13), in the words μεγάλους καὶ σκληροὺς λόγους, "great and hard words." The reference to "great" is lacking in Jude's quotation. Jude seems to have held the word "great" until the application of the prophecy in v 16 and used the word ὑπέρογκα to express it. He has used the stronger word ὑπέρογκα ("huge") which in the context is more damaging to ethos. The sectarians direct enormously arrogant words towards God. Ὑπέρογκα is used with γογγυσταί ("murmurers") to emphasize the verbal sin. This skillful use of *1 Enoch* makes the priority of Jude virtually certain, explaining the origin of ὑπέρογκα. Jude's priority here is also indicated by the fact that v 16 further explicates the proposition of the *narratio* that the sectarians deny divine authority, as do vv 8, 10, 11, and are licentious, as do vv 7, 8, 18.

2 Peter has probably borrowed the words ὑπέρογκα and ἐπιθυμία because they develop topics previously used to epitomize the sinful word and deed which characterize the false teachers. In 2:10a, immediately prior to the *digressio*, we find ἐπιθυμία and κυριότητος καταφρονοῦντες, and in the counteraccusation of 2:1-3 we find ἀσέλγεια (2:2) and πλαστοῖ λόγοις (2:3) (cf. also the topic of immorality in 2:14).

2 Pet 2:19-22

2 Pet 2:19-22 finds no counterpart in Jude. This section is the end of the *digressio* and is composed of maxims and proverbial material. A then current proverb is contained in 2:19b, a saying of Jesus in 2:20b, the proverbial form of a *Tobspruch* in 2:21, and two proverbs combined in 2:22, one from Prov 26:11 and one from *Ahikar* 8:15/18.[100] Neither the priority of Jude nor of 2 Peter can be asserted on the basis of this section, for the evidence can be used to argue for both positions.

As previously mentioned in chapter 3,[101] maxims are very useful in proof because they are considered indisputable principles drawn from practical life. Arguing for Petrine priority, Jude's lack of use of these maxims has two explanations. First Jude's purpose as outlined in the *narratio* (v 4) is to prove that those who have infiltrated the church were previously designated, and that they are ungodly and deny authority. This proverbial material does not suit his exigence since it specifically relates to the consequences of backsliding. Second, from the

---

[100] 8:15, Arabic version; 8:18, Syriac version.
[101] See ch. 3, pp. 122-23.

standpoint of invention, the use of maxims is incongruent with Jude's method of argumentation. He presents his arguments in the pesher fashion: examples or a prophecy are given (vv 5-7, 11, 14-15, 17-18), and then a specific identification is made (vv 8-10, 12-13, 16, 19). He is more interested in demonstrating who his opponents are and what their fate will be than in arguing theologically as does 2 Peter. As such, these or any other maxims do not suit Jude's inventional needs.

In 2 Peter, 2:19 is part of the premise of the enthymeme of 2:17-19, and 2:20-22 is amplification of the enthymeme. Rhetorically, the proverbial material effectively amplifies the enthymeme as well as reiterates many topics from throughout the work![102] Arguing for Jude's priority, it may be stated that this material was inserted in borrowed material by 2 Peter to end his enthymeme, and the entire *digressio,* with a plethora of maxims to further develop topics and to bolster the authority of his denunciation.

Jude 17-18 and 2 Pet 3:1-3

Jude 17-18 along with v 19 comprise an artificial proof of example based on a judgment of the subtype of supernatural oracle. Jude 17-18 constitutes the example and v 19 its application to the sectarians. Jude 17-19 also constitutes the *repetitio* or the *peroratio.* Regarding 2 Pet 3:1-3, 3:1-2 comprises a "secondary *exordium*" which is necessitated by the lengthy *digressio,* and 3:3 along with 3:4 is a prediction of scoffers denying the reality of the parousia.

As discussed previously, 2 Pet 3:2-3 is sometimes considered the source of the apostolic prophecy of Jude 17-18 because, within the testament of 2 Peter, 3:2-3 is functioning as an apostolic prophecy. Using this argument, it can be claimed that the emphasis upon the ethos of a rhetor and his sources in antiquity makes Jude's expansion in v 17 of the origin of the prediction from Peter alone to the apostles, in general, quite possible. However, he would also be expected to retain the double possessive genitive, "the commandment of the Lord and Savior through your apostles," because it give much more ethos to the apostolic prediction by showing that Christ is its origin and copossessor. Not being up against the doctrinal issue of the denial of the parousia but rather an ethical issue, Jude would have excluded the quotation of the scoffers which questions the parousia and which follows in 2 Pet 3:4.

However, this position has much to challenge it. Since Jude 17-18 functions as recapitulation within the *peroratio,* it is expected to be related to the *exordium* and *narratio,* and to reiterate key elements of the *probatio.* By its nature, like the *exordium* and the *narratio,* it is specific to the rhetorical situation and to the *probatio.* This is the case in Jude. The topic of ungodliness recurs from the *narratio* (v 4) and *probatio* (vv 14-15). Of particular note is the example of reduplication which repeats the phrase "following their own ungodly passions" in v 16 and 18. For these reasons, Jude's reliance upon another source is not

---

[102] See ch. 3, pp. 122-23.

expected here, especially the extensive reliance that would be involved if 2 Peter is posited as the source.

On the other hand, 2 Pet 3:1-3, functioning as a secondary *exordium* and the beginning of a manufactured prophecy of the apostle Peter, can be expected to be composed of borrowed elements without strict constraints imposed by the previous rhetoric. There are numerous ways for regaining audience attention, receptivity, and goodwill in the secondary *exordium*. The prophecy of the apostle Peter is a generalized introduction (3:3) and a statement of the false teachers. 2 Peter's use of Jude can be explained with regard to his exigence. Whereas in Jude the predictions are ascribed to the apostles of Christ, in 2 Peter these predictions are ascribed to the prophets, and the commandment is ascribed to Jesus and the apostles. This scheme succeeds in helping 2 Peter meet his exigence. The false teachers were undermining the apostolic preaching of the parousia by denying the divine origin of the Old Testament prophecies upon which it was partially based (1:20-21). Also, the commandment, the Christian ethical message, is denied by the false teachers (2:21). Both prophecy and the commandment are now affirmed as deserving attention and are given the ethos of the prophets, and the apostles and Christ respectively.

What is the prediction of the apostles in Jude 18, in 2 Pet 3:3 becomes the first half of a prophecy by the apostle Peter in conjunction with the format of the testament genre. The phrase "knowing this first," 2 Pet 3:3, enables a division between the references to prediction in 3:2 and the prophecy in 3:3-4 itself so that the latter is attributed to Peter and not to the prophets or apostles. In the process of adaption, 2 Peter retains the topics of following (ἐξακολουθέω) and desire (ἐπιθυμία) from Jude which are found elsewhere in his rhetoric![103] Jude 19 is not used, since it is a specific application of prophecy to the sectarians faced by Jude, and in 3:4 2 Peter shifts to rebutting a specific charge made by the false teachers, possibly relying on an apocalyptic source.

In summary, this second part of our examination has shown that rhetorical-redactional analysis yields mixed results in its attempt to determine the direction of the literary dependence between Jude and 2 Peter. Sometimes the priority of neither can be argued, and occasionally the priority of 2 Peter is indicated. Most often, however, the priority of Jude is indicated on the grounds of invention, arrangement, and style. If 2 Peter's priority is assumed, then Jude is dependent upon 2 Peter to the degree that his exigence and his own role as rhetor are unduly minimized as contributors to the rhetoric. If Jude's priority is assumed, then 2 Peter's dependence is explained by his exigence and role as rhetor. He utilizes elements of Jude that are useful to his exigence, but this by no means leads to the conclusion that 2 Peter's role as rhetor is unduly minimized.

[103] 1:16; 2:2, 15 and 1:4; 2:14, 18 respectively.

Conclusions

The rhetorical analyses of Jude and 2 Peter have demonstrated that both books are written according to the conventions of Greco-Roman rhetoric. Not only do they conform to general conventions of invention, arrangement, and style, but also are found to conform to very specific conventions, even to the point, for example, of related figures of speech and thought supporting each other as prescribed. Truly the authors of these works were familiar with the rhetorical conventions of their time, but it is unknown whether that familiarity is the product of specific training or is the outgrowth of daily interaction with spoken and written culture. If either author has formal training in rhetoric, 2 Peter is the most likely candidate. Proportionally his work exhibits many more features of rhetoric, and according to rhetorical standards, at times his rhetoric is excessive and even pedantic.

This study also shows that rhetorical criticism is an important tool for the interpretation of the New Testament. A specific pericope can be reasonably assigned to an element of arrangement, be placed in the inventional scheme, and be investigated for stylistic features. The ability of the interpreter to analyze the pericope is enhanced by the wealth of knowledge derived from the rhetoric of the whole.

In regard to redactional considerations, the study has demonstated that the union of redactional and rhetorical criticism can be a fruitful venture. Principles and probabilities deduced from rhetoric can inform redactional considerations without the initial bias of priority guiding the redaction. In the first test case, the question of the unity of 2 Peter, when examined in the light of redactional-rhetorical considerations, the question is more clearly shown to be a choice between two options that are far more opposed and polarized than they have been presented in the past. Either the form of 2 Peter is its original form, or its original form was severely defective and has undergone extensive redaction, which in places amounts to rewriting.

Concerning the second test case, the question of the direction of literary dependency between Jude and 2 Peter, the results of redactional-rhetorical criticism are mixed. Often the priority of neither can be asserted, the verbal correspondences being equally suited to the rhetoric of either work. Occasionally the priority of 2 Peter is indicated. However, by a considerable margin, the priority of Jude is strongly affirmed.

Appendixes

APPENDIX I
SPECIFIC TOPICS AND THEIR DISTRIBUTION IN JUDE

Topics	Quasi-Exordium	Exordium	Narratio	Probatio	Peroratio	Quasi-Peroratio
keeping	v 1			vv 6,13	v 21	v 24
mercy	v 2				vv 21–23	
peace	v 2			vv 12,16	v 19	
love	v 2			v 12	vv 17,20,21	
holy faith		v 3			v 20	
salvation		v 3		v 5		v 25
judgment			v 4	vv 6,15		
ungodliness			v 4	vv 14–15	v 18	
licentiousness			v 4	vv 6,7,8, 13,16	vv 18,23	
denying authority			v 4	vv 8–11, 15,16	vv 18,23	v 25
remind				v 5	v 17	
destruction				vv 5,10, 11,12		
wandering				vv 6,11,13		
fire				v 7	v 23	
reviling				vv 8,9,10		
following				vv 11,16	v 18	
gain				vv 11,16		
Spirit				cf. v 8	vv 19,20	

APPENDIX 2
SPECIFIC TOPICS AND THEIR DISTRIBUTION IN 2 PETER

Topics	Quasi-Exordium	Exordium	Probatio	Peroratio
righteousness-unrighteousness	1:1		2:5,7,8,9, 15,21; 3:13	
knowledge-ignorance	1:2	1:3,5,6,8; cf. 1:9	1:12,16,20; 2:12,20,21; 3:5,8	3:16,18
power		1:3	1:16; 2:11	
godliness-ungodliness		1:3,6,7	2:5,6,9,13; 3:7,11	3:14
glory		1:3	1:17	3:18
promises		1:4	2:19; 3:4, 9,13	
escaping corruption		1:4; cf. 1:9	2:12,18–22	
passion		1:4	2:10a,18; 3:3; cf. 2:14	
zeal		1:5,10		3:14
remember		1:12,13,15	3:1,2	
stability-instability		1:12	2:14; 3:16,17; cf. 2:18	
follow			1:16; 2:2,15	cf. 3:17
speak falsely			1:16; 2:3,19	
day			1:19; 3:3,7,8, 10,12; cf. 2:8	3:18
destruction			2:1,3,12; 3:6,7,9	3:16
denying authority			2:1,10a,18	
licentiousness			2:2,7,18; cf. 2:14	
the way			2:2,15,21	
greed			2:3,14–15	
nether gloom			2:4,17; cf. 2:9	

keeping	2:4,9,17; cf. 3:7	
lawless	2:7	3:17
reviling	2:10,11,12	
ensnare	2:14,18	
wandering	2:15,18	3:17
holy commandment	2:21; 3:2	
fire	3:7,10,12; cf. 3:11	
forbearance	3:9,15	
discovery	3:10	3:14
waiting	3:12,13	3:14

APPENDIX 3
FIGURES OF SPEECH AND THOUGHT IN JUDE

Epistolary Prescript (vv 1-2)
v 1	epithet, homoeoptoton (3)
v 2	adjunction, homoeptoton

Exordium (v 3)   metaphor, metonymy, periphrasis (2), pleonasm

Narratio (v 4)   adjunction, epithet, homoeoptoton, paronomasia, periphrasis

Probatio (vv 5-16)
v 5	homoeoptoton
v 6	adjunction, homoeoptoton (2), polyptoton, refining, reflexio, regressio, transplacement
v 7	homoeoptoton, regressio
vv 8-10	transplacement
v 8	colon, homoeoptoton, homoeoteleuton, polysyndeton
v 9-10	antithesis
v 9	epithet, exemplification, paronomasia
v 10	homoeoptoton, homoeoteleuton, similitude
vv 11, 13	transplacement
v 11	colon, exclamatio, homoeoptoton, homoeoteleuton, metaphor
vv 12, 13	asyndeton, metaphor (6)
v 12	homoeoptoton
v 13	homoeoptoton
v 14	adjunction
v 15	homoeoptoton, pleonasm, polyptoton, transplacement (2)
vv 16, 18	reduplication
v 16	asyndeton, comma, homoeoptoton

Peroratio (vv 17-23)
v 17	epithet, homoeoptoton, paronomasia
vv 19, 20	antithesis, polyptoton, transplacement
v 19	asyndeton, comma, homoeoptoton, refining
vv 20, 21	asyndeton, homoeoptoton, paronomasia, transplacement
v 20	homoeoptoton, metaphor, transplacement
vv 21-23	transplacement
vv 22-23	colon, epanaphora
v 23	emphasis, hyperbole

Epistolary Postscript (vv 24-25)
v 24	antonomasia, epithet, metaphor (2)
v 25	ellipsis, epithet (2), homoeoptoton

APPENDIX 4
FIGURES OF SPEECH AND THOUGHT IN 2 PETER

Epistolary Prescript (1:1-2)

1:1	epithet
1:2	epithet

Exordium (1:3-15)

1:3-4	transplacement
1:3	antonomasia, hendiadys, personification, synecdoche
1:4	polyptoton
1:5-7	climax, homoeoptoton, isocolon, polysyndeton, reduplication, transplacement
1:8	ellipsis, metaphor
1:9	ellipsis, homoeoptoton, homoeoteleuton, metaphor, periphrasis
1:10,11	homoeopropheron
1:10	metaphor, paronomasia, periphrasis, polyptoton, transplacement
1:11	epithet, synecdoche
1:12,13,15	paronomasia
1:12	metaphor, periphrasis
1:13,14	polyptoton, transplacement
1:13	ellipsis, metaphor, periphrasis (2)
1:14	metaphor (2), periphrasis
1:15	adjunction, metaphor, periphrasis

Probatio (1:16-3:13)

1:16-17	paronomasia
1:16	hendiadys
1:17,18	adjunction, polyptoton, transplacement
1:17	hendiadys, metonymy, periphrasis (2), polypton, transplacement
1:18	transplacement
1:19-21	paronomasia
1:19	antithesis, antonomasia, ellipsis, similitude
1:21	polyptoton, transplacement
2:1,3	transplacement
2:1	adjunction, antonomasia, irony (2) isocolon, metaphor, paronomasia (2), polyptoton
2:2-3	homoeoteleuton
2:2	metaphor
2:3	disjunction, ellipsis, isocolon, personification (2), synonymy

2:4-5	epiphora, homoeoptoton
2:4	metaphor, regressio
2:5,6	polyptoton, transplacement
2:5	antithesis
2:6-7	antithesis, paronomasia (2)
2:7-9	transplacement
2:7,8	polyptoton
2:8,9	paronomasia, polyptoton
2:8	adjunction, parenthesis, polyptoton, synecdoche
2:9	adjunction, antithesis
2:10-12	transplacement
2:10	asyndeton, comma
2:12-15	asyndeton
2:12	ellipsis, paronomasia, polyptoton, regressio, similitude, transplacement
2:13,15	reduplication
2:13	homoeopropheron, irony, metaphor, paronomasia, transplacement
2:14	emphasis (2), exclamatio, hyperbole (2), metaphor (2), metonymy, periphrasis
2:15-16	exemplification
2:15	irony, metaphor (4), polyptoton, refining, transplacement
2:16,18	transplacement
2:16	paronomasia (2), periphrasis
2:17	metaphor (2)
2:18	metaphor
2:19-22	maxim (4)
2:19	adjunction, antithesis, homoeoteleuton, irony, paronomasia, personification
2:20-21	refining
2:20	antithesis, epithet
2:21	antithesis, metaphor, synecdoche, transplacement
2:22	adjunction, ellipsis
3:1-2	aphodos, paronomasia, transitio
3:1	ellipsis, periphrasis
3:2	paronomasia
3:3	irony, paronomasia, pleonasm
3:4	dialogue, ellipsis, metaphor, rhetorical question
3:5-7	transplacement (7)
3:5,6	polyptoton
3:5	adjunction
3:6,7	polyptoton
3:7	periphrasis
3:8	antimetabole, antithesis

3:9	adjunction, distinction, ellipsis, paronomasia
3:10–12	polyptoton, transplacement
3:10,12	reduplication
3:10	adjunction, colon, homeoptoton, homoeoteleuton, onomatopoeia, parisosis, simile
3:11–12	*exclamatio*
3:12–14	polyptoton, transplacement
3:12	hendiadys, parisosis
3:13	personification

Peroratio (3:13–18)

3:14	metaphor
3:16,17	paronomasia
3:16	ellipsis, metonymy
3:17	metaphor
3:18	ellipsis, epithet

Glossary of Style

Adjunction (ἐπεζευγμένον, *adiunctio*): a figure of speech in which ". . . the verb holding the sentence together is placed not in the middle, but at the beginning or end" (Her. 4.27.38), or ". . . a number of clauses are all completed by the same verb, which would be required by each singly if they stood alone" (Quint. 9.3.62).

Antimetabole (commutatio): a figure of speech in which ". . . two discrepant thoughts are so expressed by transposition that the latter follows from the former although contrary to it . . ." (Her. 4.28.39).

Antithesis (contrapositum, contentio): a figure of speech in which ". . . either terminology or meaning, or both at once, are opposite in the opposed clauses" (*Rhet. ad Alex.* 26.1435b.25ff.).

Antonomasia (pronominatio): a trope ". . . which substitutes something else for a proper name . . ." (Quint. 8.6.29).

Aphodos: a figure of thought used to effect a transition back to the main subject after a digression (Cic. *Or.* 40.137; *De Or.* 3.53.203 = Quint. 9.1.28).

Asyndeton (dissolutio): a figure of speech in which there is an ". . . absence of connecting particles . . ." (Quint. 9.3.50).

Climax (gradatio): a figure of speech ". . . in which the speaker passes to the following word only after advancing steps to the preceding one . . ." (Her. 4.25.34).

Colon: a figure of speech which is ". . . a sentence member, brief and complete, which does not express the entire thought, but is in turn supplemented by another colon . . ." (Her. 4.19.26).

Comma: a figure of speech which occurs ". . . when single words are set apart by pauses in staccato speech" (Her. 4.19.26).

Dialogue (sermocinatio): a figure of thought which ". . . consists in assigning to some person language which as set forth conforms with his character . . ." (Her. 4.52.65), or presents ". . . imaginary conversations between men . . ." (Quint. 9.2.31).

Disjunction (disiunctio): a figure of speech occurring ". . . when each of two or more clauses end with a special verb . . ." (Her. 4.27.37).

Distinction (παραδιαστολή, *distinctio*): a figure of speech which distinguishes between similar things (Quint. 9.3.65).

Ellipsis: a figure of speech occurring ". . . when the word omitted may be clearly gathered from the context . . ." (Quint. 9.3.58).

Emphasis (significatio): a figure of thought which ". . . succeeds in revealing a deeper meaning than is actually expressed by the words" (Quint. 8.3.83).

Enargeia (φαντασία): palbability in style, vivid illustration or representation used to create a mental picture and provide vigor to style (Ar. *Rhet.* 3.11.1411b.1–1412a.3; Long. *Subl.* 15; Demetr. *Eloc.* 4.209– 220; Quint. 8.3.61–71, 88–89).

Epanaphora: a figure of speech which ". . . occurs when one and the same word forms successive beginnings for phrases expressing like and different ideas . . ." (Her. 4.13.19).

Epiphora (conversio): a figure of speech which repeats the last word in successive phrases (Her. 4.13.19).

Epithet (appositum): a trope occuring ". . . when an adjective or noun is used, which adds to the sense of the thing spoken of by simply holding forth some attribute, character, or quality descriptive of it" (Bullinger, 440).

Exclamatio: a figure of thought in which an exclamation is artfully, not genuinely, made (Quint. 9.2.26–27).

Exemplification: a figure of thought, ". . . the citing of something done or said in the past, along with the definite naming of the doer or author" (Her. 4.49.62).

Hendiadys: a figure of speech. "Two words employed, but only one thing, or idea, intended" (Bullinger, 657).

Homoeopropheron (alliteration): a figure of speech, ". . . the repetition of the same letter or syllable at the beginning of two or more words in close succession (Bullinger, 171).

Homoeoptoton (exornatio): a figure of speech occurring ". . . when in the same period two or more words appear in the same case, and with like terminations . . ." (Her. 4.20.28). Quintilian does not mandate that the case endings be identical in appearance (9.3.78).

Homoeoteleuton: a figure of speech occuring ". . . when clauses conclude alike, the same syllables being placed at the end of each . . ." (Quint. 9.3.77).

Hyperbole: a trope, ". . . a manner of speech exaggerating the truth, whether for the sake of magnifying or minifying something" (Her. 4.33.44).

Irony: a trope or figure of thought in which something understood is opposite of what is actually said. As a trope, it confesses that it implies something opposite of what it actually says, whereas as a figure, it is apparent, but not confessed that such is the case (Quint. 9.2.44–46).

Isocolon: a figure of speech ". . . comprised of cola. . . which consist of a virtually equal number of syllables" (Her. 4.20.27).

Maxim (γνώμη, sententia): a figure of speech, ". . . a saying drawn from life, which shows concisely either what happens or ought to happen in life . . ." (Her. 4.17.24).

Metaphor (translatio): a trope which ". . . occurs when a word applying to one thing is transferred to another, because the similarity seems to justify this transference" (Her. 4.34.45).

Metonymy (denominatio): a trope ". . . which draws from an object closely akin or associated an expression suggesting the object meant, but not called by its own name" (Her. 4.32.43).

Onomatopoeia: a trope ". . . which suggests to us what we should ourselves designate with a suitable word, whether for the sake of imitation or expressiveness, a thing which either lacks a name or has an inappropriate name" (Her. 4.31.42).

Parenthesis (interpositio, interclusio): a figure of speech which ". . . consists in the interruption of the continuous flow of our language by the insertion of some remark" (Quint. 9.3.23).

Parisosis: a figure of speech which ". . . occurs when a sentence has two equal members. Equality may exist between many small things and a few large things, and between an equal number of things of equal size . . . these clauses are neither like one another nor opposite, but only equal" (*Rhet. ad Alex.* 27.1435b.39ff.).

Paronomasia (adnominatio): a figure of speech, ". . . which by means of a modification of sound, or change of letters, a closer resemblance to a given verb or noun is produced, so that similar words express dissimilar things" (Her. 4.21.29), and 2) change of the preposition with which a verb is compounded (Quint. 9.3.71).

Periphrasis (circumitio): a trope occuring when ". . . we use a number of words to describe something for which one, or at any rate only a few words of description would suffice . . . a circuitous mode of speech" (Quint. 8.6.59).

Personification (προσωποποιΐα, conformatio): a figure of thought which ". . . consists in representing an absent person as present, or in making a mute thing or one lacking form articulate, and attributing to it a definite form and a language or a certain behavior appropriate to its character . . ." (Her. 4.53.66).

Pleonasm: a fault of style in which ". . . we overload our style with a superfluity of words . . ." (Quint. 8.3.53). As a figure of speech it is ". . . language fuller than is absolutely required . . ." (Quint. 9.3.46).

Polyptoton: a figure of speech where ". . . the cases and genders of the words repeated may be varied . . .," serving to mark a contrast (Quint. 9.3.36).

Polysyndeton: a figure of speech characterized by an excessive number of connecting particles (Quint. 9.3.50-52).

Reduplication (ἀναδίπλωσις, conduplicatio): a figure of speech constituted by ". . . the repetition of one or more words for the purpose of Amplification or Appeal to Pity . . ." (Her.4.28.38). It is akin to transplacement, but according to the handbook examples, the repetition is always immediate and the word used in the same part of speech (Her. 4.28.38; Quint. 9.3.28).

Refining (expolitio): a figure of thought which ". . . consists in dwelling on the same topic and yet seeming to say something ever new" (Her. 4.42.54).

Reflexio (ἀντανάκλασις): a figure of thought ". . . where the same word is used in two different meanings" (Quint. 9.3.68).

Regressio (ἐπάνοδος): a figure of speech, a ". . . form of repetition which simultaneously reiterates things that have already been said, and draws distinctions between them" (Quint. 9.3.35).

Rhetorical Question (interrogatio): a figure of thought in which a question is asked ". . . not to get information, but to emphasize our point . . ." (Quint. 9.2.7).

Simile (εἰκών): a figure of thought, ". . . the comparison of one figure with another, implying a certain resemblance between then" (Her. 4.49.62).

Similitude (παραβολή, similitudo): a figure of thought, ". . . a manner of speech that carries over an element of likeness from one thing to a different thing" (Her. 4.45.59).

Synecdoche (intellectio): a trope ". . . making us realize many things from one, the whole from a part, the *genus* from a *species,* things which follow from things which have preceded . . ." and vice-versa (Quint. 8.6.19).

Synonymy (interpretatio): a figure of speech which ". . . does not duplicate the same word by repeating it, but replaces the word that has been used by another of the same meaning . . ." (Her. 4.28.38).

Transplacement (πλοκή, traductio): a figure of speech. It is both the frequent reintroduction of the same word and when a word is used in various functions (Her. 4.14.20–21; Quint. 9.3.41–42).

Transitio: a figure of thought which ". . . briefly recalls what has been said, and likewise briefly sets forth what is to follow next . . ." (Her. 4.26.35).

Selected Bibliography

RHETORIC: PRIMARY SOURCES

Aristotle. *The "Art" of Rhetoric.* Translated by John Henry Freese. LCL. Cambridge: Harvard University Press, 1926.

———. *The Poetics.* Translated by W. Hamilton Fyfe. LCL. Cambridge: Harvard University Press, 1973. In the volume with Longinus, *On The Sublime,* and Demetrius, *On Style.*

———. *Topica.* Translated by E. S. Forster. LCL. Cambridge: Harvard University Press, 1960. In the volume with Aristotle, *Posterior Analytics.*

Augustine, Saint. *On Christian Doctrine.* Translated by D. W. Robertson, Jr. The Library of the Liberal Arts 80. Indianapolis: Bobbs-Merrill, 1958.

Bede, Venerable. "Bede's *De schematibus et tropis*—A Translation." Translated by Gussie Hecht Tannenhaus. *Quarterly Journal of Speech* 48 (1962) 237–53; also in "Concerning Figures and Tropes." Translated by G. H. Tannenhaus. In *Readings in Medieval Rhetoric.* Edited by Joseph M. Miller, Michael H. Proser, and Thomas W. Benson. Bloomington, IN/London: Indiana University Press, 1973, 96–122.

Cicero. *Brutus.* Translated by G. L. Hendrickson. LCL. Cambridge: Harvard University Press, 1939. In the volume with Cicero, *Orator.*

———. *De Inventione, De Optimo Genere Oratorum, and Topica.* Translated by H. M. Hubbell. LCL. Cambridge: Harvard University Press, 1949.

———. *Orator.* Translated by H. M. Hubbell. LCL. Cambridge: Harvard University Press, 1939. In the volume with Cicero, *Brutus.*

———. *De Oratore, Partitione Oratoriae.* Translated by E. W. Sutton and H. Rackham. LCL. 2 vols. Cambridge: Harvard University Press, 1942. In the volumes with Cicero, *De Fato, Paradoxa Stoicorum.*

Demetrius. *On Style.* Translated by W. Rhys Roberts. LCL. Cambridge: Harvard University Press, 1932. In the volume with Aristotle, *Poetics,* and Longinus, *On The Sublime.*

Hermogenes. "On Ideas of Style." in *Ancient Literary Criticism. The Principal Texts in New Translation.* Edited by Donald Andrew Russell and M. Winterbottom. Oxford: Clarendon Press, 1972, 561–79.

————. "On Stases. A Translation with an Introduction and Notes." Translated and edited by Raymond E. Nadeau. *Speech Monographs* 31 (1964) 361–424.

Longinus. *On The Sublime.* Translated by Hamilton Fyfe. LCL. Cambridge: Harvard University Press, 1932. In the volume with Aristotle, *Poetics,* and Demetrius, *On Style.*

Menandor Rhetor. Edited with translation and commentary by D. A. Russell and N. G. Wilson. Oxford: Clarendon Press, 1981.

Plato. *Phaedrus.* Translated by Harold North Fowler. LCL. Cambridge: Harvard University Press, 1977. In the volume with Plato, *Euthyphro, Apology, Crito,* and *Phaedo.*

Quintilian. *Institutio Oratoria.* Translated by H. E. Butler. LCL. 4 vols. Cambridge: Harvard University Press, 1920–22.

Rhetorica ad Alexandrum. Translated by H. Rackham. LCL. Cambridge: Harvard University Press, 1983. In the volume with Aristotle, *Problems.*

Rhetorica ad Herennium. Translated by Harry Caplan. LCL. Cambridge: Harvard University Press, 1954.

RHETORIC: SECONDARY SOURCES

Atkins, J. W. H. *Literary Criticism in Antiquity.* 2 vols. Cambridge University Press, 1934; reprint ed., Glouchester, MA: Peter Smith, 1961.

Beale, Walter H. "Rhetorical Performative Discourse: A New Theory of Epideictic." *Philosophy and Rhetoric* 11 (1978) 221–46.

Bitzer, Lloyd F. "The Rhetorical Situation." *Philosophy and Rhetoric* 1 (1968) 1–14; also in *Rhetoric: A Tradition in Transition.* Edited by W. R. Fisher. Ann Arbor: University of Michigan, 1974, 247–60.

Black, Edwin. *Rhetorical Criticism. A Study in Method.* New York: Macmillan, 1965; reprint ed., Madison: University of Wisconson Press, 1978.

Brandt, W. J. *The Rhetoric of Argumentation.* Indianapolis and New York: Bobbs-Merrill, 1970.

Burgess, Theodore C. "Epideictic Literature." *University of Chicago Studies in Classical Philology* 3 (1902) 89–261.

Burke, Kenneth. *The Rhetoric of Motives.* Berkeley and Los Angeles: University of California, 1969.

Chase, J. Richard. "The Classical Conception of Epideictic." *Quarterly Journal of Speech* 47 (1961) 293–300.

Cope, E. M. *An Introduction to Aristotle's Rhetoric with Analysis, Notes, and Appendices.* 3 vols. London and Cambridge: Macmillan, 1867; reprint ed., New York: G. Olms, 1970.

Corbett, Edward P. *Classical Rhetoric for the Modern Student.* 2nd ed. New York: Oxford University Press, 1971.

Grube, G. M. A. *The Greek and Roman Critics*. Toronto: University of Toronto Press, 1965.

Kennedy, George. *The Art of Persuasion in Greece*. Princeton: Princeton University Press, 1963.

———. *The Art of Rhetoric in the Roman World*. Princeton: Princeton University Press, 1972.

———. *Classical Rhetoric and its Christian and Secular Tradition from Ancient to Modern Times*. Chapel Hill: University of North Carolina Press, 1980.

———. *Greek Rhetoric Under Christian Emperors*. Princeton: Princeton University Press, 1983.

———. *Quintilian*. Twayne's World Author Series 59. New York: Twayne Publishers, 1969.

Kroll, Wilhelm. "Rhetorik," in *Paulys Real-Encyclopädie der classischen Altertumswissenschaft*. Supplemental vol. 7. Stuttgart: Metzler, 1940, cols. 1039–1138.

Lausberg, Heinrich. *Handbuch der literarischen Rhetorik. Eine Grundlegung der Literaturwissenschaft*. 2d ed. 2 vols. Munich: Max Hueber, 1973.

Leeman, A. D. *Orationis Ratio: The Stylistic Theories and Practice of the Roman Orators, Historians, and Philosophers*. 2 vols. Amsterdam: Adolf M. Hakkert, 1963.

McCall, Marsh. *Ancient Rhetorical Theories of Simile and Comparison*. Loeb Classical Monographs. Cambridge: Harvard University Press, 1969.

Martin, Josef. *Antike Rhetorik: Technik und Methode*. Handbuch der Altertumswissenschaft 2.3. Munich: C. H. Beck, 1974.

Oravec, Christine. " 'Observation' in Aristotle's Theory of Epideictic." *Philosophy and Rhetoric* 9 (1976) 162–74.

Perelmann, Chaim and L. Olbrechts-Tyteca. *The New Rhetoric: A Treatise on Argumentation*. Translated by John Wilkinson and Purcell Weaver. Notre Dame: Notre Dame University Press, 1969.

Russell, D. A. *Criticism in Antiquity*. Berkeley: University of California Press, 1981.

——— and M. Winterbottom, eds. *Ancient Literary Criticism. The Principal Texts in New Translations*. Oxford: Clarendon Press, 1972.

RHETORIC: THE OLD AND NEW TESTAMENTS

Betz, Hans Dieter. *Galatians: A Commentary on Paul's Letter to the Churches in Galatia*. Hermeneia. Philadelphia: Fortress Press, 1979.

———. "The Literary Composition and Function of Paul's Letter to the Galatians." *NTS* 21 (1975) 353–79.

———. *2 Corinthians 8 and 9*. Edited by George M. MacRae. Hermeneia. Philadelphia: Fortress Press, 1985.

Bradley, David G. "The *Topos* as a Form in the Pauline Paraenesis." *JBL* 72 (1953) 238–46.

Brunt, John C. "More on *Topos* as a New Testament Form." *JBL* 104 (1985) 495–500.

Bullinger, Ernest W. *Figures of Speech Used in the Bible Explained and Illustrated.* London: Eyre and Spottiswoode, 1898; reprint ed., Grand Rapids: Baker Book House, 1968.

Bultmann, Rudolf. *Der Stil der paulinischen Predigt und die kynischstoische Diatribe.* Göttingen: Vandenhoeck and Ruprecht, 1910.

Caird, G. B. *The Language and Imagery of the Bible.* Philadelphia: Westminster Press, 1980.

Ceresko, Anthony. "A Rhetorical Analysis of David's 'Boast' (1 Samuel 17:34–37): Some Reflections on Method." *CBQ* 47 (1985) 58–74.

Church, F. Forrester. "Rhetorical Structure and Design in Paul's Letter to Philemon." *HTR* 71 (1978) 17–33.

Daube David. "Rabbinic Methods of Interpretation and Hellenistic Rhetoric." *HUCA* 22 (1949) 239–64.

Dobschütz, E. von. "Zwei- und dreigliedrige Formeln." *JBL* 50 (1931) 117–47.

Donfried, K. P. "False Propositions in the Study of Romans." *CBQ* 36 (1974) 332–55; also in *The Romans Debate.* Edited by Karl P. Donfried. Minneapolis: Augsburg, 1977, 120–48.

Fischel, Henry Albert. *Rabbinic Literature and Greco-Roman Philosophy. A Study of Epicurea and Rhetorica in Early Midrashic Writings.* SPB 21. Leiden: E. J. Brill, 1973.

———. "Story and History: Observations on Greco-Roman Rhetoric and Pharisaism." *American Oriental Society, Middle West Branch, Semi-Centennial Volume.* Edited by Denis Sinor. Bloomington, IL, 1969, 59–78.

———. "The Uses of Sorites (*Climax, Gradatio*) in the Tannaitic Period." *HUCA* 44 (1973) 119–51.

Funk, Robert W. *Language, Hermeneutic, and Word of God. The Problem of Language in the New Testament and Contemporary Theology.* New York: Harper and Row, 1966.

———. *Parable and Presence. Forms of the New Testament Tradition.* Philadelphia: Fortress Press, 1982.

Gitay, Yehoshua. *Prophecy and Persuasion. A Study of Isaiah 40–48.* Forum Theologiae Linguisticae 14. Bonn: Linguistica Biblica, 1981.

———. "A Study of Amos's Art of Speech: A Rhetorical Analysis of Amos 3:1–15." *CBQ* 42 (1980) 293–309.

Hauser, Alan Jon. "Jonah: In Pursuit of the Dove." *JBL* 104 (1985) 21–37.

Hester, James D. "The Rhetorical Structure of Galatians 1:11–2:14." *JBL* 103 (1984) 223–33.

Jackson, Jared J. and Kessler, Martin, eds. *Rhetorical Criticism.* Essays in Honor of James Muilenberg. Pittsburgh: Pickwick Press, 1974.

Jeremias, Joachim. "Chiasm in den Paulusbriefen." *ZNW* 49 (1958) 145–56.

Jewett, Robert. "Romans as an Ambassadorial Letter." *Int* 36 (1982) 5–20.

Judge, E. A. "Paul's Boasting in Relation to Contemporary Professional Practice." *AusBR* 16 (1968) 37–50.

Kennedy, George A. *New Testament Interpretation Through Rhetorical Criticism.* Chapel Hill: University of North Carolina Press, 1984.

König, Eduard. *Stilistik, Rhetorik, Poetik in Bezug auf die biblische literatur.* Leipzig: T. Weicher, 1900.

Kurz, William S. "Hellenistic Rhetoric in the Christological Proof of Luke-Acts." *CBQ* 42 (1980) 171–95.

Lee, E. K. "Words Denoting 'Pattern' in the New Testament." *NTS* 8 (1961/62) 166–73.

Leon, Judah Messer. *The Book of the Honeycomb's Flow.* Edited and translated by Isaac Rabinowitz. Ithaca and London: Cornell University Press, 1982.

Lund, Nils Wilhelm. *Chiasmus in the New Testament. A Study in Formgeschichte.* Chapel Hill: University of North Carolina Press, 1942.

Lundbom, Jack R. *Jeremiah. A Study in Ancient Hebrew Rhetoric.* SBLDS 18. Missoula, MT: Scholars Press, 1975.

———. "Poetic Structure and Prophetic Rhetoric in Hosea," *VT* 29 (1979) 300–308.

Lynch, Anthony, "Pauline Rhetoric: 1 Corinthians l:10–4:21." M. A. thesis, University of North Carolina at Chapel Hill, 1981.

Moulton, J. H.; Howard, W. F.; and Turner, Nigel, eds. *A Grammar of New Testament Greek.* 3 vols. Edinburgh: T. & T. Clark, 1906–76. Vol. 4: *Style,* by Nigel Turner.

Muilenberg, James. "Form Criticism and Beyond." *JBL* 88 (1969) 1–18.

———. "The Book of Isaiah: Chs. 40–66." In *The Interpreter's Bible.* George Arthur Buttrick, gen. ed. 12 vols. New York: Abingdon, 1956, 5:381–773.

———. "A Study in Hebrew Rhetoric: Repetition and Style." in *VTSup* 1. Edited by G. W. Anderson, et al. Leiden: E. J. Brill, 1953, 97–111.

Mullins, Terence Y. "Topos as a New Testament Form." *JBL* 99 (1980) 541–47.

Norden, Eduard. *Agnostos Theos. Untersuchungen zur Formgeschichte religiöser Rede.* Leipzig and Berlin: B. G. Teubner, 1913; reprint ed., Teubner, 1956.

———. *Die antike Kunstprosa vom VI Jahrhunderts vor Christus in die Zeit der Renaissance.* 4th ed. 2 vols. Leipzig/Berlin: B. G. Teubner, 1923.

Prideaux, John. *Sacred Eloquence: The Art of Rhetoric as it is Laid Down in Scripture.* London: George Sawbridge, 1956.

Robbins, Charles. "Rhetorical Structure of Philippians 2.6–11." *CBQ* 42 (1980) 73–82.

Robbins, Vernon K. *Jesus the Teacher: A Socio-Rhetorical Interpretation of Mark.* Philadelphia: Fortress Press, 1984.

———, and Patton, John H. "Rhetorical and Biblical Criticism." *Quarterly Journal of Speech* 66 (1980) 327–50.

Schneider, Norbert. *Die rhetorische Eigenart der paulinischen Antithese.* HermUnT 11. Tubingen: Mohr-Siebeck, 1970.

Stowers, Stanley Kent. *The Diatribe and Paul's Letter to the Romans.* SBLDS 57. Chico, CA: Scholars Press, 1981.

Weiss, Johannes. "Beiträge zur paulinischen Rhetorik." In *Theologische Studien. Herrn Wirkl. Oberkonsistorialrath Professor D. Bernhard Weiss zu seinem 70 Geburtstage dargebracht.* Göttingen: Vandenhoeck and Ruprecht, 1897.

Wilder, Amos N. *The Language of the Gospel: Early Christian Rhetoric.* New York: Harper and Row, 1964; reprinted as *Early Christian Rhetoric: The Language of the Gospel.* Cambridge: Harvard University Press, 1971.

Wuellner, Wilhelm. "Greek Rhetoric and Pauline Argumentation." In *Early Christian Literature and the Classical Intellectual Tradition: in Honorem Robert M. Grant.* Edited by W. R. Schoedel and R. L. Wilken. Théologie Historique 54. Paris: Editions Beauchesne, 1979, 177–88.

———. "Paul's Rhetoric of Argumentation in Romans: an Alternative to the Donfried-Karris Debate over Romans." *CBQ* 38 (1976) 330–51; also in *The Romans Debate.* Edited by Karl P. Donfried. Minneapolis: Augsburg, 1977, 152–74.

JUDE AND RELATED SUBJECTS

Birdsall, J. N. "The Text of Jude in p[72]." *JTS* 14 (1963) 394–99.

Black, Matthew. "The Maranatha Invocation and Jude 14, 15 (*1 Enoch* 1:9)." In *Christ and Spirit in the New Testament in Honour of C. F. D. Moule.* Edited by Barnabas Lindars and Stephen Smalley. Cambridge: Cambridge University Press, 1973, 189–96.

Cantinat, J. *L'Épître de Jude.* Edited by A. George et al. Paris: Desclée, 1977.

———. *Les Épîtres de Saint Jacques et de Saint Jude.* SB Paris: Lecoffre-Gabalda, 1973.

Chase, F. H. "Jude, Epistle of." In *Hastings Dictionary of the Bible.* Edited by James Hastings. 5 vols. New York: Charles Scribner's Sons; Edinburgh: T. & T. Clark, 1911, 2:799–806.

Cladder, H. J. "Strophical Structure in St. Jude's Epistle." *JTS* 5 (1903/4) 589-601.

Ellis, E. E. "Prophecy and Hermeneutic in Jude." In *Prophecy and Hermeneutic in Early Christianity: New Testament Essays.* Edited by E. E. Ellis. WUNT 18. Tubingen: J. D. B. Mohr, 1978, 221-36.

Eybers, I. H. "Aspects of the Background of the Letter of Jude." *NeoT* 9 (1975) 113-23.

Mayor, J. B. "Notes on the Text of the Epistle of Jude." *Exp* 6/9 (1904) 450-60.

Osburn, Carroll D. "The Christological Use of *1 Enoch* 1.9 in Jude 14, 15." *NTS* 23 (1977) 334-41.

———. "The Text of Jude 5." *Bib* 62 (1981) 107-15.

———. "The Text of Jude 22-23." *ZNW* 63 (1972) 139-44.

Rowston, Douglas J. "The Most Neglected Book in the New Testament." *NTS* 21 (1975) 554-63.

———. "The Setting of the Letter of Jude." Ph.D. dissertation, Southern Baptist Theological Seminary, 1971.

Von Bieder, W. "Judas 22F. ὅυς δὲ ἐᾶτε ἐν φόβῳ. *TZ* 6 (1950) 75-77.

Wikgren, Allen. "Some Problems in Jude 5." In *Studies in the History and Text of the New Testament in honor of Kenneth Willis Clark.* Edited by B. L. Daniels and M. Suggs. SD 29. Salt Lake City: University of Utah Press, 1956, 147-52.

Wisse, Frederick. "The Epistles of Jude in the History of Heresiology." In *Essays in the Nag Hammadi Texts in Honour of Alexander Böhlig.* Edited by M. Krause. NHS 3. Leiden: E. J. Brill, 1972, 133-43.

2 PETER AND RELATED SUBJECTS

Cavallin, H. C. C. "The False Teachers of 2 Pt as Pseudo-Prophets." *NovT* 21 (1979) 263-70.

Chaine, Joseph. "Cosmogonie aquatique et conflagration finale d'après la seconda petri." *RB* 46 (1937) 207-16.

Chase, F. H. "Peter, Second Epistle of." In *Hasting's Dictionary of the Bible.* Edited by James Hastings. 5 vols. New York: Charles Scribner's Sons, 1911, 3:796-818.

Curran, John T. "The Teaching of 2 Peter 1.20: On the Interpretation of Prophecy." *TS* 4 (1943) 347-68.

Dalton, W. J. "The Interpretation of 1 Peter 3,19 and 4,6: Light from 2 Peter." *Bib* 60 (1979) 547-55.

Danker, F. W. "II Peter 3:10 and Psalm of Solomon 17:10." *ZNW* 53 (1962) 82-86.

Elliott, John H. "A Catholic Gospel: Reflections on 'Early Catholicism' in the New Testament." *CBQ* 31 (1969) 213-23.

Falconer, R. A. "Is Second Peter a Genuine Epistle to the Churches of Samaria?" *Exp* 6/5 (1902) 459–72; 6/6 (1902) 56, 117–27, 218–27.

Fornberg, Tord. *An Early Church in a Pluralistic Society. A Study of 2 Peter.* Translated by Jean Gray. ConB 9. Lund: C. W. K. Gleerup, 1980.

Grosch. *Die Eictheit das Zweite Briefes Petri Untersucht.* 2d ed. Leipzig: Deichert, 1914.

Grotius. *Adnotationes in Actus Apostolorum et in Epistolas Catholicas.* Paris, 1641.

Käsemann, Ernst. "An Apologia for Primitive Christian Eschatology." In *Essays on New Testament Themes.* Translated by W. J. Montague. SBT 41. London: SCM Press, 169–95 = "Eine Apologie der urchristlichen Eschatologie." *ZNW* 49 (1952) 272–96; also in *Exegetische Versuche und Beginnungen I.* Göttingen: Vandenhoeck and Ruprecht, 1960, 135–57 or *Bulletin du Centre Protestant d'Etude* 27 (1975) 19–45.

Klinger, Jerzy. "The Second Epistle of Peter: An Essay in Understanding." *StVladTQ* 17 (1973) 153–69.

Knoch, Otto. "Das Vermachtnis des Petrus: Der zweite Petrusbrief." In *Wort Gottes in der Zeit. K. H. Schelkle Festschrift.* Edited by H. Feld and J. Nolte. Düsseldorf: Patmos-Verlag, 1973, 149–65; also in Knoch, Otto. "Die 'Testamente' des Petrus und Paulus." SBS 62. Stuttgart: KBW Verlag, 1973, 65–81.

Lenhard, Helmut. "Ein Beitrag zur Übersetzung von II Ptr. 3, 10d." *ZNW* 52 (1961) 128–29.

———. "Noch einmal zu 2 Petr 3:10d." *ZNW* 69 (1978) 136.

Mayor, J. B. "Notes on the Text of the Second Epistle of Peter." *Exp* 6/10 (1904) 284–93.

McNamara, M. "The Unity of Second Peter: A Reconsideration." *Scr* 12 (1960) 13–19.

Molland, Einar. "La Thèse: La prophétie n'est jamais venue de la volonté de l'homme (2 Pierre 1.21) et les Pseudo-Clementines." *Studia Theologica* 9 (1955) 67–85.

Neyrey, J. H. "The Apologetic Use of the Transfiguration in 2 Peter 1:16–21." *CBQ* 42 (1980) 504–19.

———. "The Form and Background of the Polemic in 2 Peter." *JBL* 99 (1980) 407–31.

———. "The Form and Background of the Polemic in 2 Peter." Ph.D. dissertation, Yale University, 1977.

Olivier, Frank. "Une correction au texte du Nouveau Testament: II Pierre 3, 10." *RTP* 8 (1920) 237–78; also in *Essais dans le domaine du monde greco-romain antique et dans celui du Nouveau Testament.* Geneva: Libraire Droz, 1963, 129–52.

Robson, E. Iliff. *Studies in the Second Epistle of St. Peter.* Cambridge: Cambridge University Press, 1915.

Smitmans, A. "Das Gleichnis vom Dieb." In *Wort Gottes in der Zeit: Festschrift Karl Hermann Schelkle, zum 65 Geburtstag.* Edited by H. Feld and J. Nolte. Düsseldorf: Patmos-Verlag, 1973, 43–68.

Spicq, Ceslas. *Les Epîtres de Saint Pierre.* SB. Paris: Gabalda, 1966.

Strobel, A. *Untersuchungen zum eschatologischen Verzögesungsproblem auf Grund der spätjüdisch-urchristlichen Geschichte vom Habakuk 2, 2ff.* NovTSup 2. Leiden: E. J. Brill, 1961.

Talbert, C. H. "II Peter and the Delay of the Parousia." *VC* 20 (1966) 137–45.

Ullmann, Karl. *Der zweite Briefe Petri, Kritisch Untersucht.* Heidelberg: A. Oswald, 1821.

Vögtle, Anton. *Das Neue Testament und die Zukunft des Kosmos.* KomBeiANT Dusseldorf: Patmos-Verlag, 1970.

———. "Die Schriftwerdung der apostolischen Paradosis nach 2. Petr 1, 12–15." In *Neues Testament und Geschichte: Historisches Geschehen und Deutung im Neuen Testament. Oscar Cullmann Festschrift.* Edited by Heinrich Baltensweiler and Bo Reicke. Zurich: Theologischer Verlag/Tübingen: J. C. B. Mohr, 1972, 297–305.

von Allmen, Daniel. "L'Apocalyptique juive et le retard de la parousie en II Pierre 3:1–13." *RTP* 99 (1966) 255–74.

Witherington, Ben. "A Petrine Source in Second Peter." *SBLSP* Edited by Kent Richards. Atlanta: Scholar's Press, 1985, 187–92.

JUDE AND 2 PETER AND RELATED WORKS

Balz, H., and Schrage, W. *Die "Katholischen" Briefe. Die Briefe des Jakobus, Petrus, Johannes und Judas.* NTD 10. 12th ed. Göttingen: Vandenhoeck and Ruprecht, 1980.

Bauckham, Richard J. *Jude, 2 Peter.* WBC 50. Waco, TX: Word Books, 1983.

Bigg, Charles. *Epistles of St. Peter and St. Jude.* ICC. New York: Charles Scribner's Sons, 1901.

Chaine, J. *Le épîtres catholiques: la seconde épître de saint Pierre, les épîtres de saint Jean, l'épître de saint Jude.* 2nd ed. EBib Paris: Gabalda, 1939.

Fuchs, Eric, and Reymond, P. *La deuxième Épître de saint Pierre, L'Épître de saint Jude.* CNT 2/13b. Neuchatel and Paris: Delachaux and Niestlé, 1980.

Green, E. M. B. *The Second Epistle General of Peter and the General Epistle of Jude.* TNTC 18. Grand Rapids: William B. Eerdmans, 1968.

———. *2 Peter Reconsidered.* London: Tyndale Press, 1961.

Grundmann, W. *Der Brief des Judas und der zweite Brief des Petrus.* THKNT 15. Berlin: Evangelische Verlagsanstalt, 1974.

Huther, J. E. *Kritische exegetische Handbuch über den I. Brief des Petrus, den Brief des Judas und den 2. Brief des Petrus.* 5th ed., revised by E. Kühl. MeyerK 12. Göttingen: Vandenhoeck and Ruprecht, 1887.

Kelly, J. N. D. *The Epistles of Peter and Jude.* BNTC. London: Adam and Charles Black, 1969; HNTC. New York and Evanston: Harper and Row, 1970; reprint ed., Grand Rapids: Baker Book House, 1981.

Krodel, Gerhard, ed. *Hebrews, James, 1 and 2 Peter, Jude, Revelation.* PC. Philadelphia: Fortress Press, 1977.

Kühl, Ernst. *Die Briefe Petri und Judä.* MeyerK 12. 6th ed. Göttingen: Vandenhoeck and Ruprecht, 1897.

Mayor, Joseph B. *The Epistle of St. Jude and the Second Epistle of St. Peter.* London: Macmillan and Co., 1907; reprint ed., Grand Rapids: Baker Book House, 1979.

Michl, Johann. *Der Katholischen Briefe.* RNT 8. 2nd ed. Regensburg: Friedrich Pustet, 1968.

Reicke, Bo. *The Epistles of James, Peter, and Jude.* 2d ed. AB 37. Garden City: Doubleday, 1964.

Schelkle, K. H. *Die Petrusbriefe, der Judasbrief.* 3d ed. HTKNT 13/2. 4th ed. Frieburg/Basel/Vienna: Herder, 1976.

Schrage, W. *Die "katholischen" Briefe: Die Briefe des Jakobus, Petrus, Johannes und Judas.* NTD 10, 12th ed. Göttingen: Vandenhoeck and Ruprecht, 1961.

Senior, Donald. *1 & 2 Peter.* NTM 20. Wilmington, DE: Michael Glazier, 1980.

Sidebottom, E. M. *James, Jude, and 2 Peter.* NCB. London: Thomas Nelson and Sons, 1967; reprint ed., London: Marshall, Morgan and Scott/Grand Rapids: Eerdmans, 1982.

Spitta, F. *Die zweite Briefe des Petrus und der Brief des Judas.* Halle: Waisenhauses, 1885.

———. "Spätapostolische Briefe und Frühkatholizimus." In *Neutestamentliche Aufsätze für J. Schmid.* Edited by J. Blinzler, O. Kuss, and F. Mussner. Regensburg: Friedrich Pustet, 1963, 225–32.

Wand, J. W. C. *The General Epistles of St. Peter and St. Jude.* Westminster Commentaries. London: Methuen, 1934.

Windisch, H. *Die katholischen Briefe erklärt.* 3d ed. HNT 15. Tubingen: J. C. B. Mohr, 1951.

SUPPLEMENTAL WORKS

Aubineau, M. "La thème du 'bourbier' dans la Litterature grecque profane et chrétienne." *RSR* 33 (1959) 201–4.

Aune, David E. *Prophecy in Early Christianity and the Ancient Mediterranean World.* Grand Rapids: Eerdmans, 1983.

Baltzer, Klaus. *The Covenant Formulary.* Translated by David E. Green. Oxford: Basil Blackwell, 1971.

Berger, K. "Hartherzigkeit und Gottes Gesetz, die vorgeschichte des anti-jüdischen Vorwurfs in Mc 105." *ZNW* 61 (1970) 27-36.

Deissmann, G. Adolf. *Bible Studies.* Translated by Alexander Grieve. 2d ed. Edinburgh: T. & T. Clark, 1903.

Donfried, Karl. *The Setting of Second Clement in Early Christianity.* NovTSup 38. Leiden: E. J. Brill, 1974.

Grelot, P. "Les Targums du Pentateuque: Étude comparative d'apres Genèse, IV, 3-16." *Sem* 9 (1959) 59-88.

Guthrie, Donald. *New Testament Introduction.* 3d ed., rev Downers Grove, IL: Inter-Varsity Press, 1970.

Kolenkow, A. B. "The Genre Testament and Forecasts of the Future in the Hellenistic Jewish Milieu." *JSJ* 6 (1975) 57-71.

Marshall, I. H. "The Development of the Concepts of Redemption in the New Testament." In *Reconciliation and Hope, L. Morris Festschrift.* Edited by R. Banks. Exeter: Paternoster/Grand Rapids: Eerdmans, 1974, 153-69.

Moffatt, James. *An Introduction to the Literature of the New Testament.* International Theological Library. 3d ed. New York: Charles Scribner's Sons, 1923.

Mullins, T. Y. "Petition as a Literary Form." *NovT* 5 (1962) 46-54.

Munck, Johannes. "Discours d'adieu dans le Nouveau Testament et dans la litterature biblique." In *Aux Sources de la Tradition Chrétienne, M. Goguel Festschrift.* Neuchatel: Delachaux and Niestlé, 1950, 155-70.

Nineham, D. E. "Eyewitness Testimony and the Gospel Tradition III." *JTS* 11 (1960) 254-64.

Picirelli, Robert E. "The meaning of 'Epignosis.' " *EQ* 47 (1975) 85-93.

Schlosser, J. "Les jours de Noé et de Lot: A propos de Luc, XVII, 26-30." *RB* 80 (1973) 126-34.

Vermes, Geza. "The Targumic Versions of Genesis 4:3-16." In *Post Biblical Jewish Studies.* SJLA 8. Leiden: E. J. Brill, 1975, 92-126.

White, John L. *The Form and Function of the Greek Letter: A Study of the Letter-Body Form in the Non-Literary Papyri and in Paul the Apostle.* SBLDS 2. Missoula, MT: Scholars Press, 1972.

Zahn, Theodor. *Introduction to the New Testament.* Translated by M. W. Jacobus, et al. 2 vols. Edinburgh: T. & T. Clark, 1909.

TEXTS, TRANSLATIONS, AND GENERAL REFERENCE

Aland, Kurt et al., eds. *The Greek New Testament.* 3d ed. New York: United Bible Societies/American Bible Society, 1975.

The Apostolic Fathers. Translated by Kirsopp Lake. LCL. 2 vols. Cambridge: Harvard University Press, 1913.

The Babylonian Talmud. Translated and edited by I. Epstein. 17 vols. London: Soncino Press, 1935–53.

Bauer, W. *A Greek-English Lexicon of the New Testament and Other Early Christian Literature.* Translated and edited by W. F. Arndt and F. W. Gingrich. 2d ed, rev. Chicago: University of Chicago Press, 1957.

Blass, F., and Debrunner, A. *A Greek Grammar of the New Testament and Other Early Christian Literature.* Translated and revised from the 9th and 10th German edition by Robert Funk. Chicago and London: University of Chicago Press, 1961.

Charles, R. H., ed. *The Apocrypha and Pseudepigrapha of the Old Testament in English.* 2 vols. Oxford: Clarendon, 1913.

Charlesworth, James M., ed. *The Old Testament Pseudepigrapha.* 2 vols. Garden City: Doubleday and Company, 1983–85.

Elliger, K. and Rudolph, W. eds. *Biblia Hebraica Stuttgartensia.* Stuttgart: Deutsche Bibelstiftung, 1977.

Etheridge, J. W. *The Targums of Onkelos and Jonathan Ben Uzziel on the Pentateuch with the Fragments of the Jerusalem Targum.* New York: KTAV, 1968.

Eusebius. *Ecclesiastical History.* Translated by J. E. L. Oulton. LCL. Cambridge: Harvard University Press, 1932.

Gaster, Theodor H. *The Dead Sea Scriptures in English Translation with Introduction and Notes.* 3d. ed., rev. and enl. Garden City: Doubleday, 1976.

Hennecke, Edgar, and Schneemelchor, Wilhelm. *New Testament Apocyrpha.* Translated by A. J. B. Higgins et al. English edition edited by R. McL. Wilson. Philadelphia: Westminster Press, 1963–65.

Kittel, Gerhard, and Friedrich, Gerhard, eds. *Theological Dictionary of the New Testament.* Translated and edited by Geoffrey Bromiley. 10 vols. Grand Rapids: Wm. B. Eerdmans Publishing Company, 1964.

Metzger, Bruce. *A Textual Commentary on the Greek New Testament.* New York: United Bible Societies/American Bible Society, 1971.

Midrash Rabbah. Translated and edited by B. A. Freedman and M. Simon. 10 vols. London: Soncino Press, 1939.

Mishnah. Translated by Herbert Danby. Oxford: Oxford University Press, 1933.

Moulton, J. H., Howard, W. F., and Turner, Nigel, eds. *A Grammar of New Testament Greek.* 4 vols. Edinburgh: T. & T. Clark, 1906–76.

Rahlfs, Alfred, ed. *Septuaginta: Id est Vetus Testamentum graece iuxta LXX interpretes.* 8th ed. 2 vols. Stuttgart: Württemberigische Bibelanstalt, 1965.

Vermes, Geza. *The Dead Sea Scrolls in English.* 2d ed. Baltimore: Penguin Books, 1975.